Christian Ethics

A Historical Introduction

Christian Ethics

A Historical Introduction

J. Philip Wogaman

WESTMINSTER
JOHN KNOX PRESS
LOUISVILLE · KENTUCKY

Jacket design by Kevin Darst, KDEE Inc.

Book design by Drew Stevens

First edition

Published by Westminster/John Knox Press
Louisville, Kentucky

This book is printed on acid-free paper that meets the American National Standards Institute Z39.48 standard. ∞

PRINTED IN THE UNITED STATES OF AMERICA
9 8 7

Library of Congress Cataloging-in-Publication Data

Wogaman, J. Philip.
    Christian ethics : a historical introduction / J. Philip Wogaman.
        p.   cm.
    Includes bibliographical references and index.
    ISBN 0-664-25163-3 (alk. paper)

    1. Christian ethics—History.   2. Christian ethics—Methodist authors.   I. Title.
BJ1201.W64   1993
241'.09—dc20   93-3259

This book is gratefully dedicated to
the faculty of Wesley Theological Seminary
and
the congregation of Foundry United Methodist Church
both of which embody the best in this history

CONTENTS

INTRODUCTION

I welcomed the publisher's invitation to contribute this history of Christian ethics, not out of any illusions about how easy such a task would be, but because I think it important for each generation of Christians to be reintroduced to its immense legacy. The legacy is not altogether positive. In defining and addressing moral problems, Christians have sometimes illustrated James Russell Lowell's line that "time makes ancient good uncouth." But if Christians are to accept the responsibilities of their own era, they need to know something of the mistakes as well as the insights and triumphs of Christian witness in previous generations.

We stand, now, at the conclusion of two thousand years of Christian history. That is a vast expanse of time, in human if not in cosmic terms. But there has scarcely been a moment in those two millennia when Christians have not had to confront moral questions. The result is a rich legacy of thought, much of which proves strikingly relevant to contemporary issues and most of which can at least help us address our own time with greater clarity. My hope is that this volume will open the door on a treasure house no one book can hope to contain. It is designed to introduce, not to conclude, the history. A history of this kind, while it cannot be encyclopedic, must at least be dependable, and if it is to accomplish its purpose, it must be interesting.

In striving to make the book dependable, I must acknowledge my dependence upon the prior work of many scholars. There is a sense in which all of us who work at Christian ethics should be historians of ideas. But in that we are particularly dependent upon those whose full-time work is historical study.

In writing a book such as this, I am freshly conscious of how inadequate even the most thorough work of history must be. For one is selecting out of an immense sea those buckets of fact and insight that seem, to the writer, to be particularly significant. There is so much that must be neglected! But if it is a sin to be more superficial than we have to be, it may even be worse to allow ourselves to be paralyzed by the fear of necessary incompleteness. If incompleteness is inevitable, so too, lamentably, is bias. One does not have to attribute all knowledge to social location to grasp the point that we are deeply influenced by our social situation, with its peculiar pattern of needs, interests, and privileges. One cannot write a history of anything, and particularly a history of Christian ethics, without selecting out what seems most important. And we do not always know why we regard something as more important than something else! Church history, like all history, is so often the chronicle of those who prevailed. It sometimes neglects the losers or the disregarded. A result of this is that the children of the losers may find little with which to identify in the remembered story of the community. In our own century that is dramatically the case for oppressed ethnic groups and women, who have had to struggle to reclaim their proper share in the past.

I do not know whether this book will prove helpful in enlarging our understanding of the story. But I will not hesitate to bring twentieth-century questions and problems to bear in examining the thinkers of earlier periods. That is, in a sense, unfair. But if our purpose is less one of judging the morality of earlier times and more one of appropriating a history into contemporary existence, the issue of fairness may not be so important. We must not allow ourselves to be distracted by the question whether Paul or Augustine or Martin Luther was better or worse than Christians today. We do need to learn from the experience and insights of earlier Christians while coming to understand more clearly how their thoughts have helped shape what we are.

One point should be stressed at the outset. Few, if any, Christian thinkers have been perfectly consistent. It is possible to quote most thinkers against themselves. One could almost argue that the more profound a thinker is in challenging the root assumptions of an age, the more likely there is to be a gap between the central insights and the way in which that thinker responds to particular problems. Paul's understanding of women may be a case in point. At the deeper levels of his theology, Paul acknowledges that there is no essential difference between women and men: "there is neither male nor female; for you are all one in Christ Jesus" (Gal. 3:28). But in his response to practical problems (as he saw them) in the life of the church, he can still write that women "are not permitted to speak, but should be subordinate" (1 Cor. 14:34). Which is the "real" Paul? Both, probably. But we do have to form a judgment as to which represents Christian ethics in the more profound way.

Such complexities mean that sorting out the history of Christian moral thought cannot be reduced to technical exegesis of the work of a few key figures. We are challenged to encounter that history from the depths of our own spirits seeking, if indeed we may, the truth that an earlier time may have conveyed without fully understanding it. Still, while technical accuracy is not a sufficient objective, it is a worthy goal to avoid inaccuracy! In that respect, the present work seeks to be dependable even as it endeavors to draw the reader into the deeper treasures presented by a great inheritance.

I wish to acknowledge my specific indebtedness to the following scholars who have read all or part of the manuscript: Mark S. Burrows, Victor Paul Furnish, Alan Geyer, John D. Godsey, James A. Nash, Douglas M. Strong, Leo Maley III, and (my ever-helpful editor) Davis Perkins. Such improvements as have been made in the manuscript are to be counted to their credit; remaining flaws are my own responsibility. I am grateful to Ann Rehwinkel, Shirley Dixon, Susan Bender, and Jane Martin for secretarial assistance, and to my wife, Carolyn, for her typical supportiveness throughout the writing process.

Christian ethics, while largely an academic undertaking, is unthinkable apart from the community of faith, the church. My writing of this book was begun at Wesley Theological Seminary and concluded after I had begun serving Foundry United Methodist Church in Washington, D.C. I have found both institutions wonderful places in which to engage in dialogue about issues that matter, and I gratefully dedicate this volume to my colleagues at the seminary and to the great congregation I now serve.

PART I

The Legacies of Christian Ethics

The New Testament, as the product of earliest Christian thought and tradition, is itself a part of the history of Christian ethics. It is possible, by careful study of the setting, date, and authorship of New Testament writings, to form some initial impressions about the developing moral traditions of the early church in its formative decades. Such a study also reveals that the earliest Christian writers depended heavily upon Hebrew scripture, eventually known among Christians as the Old Testament. Indeed, when earliest Christian thinkers referred to "scripture" they invariably meant the Hebrew scriptures, for at that time the New Testament canon, as such, did not exist.

But even though the biblical materials are part of an evolving story, they constitute en bloc the most important source for the work of subsequent Christian moral thought. In this first part of our study, we shall look at the Bible in this way—as a received tradition that has exerted formative influence on all Christian ethics through the centuries.

It is also evident that Christian ethics was, perhaps from the very beginning, substantially influenced by ancient philosophical traditions. It may help to set the stage for the later history for us to be reminded of essential contributions of some of those traditions, while noting that the degree to which such sources should be used in Christian moral thought is itself a matter of dispute.

1

THE BIBLICAL LEGACY
OF CHRISTIAN ETHICS

The product of more than a thousand years of development, the Bible presents us with an extraordinary mixture of materials with which to think ethically. The span of time encompassed in biblical writing tends to be compressed in our minds because it took form so long ago. How long ago? While nobody knows for sure, the exodus of the Hebrews from Egypt may have occurred around 1300 B.C. (with the stories about Abraham, Sarah, etc. referring to a still earlier period). The reign of King David began around 1000 B.C. The Babylonian exile began around 587 B.C. The latest of the writings of Hebrew scripture came around 300 B.C. The life of Jesus spanned about the first third of the first century A.D. And the last of the New Testament writings dates from early in the second century A.D. It might be helpful to think of all that has happened in the Western world in the five hundred years since Columbus first set sail from Spain in 1492—and then to remember that it took more than twice that length of time for the Bible to take shape.

Impressed by the different periods of history, the different social settings, and the different genres of the writings themselves, many biblical scholars today are happier to speak of diversity than of unity in the scriptures. The Bible does not have a theology—it has theologies. The Bible does not have a single ethical perspective—it has a variety of ethical perspectives. To do justice to the actual texts, one must acknowledge first the diversities, letting them speak for themselves.

And yet, those who regard the Bible as speaking with some authority in theology and ethics cannot be content to leave it as a collection of diverse writings. For the Bible to be appropriated into the work of Christian ethics, it must be seen to have some core of unity. Otherwise, there would be no basis in the Bible itself for dealing with apparently conflicting elements in the biblical canon.

One way of establishing such an essential core is to impose arbitrary uniformity upon the writings, running roughshod over the evidences of difference and inconsistency. Few biblical scholars countenance such intellectual dishonesty, whatever its values may seem to be in protecting the pieties of the innocent. Another way is to interpret the Bible on the basis of a moral hermeneutic, recognizing that by doing so one necessarily gives higher priority to some texts or passages than to others. In a word, one has established a kind of canon within the canon. That approach is clearly followed by most Christian ethics. For instance, a pacifist Christian is likely to emphasize the Sermon on the Mount and all other teachings about loving one's enemies while discounting or disregarding the wars of the ancient Israelites and the prospect of an eschatological Armageddon.

In telling the story of Christian ethics, however, it is well not to press any given set of interpretations upon the Bible too soon. It is better, when we speak of the Bible as a legacy upon which Christian ethics has drawn through the centuries, to try to understand the tensions within which creative thought has occurred. These are the points of conflict, where both "sides" have to be taken into account. Six of these biblical points of tension may be especially helpful to us in understanding the Bible as a legacy for Christian ethics.

Tension One: Revelation Versus Reason

In one sense, the very first question to ask about the biblical legacy is the basis of its moral claims. In part, it makes claims for special revelation—knowledge or insight that has been given to persons of faith and that is not available to those who are outside the community of faith. But in part it also relies upon knowledge that is available to any person of normal intelligence, reflecting on experience common to humanity.

It might seem, at first glance, that the biblical tradition rests entirely upon revelation. The story of the ancient Israelites is the constant narration of God's interaction with a chosen people. Abraham, Isaac, Jacob, Joseph, Moses, Miriam, Joshua, Deborah, Samuel, David, Ezra, Nehemiah—all are depicted as basing their judgments and actions upon direct communication from God. The Ten Commandments are presented as the gift of God to Moses on Mount Sinai. The great prophets validate their moral teachings with "thus says the Lord." The New Testament picks up with Mary's special communication from the angel Gabriel and includes a variety of miracle stories bespeaking God's intervention in human history. Jesus Christ is, himself, seen to be the perfect revelation of God—"The Word became flesh and dwelt among us" (John 1:14). Paul's moment of truth is depicted as a flashing confrontation with the risen Christ on the road to Damascus. Paul, whose New Testament writings plainly bespeak a penetrating mind, still seems to disdain rational argumentation:

> Where is the wise man? Where is the scribe? Where is the debater of this age? Has not God made foolish the wisdom of the world? For since, in the wisdom of God, the world did not know God through wisdom, it pleased God through the folly of what we preach to save those who believe. For Jews demand signs and Greeks seek wisdom, but we preach Christ crucified, a stumbling block to Jews and folly to Gentiles. (1 Cor. 1:20–24)

Of course, the term "revelation" itself need not be restricted to dramatic interventions, special miracles, and communication with angels—though the biblical legacy has much of that. The claim is also implicit that we gain the really important truths, not through reasoning but through encounter with moral realities in human form. So Paul understands "Christ crucified" to provide a more compelling moral vision than any rational analysis could possibly hope to do.

Still, while the biblical narrative rests decisively upon revelation, it also makes appeal to reason. In most rudimentary form, that includes the delightful stories of Hebrew herdsmen, rulers, warriors, and so on bargaining with or reasoning with their trading partners, subjects, fellow rulers, or adversaries. The rationale for commandments and moral admonitions is not infrequently pragmatic—the negative consequences of not doing what is commanded. Some of the great prophets, notably Amos and the unknown prophet of exile (Deutero-Isaiah), develop a universal understanding of God in contrast with crude polytheisms. The books in the Hebrew wisdom tradition—Proverbs, Ecclesiastes, Job—are more philosophical in cast than the rest of the Hebrew scriptures. And much of the rest could be said to "make sense" to a non-Jew on grounds of human justice.

While Jesus Christ is understood by the New Testament writers to be the decisive revelation of God to humanity, it is interesting how even this revelation is presented in the thought categories of Hellenistic philosophy. Thus, in speaking of Christ as the "Word" made flesh, the allusion of the Fourth Gospel may be to the Greek "Logos," understood by the Stoic rationalist tradition as the universal structure of reason. Paul's Mars Hill address (Acts 17:22–31) is similarly couched in Stoic language, though it is punctuated by appeal to the resurrection. In that address, Paul ridicules the pretensions of idolatry, while appealing reasonably to a universal conception of God. Paul, as a matter of fact, also appealed to a universal conscience (Romans 1) and argued against certain practices as being unnatural (especially in 1 Corinthians).

The biblical legacy, taken as a whole, would seem to suggest that serious thought about ethics must employ both revelation and reason, although the meaning of revelation, the nature of reason, and the proper way to employ the two together have been elaborated in very different ways through Christian history.

Tension Two: Materialism Versus the Life of the Spirit

Viewed from one standpoint, the biblical legacy is very "materialistic"; viewed from another, it is quite "spiritual." The materialistic side is anchored in the traditions of creation. God created the world in all of its material detail, observing that "it was good." The nature psalms proclaim this work of God the creator ("When I look at thy heavens, the work of thy fingers, the moon and the stars which thou hast established"—Ps. 8). Nor is this materialism only on the grand scale of creation; it is reflected in the earthiness of the heroes of faith and ordinary people alike. The Song of Songs depicts the sensual aspects of human love. The blessedness of divine favor is depicted in terms of material prosperity. The loss of material well-being, as in the story of Job, is depicted as outright disaster. The neglect of the material well-being of ordinary people is treated by the great prophets as altogether contrary to the will of God. Nor is this materialistic theme suddenly reversed by the New Testament. The ministry of Jesus depicts the healing of the sick, the feeding of the multitudes, the celebration of God's loving concern for the sparrows, and the use of other images drawn from nature. Jesus' followers are taught to pray "give us this day our daily bread," and Jesus is characteristically known in the "breaking of bread." When the Fourth Gospel refers to the advent of Jesus, it is in the proclamation that "the word became flesh and dwelt among us." When Colossians sought to interpret the meaning of Christ, it made connection with the inherited Hebrew tradition by asserting that he is "the first-born of all creation; for in him all things were created, in heaven and on earth, visible and invisible" (Col. 1:15b–16a). However such passages are interpreted, they certainly are not a denial of the divine origins and purposes of this quite material world.

But biblical materialism does not value the material as the end purpose of human existence. The first sin catalogued in the Ten Commandments is the sin of idolatry—worshiping something else in place of God. The great prophets, while affirming the importance of material well-being, were clear about the corruptions of idolatry and materialism. Amos was, perhaps,

5

especially clear: "Woe to those who lie upon beds of ivory, and stretch themselves upon their couches, and eat lambs from the flock, and calves from the midst of the stall; who sing idle songs to the sound of the harp . . . but are not grieved over the ruin of Joseph!" (Amos 6:4–6). Amos thus would not allow materialistic self-indulgence to compensate for loss of deeper human values identified with the well-being of the community.

The many New Testament references to the life of the spirit preclude any altogether materialistic interpretation of Christian scripture. Thus, the Fourth Gospel insists that true worship is "in spirit and truth" (John 4:24). And Paul characteristically contends that "the mind that is set on the flesh is hostile to God; it does not submit to God's law, indeed it cannot; and those who are in the flesh cannot please God" (Rom. 8:7–8). New Testament warnings against worldliness appear quite antithetical to any materialism. Thus Jesus' admonition, as reported in the Synoptic Gospels, that it is a dangerous thing to gain the whole world at the cost of one's life; and Jude's reference to "worldly people, devoid of the Spirit" (Jude 1:19).

So here we have a biblical tension between strong affirmation of the goodness of created, physical, even sensual existence, on the one hand, and the assertion of spiritual values transcending the material, on the other. Much of the work of twenty centuries of Christian ethics has also been occupied with creative efforts to resolve this tension.

Tension Three: Universalism Versus Group Identity

The question here is whether one's ultimate significance is established by membership in the chosen or redeemed community (Israel or the church) or by being created and loved by the God of all people. Hebrew scripture is, of course, deeply grounded in the notion of the chosenness of Israel. This elect nation is liberated from Egypt, formed by the special Covenant of Sinai, and given the Promised Land. The tension between universalism and group identity as conflicting interpretations of the meaning of Israel is played out in various ways in Hebrew scripture. Thus, Amos, acknowledging that this is the chosen people, can nevertheless bring a word of judgment with universalistic overtones: "You only have I known of all the families of the earth; therefore I will punish you for all your iniquities" (Amos 3:2). There is a kind of universalism implicit in Isaiah's announcement that "out of Zion shall go forth the law" and that "all the nations shall flow" to "the mountain of the house of the LORD" (Isa. 2:3, 2; paralleled in Micah 4:1–3), although this smacks of triumphalism or even imperialism and might be taken to be a heightening of group identity. Such pronouncements do at least suggest that God is God of all peoples and that Israel's mission—its reason for existence as a group—has universal significance. In the case of Isaiah and Micah, this is emphasized by the theme of universal peace among the nations: "they shall beat their swords into plowshares."

The tension between universalism and group identity is perhaps most strongly felt in the crisis of the exile of 587 B.C., when the nation Israel was devastated and all hope of real group identity appeared lost ("How shall we sing the LORD's song in a foreign land?" Ps. 137:4). The reassertion of faith in that moment of defeat took a strongly universalistic turn in the writings of Ezekiel and the unknown prophet who wrote several chapters beginning with Isaiah 40 (the so-called Deutero-Isaiah). Ezekiel is a good reminder that universalism is often expressed as individualism. Personal responsibility before the universal God can be substituted for a relationship with God that is mediated through the group. Ezekiel takes pains to assert personal moral responsibility and to repudiate the notion that anyone is to be blamed for the actions of others.

The contrast between universal and group-centered forms of identity is nowhere more vividly expressed in Hebrew scripture than in the period of restoration under the Persian Empire during the fifth century B.C. The books of Ezra, Nehemiah, and Esther emphasize Jewish group identity almost to the point of chauvinism, with genealogies making it easier to establish who did and who did not belong and with Ezra's high-priestly prayer and its call to the men of Israel to put away their foreign wives and children. The books of Jonah and Ruth represented a reaction against such chauvinism. Ruth portrays the goodness and faithfulness of such a foreign wife, even depicting her as great-grandmother to King David. Jonah pokes fun at an explicitly chauvinistic character named Jonah, contrasting his narrowness with God's compassion for even the hated Assyrians.

The tension between universalism and group identity is expressed in two ways in the New Testament. First, in Paul's struggle with the "Judaizers." The issue was whether newly converted Gentile Christians should be required to observe Jewish ritual requirements. In practical terms, that issue was settled through the successful missionary efforts of Paul and others in establishing Christianity among Gentiles. Theologically, the issue was addressed in Paul's doctrine of grace, to which we shall return below.

But if being a Christian does not require that one be a Jew, there remains the question whether Christianity constitutes a new group identity of its own. Is Christian identity now grounded in the church and, if so, is the church understood in broadly universal or more narrowly sectarian terms? Again, one may note a tension. The God of the New Testament is clearly universal. Through Christ, the "dividing wall of hostility" (Eph. 2:14) has been broken down, the alienations overcome, both between humanity and God and among persons. But to the extent this is seen as an event in the life of Christians within the church, a new form of group identity could be seen to have replaced the older Jewish one. Here and there, Christians are referred to as the "elect" (e.g., Rom. 8:33 or Matt. 24:22), implying that God has chosen some to be saved within the church while others are excluded. But the strong evangelistic, missionary theme implies that the gospel should be proclaimed to all—a point that becomes quite explicit in Luke-Acts. Interactions between Christians and non-Christians on substantive moral and legal questions imply New Testament recognition of a wider community of discourse.

Tension Four: Grace Versus Law

A related tension concerns the basis of salvation itself. In one sense, biblical religion emphasizes morality throughout. The prophets all stressed moral action as essential to faithfulness and human fulfillment. God, as seen by them, utterly rejects unrighteousness and injustice and blesses the lives of all who obey God's moral demands. The Hebrew law codes, such as expressed in Leviticus and Deuteronomy, embody this prophetic standard, applying it to the circumstances of life in the Hebrew community. Even the Psalms celebrate righteous behavior. Unrighteousness is, throughout Hebrew scripture, subject to the stern judgments of God. A variety of offenses are taken to merit harsh punishments, including stoning to death, while long life, prosperity, and many children are considered the reward for a good life. God, as lawgiver and judge, has high moral expectations. The Ten Commandments (Ex. 20:2–17; Deut. 5:6–21) represent the essence of these expectations. The moral requirements, such as the commandments against murder and adultery, are combined there with the fundamental insistence upon single-minded worship of the one God. Thus, the moral commandments are set in the context of devotion to God, and violations of those commandments can now be understood as forms of idolatry.

That picture, while sometimes contrasted with New Testament emphases upon grace, actually is presupposed and expressed in much of the New Testament. At points, the New Testament even appears to increase the moral demand. For instance, Matthew reports Jesus' sayings:

> Think not that I have come to abolish the law and the prophets; I have come not to abolish them but to fulfil them. . . . Whoever then relaxes one of the least of these commandments and teaches men so, shall be called least in the kingdom of heaven; but he who does them and teaches them shall be called great in the kingdom of heaven. For I tell you, unless your righteousness exceeds that of the scribes and Pharisees, you will never enter the kingdom of heaven. (Matt. 5:17, 19–20)

To emphasize the point, that passage is followed by the assertion that attitudes of anger and lust are the moral equivalents of killing and adultery. Paul makes clear that certain forms of behavior and attitude are inconsistent with life in the spirit. The epistle of James reads like the Old Testament prophets in its emphasis upon righteousness. And moral demands are typical of the other New Testament writings as well.

In some tension with this long, rich biblical tradition of moral law, there is also a deep expression of God's love for undeserving sinners. Nor is that exclusively a New Testament emphasis. The formation narratives of Genesis and Exodus portray this love, often in contrast with the moral weakness, even the unscrupulousness, of Israelites. Hosea is depicted as loving and redeeming a faithless, licentious woman, and finding in her a metaphor for Israel's own faithlessness in contrast to the steadfast love of God. A similar sense of God's forgiving love activates Jeremiah and the unknown prophet of the exile as well as other Hebrew writings.

The transforming, redeeming love of God permeates New Testament writings, such as the parables of Jesus and the letters of Paul. Often, this love is portrayed as utterly undeserved—a love given prior to considerations of merit. Paul's own word for it, derived from Roman law, is "grace": being treated as innocent when one is in fact guilty. And this is a "gift," given freely to humanity through Jesus Christ: "For there is no distinction, since all have sinned and fall short of the glory of God, they are justified by his grace as a gift, through the redemption which is in Christ Jesus, whom God put forward as an expiation by his blood, to be received by faith" (Rom. 3:22–25).

This biblical emphasis upon unmerited love is in obvious tension with the portrayal of God's moral demands and judgments upon the unrighteous. The tension is reflected more or less directly in the epistle of James, where the writer responds to a certain interpretation of Paul with caustic words:

> What does it profit, my brethren, if a man says he has faith but has not works? Can his faith save him? If a brother or sister is ill-clad and in lack of daily food, and one of you says to them, "Go in peace, be warmed and filled," without giving them the things needed for the body, what does it profit? So faith by itself, if it has no works, is dead. (James 2:14–17)

Part of the biblical legacy of Christian ethics is the necessity somehow to do justice to both sides of the tension.

9

Tension Five: Love Versus Force

A somewhat related conflict is between reliance upon love and trust in God and the acceptance of coercive power and political authority to gain moral objectives. Love itself is central to the ethics of both Old and New Testaments. Both testaments emphasize the love commandment, grounding love of neighbor with love of God. Through the parable of the Good Samaritan Jesus specifically applied the commandment to love one's neighbor to an alien people.

Superficially, the Old and New Testaments appear to be in conflict over the question whether it is ever permissible to use force. Hebrew scripture is, after all, the expression of a nation, a political community; the New Testament is not. The ancient Hebrews are depicted as fighting wars, with Yahweh leading them to victory. Joshua, in obedience to God, obliterates the men, women, and children of Jericho—and many other residents of Canaan, whose country has been given as the "promised land" to the Israelites. Deborah, a judge and prophet, urged the Hebrews on into battle, then celebrated the victory (and a subsequent act of treachery) in what scholars consider to be one of the oldest oracles of the Old Testament (Judges 5). King David, despite human flaws that the Bible does not pass over, is depicted overall as God's servant for the upbuilding of the nation. Within the nation, law is presented not simply as moral exhortation but as commandments that are to be enforced by the community with real sanctions.

The New Testament is not, of course, the product of a political community. The first Christians were subjects of a political empire encompassing most of the world known to them; they were definitely not in charge. There was no occasion for their writings to deal with problems of state on the grand scale, no Jeremiah advising a King Zedekiah nor a Nathan confronting King David. It is noteworthy, however, that New Testament writing occasionally expresses respect for the Roman authority and its agents. Even the ascetic John the Baptist is not portrayed as requiring Roman soldiers to change careers, but only to "rob no one by violence or by false accusation, and be content with your wages" (Luke 3:14). Jesus, in the familiar story, advises his clever questioners to "render . . . to Caesar the things that are Caesar's" (Matt. 22:21, etc.), without any suggestion of the illegitimacy of the Roman state. Paul commands his readers to "be subject to the governing authorities. For there is no authority except from God," and he identifies the ruler as "God's servant for your good" (Rom. 13:1, 4). In this famous passage, Paul makes clear that even the coercive power of the state has divine sanction: The ruler "does not bear the sword in vain; he is the servant of God to execute his wrath on the wrongdoer" (v. 4). The theme is echoed in 1 Peter: "Be subject for the Lord's sake to every human institution, whether it be to the emperor as supreme, or to governors as sent by him to punish those who do wrong and to praise those who do right" (1 Peter 2:13–14).

These, and other biblical writings, suggest that political authority, even when expressed through the power of the sword, is a part of the divine scheme of things.

But here, too, there is another side to the biblical story. It begins with a strong theme of criticism of kings in Hebrew scripture; one tradition conveys strong opposition to establishment of monarchy in the first place, implying that by doing so the people have rejected God. The story is worth quoting:

> Then all the elders of Israel gathered together and came to Samuel at Ramah, and said to him, "Behold, you are old and your sons do not walk in your ways; now appoint for us a king to govern us like all the nations." But the thing displeased Samuel when they said, "Give us a king to govern us." And Samuel prayed to the LORD. And the LORD said to Samuel, "Hearken to the voice of the people in all that they say to you; for they have not rejected you, but they have rejected me from being king over them." (1 Sam. 8:4–7)

Samuel then predicts in detail the abuses to be expected from monarchy, but the people nevertheless insist upon the naming of a king. Concrete Hebrew experience with monarchy, possibly reflected back into the Samuel narrative, amply bore out his dire predictions. Hosea may have been thinking of this when he declared that "from the days of Gibeah, you have sinned, O Israel" (Hos. 10:9). Gibeah was the place where Israel's first king, Saul, made his headquarters. In the Chronicler's catalog of the virtues and vices of Israel's kings, there were many more of the latter than of the former, and a large majority of the kings are put down as evil.

Still, even this tradition cannot exactly be said to be opposed to political power as such. The development of the Hebrew monarchy was against the background of the rule of charismatic judges, designated more or less democratically by the people who were convinced that these special people possessed the spirit of God. The fundamental design was theocratic; the question was not whether God would rule through certain people but who those people would be, how they would be chosen, what limits would be placed upon them.

The real contrast, within the biblical narrative, is between reliance upon state power (however designated and restrained) and trust in God and obedience to the ways of peace and love. It is difficult to interpret the Old Testament from any angle as pacifist literature. But there are poignant appeals to the ways of peace all the same. Isaiah is particularly noteworthy, with memorable passages such as "they shall beat their swords into plow-shares, and their spears into pruning hooks" (2:4) and "the wolf shall dwell with the lamb, and the leopard shall lie down with the kid. . . . They shall not hurt or destroy in all my holy mountain" (11:6, 9). In prospect is a time when "every boot of the tramping warrior in battle tumult and every gar-ment rolled in blood will be burned as fuel for the fire," for the government will be in the hands of one who will be called "Prince of Peace" (9:5, 6). Isaiah's vision of such a peaceful future is combined with sharp criticism of reliance upon military methods: "Woe to those who go down to Egypt for help and rely on horses, who trust in chariots because they are many and in horsemen because they are very strong, but do not look to the Holy One of Israel or consult the Lord" (31:1).

While the Old Testament vision of divine presence often uses military metaphors (such as "the LORD, mighty in battle" of Ps. 24), such imagery is replaced by the concept of a suffering servant who was "despised and rejected" (see esp. Isa. 53). The unknown writer(s) of the great exile con-cluded that God's deeper purposes for the redemption of the people could come through loving vulnerability that is very different from reliance upon physical power. And, anticipating some key New Testament writings, the book of Proverbs argues that "if your enemy is hungry, give him bread to eat; and if he is thirsty, give him water to drink; for you will heap coals of fire on his head, and the Lord will reward you" (Prov. 25:21–22).

Such a conception comes to full flower in the New Testament with pas-sages calling for love of enemy. The Sermon on the Mount contains some of the most remarkable words in ancient literature: "You have heard that it was said, 'An eye for an eye and a tooth for a tooth.' But I say to you, Do not resist an evildoer. But if anyone strikes you on the right cheek, turn the other also. . . . You have heard that it was said, 'You shall love your neigh-bor and hate your enemy.' But I say to you, Love your enemies and pray for those who persecute you, so that you may be children of your Father in heaven; for he makes his sun rise on the evil and on the good, and sends rain on the righteous and on the unrighteous" (Matt. 5:38–39, 43–45, NRSV).

The theme is echoed by Paul in a similar passage, which comes imme-diately before the call in Romans 13 for obedience to governing authorities: "Bless those who persecute you; bless and do not curse them. . . . Repay no one evil for evil, but take thought for what is noble in the sight of all. . . . Do not be overcome by evil, but overcome evil with good" (Rom. 12:14, 17, 21).

How are such passages to be reconciled with the acceptance of force and state authority, even within the confines of the book of Romans? That ques-tion has fueled debates through twenty centuries of Christian history! Clearly, this is a tension to be struggled with.

Tension Six: Status Versus Equality

We have already referred to the different conceptions of political authority in the Bible. Those who support Hebrew royalty and Roman emperors obviously accept great differences of human status. That is also true of attitudes toward wealth and poverty. Stories of the patriarchs in Genesis treat their relative material wealth (flocks, retinue, etc.) with deference. The Bible does not apologize for Abraham, Isaac, Jacob, Joseph, and other such figures —at least not for their wealth. At various points in the Old Testament wealth is, in fact, portrayed as a sign of God's favor. For instance, Psalm 1 praises those whose "delight is in the law of the LORD" and who "do not follow the advice of the wicked," concluding of such people that "in all that they do, they prosper" (NRSV). Adversity and poverty, however, are sometimes taken as prima facie evidence of God's disfavor—an attitude that helps set the stage for the probing drama of Job.

Nor can the New Testament be described as altogether egalitarian. In his parables, Jesus sometimes depicts persons of wealth and power without interjecting that such status is, as such, to be rejected. At points in the New Testament narrative, wealthy people like Joseph of Arimathea are portrayed in an altogether favorable light (Mark 15:43), and not all of the personal interactions between Jesus or Paul and such persons are treated negatively. In the celebrated attempt by James and John to curry special favor (status) with Jesus, the rebuke is not based on the denial of status as such but upon the exclusive power of God to decide questions of rank (Mark 10:35–40).

Nevertheless, the theme of equality is also emphasized to a remarkable degree in both the Old and New Testaments. It can be called remarkable because it is so at variance with the culture of most of the ancient world. We have already noted this in relation to questions of political power. It is also true of economics. The Hebrew prophets do not appeal to an abstract principle of equality, but they are obviously offended by existing inequalities and especially by the indifference of the rich over the plight of the poor. Amos condemns the heartless practices of those "who trample upon the needy, and bring the poor of the land to an end . . . [who] buy the poor for silver and the needy for a pair of sandals" (Amos 8:4, 6). Micah, in the same vein, condemns those who "covet fields, and seize them; and houses, and take them away; they oppress a man and his house, a man and his inheritance" (Micah 2:2).

Reflecting this tradition, the Levitical laws made important provisions for the poor:

> When you reap the harvest of your land, you shall not reap your field to its very border, neither shall you gather the gleanings after your harvest. And you shall not strip your vineyard bare, neither shall you gather the fallen

grapes of your vineyard; you shall leave them for the poor and for the sojourner: I am the LORD your God. (Lev. 19:9–10)

The Hebrews were commanded not to oppress their neighbors and, reflecting upon the practical plight of the poor, wages were to be paid promptly, the very same day on which they were earned (19:13). Provision is even made for the forgiveness of debts and the redemption of indentured servants in the year of "jubilee"—specified to occur each fifty years. And those who are forced to borrow should be charged no interest (Leviticus 25). A high standard of justice was to be maintained: "You shall do no injustice in judgment; you shall not be partial to the poor or defer to the great, but in righteousness shall you judge your neighbor" (19:15). Nor is such a sense of justice understood in merely abstract terms; it is grounded more deeply in the moral reality of interpersonal life: "you shall love your neighbor as yourself" (19:18).

New Testament writings emphasize these themes. The Magnificat of Mary reflects the leveling implications of belief in the biblical God: "he has scattered the proud in the imagination of their hearts, he has put down the mighty from their thrones, and exalted those of low degree; he has filled the hungry with good things, and the rich he has sent empty away" (Luke 1:51–53). Jesus commands a rich ruler to "sell all that you have and distribute to the poor" as a condition of inheriting eternal life. When this man turns away sadly, Jesus remarks on "how hard it is for those who have riches to enter the kingdom of God! For it is easier for a camel to go through the eye of a needle than for a rich man to enter the kingdom of God" (Luke 18:18–25). In his parable of the rich man and the poor man Lazarus, the earthly stations of wealth and poverty are absolutely reversed after death, and Jesus makes clear that this teaching is fundamental to the whole Hebrew religious heritage (Luke 16:19–31). In the parable of the last judgment, the true test of religious commitment is seen to be whether one has aided the suffering, including the poor, the sick, the stranger, and the imprisoned (Matthew 25).

The practices of the earliest church, as reported in Acts, evidently included a sharing of material resources: "and no one claimed private ownership of any possessions, but everything they owned was held in common. . . . There was not a needy person among them, for as many as owned lands or houses sold them and brought the proceeds of what was sold. They laid it at the apostles' feet, and it was distributed to each as any had need" (Acts 4:32–35, NRSV). Emphasizing the point, Acts tells of a man and woman who withheld some of their resources and then lied about it, who spontaneously died upon being confronted about this deception (5:1–11). The epistle of James, reflecting a somewhat different church situation in which status distinctions had begun to be made, speaks of this with bitter sarcasm:

My brothers and sisters, do you with your acts of favoritism really believe in our glorious Lord Jesus Christ? For if a person with gold rings and in fine clothes comes into your assembly, and if a poor person in dirty clothes also comes, and if you take notice of the one wearing the fine clothes and say, "Have a seat here, please," while to the one who is poor you say, "Stand there," or "Sit at my feet," have you not made distinctions among yourselves, and become judges with evil thoughts? Listen, my beloved brothers and sisters. Has not God chosen the poor in the world to be rich in faith and to be heirs of the kingdom that he has promised to those who love him? But you have dishonored the poor. Is it not the rich who oppress you? Is it not they who drag you into court? Is it not they who blaspheme the excellent name that was invoked over you? (James 2:1–7, NRSV)

Paul's writings in the New Testament do not emphasize the theme of equality, but the equality is implied at many points: All are sinners; none should boast, except of the saving act of Jesus Christ on the cross; "There is neither Jew nor Greek, there is neither slave nor free, there is neither male nor female, for you are all one in Christ Jesus" (Gal. 3:28); the church is the "body of Christ" in which "if one member suffers, all suffer together; if one member is honored, all rejoice together" (1 Cor. 12:26).

So, there also exists some tension between status and equality in the biblical legacy—enough to provide grounds for enduring controversy in subsequent Christian ethics.

A brief recital of these six tension points in the biblical legacy does not exhaust the possibilities, for that legacy is vast and it has been drawn upon in many different ways. Nevertheless, this will serve to illustrate the richness of the biblical reference points to which Christian moral thought has constantly returned.

2

PHILOSOPHICAL LEGACIES

Biblical legacies have exerted formative influence throughout the history of Christian ethics. But they have not been the only important influences on that history. In particular, we cannot overlook the sometimes intimate, sometimes uneasy relationship between Christian ethics and traditions of secular philosophy. Virtually from the beginning, Christian thinking has interacted with important legacies of Greek and Hellenistic philosophy.

The origin of those legacies is itself an intriguing subject, though we cannot explore it adequately here. Why was it that the dominant minds of the Aegean world, beginning around 600 B.C. (roughly, the time of Jeremiah), cut loose from religious mythological traditions and attempted to explain the world in conceptual terms? Their project was to bring unity to thought without reference to particular forms of revelation or inherited myths about gods and goddesses. At least it can be said that they had come to find such myths inadequate in face of increased knowledge and moral sensitivity.

The drive toward intellectual unity first took the form of the search for the one substance from which all else is derived—with Thales, the first of the great nature philosophers, that substance was water. To Heraclitus, the fundamental principle was motion or change; to Parmenides it was permanence; to Democritus it was tiny, irreducible atoms. All of these early philosophers were convinced that rationally explainable principles could be found to bring coherence to human conceptions of the world and human life itself.

Influential Forms of Greek Philosophy

The most influential forms of Greek thought trace their origins to the great philosophers Socrates (469–399 B.C.), Plato (427–347 B.C.), and Aristotle (386–322 B.C.). Socrates left no writings, and his thought is known only through the writings of his pupils, especially Plato.[1] Nevertheless, his inquiring mind and his efforts to discern universal principles governing the moral life exerted profound influence on Plato and Plato's own pupil Aristotle. Socrates subjected attitudes on human values and virtues to relentless scrutiny, confident that moral truth could be gained through critical reflection. In Plato's "Apology" Socrates is quoted as saying that "the unexamined life is not worth living."[2] With Socrates, knowledge and virtue were closely connected. At the same time, Socrates affirmed the importance of obeying one's conscience: We are morally bound by what we believe to be right, even when it conflicts with our interests or inclinations. Thus, in the "Crito," Socrates refuses to violate his convictions even to save himself from unjust execution, asking "ought a man to do what he admits to be right, or ought he to betray the right?"[3]

Despite the injustice inflicted upon him, Socrates saw himself as committed to the laws of the Athenian state. It was by these laws that he had been begotten and nurtured and educated. And having benefited in every way through the laws, he had "entered into an implied contract" by not leaving Athens.[4] This covenantal understanding of citizenship was destined to have enormous importance in Western thought. In a later dialogue, Plato also depicts Socrates as defending a universal conception of justice.[5] In the dialogue, Thrasymachos asserts that "justice is nothing else than the interest of the stronger."[6] Socrates, in a fascinating exploration of the implications of this doctrine of might makes right, forces Thrasymachos to acknowledge that the powerful can be quite mistaken about their own true interests. In fact, the true interest of the ruler is the well-being of the ruler's subjects. Power does not validate itself. Those who govern must do so on the basis of a higher conception of the good.

Such ideas appear in embryonic form in the thought of this great Athenian teacher, but his questions and conclusions helped shape the work of subsequent Greek and Hellenistic thought.

Plato and Platonism

Born into a prominent Athenian family, Plato had an opportunity to play a leading role in public life even as a young man. He was, however, disillusioned by the corruption of politicians and the enormous injustice inflicted upon Socrates. Withdrawing from the public arena, he devoted his life to teaching, writing, and the founding of his Academy. Most of his writings survived to exert a profound influence, his teaching gave us the great Aristotle, and even his Academy lasted for nine hundred years.

Truth, to Plato, is universal and eternal. The world of things is fleeting and corruptible, manifesting briefly and imperfectly the realm of pure ideas. However, Plato had great confidence in the capacity of the human mind to discover truth through reason. Critical thought exposes the contradictions and fallacies of conventional opinion and separates the temporal from the eternal. Not all are equally gifted as thinkers, but true philosophers enlighten the whole society.

Plato in fact thought of society as containing, broadly speaking, three classes of people: the artisans, the guardians, and the thinkers. These classes correspond to the three aspects or faculties of the human psyche: the appetitive, the spirited, and the rational. The appetitive is the need-fulfilling faculty, and the class to which it corresponds are the farmers and artisans who provide for the physical needs of society. The spirited is the faculty of vigorous activity, and the class to which it corresponds are the guardians or warriors who protect the community. The rational is the faculty of thinking, and its corresponding class is made up of the philosophers or thinkers. All people have each of the three faculties in their makeup, but everyone has one of the three as a dominant tendency. It is both interesting and important that Plato regarded women, as well as men, as possessing each of the faculties. And women, as well as men, could be found in each of the three classes. In the well-ordered society, the young all receive education appropriate to each of the three faculties. But the educational process eventually classifies each young person in accordance with his or her dominant gifts. The highest class, the philosophers, receive education over the longest period of time. In the well-ordered society they eventually become the rulers. Again, women can be numbered in this class as well as men. It is also noteworthy that Plato toyed with a form of communism through the sharing of property and limitations on permissible disparities of wealth and that he contemplated communal sharing of marriage partners.

Plato's understanding of virtue and vice corresponds to the human faculties and classes. Thus, the virtue of temperance is intended to hold the appetites and the vice of intemperance in check. The virtue of courage focuses the spirited aspect and preserves one from the vice of cowardice. The virtue of prudence represents the reason properly governed in contrast to the vice of folly. The crowning virtue is justice, which consists in the proper relating of the three faculties of the person and the three classes of society so that each is accorded its due.

The state, as a whole, should be governed by reason. Ideally, the governors should be "philosopher kings." Plato had little confidence in the passions exhibited in the rule of the masses nor in the dictates of a military elite. His own brief efforts to implement his ideas, on invitation, in Syracuse were not successful, and there is no evidence that the Athenians were attracted by them. Nevertheless, the concept of a civil order governed by reason and not by passion or selfish interests was to have enduring influence.

Aristotle

Plato's great pupil Aristotle also exerted enormous influence in the development of Western ethical thought. While he was obviously influenced by Plato at many points, such as the designation of virtues and vices, Aristotle deviated at important points. To begin with, things are not a pale image of ideas; ideas are a reflection of things. This reversal, which anticipates one of the longest-standing conflicts in the history of philosophy, has important implications for ethics. To Plato, the moral life consists in patterning one's behavior in accordance with universal ideals. To Aristotle, it consists in the realization of the ends potential to one's nature. The distinction can be overstated, of course, since Plato recognizes the particularities of human existence and Aristotle has universal ideas about human nature and destiny. Nevertheless, Aristotle's starting point in the analysis of the ends given in our nature gave rise to a more rigorous examination of actual human life and to observable social, economic, and political institutions. So we are not surprised to find whole chapters of his *Politics* outlining criticisms of Plato's ideas as unworkable.[7] We also find Aristotle seeking reasonable explanations for existing inequalities, including those inherent in slavery. Aristotle's quest for the end or goal of all things as the way to understand them includes social institutions such as the family and the state. Each has a good in the fulfillment of which its nature is made complete. The understanding of that ultimate end or good is the key to understanding every institution or practice, just as it is the key to understanding human life itself.

Two of Aristotle's contributions to ethics are especially important. One is his observation, also in the *Politics*, that human beings are by nature social or political.[8] Social and political institutions are not, to Aristotle, mere conveniences to serve the interests of isolated individuals. They are an expression of the fact that we are social beings.

The other noteworthy contribution is his idea that the moral life aims at the "golden mean" between excess and deficiency.[9] The various virtues can be understood in this way. True courage, for example, lies between the excess of foolhardiness and the deficiency of cowardice.

Stoicism

Immediately prior to the time of Christ, several important philosophical movements came into being that were also destined to influence Christian thought. Stoicism was among the most important of these. This philosophy involved much more than the "stiff upper lip" with which the word "stoic" is popularly associated in our time, though Stoicism did teach its followers to be self-disciplined in the face of adversity. Thoroughly rationalistic in its basic assumptions, Stoic thought depicted a cosmos grounded in the mind of a rational God. Human beings were understood to reflect this same rationality. In essence they are also rational beings, although when corrupted by the flesh they can deviate from that rational essence. To be true to one's humanity is to center oneself on reason, thereby transcending the accidents and circumstances of birth, station, and life experience. Since all are, by nature, rational beings, all are fundamentally equal. The fundamental, essential equality of human beings is belied by human society, corrupted as it has been by the flesh. Nevertheless, that equality remains the basic moral reality. Thus, among the great Stoic thinkers there could be numbered the slave Epictetus and the Roman emperor Marcus Aurelius, along with the writer Seneca and the orator Cicero.

Stoic thought lay behind the theoretical development of Roman law. The Roman lawyers, whose work proceeded in the centuries following Christ, understood all true law to be a reflection of the universal reason of God. This natural law finds imperfect expression in the law of peoples—the universal laws and customs to be observed across many cultures—and the civil law enacted by particular rulers. But civil law and the law of peoples are to be judged by the universal natural law.

Stoic political thought was basically covenantal, which might seem surprising since its major development occurred in the era of the Roman emperors. The state, made up as it is of equal beings possessed of the gift of reason, is a contract among those who belong to it. Those who rule, including the emperors, do so by the consent of the people. This notion reflected in part the legal fiction from the time of Julius Caesar that the emperors were empowered by the Roman Senate. But more basically it reflected the underlying conceptions of rationality and equality.

There is no evidence that Stoicism ever gained a mass following in the Hellenistic and Roman world. Nevertheless, it was very influential in defining that world.

Epicureanism

The movement influenced by the Greek philosopher Epicurus is often thought of as pleasure seeking and morally irresponsible. That stereotype is not altogether inaccurate. Believing that human beings are but chance configurations of material particles, the Epicureans did not consider life to have any enduring meaning. The best we can hope to do is to enhance life's pleasures while minimizing its pains. That principle is the heart of the ethics of Epicureanism. The irony is that Epicurus and many of his followers lived simple, austere lives. They avoided gross excess on the sensible ground that that only leads to greater pain in the long run. A simple life-style contributes more to peace of mind and to the more satisfying pleasures of intellectual activity.

Nevertheless, adoption of pleasure as the central moral principle made it inevitable that many Epicureans would make *physical* pleasure their highest value. And Epicureans in general avoided social relationships and political responsibilities that might complicate their lives. Friendship could be affirmed as a source of pleasure. But on the basis of the pleasure principle one would hardly want to invest further time in the life of a dying friend or in otherwise contributing something that could not be returned. As for political responsibility, that could only lead to further stress. Certainly the honors and glory associated with political or military life were understood to be devoid of meaning. Nor would it make much sense to die for somebody else unless one had already concluded that there was no longer anything worth living for.

Ultimately, of course, we all die, and that, for the Epicureans, was absolutely final. Death was not to be feared, however. For, as Epicurus remarked, "where death is, I am not, and where I am, death is not." Death, by definition, is not something that one can experience, so why be preoccupied by its supposed terrors? It is enough to cultivate the simple pleasures of body and mind and to avoid all unnecessary pain. Epicureanism could thus be described as a kind of principled selfishness or enlightened self-interest.

Influence of Greek Philosophy on Biblical Writings

Each of these movements was to help set the agenda for Christian ethics, as were Neoplatonism and assorted other quasi-religious and philosophical movements of the Greco-Roman world.

Did these nonbiblical sources exert as much influence as the Bible? That is doubtful. But one does not want to overstate the degree to which biblical and nonbiblical legacies were contradictory. Nor would one want to ignore the extent to which extrabiblical resources affected the later assimilation of biblical writings. At one time it was fashionable to draw a sharp contrast between "Hebrew" and "Greek" ways of thinking, associating the former with biblical writings and the latter with Greek philosophy. We now know that this contrast can be overdrawn. Certainly the New Testament writings themselves betray occasional influences from Greek philosophical sources. Here and there the fingerprints of Greek philosophy can be found. The eleventh chapter of Hebrews betrays Platonic influence ("what is seen was made out of things which do not appear"). The striking interpretation of Christ at the beginning of the Fourth Gospel ("in the beginning was the word" [Greek, *logos*]) suggests the influence of Stoicism (mediated, in part, through the channels of Hellenistic Judaism). Even Paul's "now we see in a mirror dimly, but then face to face" in a passage of 1 Corinthians 13 carries overtones similar to Plato's celebrated parable of the cave, which depicts perceived reality as only a reflection of the pure realm of ideas— though Paul's theological frame of reference was very different. The reference in Colossians to Christ as "the image of the invisible God, the first-born of all creation" seems to be using a Greek philosophical manner of speaking. In the first chapter of 1 Corinthians, Paul takes pains to distance himself from Greek thought, but in doing so he betrays familiarity with it. Paul's speech in the Athenian Areopagus (Acts 17:16–34) is depicted as being addressed to Epicurean and Stoic philosophers, and the lines "from one ancestor he made all nations to inhabit the whole earth" (NRSV) and "in him we live and move and have our being" are probably Stoic in origin. And in Romans 2, and elsewhere, Paul evidently makes use of natural law in a universal conception of the moral conscience.

I do not wish to overstate the influence of Greek philosophy on the New Testament. But Greek influence permeated the world in which the Christian church and its writings took shape. In noting that this was a part of the legacy of subsequent Christian ethics we must not regard that necessarily as a departure from the biblical legacy.

PART II

The Ethics of Early Christianity

Christians, as the second-century *Letter to Diognetus* reminds us, "dwell in the world, but do not belong to the world." This paradox of being in but not of the world has usually compelled Christians to respond to issues and problems in the world but not to do so entirely on the world's own terms.

The world of the earliest Christian centuries was framed by the Roman Empire. Christians, at first, had scant influence in that political order; indeed, they were subjected to occasional persecution by political authorities. For the first three or four centuries, the church was part of a relatively stable and unified civilization. Within, however, Roman civilization was in ferment. Highly sophisticated philosophical movements jostled for influence with various religious cults. Lacking a cohesive set of religious values, the empire experimented with worship of emperors—a practice that few of the emperors themselves took personally but that made the nonparticipating Christians seem subversive. Economic life was increasingly polarized between rich and poor, with the imperial centers feeding upon the resources and production of vassal territories. Slavery was widespread. Public morals were at low ebb. Entertainments in urban centers came to include mortal combat between trained gladiators and the slaughter of condemned peoples. Women were held in low regard, and unwanted babies—especially girl babies—were sometimes abandoned to the elements in a primitive form of after-the-fact birth control.

In short, many facets of ordinary life were in tension with central aspects of the faith of the earliest Christians, and it became necessary for the church to respond. The response included efforts to think through the meaning of

23

Roman civilization in Christian terms, and it included moral instruction on specific problems and practices. In addition to the New Testament itself, early Christian writings exemplify a vivid reaction to the social setting. Some of these come down to us in the form of letters from figures like Clement of Rome or Ignatius of Antioch; others, like the *Didache*, are small collections of moral teachings. These writings are not sophisticated ethical analyses so much as efforts to confront issues by more or less direct application of the teachings and example of Jesus and the writings eventually canonized as scripture. Toward the end of the second century, more sophisticated thinking about the meaning and implications of Christian faith began to appear. The intellectual capstone of the ancient Christian world was supplied by the writings of Augustine.

3

THE FORMATIVE YEARS

Our understanding of the early, formative period of the church (roughly the first century and a half) partly depends on the emergence and interpretation of New Testament writings, which span the latter half of the first century and the early part of the second. We can also learn from other writings that are not a part of the New Testament. Some of these were written before A.D. 100 and some are from the first decades of the second century. These writings were infused with ethical teachings. Most such writings that have come down to us were occasional letters—written for specific individuals or groups and addressing particular problems. Some were apologies written to defend Christianity before its critics or simple outlines of moral instruction. There were also "gospels" written later than the four canonical gospels and never included in the New Testament canon. What do we learn about the moral teaching of the early church from such writings?

The most obvious point is that the early church was deeply engaged in moral teaching! Moral instruction was not a side interest; it was at the heart of the presentation of the gospel to believers and nonbelievers alike.

Attitude Toward the Material World

In some ways, the most fateful moral issue before the earliest Christians was the question how they should interpret and relate to the material world, as such. Some voices, among them Basilides and Marcion, interpreted the world in essentially negative terms. The world in no way represents the

God who is revealed through the preexistent and risen Christ. Christ himself is to be understood in altogether spiritual terms and faithful Christian life is to be lived entirely on that plane.

Such a view, had it been sustained in the early church, would have had profound effects on all the church's moral teaching. Economic life would have become inconsequential. What importance could any longer be given to the plight of the poor or to teachings about stewardship? Everything material, having been dismissed as evil or unreal, would no longer count to a life lived in the spirit. Similarly, political questions, preoccupied as they generally are with distribution of resources, protection of property, and regulation of the material circumstances of a society, would lose moral relevance. Human sexuality might be treated as necessary to the propagation of the species, though some forms of early Gnosticism denied even this, but the subject otherwise could only be seen as disgusting. In short, since the material world is what gives factual substance to morality, Christian ethics would no longer have much to talk about.

So we must not be surprised at the vigor with which the bits and pieces of early Christian writings respond to that challenge. These early voices sharply condemned, even ridiculed, the notion that the physical world is evil or that it has nothing to do with life in the spirit. Various of the letters of Ignatius of Antioch[1] make the point. In one, he emphasizes physical details in the life of Jesus, "who was really born, ate, and drank; was really persecuted under Pontius Pilate; was really crucified and died."[2] In another, he ridiculed the idea that Jesus was only an appearance, a sham. Those who say this are themselves a sham.[3] The so-called first letter (*I Clement*) of Clement of Rome, probably from the last decade of the first century, contains a poetic affirmation of the grandeur of God's creation of the heavens and earth. God has decreed, Clement writes, that "the earth becomes fruitful at the proper seasons and brings forth abundant food for (humanity) and beasts and every living thing upon it." By this same decree, "the basin of the boundless sea is . . . constructed to hold the heaped up waters, so that the sea does not flow beyond the barriers surrounding it. . . . Perennial springs, created for enjoyment and health, never fail to offer their life-giving breasts to [humanity]. The tiniest creatures come together in harmony and peace. . . . All these things," he concludes, "the great Creator and Master of the universe ordained to exist in peace and harmony."[4]

The early church's response to Marcion is especially interesting. Heavily influenced by Gnostic dualism, that second-century Christian teacher was repudiated by the church around A.D. 144. Forming a separate Christian movement, Marcion attracted many followers. Having rejected Jewish law, he came to interpret the God of the Hebrews as a lesser deity, in no way to be identified with Christianity. By the same token he rejected the created world as the work of this lesser god and affirmed instead the spiritual realm revealed by Christ. The struggle with Marcionism was, in many ways, decisive in establishing whether the church would regard the created world as an expression of divine spirit and love or somehow in opposition to the God of salvation.

Mid-second-century Christian writers like Justin and Irenaeus specifically and vigorously condemned Marcion's ideas. Justin wrote that "the wicked demons have also put forward Marcion of Pontus, who is even now teaching men to deny that God is the Maker of all things in heaven and earth and that the Christ predicted by the prophets is his Son."[5]

In a similar and more extensive condemnation of the Gnostics and Marcion, Irenaeus reasserted the connection between Jesus Christ and the God of the Old Testament who created the world. Marcion was guilty of "shamelessly blaspheming the God whom the Law and the Prophets proclaimed."[6] Marcion had mutilated the Gospel narratives and the writings of Paul, "removing whatever the apostle said clearly about the God who made the world."[7] In a summary of the church's true message, Irenaeus affirms "faith in one God, the Father Almighty, who made the heaven, and the earth, and the seas, and all that is in them, and in one Christ Jesus, the Son of God, who was made flesh for our salvation, and in the Holy Spirit."[8] Such affirmations might appear to be platitudes, unrelated to the real existence of people. In fact, their affirmation of the material realm as an expression of God's creative and redemptive purposes is fundamental to the whole structure of Christian moral teaching.

It is difficult to see how the church could have survived over the long run if it had followed the Marcionites in cutting the connection between God and the physical universe. Without that connection, the faith would have become irrelevant to the actual existence of people since existence has, after all, so many physical aspects.

Wealth and Poverty

The early church, in fact, underscored the importance of the material world to God's purposes and human well-being by giving enormous attention to the relationships of rich and poor. The possession of wealth is generally portrayed as spiritually and morally dangerous. Poverty is a plight to which faithful Christians, especially those with wealth, must respond. The spiritual danger of wealth is partly in its temptation toward idolatry, thus substituting worship of material things for worship of God. So Polycarp emphasizes that "if anyone does not refrain from the love of money he will be defiled by idolatry and so be judged as if he were one of the heathen, 'who are ignorant of the judgment of the Lord.' "[9]

The spiritual peril of wealth is also in the barrier it can so easily create between rich and poor. Rich people tend to neglect their need to love poor people, and failure to love is a deeply spiritual issue. Love itself is grounded in recognition that rich and poor are sisters and brothers. One of the earliest of the church's surviving manuals of instruction, the *Didache*,[10] commands Christians to "share everything with your brother and call nothing your own. For if you have what is eternal in common, how much more should you have what is transient!"[11] Clement of Rome writes of the responsibility of neighbor love, with each bound to the needs of the other in proportion to each's special gifts: "The rich must provide for the poor; the poor must thank God for giving him someone to meet his needs."[12] Ignatius sharply criticizes those "who have wrong notions about the grace of Jesus Christ." Such people "care nothing about love: they have no concern for widows or orphans, for the oppressed, for those in prison or released, for the hungry or the thirsty."[13]

Such ideas are not expressed with systematic clarity in most of the writings of the early church; certainly they are not expounded with economic sophistication. The church's economic ethic was more distribution than production oriented. Even the distributional side of economics was seen more in terms of the moral responsibility for acts of charity than as a problem for systemic reform—although, as we shall see, there appear to have been some efforts toward systematic sharing of wealth within the churches themselves. The moral urgency of acts of charity was often grounded in direct appeals to earlier apostolic traditions, including the teachings of Jesus and what were to become the New Testament epistles. Thus Polycarp makes direct reference to 1 Timothy and 2 Corinthians in a brief passage condemning materialism: "But 'the love of money is the beginning of all evils.' Knowing, therefore, that 'we brought nothing into the world, and we cannot take anything out,' let us arm ourselves 'with the weapons of righteousness.' "[14]

In the modern church, charitable giving is termed an act of stewardship, grounded on Jesus' parable of the talents (Matt. 25:14–28; Luke 19:11–27). The idea is that we give what God has first given to us. This idea is implicit in many of the teachings on the sharing of wealth in the early church. Occasionally, as in the *Shepherd of Hermas*, it is made explicit. According to that mid-second-century writing, it is God who gives us the reward for our labors. And God wishes these gifts "to be shared among all. . . . They who receive, will render an account to God why and for what they have received. . . . He, then, who gives is guiltless. For as he received from the Lord, so has he accomplished his service in simplicity."[15] Not surprisingly, this writing seems to have been addressed more directly to the few Christians possessing wealth.[16]

To what extent did the first- and second-century church institutionalize sharing? There is little evidence of any widespread pattern of out-and-out communism. To be sure, the book of Acts depicts the church at the very beginning in almost such terms: "All who believed were together and had all things in common; and they sold their possessions and goods and distributed them to all, as any had need" (Acts 2:44–45). But even that primitive church was to encounter conflicts over the "daily distribution," as references to the dispute between the "Hellenists" and the "Hebrews" makes clear (Acts 6:1–2). The many exhortations to give to the poor contained in the writings of the first two centuries suggest individual acts of charity, rather than institutional schemes for sharing, as the dominant pattern. Still, the testimony of Justin from the middle of the second century indicates some institutionalization of sharing. In discussing the transformations brought about by the gospel, Justin comments that "we who once took most pleasure in the means of increasing our wealth and property now bring what we have into a common fund and share with everyone in need."[17] The voluntary character of this sharing is, however, indicated by this subsequent passage:

> Those who prosper, and who so wish, contribute, each one as much as he chooses to. What is collected is deposited with the president, and he takes care of orphans and widows, and those who are in want on account of sickness or any other cause, and those who are in bonds, and the strangers who are sojourners . . . and, briefly, he is the protector of all those in need.[18]

Despite the early Christian stress on the perils of wealth and the importance of sharing with those in need, these writings seldom venture any criticism of slavery. The institution of slavery was an important economic fact of life in the Roman world. Many Christians were, themselves, slaves. The institution, as such, was accepted as a given. Ignatius's letter to Polycarp may have reflected a prevailing Christian moral view. In this letter, Ignatius advises his fellow bishop not to "treat slaves and slave girls contemptuously." At the same time, slaves must not "grow insolent." Instead, "for God's glory they must give more devoted service, so that they may obtain from God a better freedom." Moreover, he continues, "they must not be over-anxious to gain their freedom at the community's expense, lest they prove to be slaves of selfish passion."[19] In a similar vein, the *Didache* instructs Christian slaveowners not to "be harsh in giving orders to your slaves and slave girls. They hope in the same God as you, and the result may be that they cease to revere the God over you both. For when he comes to call us, he will not respect our station, but will call those whom the Spirit has made ready." While such a relativizing of status could be a first step

29

toward challenging the institution itself, that door is slammed shut with the *Didache*'s further admonition: "You slaves, for your part, must obey your masters with reverence and fear, as if they represented God."[20] The resemblance between these teachings on slavery and the language of Ephesians and Colossians cannot be accidental.

The failure to question the institution of slavery, with its manifest challenge to the Christian notions of kindredship and community that are so evident in other writings on economic life, comes as yet another reminder that the early church did not—could not—think systematically about an economic ethic for society at large. Christians had to accept their lot. But within the parameters set by economic circumstance, they were challenged again and again by their leaders to share generously with those in need.

Sexual Ethics

The evidence we have suggests that the Roman world of those early Christian centuries was not a very inhibited sexual environment. Against the loose sexual morality of the wider civilization, early Christian writings advocate—even command—very strict standards. Following in the wake of Paul's writings on the subject, and often quoting them directly, the surviving instructions insist upon the correlation between spiritual wholeness and sexual self-discipline. The instructions are largely couched in negative terms. It would have been easy for early Christians to conclude from this literature that sex is more fraught with spiritual danger than with blessings from the Creator.

Representative of the instructions is the *Didache*'s "My child, do not be lustful, for lust leads to fornication. Do not use foul language or leer, for all this breeds adultery."[21] And Ignatius's blunt statement: "Make no mistake, my brothers: adulterers will not inherit God's Kingdom."[22] And from Clement of Rome: "Since, then, we are a holy portion, we should do everything that makes for holiness. We should flee from slandering, vile and impure embraces, drunkenness, rioting, filthy lusts, detestable adultery, and disgusting arrogance."[23] In this vein, Justin points with pride to the "many men and women now in their sixties and seventies who have been disciples of Christ from childhood [who] have preserved their purity" and to "the uncounted multitude of those who have turned away from incontinence and learned these things."[24]

Sexual relations between persons of the same gender, while not as major a preoccupation of these writings as lust, fornication, and adultery, are also condemned. Polycarp quotes Paul's statement in 1 Corinthians 6:9–10 that "neither fornicators nor the effeminate nor homosexuals will inherit the Kingdom of God."[25] The *Didache*, in its lengthy listing of sins to be avoided, includes the admonition not to "corrupt boys."[26] Justin refers to the mutilation of children for purposes of sodomy.[27]

Marriage, while accepted, is not always depicted in positive terms. Justin remarks that "we do not marry except in order to bring up children, or else, renouncing marriage, we live in perfect continence."[28] And he notes that "those who make second marriages according to human law are sinners in the sight of our Teacher."[29] Ignatius commands women to be "contented with their husbands" and (following Ephesians) husbands "to love their wives as the Lord loves the Church." A life in chastity is to be especially commended; still, "it is right for men and women who marry to be united with the bishop's approval" so that their marriage "will follow God's will and not the promptings of lust."[30] The unknown author of the *Letter to Diognetus* suggests, however, that Christian marriage is similar to marriage among non-Christians, except that Christians do not abandon their children.[31]

The Status and Role of Women

So far as the status relationships of men and women are concerned, the early church was generally male-dominated. Insofar as the status of women is referred to, it is usually in the terms expressed by such New Testament writings as Ephesians and 1 Timothy. Writing about the same time, Clement of Rome commends the Corinthian church in this vein: "You instructed your women to do everything with a blameless and pure conscience, and to give their husbands the affection they should. You taught them, too, to abide by the rule of obedience and to run their homes with dignity and thorough discretion."[32]

The so-called second letter of Clement (*II Clement*) does, however, have an enigmatic passage saying that God's kingdom will come "when the two shall be one, and the outside like the inside, and the male with the female, neither male nor female." This will be "when a brother sees a sister [and does] not think of her sex, any more than she should think of his."[33] There may be a hint, here, of the "there is neither male nor female; for you are all one in Christ Jesus" of Galatians (3:28). On the other hand, *II Clement* later identifies the male principle with Christ and the female principle with the church, while also identifying the church with flesh and Christ with spirit.[34] The union of male and female, then, becomes the reunion of spirit and flesh—not exactly the same thing as a proclamation of the *equality* of men and women!

The general, underlying superiority of men to women is conveyed on a more routine basis in all of these writings by habitual use of male metaphors and pronouns in speaking of God (Father, Him, etc.). Still, it is a mistake to think of this literature, on the whole, as dehumanizing women. Women are frequently addressed as responsible, thinking moral beings, quite capable of responding in faith and service to God's love. Women are sometimes commended for their faith and love—as in the slightly backhanded compliment in *II Clement* that "many women, empowered by God's grace, have performed deeds worthy of men."[35] They are fully human in the sense in which the early church thought of humanity, and their destiny in the divine kingdom is ultimately indistinguishable from that of men. But their status was undeniably seen to be lower than that of men.

Violence and the Political Order

Some historians of the period have commented that the church was essentially pacifist during the first two centuries.[36] In his classic study of Christian views of war, Roland Bainton distinguishes three basic Christian positions on war: pacifism (which rejects war), the just war (which prescribes circumstances under which war can be regarded as justified), and the crusade (which glorifies warfare waged against the enemies of God). The three positions matured in that order, according to Bainton, with pacifism dominating the life and thought of the church up to the time of Constantine.[37]

The available evidence does support this characterization of the early church. No Christian is known to have served in the imperial armies until about A.D. 170. Around that time, as reported later by Origen, the pagan critic Celsus criticized Christians for being unwilling to serve: "If all were to do the same as you, there would be nothing to prevent [the king from] being left in utter solitude and desertion and the affairs of the earth would fall into the hands of the wildest and most lawless barbarians. . . ."[38]

Insofar as the writings of the first two centuries deal with war or violence, they tend to sustain this judgment. The New Testament emphasis upon love, upon not returning evil for evil, upon love of enemies finds ample reinforcement during these years. Repeating the moral demands of Jesus in Matthew and Luke, the *Didache* underscores that the "way of life" includes blessing "those who curse you," prayer for one's enemies, fasting "for those who persecute you," loving "those who hate you" (adding that "then you will make no enemies"). "If someone forces you to go one mile with him, go along with him for two; if someone robs you of your overcoat, give him your suit as well. If someone deprives you of your property, do not ask for it back" (noting, practically, that "you could not get it back anyway!").[39] *II Clement* repeats the commandment about loving enemies as though this were standard church teaching by which outsiders are impressed. But that writer then exhorts the faithful to put this into practice, for "when they [the outsiders] see that we fail to love not only those who hate us, but even those who love us, then they mock at us and scoff at the Name."[40] Justin comments on the courage as well as nonviolent character of Christians: "we who once killed each other not only do not make war on each other, but in order not to lie or deceive our inquisitors we gladly die for the confession of Christ."[41] And he claims that "we who were filled with war, and mutual slaughter, and every wickedness, have each through the whole earth changed our warlike weapons,—our swords into ploughshares, and our spears into implements of tillage."[42] Later, in response to some standard criticisms of the Christians, Athenagoras pleads that "we have learned not only not to return blow for blow, nor to sue those who plunder and rob us, but to those who smite us on one cheek to offer the other also, and to those who take away our coat to give our overcoat as well."[43]

Such texts from the first two centuries clearly have a pacifist tone. That tone is modified, here and there in the writings of the early church, only to the extent that the wars of ancient Israel are referred to without reproach, military metaphors are sometimes used to describe service to the Lord, and the apocalyptic consummation is portrayed in the language of battle. Overall, the early Christians were seriously committed to peace.

One may still question whether the issue of military force, as such, was fully engaged during this period. Most of the quotations refer to the *personal* response expected of Christians. On that level, they were almost uniformly expected to love their enemies and return good for evil. We do not know of Christians in the imperial armies prior to around A.D. 170, but that could partly be accounted for by the potential conflict of loyalties such service would demand: to serve in the army, one was expected to pay homage to Caesar in forms of worship that Christians took to be idolatry. It is interesting that the question of military service, as a potential option or decision for Christians, does not arise in the writings of this period. For most Christians, over most of these years, it probably was not a morally or politically feasible option.

The more serious and difficult question is whether Christians considered the coercive power of the state to be morally legitimate. Here the evidence is more mixed. Obviously Christians regarded the periodic waves of persecution as an outrage. To the extent the state set itself against the church, it set itself against God. But what about when the state attempted to maintain order within the empire and to protect the frontiers of the empire from periodic barbarian incursions? The Roman state, after all, was not one nation in a world of many interacting and competing nations. Warfare, in this period, was not between nations; it was to quell disturbances and protect the periphery. What was at stake, more or less, was the maintenance of order in a unified civilization representing to its inhabitants the Mediterranean world.

Reading the Christian literature of the first two centuries with this reality in mind, one is struck by the frequency of Christian assurances that they were not the enemies of the state. For one thing, the gentle, unselfish character of Christians could itself be no problem for the state (apart from the state's own overreaching violation of the religious conscience of Christians). Writings during this period point out that Christians are easily governed people. As the *Letter to Diognetus* puts it, Christians "obey the established laws, but in their own lives they go far beyond what the laws require."[44]

But more than that, there is a recurrent note of positive appreciation for the state in the pursuit of its appointed task. Note this remarkable prayer contained in *I Clement* concerning "our rulers and governors on earth":

> You, Master, gave them imperial power through your majestic and indescribable might, so that we, recognizing it was you who gave them the glory and honor, might submit to them, and in no way oppose your will. Grant them, Lord, health, peace, harmony, and stability, so that they may give no offense in administering the government you have given them. For it is you, Master, the heavenly "King of eternity," who give the sons of men glory and honor and authority over the earth's people.[45]

That authority is to be exercised with "peace, considerateness, and reverence." But still this passage clearly affirms imperial power. Justin's appeal to the emperor contains a similar affirmation of imperial authority: "So we worship God only, but in other matters we gladly serve you, recognizing you as emperors and rulers of men, and praying that along with your imperial power you may also be found to have a sound mind."[46]

Such passages do not contain a consistently developed political philosophy, nor do they specifically deal with the state's use of coercive force with its armies and police. But they do provide striking evidence of theologically grounded support for the state—and the only state known to these writers was one that had armies and police!

Portrait of Christians in the World

What were Christians *like* in those early years of the church's existence?

Obviously they did not wholly conform to the moral rhetoric of their teachers, else the teachings would not have been expressed in such forceful language. Nor was their community devoid of conflict and controversy. Fateful controversies over the fundamental attitude Christians should have toward the world were fought, with echoes destined to affect the whole later development of the church. Nor could all of the specific teachings of the early church still be viewed as morally sensitive and insightful. Strident moralism sometimes overtakes the rhetoric of love.

Nevertheless, running through most of these documents is a picture of people who believe in a loving Savior and who are themselves committed to a life of love. Echoing the familiar words of Paul's 1 Corinthians 13, *I Clement* describes the heart of Christian morality in these terms:

> Who can describe the bond of God's love? Who is capable of expressing its great beauty? The heights to which love leads are beyond description. Love unites us to God. "Love hides a multitude of sins." Love puts up with everything and is always patient. There is nothing vulgar about love, nothing arrogant. Love knows nothing of schism or revolt. Love does everything in harmony. By love all God's elect were made perfect. Without love nothing can please God. By love the Master accepted us. Because of the love he had for us, and in accordance with God's will, Jesus Christ our Lord gave his blood for us, his flesh for our flesh, and his life for ours.[47]

It is sometimes argued that the early Christians captivated people by upholding high moral standards. Admittedly their standards were in vivid contrast with the decadence of so much of the surrounding culture. The contrast must have impressed many people. Yet one wonders whether, beyond the negative moral commandments that abound in the literature of the period, the magnetism of the life of love may not have constituted the deeper appeal.

The paradoxical witness of that life is expressed with unusual power in the anomymous *Letter to Diognetus* written, we think, in the latter part of the second century. Acknowledging that "Christians cannot be distinguished from the rest of the human race by country or language or customs" and that "they do not live in cities of their own" or "use a peculiar form of speech" or "follow an eccentric manner of life," the writer of this letter claims that Christians "give proof of the remarkable and admittedly extraordinary constitution of their own commonwealth."[48] The letter continues:

> They live in their own countries, but only as aliens. They have a share in everything as citizens, and endure everything as foreigners. Every foreign land is their [native] land, and yet for them every [native] land is a foreign land. They marry, like everyone else, and they beget children, but they do not cast out their offspring. They share their board with each other, but not their marriage bed. It is true that they are "in the flesh," but they do not live "according to the flesh." They busy themselves on earth, but their citizenship is in heaven. They obey the established laws, but in their own lives they go far beyond what the laws require. They love [everyone], and by [everyone] they are persecuted.[49]

"To put it simply," this eloquent author concludes, "What the soul is in the body, that Christians are in the world. . . . The soul is shut up in the body, and yet itself holds the body together; while Christians are restrained in the world as in a prison, and yet themselves hold the world together."

The writings of these first centuries are not developed with great systematic power, but the *Letter to Diognetus* has nicely captured the depth of the witness of early Christians to a moral reality transcending conceptualization. It was perhaps enough, in those first centuries, that Christians protected their movement from world-denying Gnosticism, accepted responsibility for the poor, struggled with issues of sexual life in a time of loose morality, affirmed the legitimacy of the state, and above all grounded their faith in love.

4

SEMINAL THINKERS AND TRANSITIONS

In some respects, Ignatius of Antioch may have spoken for most of the church of the first two centuries with his comment that "the greatness of Christianity lies in its being hated by the world, not in its being convincing to it."[1] The church's objective was not to persuade the world of the reasonableness of the new faith. The point was to be a contagious example—which early Christianity obviously was.

Nevertheless, the time inevitably came when Christian thought had to engage the mind of the world. Thinking people, unconvinced by the truth of this new faith, could not have adopted it wholeheartedly. They could have been attracted by the love and the heroism of believers. But having acknowledged that Christianity was attractive, they could not have believed that it was also true. That may not have been a problem with very many people in the Roman world. The great philosophical movements, like Stoicism and Neoplatonism, did not enjoy mass followings. Nevertheless, their thinkers were also the political and cultural leaders. In the long run, the inability of Christians to be convincing to thoughtful Romans might have placed limits on their ability to influence the culture.

In any event, by the end of the second century, highly educated Christian thinkers were hard at work addressing the mind of the Roman world. The result was the emergence of a body of theological reflection that combined the faith of the primitive Christian church with sophisticated Graeco-Roman thought. In the development of a Christian ethics, this meant that more serious attention could now be given to reasons why a Christian morality could and should be adopted. Values, principles, practices, and virtues were now discussed more clearly on their merits, with less reliance upon revealed authority.

The Alexandrians

Alexandria, site of the greatest library of antiquity and center of Hellenistic thought, also became a major focal point of creative theology in the early church. Clement of Alexandria (c. A.D. 145 to c. 215) and his pupil Origen (c. A.D. 182 to c. 251) are particularly noteworthy. Both were deeply grounded in Hebrew and Christian traditions and in classical literature and philosophy. Both were superbly equipped to interpret Christian faith to sophisticated Greco-Roman audiences.

There is, in Clement's view, no necessary conflict between faith and reason. Since truth is one, the truths of philosophy support and prepare the way for the Christian faith: "Before the advent of the Lord, philosophy was necessary to the Greeks for righteousness. And now it becomes conducive to piety; being a kind of preparatory training to those who attain to faith through demonstration."[2] Even for believers, philosophy helps in understanding the faith. It is possible for an uneducated person to be a believer, according to Clement, but it is not possible for such a person to understand the faith believed.[3] While Clement thus does not confuse Christian piety and morality with knowledge and understanding, he insists that being "conversant with the art of reasoning" is very important in "confuting the deceitful opinions of the sophists."[4] And "demonstrations from the resources of erudition strengthen, confirm" us when our minds "are in a wavering state."[5] Clement finds much to approve in the inherited classical traditions of ethics, which he mines with great erudition. At the same time, he makes ample use of the tools of critical reasoning to unmask flaws in the views of the sophists and Epicureans. To the extent his work was known by contemporaries, the intellectually and morally serious non-Christians of the age could have been impressed by Clement.

Much of his writing seems designed to remove stumbling blocks to belief by non-Christians. At the deepest philosophical levels, his thought spoke to those who might have found Christian claims less than credible. Following in the older Alexandrian tradition of the Jewish philosopher Philo, he offered his sophisticated readers the possibility of allegorical interpretation where literal readings of scripture strained their credulity. Above all, he emphasized that God transcends all human symbols and concepts. The first principle or cause of everything cannot be exhibited as an object in space and time since it precedes and supports everything that exists in space and time. How, he asks, "can that be expressed which is neither genus, nor difference, nor species, nor individual, nor number; nay more, is neither an event, nor that to which an event happens?"[6] Thus he speaks of God:

> No one can rightly express Him wholly. For an account of His greatness He is ranked as the all, and is the Father of the universe. Nor are any parts to be predicated of Him. For the One is indivisible; wherefore also it is infinite, not considered with reference to inscrutability, but with reference to its being without dimensions, and not having a limit. And therefore it is without form and name. And if we name it, we do not do so properly, terming it either the One, or the Good, or Mind, or Absolute Being, or Father, or God, or Creator, or Lord. We speak not as supplying His name; but for want, we use good names, in order that the mind may have these as points of support, so as not to err in other respects. For each one by itself does not express God; but all together are indicative of the power of the Omnipotent.[7]

Clement grapples with the implications of this for Christians. "If, then, abstracting all that belongs to bodies and things called incorporeal, we cast ourselves into the greatness of Christ, and thence advance into immensity by holiness, we may reach somehow to the conception of the Almighty, knowing not what He is, but what He is not."[8] Clement himself shows a remarkable flexibility, at least for the times, in his choice of symbols and descriptive metaphors for God. Thus, while typically referring to God in masculine terms, he can write that "In His ineffable essence He is Father; in His compassion to us He became Mother. The Father by loving became feminine."[9]

Clement's writings address a variety of moral issues. He is especially famous for his interpretation of wealth in the essay "Who Is the Rich Man That Shall Be Saved?" That writing explores the ethical/theological meaning of the story of the rich young man (Mark 10:17–27) with its culminating observation that "it is easier for a camel to go through the eye of a needle than for a rich man to enter the kingdom of God" (Mark 10:25). Clement argues that this is not to be taken literally. Christ did not mean that a rich person could not be saved, but meant only that one who is attached to wealth, one whose life is centered on wealth, is separated from God's kingdom. Wealth as an idolatry and distraction is a grave spiritual danger. But the problem is not with wealth itself; it is with our *attitude* toward wealth. So, when Jesus says "sell thy possessions," the point is not to get rid of the property itself but to "banish from his soul his notions about wealth, his excitement and morbid feeling about it, the anxieties, which are the thorns of existence, which choke the seed of life."[10] Indeed, Clement observes, it does no good simply to get rid of one's wealth if one continues to grieve over the loss:

One, after ridding himself of the burden of wealth, may none the less have still the lust and desire for money innate and living; and may have abandoned the use of it, but being at once destitute of and desiring what [one] spent, may doubly grieve both on account of the absence of attendance, and the presence of regret.[11]

Material resources are necessary to life. Those who lack such necessities are harassed in mind and distracted from "better things." Moreover, lacking wealth, we lack the power to do good things.

In comparison with the bulk of earlier Christian writings on wealth and poverty, Clement's essay appears to rationalize an easier ethic for rich people. Certainly, it gives evidence of the growing attractiveness of the new faith to persons of greater affluence and power and of the gathering impulse among Christian leaders to attract such people. But it is more than this. Clement's essay is not perfunctory in its condemnation of materialism. Here, and in his *The Instructor*, Clement hammers away at the idolatries of wealth. In the latter writing, his criticisms of luxury and gluttony are almost as biting as those of an Amos or a James. (He refers to the "unhappy art— that of cookery, and the useless art of making pastry," noting that "people dare to call by the name of food their dabbling in luxuries, which glides into mischievous pleasures" and gives rise to disease.[12] And he lays a considerable burden on the rich to use their wealth for good ends, including the relief of the poor.

Clement is also famous in the history of Christian ethics for his detailed instructions on trivial details of social life, such as table manners: "From all slavish habits and excess we must abstain, and touch what is set before us in a decorous way; keeping the hand and couch and chin free of stains; preserving the grace of the countenance undisturbed, and committing no indecorum in the act of swallowing; but stretching out the hand at intervals in an orderly manner."[13] Does such advice betray the writer's wish not to be embarrassed by the less cultured of his fellow Christians?

Comparing Clement with earlier Christian writers, one is struck by the extent to which he evidently sought to bring the church into the social and cultural mainstream of Graeco-Roman civilization. But his views were not merely accommodations to that civilization. He sufficiently mastered its greatest thought and literature to be able to offer discriminating theological judgments while yet presenting an attractive case for Christianity among thoughtful contemporaries.

One final observation: It is very interesting that Clement has so little to say about politics and issues of war and peace. In the surviving corpus of his writings, not much is said about civil authority nor about the acceptability of military power. That may be all the more surprising in light of the sporadic outbreaks of persecution with which Christians had still to contend. But if Clement's main goal was to bring Christian influence to bear upon the cultural leadership of the Roman world, one would not expect him to have challenged the basic legitimacy of that world's institutions of government.

Clement's great pupil and successor Origen also drew heavily upon classical literature and philosophy. His vast corpus of writings also makes substantial use of the allegorical method of scriptural interpretation— which spares him some embarrassment in interpreting scriptural teachings that are in conflict with his own moral sensibilities. Those sensibilities are, however, formed through and through by scriptural teaching, in which Origen has been steeped. Familiar Christian virtues of love, kindness, generosity, and humility infuse his writing, gaining substance through thoughtful interpretations of scripture.

In an exploration of the moral significance of the Trinity, Origen speaks of the Father as source of our existence, of the Son as the word of reason by which we become rational beings, and of the Holy Spirit as the basis for receiving the righteousness of God. All humanity possesses existence and rationality, but the Holy Spirit is given only to the faithful: "The working of the power of God the Father and of the Son extended without distinction to every creature; but a share in the Holy Spirit we find possessed only by the saints."[14] In one very complex and lengthy sentence, Origen summarizes his trinitarian conception of Christian growth toward perfection or sanctification:

> Whence also the working of the Father, which confers existence upon all things, is found to be more glorious and magnificent, while each one, by participation in Christ, as being wisdom, and knowledge, and sanctification, makes progress, and advances to higher degrees of perfection; and seeing it is by partaking of the Holy Spirit that any one is made purer and holier, he obtains, when he is made worthy, the grace of wisdom and knowledge, in order that, after all stains of pollution and ignorance are cleansed and taken away, he may make so great an advance in holiness and purity, that the nature which he received from God may become such as is worthy of Him who gave it to be pure and perfect, so that the being which exists may be as worthy as He who called it into existence.[15]

Such a conception of the Trinity is interesting as a theological explanation of sanctification and moral growth. It is also interesting as a theological basis for entering into conversation with Greco-Roman moral philosophy, especially in its Stoic form. By treating the Second Person of the Trinity as reason, the possession of all human beings as rational creatures, Origen has provided a theological basis for moral thought that is not exclusively

Christian. Christ is the Word or *logos* to which the Stoics referred in their conception of the fundamental rationality of being. To the Stoics, humanity participates in the divine reason that is at the center of being. To Origen, Christ is the aspect of the Trinity manifesting the reason of God in which all humanity, whether or not Christian, shares. Interpreting Paul, Origen exclaims that "all have a share in Christ. . . . [Christ] is in the heart of all, in respect of His being the word or reason, by participating in which [all] are rational beings."[16] Thus, Origen can quote several biblical passages to emphasize that even non-Christians can, as rational beings, have no excuse for sin. But he can also enter into serious conversation with classical moral philosophy without having to invoke special revelation.

In doing so, Origen appeals to the concept of natural law. This is the moral law, promulgated by God the legislator, known by universal human reason. This law of nature stands in judgment over all human laws. When it is in conflict with human law, the former, not the latter, must be obeyed. Thus, Origen can appeal to reason in his defense against the charge that Christians do not obey the laws of countries in which they dwell. In one celebrated passage, Origen anticipates later theories of civil disobedience:

> As there are, then, generally two laws presented to us, the one being the law of nature, of which God would be the legislator, and the other being the written law of cities, it is a proper thing, when the written law is not opposed to that of God, for the citizens not to abandon it under pretext of foreign customs; but when the law of nature, that is, the law of God, commands what is opposed to the written law, observe whether reason will not tell us to bid a long farewell to the written code, and to the desire of its legislators, and to give ourselves up to the legislator God, and to choose a life agreeable to His word, although in doing so it may be necessary to encounter dangers, and countless labours, and even death and dishonour.[17]

In his *Against Celsus*, a reply to an earlier second-century pagan critic, Origen confronted the charge that Christians were politically and militarily irresponsible. According to Celsus (as reported by Origen), Christians were setting a disastrous example through their pacifism and aloofness toward public service: "For if all were to do the same as you," Celsus complained, "there would be nothing to prevent [the king from] being left in utter solitude and desertion, and the affairs of the earth would fall into the hands of the wildest and most lawless barbarians."[18] In his reply, Origen commented that if *all* were to do as the Christians, then "even the barbarians, when they yield obedience to the word of God, will become most obedient to the law, and most humane."[19] Christians, far from being aloof from the needs of the state, support it best through their prayers. "When the occasion requires," he writes, "we do . . . give help to kings, and that, so to say, a divine help."[20] Obedient to Paul's injunction to pray for those in authority, Christians offer "the more effective help . . . to kings, even more than is given by soldiers, who go forth to fight and slay as many of the enemy as they can."[21] If all the Romans were to do as the Christians, "they will, when they pray, overcome their enemies; or rather, they will not war at all, being guarded by that divine power which promised to save five entire cities for the sake of fifty just persons."[22] Those who serve God are the salt of the earth who "preserve the order of the world" as long as they remain uncorrupted. That order will, indeed, one day prevail over the whole world: "it will surely come to pass, that all who are endowed with reason shall come under one law. . . . [O]ur belief is, that the Word shall prevail over the entire rational creation, and change every soul into His own perfection."[23]

So, though Christians admittedly do not fight under the king, even when he requires them to, they still "fight on his behalf, forming a special army—an army of piety—by offering [their] prayers to God."[24]

Origen's reply to Celsus is interesting for two reasons: first it is confirmation that as late as the middle of the third century (when this was likely written) the pacifist witness remained a dominant Christian commitment, and second, it is a limited but real recognition of the legitimacy of civil authority. Origen speaks of the church as though it were "another national organization, founded by the Word of God,"[25] existing within each state. But the state itself is legitimately a part of the world order that God has created. Here there is some anticipation of Augustine's two cities and Luther's two kingdoms.

Tertullian

A younger contemporary of Origen, Tertullian (whose specific dates remain uncertain), influenced Christian ethics in the Latin world in very different ways. While the Alexandrians had sought where possible to bridge the gap between Christian thought and classical learning, Tertullian emphasized the conflicts and discontinuities. To be a Christian is to be estranged from pagan culture. Tertullian's often brilliant pen exposed the barbarities and idolatries of Roman civilization to scathing criticism. Nor did he neglect idolatries and apostasies he found in the church itself; his work on heresies remains an excellent source of information on diverse movements and opinions within the church at the close of the second century. Tertullian's sweeping attack on Roman civilization could be taken as a reversion to earlier forms of anti-intellectualism. But that would be to miss the depth of his familiarity with classical intellectual traditions and the intellectual brilliance of his criticism.

His first major writing, the *Apology*, written around 197, defends Christian morality and practice against calumnies and persecutions by Roman authorities while rebuking the latter for the crude immoralities into which Rome has fallen: the exposure of infants, the "madness of the circus," the "immodesty of the theatre," the "atrocities of the arena."[26] The Roman deities are themselves flagrantly immoral, and Roman life has fallen below even its own previous standards.

By contrast, the oppressed Christians are virtuous, caring, self-disciplined people, a great asset to the society that persecutes them. "We are," he writes, "a body knit together as such by a common religious profession, by unity of discipline, and by the bond of a common hope." He continues, "One in mind and soul, we do not hesitate to share our earthly goods with one another. All things are common among us but our wives."[27] "As it is with God himself, a peculiar respect is shown to the lowly" in the common meals of the Christians.[28] Nor is this close-knit body any threat to the political authority. In a remarkable passage, Tertullian writes of "the reverence and sacred respect of Christians to the emperor, whom we cannot but look up to as called by our Lord to his office. . . . [S]o that on valid grounds I might say Caesar is more ours than yours, for our God has appointed him."[29] Such respect is expressed in the constant prayers of the Christian community: "Without ceasing, for all our emperors we offer prayer. We pray for life prolonged; for security to the empire; for protection to the imperial house; for brave armies, a faithful senate, a virtuous people, the world at rest, whatever, as man or Caesar, an emperor would wish."[30] The emperor, he concludes, "gets his sceptre where he first got his humanity; his power where he got the breath of life."[31]

In this early writing, Tertullian obviously does not challenge the moral legitimacy of military activity. That point is underscored by Tertullian in one of the earliest references to the existence of Christian soldiers in the imperial armies. Tertullian asserts that the emperor Marcus Aurelius had written of the end of a drought "by the rains obtained through the prayers of the Christians who chanced to be fighting under him."[32] Later, Tertullian was to express strong opposition to military service. In his *On Idolatry*, he writes that this is inherently idolatrous: "One soul cannot be due to two *masters*, God and Caesar." He concludes that "in disarming Peter," the Lord "unbelted every soldier."[33]

In his later writings, under the influence of Montanism, Tertullian's ethics became more uncompromising. In all areas of life—sexual, economic, cultural, political, military—the gulf between Christian standards of holiness and the world's enslavement to idolatries and demonic forces becomes more absolute. To be a Christian is to accept those standards and to renounce those idolatries. Those who take on this commitment and then fall away from it are not again to be received into the Christian community.

The Constantinian Watershed

It would be difficult to exaggerate the importance of the events whereby Christianity changed its status from a despised and often persecuted sect into the dominant and favored religious force in Roman civilization. The judgment that Constantine effected "the greatest revolution in mind and manners that has ever been known among men"[34] may be such an exaggeration. But the transformation of both Christianity and the Roman Empire decisively changed all subsequent Western history.

The details of the events need not be elaborated here. Though still a minority of the empire's inhabitants, the church had obviously grown by leaps and bounds during its first three centuries. By A.D. 313 when Constantine became undisputed emperor under the Christian insignia, the Christian population may have numbered in the millions. The church's credentials had, by that time, acquired some respectability through the writings of figures like Clement, Origen, and Tertullian. The moral virtue of the Christians contrasted impressively with the cruelty and decadence of the popular culture. Even the occasional outbursts of persecution contributed to the church's growing attractiveness, for it gave the Christians opportunity to demonstrate the seriousness of their commitment. The blood of the martyrs became, as Tertullian said, the seed of the church. So the Edict of Milan, whereby Constantine granted recognition and freedom to the Christians, did not occur in a vacuum. And the subsequent moves conferring preferred status on the church came only after the church had become a force to be reckoned with.

Still, this vast reversal of fortune and the eagerness with which it was received by Christians posed new questions that have continued to haunt Christian ethics. The union of religious faith with cultural and political power is not an unmixed blessing. Under the new order, how could one be sure who were and who were not truly committed? If being a Christian confers respectability and power, then is it not a ready temptation for those who are not really Christian to pretend that they are? Is there not a corresponding temptation for Christian thinkers to accommodate the faith to the cultural and political interests of those in power? How can the purity of the faith be safeguarded against cultural idolatries?

The question cannot be answered on the basis of the events and writings of that era alone. Given the fact of the Constantinian reversal and its effects on subsequent Western history, each subsequent age has had to struggle with the question in fresh ways.[35] Efforts to influence the course of history entail interactions with centers of power and, if successful, lead to the empowerment of particular views and those who hold them. Efforts to maintain moral purity by sectarian withdrawal from the fallen world contribute to self-righteousness and illusions about the church's own moral perfection. The dilemmas are, in a sense, perennial; they are addressed in one way or another by every generation of Christian ethics.

We do well to remember, therefore, that dilemmas involving the attempt to influence the world with the gospel did not begin with the Edict of Milan. Earliest Christianity, despite certain obviously sectarian tendencies, had to come to terms with the world it sought to influence. That is even more obvious in the case of the formative thinkers whose work is illustrated in this chapter. Figures like Clement and Origen sought to present the Christian case intelligibly. Although their ideas were often in conflict with the dominant moral currents of the age, they accepted many of the classical thought patterns and political institutions of the time. Even Tertullian, as we have seen, gave early legitimation to the very powers that were persecuting the church. The church did not simply change its mind in order to accept its new sociopolitical circumstances. The way had been prepared. Nevertheless, the realities of success did pose new problems for Christian thought in the last years of the Roman Empire.

Lactantius

One of the first Christian thinkers to respond to the new situation was Lactantius (c. 260–330). Employed as a tutor to Constantine's son, Lactantius addressed his principal theological work, *The Divine Institutes,* to the emperor. The changed situation is suggested in Lactantius's effusive words to Constantine as the first Roman emperor "to acknowledge and honour the majesty of the one and only true God. For when that most happy day had shone upon the world, in which the Most High God raised you to the prosperous height of power, you entered upon a dominion which was salutary and desirable for all, with an excellent beginning, when, restoring justice which had been overthrown and taken away, you expiated the most shameful deed of others."[36]

The work itself is an extended critique of Greek and Roman deities and philosophies, defending throughout the superiority of Christian worship. The chief good of humanity, as explored by Lactantius, is not to be found in the theories of the philosophers, for these have to do with things common to animals as well as humans or things not available to all humans.[37] So pleasure, riches, and power are not the chief good. These have to do with the body, which ultimately perishes. The chief good is the imperishable good of the soul, which is from God. We are born to worship and serve God, and "to serve God is nothing else than to maintain and preserve justice by good works." Justice, to Lactantius, is not conceivable apart from God. His basically theological conception of justice is emphasized in these words: "For what is humanity itself, but justice? what is justice, but piety? And piety is nothing else than the recognition of God as a parent."[38] The philosophers have failed to grasp that their conceptions are transitory; only an understanding of justice that grounds it in the source of all reality can fittingly be called the chief good.

Lactantius's moral conception makes much of God as the divine parent of all humanity, thereby implicitly emphasizing that humankind is a single moral community. "Divine religion," he argues, "which alone effects that man should esteem man dear, and should know that he is bound to him by the tie of brotherhood, since God is alike a Father to all, so as to share the bounties of the common God and Father with those who do not possess them; to injure no one, to oppress no one, not to close his door against a stranger, nor his ear against a suppliant, but to be bountiful, beneficent, and liberal. . . . This truly is justice."[39] In a world in which God were truly and universally worshiped, he writes, "there would be no need of so many and varying laws to rule men, since the law of God alone would be sufficient for perfect innocence; nor would there be any need of prisons, or the swords of rulers, or the terror of punishments, since the wholesomeness of the divine precepts infused into the breasts of men would of itself instruct them to works of justice."

While Lactantius's praise of Constantine might appear to be an easy capitulation to the "principalities and powers" of the new age, in substance he sought rather to define the new situation and to do so in theological terms. If anything, he may have overstated his objections to classical theories of justice in order to emphasize that no culture is adequately formed unless it is grounded in faith in God. The speed with which Roman law reformed many of the practices criticized by Christian moralists suggests that, in the beginning at least, Constantinianism was less the capture of Christianity by imperial power than the transformation of imperial power by Christianity.[40]

Other Formative Thinkers

A succession of other notable Christian thinkers also graced this age. The fourth-century Cappadocians—Basil of Caesarea, Gregory of Nazianzus, and Gregory of Nyssa—all made significant contributions to Christian moral teaching, especially on issues touching on economics. All three emphasize sharing with the poor. Wealth is spiritually dangerous if hoarded or spent selfishly. Money given to the poor is an investment in eternal treasure; it is faithful stewardship of what actually belongs to God. Basil elaborated the traditional rejection of usury, reminding his readers that "in many passages of the Scripture, lending with interest is condemned as sinful" and arguing that "it is extremely inhuman that one has to beg for the most basic necessities to support his life while another is not satisfied with the capital he has, but excogitates ways of increasing his opulence at the expense of the poor in distress."[41] Basil grounded his moral teaching both on theological teaching ("our Lord invites us to adopt the spirit of sharing, mutual love") and a conception of human nature ("Man, indeed, is a political and social animal. Now, in social relations and in common life, a certain disposition to share one's goods is necessary in order to assist the needy").[42] As bishop, Basil put his economic views into practice with the development of an impressive set of institutions designed to aid the ill and disabled, travelers, and the unemployed.[43]

Gregory of Nyssa is especially noteworthy for his vigorous rejection of slavery, which he ridicules as a vain attempt to put a price on persons created in the image of God: "Now, tell me, who is the one who buys, who is the one who sells the one who is God's image, who must rule over the whole earth, who has received from God the dominion over all that exists on earth as heritage?"[44] In a poignant homily on the virtue of mercy, Gregory portrays the kind of social existence that would be possible if "such an attitude of mind to our inferiors were innate in all of us": "there would no longer be either superfluity or want. Life would no longer be lived in diametrically opposite ways; man would no longer be distressed by want or humiliated by slavery, nor would dishonor sadden him. For all things would be common to all, and man's life as a citizen would be marked by complete equality before the law, since the person who was responsible for the government would of his own free will be on a level with the rest." In such a world, indeed, peace and justice would prevail, for there would no longer be any cause for enmity.[45]

In addition to their theological contributions, which cannot be explored here, the Cappadocians thus provide a striking illustration of Christian ethical thought in an age when social power need no longer be confronted in simply adversarial terms.

Similar things could be said concerning Saint John Chrysostom, whose many homilies strongly condemn unshared wealth, while affirming the legitimacy of government. Chrysostom distinguishes between specific unjust rulers, who may not have been chosen by God, and political authority itself which, as Paul had said, was a part of God's providence: "I am not speaking about individual rulers, but about authority in itself. I mean to say that it is the will of God's wisdom that there should be authority, that some govern and others obey, and that things should not be carried on in confusion, the people swaying like waves in this direction and that."[46] Despite a strongly egalitarian flavor in some of his economic writings, Chrysostom could still assert that "God has established different degrees and forms of subjection, as that, for instance, of husband and wife, of son and father, of old and young, of free and slaves, of ruler and ruled, of master and disciple." This is necessary, he argues, "since equality and power and honor lead many times to fighting."[47]

Bishop Ambrose of Milan (339–397) was a particularly striking representative of the new establishment Christianity of the fourth century. A Roman governor prior to his baptism and designation as bishop, Ambrose was thoroughly grounded in political practice and steeped in classical learning. Much of his writing, in fact, is consciously dependent on Stoic works as well as Christian sources. His writings range from trivialities of etiquette that are reminiscent of Clement (e.g., "An appropriate stride gives the appearance of authority, stability, and dignity, and reflects tranquillity. It should be simple and natural so that it does not appear to be intentional, conceited, or artificial"[48]) to serious reflections on the meaning of justice.

Justice, to Ambrose, is a profoundly communitarian concept. Noting that both justice and humanitarianism are needed to hold society together, Ambrose regards justice as the more important: "The splendor of Justice is great," he writes. "Justice exists for the good of all and helps to create unity and society among us. It is so high that all else must fall beneath its authority."[49] Applying these ideas of justice specifically to economic matters, Ambrose does not hesitate to arrive at radical conclusions:

> The philosophers also believe that justice requires that public property be treated as public and private property as private. But this is not what nature illustrates, for nature has provided all things for common use. God has decreed that all things are produced so that food is available to all and the earth is possessed by everyone equally. Nature provides for everyone, but greed has restricted the supply to only a few.[50]

"When," however, "our goal is to make money and accumulate possessions, to buy more land and be the richest of all, we have rejected the virtue of justice and are not able to be a blessing to others. How can you be just," he asks, "if you attempt to add to yourself what you take from others?"[51]

Ambrose is characteristic of the age in no longer writing as a pacifist. Still, he approves violence only when necessary in the defense of others. Violent self-defense is rejected as contrary to the virtue of love.[52]

Unquestionably, the transformation wrought by the triumph of Constantine was enormously important in the development of early Christianity. Whether it effected a sea change in Christian ethics may not be as clear as some have supposed. Most of the ideas of post-Constantinian thinkers are anticipated in earlier Christian thought, and those same post-Constantinian thinkers clearly did not simply capitulate to political leadership. In certain matters, especially relating to sexual morality, the changes may have been more dramatic.

5

THE MORAL VISION OF SAINT AUGUSTINE

Assessments of Augustine vary. An otherwise appreciative John Mahoney can write that "for all his tenderness and mystic yearning, there is also to be found a violence, not only of language, but also in Augustine's very way of thinking."[1] Or Peter C. Phan can speak of him as "certainly the greatest Latin Father and one of the greatest theologians of all times."[2] Certainly his influence is almost without parallel in the history of Christian thought. Asked to name the three most important theologians of Christian history, some might dispute the identity of the other two, but virtually all knowledgeable people would include Augustine in the list.

Augustine's lifetime (354–430) began some forty years after the Edict of Milan and ended some twenty years after the sack of Rome by Alaric's Goths. The first of these events had brought relief and new legal status to the church, challenging Christian thinkers to address moral questions from inside the circle of power in a great world empire. The second signaled the fragility of that empire, a first sign of its coming disintegration. Augustine's work was directly relevant to both. It uniquely marked the transition from early to medieval Christian thought in the West. More than that, his mind dominated Western Christian theology for the next millennium and, in various ways, continues to be very influential.

The Moral Will

To Augustine, there is no evil outside the will. God the Creator has created only good things, and there is no other creator alongside God. Breaking

51

with the Manichaeans—by whom he had been influenced for nearly a decade—Augustine rejected every form of theological or metaphysical dualism. God alone is the source of all being, and God is wholly good. All of God's works, as an expression of God's nature, are themselves good. Evil, as such, is therefore not created by God. But neither does it have an independent source outside of God. Rather, it exists as a movement away from the good or, as he puts it in the *Confessions*, evil is "nothing but a privation of good, until at last a thing ceases altogether to be."[3] In these points Augustine was deeply influenced by Neoplatonic doctrine.

When we are attracted by evil, he argued, it is because we perceive it to be good. Indeed, insofar as it has existence it is good. But it is a lesser good, and it becomes evil because it is a substitute for God. Evil, thus, exists in our inordinate love of a lesser good. Evil is not a property of objects outside the will. The lesser good is a good, but it is good only as it is good to God. We love the lesser good appropriately only when we love it through our love for God. We do not love other people for themselves, but for what they are to God. It is not inaccurate to say that we love God in the other. Similarly, we love lesser objects as they are for God. There is thus a ground for loving all things, not as ends in themselves, but as they are to their Creator.

An evil will thus is a will directed away from God; it is simply a misdirected will. But its misdirection is away from its own well-being, its own salvation.

Sin, therefore, is error or untruth. It is based upon a mistaken conception of what is good for us. Augustine's view is set forth graphically in this passage:

> Man indeed desires happiness even when he does so live as to make happiness impossible. What could be more of a lie than a desire like that? This is the reason why every sin can be called a lie. For, when we choose to sin, what we want is to get some good or get rid of something bad. The lie is in this, that what is done for our good ends in something bad, or what is done to make things better ends by making them worse. Why this paradox, except that the happiness of man can come not from himself but only from God, and that to live according to oneself is to sin, and to sin is to lose God?[4]

But sin is not simply intellectual error; it is misdirection of the will. Augustine writes that human pride is the root of all sin. "And what is pride," he asks, "but an appetite for inordinate exaltation? Now, exaltation is inordinate when the soul cuts itself off from the very Source to which it should keep close and somehow makes itself and becomes an end to itself." "This takes place," he continues, "when the soul becomes inordinately pleased with itself, and such self-pleasing occurs when the soul falls away from the unchangeable Good which ought to please the soul far more than the soul can please itself."[5] Original sin was the falling away of "our first parents" (Adam and Eve), who had fallen away even before eating the forbidden fruit. That is, they had fallen away from God. Still, the fall was not complete, or they would have become "absolutely nothing." But "no longer to be in God but to be in oneself . . . is not to be wholly nothing but to be approaching nothingness."[6] In an eloquent passage on humility, Augustine concludes that "there is, then, a kind of lowliness which in some wonderful way causes the heart to be lifted up, and there is a kind of loftiness which makes the heart sink lower. . . . The kind of lowliness that makes us close to God exalts us," but the "loftiness" that falls away from God causes us to be lower.[7]

Augustine, thus, grounds Christian ethics in the moral will, not in the goodness or evil of objects outside the will. The will is good or bad in accordance with what it worships and loves. A will directed by its love for God is good, while a will directed by love of self and lesser goods is evil—even though those lesser goods are not, in themselves, evil.

Augustine's writing is one of the first in the history of Christian thought to grapple with the problem of freedom of the will. Acknowledging that there can be no moral obligation where there is no freedom to choose and to do, Augustine nevertheless insisted upon God's absolute foreknowledge of the choices all people will in fact make. To God, past, present, and future exist in timeless eternity.[8] To Augustine, God's foreknowledge does not minimize human freedom: God just knows how that freedom will be exercised. In these views, Augustine consciously disagrees with the Stoic philosopher Cicero, who held that divine foreknowledge logically implies the necessity of fate. "Be these tortuous strifes and disputations of the philosophers what they will," Augustine replies, "we who profess belief in the supreme and true God confess, likewise, His will, His supreme power, His foreknowledge. Nor are we dismayed by the difficulty that what we choose to do freely is done of necessity, because He whose foreknowledge cannot be deceived foreknew that we would choose to do it."[9] Accusing Cicero of giving up God in order to affirm human freedom, Augustine insisted that people of faith want both God and freedom. "Our conclusion is that our wills have power to do all that God wanted them to do and foresaw they could do. Their power, such as it is, is real power. What they are to do they themselves will most certainly do, because God foresaw both that they could do it and that they would do it and His knowledge cannot be mistaken."[10]

The Two Cities

This conception of the moral will became the basis of Augustine's social ethic, expressed in its most mature form in *The City of God*. The immediate occasion for his writing of this great work was the need for a Christian explanation of Rome's new vulnerability in the fifth century. After the sack of Rome by Alaric in A.D. 410, Augustine was challenged to show that this catastrophe was not the result of the rise of Christianity. Pagan writers argued that Rome had been weakened by the embrace of the soft Christian virtues—love, kindness, patience, etc.—and the corresponding neglect of the gods and great civic virtues of pagan Rome, which had stressed leadership and manly courage. Christianity was causing Roman civilization to disintegrate. The only thing that could prevent further catastrophe was a return to Rome's traditional religions and moral virtues.

Augustine, in reply, roundly criticized the injustices and depravities of pre-Christian Rome. But the heart of the matter was the illusions upon which Rome had been based. Even the noblest of the pagans, being devoted to self-love, contributed to the undermining of the commonweal. In a classic passage, Augustine distinguished between the city of earth and the city of God. The former, based on self-love and transitory goods, is destined to perish. The latter, based upon the worship of God, is eternal.

> Accordingly, two cities have been formed by two loves: the earthly by the love of self, even to the contempt of God; the heavenly by the love of God, even to the contempt of self. The former, in a word, glories in itself, the latter in the Lord. For the one seeks glory from men; but the greatest glory is God, the witness of conscience. The one lifts up its head in its own glory; the other says to its God, "Thou art my glory, and the lifter up of mine head." In the one, the princes and the nations it subdues are ruled by the love of ruling; in the other, the princes and the subjects serve one another in love, the latter obeying, while the former take thought of all. . . . And therefore the wise men of the one city, living according to man, have sought for profit to their own bodies or souls, or both. . . . But in the other city there is no human wisdom, but only godliness, which offers due worship to the true God, and looks for its reward in the society of the saints, of holy angels as well as holy men, "that God may be all in all."[11]

The earthly city, corrupted by self-love, is destined to fail. In this respect Rome is but one illustration. Nevertheless, in the providence of God, the earthly city does contribute to the temporal well-being of humankind, however imperfectly. Even the Roman republic, in its day, was an "exquisite masterpiece," although it was flawed by the absence of true justice.[12] God, in fact, granted the Romans "the temporal glory of a splendid empire" as "reward for the praiseworthy efforts or virtues by which they strove to attain that glory." Even the pagans were devoted to the common good, subordinating their private property to the community, resisting avarice, refraining from crime. Their laws have governed many peoples.[13] Thus, while destined to fail, the city of this world "has a finality of its own; it reaches such happiness by sharing a common good as is possible when there are no goods but the things of time to afford it happiness. . . . [T]he aims of human civilization are good, for this is the highest end that [humanity] can achieve."[14]

To what extent is the city of God a possibility within human history? Clearly Augustine does not believe it possible for that city to reign in pure form until the consummation of history. Nevertheless, it does exist, alongside its earthly counterpart, among those for whom love of God takes precedence over love of self. Such people exist within the earthly city as a foretaste of the eternal city. The heavenly city is, in its earthly existence, a city of pilgrims, a wayfaring company. In some respects, Augustine is referring to the church[15]—and thus Augustine's work was often interpreted over the next millennium of Christian history. But he seems well aware that there are people within the church for whom love of self is dominant while some of the church's apparent enemies are destined to be its friends: "On earth, these two cities are linked and fused together, only to be separated at the Last Judgment."[16]

The city of God rises above human diversities to affirm what is universally good, even within the temporal order. Augustine writes that "this heavenly city . . . while it sojourns on earth, calls citizens out of all nations, and gathers together a society of pilgrims of all languages, not scrupling about diversities in the manners, laws, and institutions whereby earthly peace is secured and maintained, but recognizing that, however various these are, they all tend to one and the same end of earthly peace." The heavenly city "preserves and adapts" human diversities, "so long as no hindrance to the worship of the one supreme and true God is thus introduced." Thus, the heavenly city "avails itself of the peace of earth, and, so far as it can without injuring faith and godliness, desires and maintains a common agreement among men regarding the acquisition of the necessaries of life, and makes this earthly peace bear upon the peace of heaven."[17]

This portrait of the city of God, as it interacts in and with the earthly city, is suggestive of the catholic or universal church. As a catholic society, the church gathers up and affirms all human diversities that are not in conflict with the worship of God. This is but an expression of Augustine's basic ethic, for the diversities represent not competing but complementary goods inasmuch as they are all good to God and represent human good, too, insofar as they are affirmed through God. In this sense, Augustine's doctrine of the church is an expression of his view of human society as it is intended by God. The church, except for its own involvement in sin, is a manifestation on earth of God's intention for human life.

Peace and Justice

Augustine writes of peace as the universal goal of humankind. "There is no such thing," he insists, "as a human heart that does not crave for joy and peace." That is even so of those who seek war, for "what they want is to win" and "their battles are but bridges to glory and to peace." That is to say, peace is the *purpose* of war. And even those who plot to disturb peace merely do so "to fashion a new peace nearer to the heart's desire; it is not because they dislike peace as such. It is not that they love peace less, but that they love their kind of peace more." Even robber bands are bound together by a kind of peace: "The more violence and impunity they want in disturbing the peace of [others] the more they demand peace among themselves." When such people succeed in dominating cities or nations, they "impose on [their enemies] the victor's will and call it peace."[18]

So peace, taken in this broader sense, is not a sufficient moral norm. It must be defined by justice as well. Ultimately, of course, the only peace that counts with Augustine as real peace is the peace of God, which also contains perfect justice. On earth, however, there is need for specific attention to justice. For "justice being taken away, then, what are kingdoms but great robberies. For what are robberies themselves, but little kingdoms."[19]

In agreement with Aristotle's formal definition, Augustine writes of the task of justice as assuring "that to each is given what belongs to each."[20] Within the self, justice is the subordination of the body to the soul and of the soul to God. Within society, justice is subordination of the people to authorities and of authorities to God. In an address to Christian emperors, Augustine spells out the implications:

> We call those Christian emperors happy who govern with justice, who are not puffed up by the tongues of flatterers or the services of sycophants, but remember that they are men. We call them happy when they think of sovereignty as a ministry of God and use it for the spread of true religion; when they fear and love and worship God; when they are in love with the Kingdom in which they need fear no fellow sharers; when they are slow to punish, quick to forgive; when they punish, not out of private revenge, but only when forced by the order and security of the republic, and when they pardon, not to encourage impunity, but with the hope of reform; when they temper with mercy and generosity the inevitable harshness of their decrees.[21]

Taking note of the tendencies of power to corrupt, Augustine adds that "we call those happy who are all the more disciplined in their lusts just because they are freer to indulge them; who prefer to curb the waywardness of their own passions rather than to rule the peoples of the world, and who do this not out of vainglory but out of love for everlasting bliss."[22]

The Doctrine of "Just War"

In his voluminous writings, Augustine commented on many specific moral questions. On some of these, such as slavery (which he did not condemn), Augustine reflected conventional Christian thinking of his time. At two or three points, however, his thought was destined to have enduring influence.

He was, for instance, one of the first to articulate a Christian doctrine of just or justified war. While he did not write a systematic treatise on that subject, his scattered discussions of the circumstances under which Christians could approve of war formed a substantial base for thought by later generations.

Augustine clearly was not a pacifist, but his devotion to peace is evident throughout his writings. He uses biting language to characterize even the military requirements for preserving the Roman peace: "There is one war after another, havoc everywhere, tremendous slaughterings of men." And this has led to civil wars, with attendant massacres and other ravages of war, giving rise to "even more wretched anxieties for human beings." Anyone, he concludes, "who will consider sorrowfully evils so great, such horrors and such savagery, will admit his human misery. . . . [I]t is only the loss of all humane feeling that could make [anyone] call such a life 'the happy life.' "[23]

In face of this reality, "a good ruler will wage wars only if they are just," and "he will begin by bewailing the necessity he is under of waging even just wars." War is a moral exception. It "is justified only by the injustice of an aggressor."[24] Even then, he writes in his treatise *Against Faustus*, war can be undertaken only by the legitimate authority:

> It makes a difference for what reasons and under whose authority men undertake wars that are to be waged. The natural order of things, which is designed for the peace of mankind, requires that the authority for waging war, and the planning of it, rest with the chief of state. Soldiers, in turn, for the sake of the peace and safety of all are obliged to carry out a war that has been decided on.[25]

In the conduct of war or the inflicting of harsh punishments (such as capital punishment, of which Augustine approved), the motive of rulers, soldiers, and police must be loving. He explains this apparent paradox in a homily on 1 John:

You may chastize but it is love that does this, not cruelty. You may strike but you do it for disciplinary reasons because your love for love itself does not permit you to leave the other person undisciplined. At times what comes from love and hatred seems self-contradictory. Hatred sometimes comes out in sweet tones and love in harsh ones.[26]

The point is applied specifically to those instances when a ruler must inflict coercion upon heretics—which Augustine had opposed earlier in his life but came later to support. While acknowledging that coercion does not of itself change people's minds, Augustine supposed that "the difficulty or pain a [person] endures serves as an incentive" to that person to think about the reasons for the suffering. Heretics, such as the Donatists to whom these words are addressed, should reflect that "howsoever we treat you we do so out of love for you . . . even when we are acting contrary to your own desires."[27]

The importance of love is underscored by Augustine's disapproval of the use of force in self-defense: "I do not approve of killing another man in order to avoid being killed oneself unless one happens to be a soldier or public official and thus acting not on [one's] own behalf but for the sake of others, or for the city in which [one] lives."[28]

Furthermore, while legitimate uses of military force may be undertaken without guilt or apology, Augustine urges authorities to be merciful whenever possible: "Just as we use force on a man as long as he resists and rebels, so, too, we should show him mercy once he has been vanquished or captured, especially when there is no fear of a future disturbance of the peace."[29]

In summary, Augustine approved of war as a last resort, when necessary to prevent or punish aggression (or heresy), when undertaken by rightful authority, when motivated by love, when pursued with mercy and restraint. These principles, never fully developed by Augustine, were to be expanded and elaborated by the church into the doctrine of just war.

Human Sexuality

Augustine's teachings on sexuality were also destined to have major influence in subsequent Christian history. Perusal of Augustine's autobiographical *Confessions* makes clear that he had serious problems with this subject. Evidently having himself very strong sex drives, the control of those drives was a fundamental aspect of his religious conversion in his early thirties. Prior to that he had lived for some years with a concubine, the mother of his only child. Resolved to marry in a proper way, he dismissed the concubine, only to take up with another before finally deciding not to marry. He did not conclude that marriage is somehow immoral, but he condemned sexual intercourse for any purpose other than procreation. That point was underscored by his disapproval of abstention from intercourse during the fertile periods (an earlier version of the rhythm method of birth control).[30] All sexual intercourse not for procreation is an expression of lust.

While sexual lust or concupiscence assumes enormous importance in Augustine's discussions of sin, it should be remembered that even this powerful drive is not, to him, the *cause* of sin. The cause of sin is our turning away from God. Sexual lust is an occasion for such rebellion, albeit a particularly compelling one.

It is a debatable question whether Augustine's pervasive sense of the sinfulness of lust served indirectly to distort his attitude toward women. However, John Mahoney's interpretation of Augustine at this point may not be far wide of the mark:

> Lacking, of course, from Augustine's introspective makeup was any positive appreciation of women, and he seems to have considered them as little more than sex objects. He could not for the life of him think of any reason why woman should have been given to man other than for the procreation of children, "as the soil is a help to the seed." She was physically weaker and her friendship could not compare with that of another man.[31]

In any event, Augustine, like Paul before him, elected to maintain a life of strictest celibacy for himself, and the net effect of his teaching is to suggest that that is morally the higher course for those for whom it is possible.

The Use and Enjoyment of Riches

In his writings on economic questions, Augustine reflected both the traditional Christian suspicion of riches and the (then) more recent tendency to find ways of justifying the possession of wealth. His distinction between "use" (*uti*) and "enjoy" (*frui*) had the latter effect. Wealth is not evil in itself; it is a part of God's creation and, like the rest of creation, it is good. But like the rest of creation it is good as it is good to God; it is not good in itself. "To enjoy anything means to cling to it with affection for its own sake. To use a thing is to employ what we have received for our use to obtain what we want, provided that it is right for us to want it."[32] The problem is that we often enjoy what we should be using (worldly goods) but use what we should enjoy (God). "It is a perversion for people to want to enjoy money, but merely to make use of God. Such people do not spend money for the sake of God, but worship God for the sake of money."[33] Wealth, accordingly, is an instrumental value, not an intrinsic one. When we make it intrinsic, it becomes an idol in place of God. When we treat it instrumentally, it can be a facility for a life centered on God. When so used, the rich are generous to the poor, refuse to take interest on loans (usury), and above all never surrender to greed.

The practical consequences of this distinction—and Augustine's own disenchantment with wealth—are illustrated in this passage from the *City of God*:

> Let us imagine two . . . men, let us suppose that one is poor, or, better, in moderate circumstances; the other, extremely wealthy. But, our wealthy man is haunted by fear, heavy with cares, feverish with greed, never secure, always restless, breathless from endless quarrels with his enemies. By these miseries, he adds to his possessions beyond measure, but he also piles up for himself a mountain of distressing worries. The man of modest means is content with a small and compact patrimony. He is loved by his own, enjoys the sweetness of peace in his relations with kindred, neighbors and friends, is religious and pious, of kindly disposition, healthy in body, self-restrained, chaste in morals, and at peace with his conscience. I wonder if there is anyone so senseless as to hesitate over which of the two to prefer.[34]

Still, Augustine does not consider the coexistence of rich and poor to be a theological or moral scandal. It is a part of God's plan: "Who made the two? The Lord made the rich so they could find help in the poor, and the poor to test the rich."[35] In this respect, as in so many others, Augustine marks the transition from early Christianity to the Christianity of the medieval world.

PART III

Medieval Christianity

Augustine was doubtless right in protesting that Rome's political and military vulnerabilities should not be attributed to its becoming Christian. The church may, indeed, have deepened the basis of unity in Roman civilization, helping thereby to stabilize its political institutions. The disintegration of empire did, however, follow closely on the heels of Christian triumph. The division of East and West had already begun, and imperial centers in Constantinople and Rome (or Milan) signaled what was to be a major split within the church as well as in the political order. In the West, the victory of the Visigoths at the battle of Adrianople in 378, the sack of Rome by Alaric's Goths in 410, and subsequent establishment of federated kingdoms in Gaul, Spain, and Africa by assorted Visigoths, Vandals, Franks, and Burgundians effectively signaled the end of the Roman Empire as it had existed for centuries. The integrated civil and economic life of that empire—symbolized by the fact that at the height of imperial power it was possible to transmit a message from England to Rome by relay riders over the superb roads in scarcely more than a day's time—was no longer sustainable. Politically, militarily, economically, territorial rule replaced empire.

Remarkably, this did not particularly diminish Christian influence. The various Germanic tribes were positively attracted by Roman civilization, of which Christianity was now an essential part. Their conversion to Christianity meant that the territorial kingdoms and principalities were Christian even though no longer directly subject to Roman rule. Thus, the church, which had been so shortly before a limited community within a great political empire, now had a universal reach within which the remnants of that empire were a limited part.

What was this new Christian reality? Was it the "Dark Ages" of popular imagination, a period of intellectual starvation and religious repression? Or did it correspond to the romantic vision of a Christopher Dawson, who wrote of the thousand years of medieval Christian civilization as "a living and growing organism—a great *tree of culture* which bore rich fruit in its season"?[1]

That is a difficult question to answer since both characterizations are partly true. It is important to remember that the thousand years, more or less, of medieval Christianity was a very long time. The reality of those centuries was very complex. It includes centuries of effective isolation of various territorial churches, the eventual achievement of a unified church under strong papal rule, centuries of struggle between religious and civil authorities, a flowering of Christian movements (some defined as heretical or schismatic, some incorporated within the catholic whole), the challenge of Islam that affected Eastern and Western Christendom in different ways, the development of feudalistic economies. If Augustinian thought had dominant influence in this world, that was largely because it was functionally so relevant to its realities. The conception of the city of God, a wayfaring community, in but not altogether of the world, beautifully anticipated the needs of the church in a disintegrating empire. The church, Augustine had effectively said, can function anywhere, under any circumstances. Augustine's basic moral conception, centering in love of God and the renunciation of self, provided a grounding for the increasingly important monastic movement around which so much of the life of church and community spiritually centered. Augustine's doctrine of just war provided a groundwork of rules to govern the quarrels of rival Christian kingdoms and principalities. Augustine's economic ethic laid a kind of foundation for the moral assumptions of medieval feudalism. Whether or not Augustine's sexual ethic was entirely functional, it clearly dominated much of the morality of the medieval world.

At its best, that medieval world may have been something of the theonomous culture of which Paul Tillich has spoken—a culture that is transparent to the ground of its being. At its worst, it may have been repressive to the point of suffocation.

It is also possible to record significant developments in the ongoing history of Christian ethics—always bearing in mind the vast period of time from which a few such developments are selected for discussion.

6

MONASTIC AND MYSTICAL CONTRIBUTIONS

Monasticism and mysticism did not originate with medieval Christianity. Both are recurrent, in one form or another, throughout Christian history, with origins back in Judaism. (For that matter, most of the great world religions have monastic and mystical currents.) But, if these tendencies are not unique to medieval Christianity, they are among its most striking features.

Moral Themes in Monasticism

Monasticism itself took more than one direction. Some of the earliest monks, such as Anthony of Egypt and Simeon Stylites, withdrew as individuals from ordinary society in order to purge themselves of contamination from worldly idolatries and attain personal holiness. Impressed by the Gospel story of the rich young man and the commandments of Jesus to renounce this world, these "anchorite"[1] monks were not motivated so much by the desire to influence others as they were by their quest for personal salvation. Other monks, such as the great Basil of Caesarea, were more communal. Their aim was to recapture the community of sharing as depicted in the accounts of the primitive church in the book of Acts. These "cenobite"[2] monks were far less individualistic than the anchorites, though they, too, embraced the *via negativa* of renunciation.

While the monastic impulse by no means originated with Augustine, it is worth noting that his ethic undergirded both of these monastic tendencies in striking ways. The ascetic side of Augustine, with its profound mistrust of the flesh and its stern sense of discipline, corresponded to the renunciations if not to the individualism of the anchorites. But Augustine's social ethic, summarized in the concept of the city of God, had much in common with the cenobitic ideal: to create, on earth, a communal expression of God's intended community. If the church as a whole continues to be corrupted by some within it whose love of self predominates over the love of God, the monastic community can be a company of the truly committed.

The cenobitic ideal in fact came to encompass the renunciations of the anchorites without succumbing to their individualism, and medieval monasticism was by and large a communal presence. Its announced threefold ethic of poverty, chastity, and obedience was an understatement of its moral aims. For it existed as a *koinonia*, a community of caring, as well. The love ethic manifested itself first within the community, but it also was expressed through hospitality and ultimately a considerable sense of mission. Still, the disciplined life, as summarized in poverty, chastity, and obedience, was not understood to be in tension with the love ethic but rather as necessary means to the end of union with God in heaven and with one's fellows on earth.

The ethic of medieval monasticism is illustrated in the influential Rule of Benedict of Nursia for the monastery he founded in the sixth century.[3] Above all else, the rule emphasizes the importance of conquering one's pride, thereby opening oneself to God's loving direction. The rule sets forth the steps by which a monk can expect to arrive at true humility. The rule emphasizes absolute obedience to one's superior, a total putting aside of one's self-will, patient acceptance of abuse from others, belief in one's personal inferiority to others, speaking only when spoken to, refraining from laughter. The twelfth and last step in this moral ladder to heaven conveys the tone of the whole: "The twelfth step in humility is if a monk not only be humble in heart, but also always in his very body evince humility to those who see him, that is, that in the Work of God, in the oratory, in the monastery, in the garden, on the road, in the field or elsewhere, sitting, walking, or standing, his head be always bent, his eyes cast down, accounting himself at all times as one convicted of his sins."[4] Benedict promises that, having ascended these steps, the monk "will presently arrive at that love of God which, being perfect, puts fear right outside," doing through force of habit and out of "delight in virtue" what he previously had done through fear of hell. In respect to the economic ordering of the monastery, Benedict's Rule specifies that "this vice of private ownership [is] to be cut off from the monastery by the roots." The monk is not "to have anything as his own, nor anything whatsoever, neither books, nor writing-tablet, no pen; no, nothing at all, since indeed it is not allowed them to keep either body or will in their own power, but to look to receive everything necessary from their monastic father; and let not any be allowed to have what the abbot has not either given or permitted. And let all things be common to all."[5]

Paradoxes in the Monastic Ethic

The monastic ethic, thus summarized, is not without its paradoxes. The central paradox may be reflected in the "humility and how I attained it" theme. Each monk is to think himself more undeserving than any other, but he is also to recognize that such an attitude is in fact a spiritual accomplishment. The various disciplines, many of which exhibit an extraordinary degree of asceticism, are designed to exterminate every vestige of pride or enslavement to the things of this world. But how easily can one slip into pride over such heroic accomplishments, how readily will one even begin to compete with the brethren! That may have been especially true of some of the Egyptian and Syrian anchorites. C. H. Lawrence's history of medieval monasticism records a fascinating account of one Macarius, a monk of legendary self-discipline. Hearing that another monastery had a great reputation for the ascetic practices of its monks, Macarius entered in disguise as a novice to test the competition. When some of the monks fasted for two days or even a week at a time during Lent, Macarius outdid them by standing in a corner "and remained there praying and plaiting mats, without food, drink, or sleep, until Easter."[6] This feat of monastic athleticism evidently caused consternation among the other monks and led to his being asked to leave. A story of this kind is bound to have gained much in the telling. But it nicely portrays the irony of how practices designed to enhance one's humility before God instead could contribute greater pride.

There are other paradoxes. For instance, there is the interesting point that this form of spiritual elitism, with its implied (and sometimes bluntly stated) criticism of the rest of the church, should contribute to the unity of the church rather than its disintegration. Monks took up the religious life in order to be saved. Ordinary Christians, living in a more worldly environment, were understood to be corrupted by the evils abounding in the world. The monks' withdrawal from the world was clearly a judgment upon the world and upon those who did not withdraw. It is a nice question why this did not break the church apart—at least, it is a nice question how the monastic movements could still be a part of the church. The threat was certainly there, and now and again particular movements did seem on the verge of separation.

That they generally did not do so owes something to the continuing need of even the most ascetic monks for some worldly support, of course. But, more than that, it came to be understood that the prayers of the monks contributed to the spiritual well-being of those who were not monks. In an intriguing interpretation of this, Ernst Troeltsch refers to "the spiritual treasury of the Church, into which those surplus offerings are poured, to be shared out again as indulgences." The contribution of those who must live a more worldly life "is that of preserving and procreating the race—a task in which ascetics cannot share." But the ascetics "for their part have the duty of showing forth the ideal in an intensified form, and of rendering service for others through intercession, penitence, and the acquisition of merit." That, Troeltsch observes, "is the reason for the enormous gifts and endowments to monasteries; men wanted to make certain of their own part in the oblation offered by monasticism."[7]

That point is made very clearly by Duke William III of Aquitaine in the charter establishing Cluny in A.D. 909.

> Desiring to provide for my own salvation while I am still able, I have considered it advisable, indeed most necessary, that from the temporal goods which have been conferred upon me I should give some little portion for the gain of my soul . . . [by supporting] at my own expense a congregation of monks. And this is my trust, this my hope, indeed, that although I myself am unable to despise all things, nevertheless by receiving those who do despise the world, whom I believe to be righteous, I may receive the reward of the righteous.[8]

The monks, for their part, while despising the world do not appear to have despised the duke's endowment! But Troeltsch's point is that that is not cynicism; it is the consequence of a genuinely organic understanding of church and society. Each part of the whole contributes to every other part. At times and places where the radical criticism of the world typified by monasticism was not thus successfully incorporated in a larger, more catholic conception of the church, sectarian, heretical movements developed—as in the case of the Cathars, of the twelfth to fourteenth centuries, whose dualistic teachings were reminiscent of Gnosticism and Manichaeanism.

The organic wholeness of the church, of which the monastic movement existed as a part, included the church's sacramental gifts. Even in its most extreme forms, the monastic orders did not contemplate an existence apart from that. Originally most of the orders were primarily lay, not clerical. But provision was made for the Eucharist and, in time, many of the male orders were primarily peopled by priests. The continued belief in the efficacy of the sacraments always qualified, to some extent, the reliance of monasticism upon its own "works" for salvation.

Yet another paradox resulted from monastic economics. Committed by the Benedictine Rule or similar monastic rules to utter poverty, individual monks nevertheless were a part of monastic communities that in many instances became very wealthy. The wealth came partly from endowments or bequests from those anxious thereby to ensure their own salvation and partly in the form of gifts brought by novices (or by parents dedicating their young children to the religious life). Over time, many of the monasteries accumulated vast holdings of land and wealth. Individual monks would die, but the monastic communities continued to exist. In time, monasteries found themselves leading economic actors on that worldly stage their monks had sworn to renounce. This reality contributed over the centuries to the periodic need for reformation, with prophetic new monastic figures like Saint Dominic (c. 1171–1221) and Saint Francis (c. 1181–1226) arising to found new orders or to urge existing ones back to their original calling.

Still another paradox is suggested by the fact that the spiritual impetus for the Crusades (1096–1291) was largely derived from monastic themes of idealism, self-sacrifice, and total devotion to Christ while its military agenda was so at variance with the monastic commitments to love and peace. Those who summoned Western Christendom to recover Jerusalem from Muslim infidels were, in many cases, persons who had been deeply influenced by the monastic movements of the time—including specifically Bernard of Clairvaux, who enthusiastically preached the Second Crusade. The Crusades gave birth to two military orders, the Knights Templar and the Knights Hospitallers, both largely modeled on monastic lines. (Bernard himself prepared a rule for the Knights Templar.) The crusading spirit, in its military ethic, greatly exceeded the bounds of the Augustinian just war theory, not least by treating the Muslim adversaries (and many Jews who got caught in the middle) as the enemies of God and by slaughtering even the defeated enemies. The paradox is not easily resolved. It does suggest the ambiguity, in human terms, of even the purest forms of idealism.

A final paradox is suggested by the conflict between withdrawal from the world and service to the world. The monasteries never wholly discarded the anchorite ideal. Often, individual monks would take the eremitical route, sometimes dwelling in hermit cells attached in sealed-off fashion to the monasteries. Even those who continued in the monastery community were committed to disciplines of silence and, as a whole, the community was more or less withdrawn from the surrounding society. As we have seen, the gathering wealth of monasteries made that increasingly problematical; the monks were an important part of medieval economy. But there was a deeper conflict between the ideals themselves: the renunciation of the world, on the one hand, and the doing of good works for fellow humanity, on the other hand. That conflict was characteristically resolved through hospitality. The monastery itself was a place from which the sojourner, the destitute, the sick, the troubled, the fugitive would not lightly be turned away. If the monastery had withdrawn from the world, the world was welcome, in its need, to come to the monastery.

It belonged, however, to the followers of Francis of Assisi to overcome this conflict in principle. The Franciscans withdrew from the world spiritually, taking their vows of renunciation and poverty very seriously. But they did not simply wait for the world to come to them; they were to be pilgrims in that world, accumulating no property or wealth, living simply off the alms offered by others each day, preaching the simple gospel of the Lord, and doing works of kindness. According to the rule of Saint Francis,

> the brothers shall appropriate nothing to themselves, neither a place nor anything; but as pilgrims and strangers in this world, in poverty and humility serving God, they shall with confidence go seeking alms. Nor need they be ashamed, for the Lord made himself poor for us in this world. This is that summit of most lofty poverty which has made you, my most beloved brothers, heirs and kings of the kingdom of heaven.[9]

The *Little Flowers of Saint Francis,* a medieval collection of stories about Francis and his followers, conveys the spirit of this monastic ethic. Francis is depicted in Christlike terms as one who trusted God absolutely for bodily needs and physical safety while devoting himself to acts of charity and reconciliation. His winsome spirituality is credited with the conversion of all with whom he had contact, including a Muslim sultan and even a wolf who had terrorized a village. Many of the stories are of doubtful historicity; they nevertheless embody the values of the movement and the way the movement registered with medieval society. The stories are full of renunciation of the idolatries of this world, but they are far from otherworldly. Francis actively ministered to people in the world. The stories, as well as the hymn credited to the saint ("All creatures of our God and King"), also suggest a remarkable empathy for nature. Animals and birds, the sun, moon, stars, and earth itself are depicted in personal terms as "sister," "brother," "mother." These are all God's creatures, in which God and humanity may take delight and from which we should not be alienated. (The Franciscan ethic is one of the most relevant chapters in the history of Christian ethics for contemporary ecological sensitivity.) The net impression is that the world is to be affirmed as God's world. Renunciation is not abandonment of the world but of a prideful relationship to it. Of course in sexual matters the Franciscans, in common with other monastic orders, did renounce an important aspect of life in the world.

The Monastic Ideal and Women

The monastic treatment of women was also something of a paradox. On the one hand, the movement generally regarded women as the weaker sex, even as the offspring of Eve who tempted Adam. Something of Augustine's thoroughly sexist conception of women continued to influence monasticism throughout the medieval centuries. Still, it was understood that women could also aspire to monastic life. Many did. Basil had organized a community for women religious alongside his monastic community. One of the earlier rules by which Benedict was influenced in the compilation of his own famous Rule was one developed by Caesarius of Arles for women religious. Cenobitic communities for women proliferated throughout Europe. In many cases, such convents developed alongside monasteries, upon which they were dependent for supervision and the sacramental ministries of the church. Sometimes the foundations were separate. While women were wholly excluded from the priesthood, some nuns exhibited remarkable gifts for leadership.

The early appearance of such leadership owes something to the fact that many of the early medieval nuns were of noble or even royal upbringing. The aristocratic background of a number of the abbesses or prioresses contributed to a degree of assertiveness otherwise seldom encountered in medieval society. In a few instances, women religious exerted striking spiritual and theological leadership in the wider church.

Hildegard of Bingen (1098–1179) is illustrative of such leadership.[10] Abbess of a Benedictine convent, she exhibited remarkable and independent administrative talents. She is better known, however, for her influential writings on theological subjects and for the correspondence she maintained with notable religious and secular rulers. Her writings on spirituality and theology were accepted and appreciated by male church leadership in part because they were offered as spiritual visions she had been given directly by God. Presented in this way, her writings did not have to be perceived as a contradiction to the general view of the nature of women. As her biographer, Sabena Flanagan, shrewdly observes,

> There were both biblical and early Christian precedents for the role of female prophet. Moreover, a woman could be a prophet without upsetting the perceived natural order, since no particular attributes of her own were required, except, possibly, humility. Indeed, there was some suggestion that God might specifically choose the weak and despised to confound the strong. Thus to be a female prophet was to confirm women's inferiority, rather than to deny it.[11]

Indeed, Hildegard herself occasionally took pains to confirm the general assessment, as in her comment that "man needed a helper in his likeness.

So God gave him a helper which was his mirror image, woman, in whom the whole human race lay hidden." And "woman is the work of man, and man the form of woman's consolation. Neither can exist without the other. And man signifies the divinity of the Son of God; woman his humanity."[12] Such comments do not reflect the most negative medieval views of women, but they do confirm the generally secondary status to which women were consigned.

Still, having made such concessions, a Hildegard could assert her views freely on a variety of subjects, including those quite removed from her visions.

Ethical Contributions of the Medieval Mystics

It is not altogether accurate to refer to the contributions of mysticism in contrast to those of monasticism, as some have done,[13] for most of the medieval mystics were monks or nuns who fully accepted the general monastic ethic. Still, if mysticism is understood as the single-minded endeavor to achieve a direct union with or vision of God, its effects on medieval ethics is worth additional comment.

Bernard of Clairvaux, probably the preeminent leader of twelfth-century monasticism, is also generally regarded as the foremost mystic of that age. His work on love is something of a classic in delineating the stages or degrees through which love passes in the movement from love of self to the love of God.[14] Love, according to Bernard, is an altogether "natural affection," but in its first degree it appears as "love for self." So in this stage, even the love of God is for the sake of oneself. The second stage of "love of God for what God gives" occurs as one discovers one's limitations and one's need of God's help. "Recurrent troubles throw us back on God, and each occasion proves how kind he is. And this experience of His sweetness provides an urge to the pure love of God, more powerful than the impetus our trouble gave before."[15] We are then led by the graciousness of God into "the love of God *for* God, not merely for oneself." Thus, "the third degree is that in which the love of God is purely for Himself."[16] Finally, in the fourth stage, we come to love even ourselves only for God's sake. In describing the fourth stage, Bernard gives full vent to the mystic impulse:

> When shall I know this kind of love, when will my soul, inebriated by His love, forget herself, yea, know herself but as a broken vessel, and go clean out to God and cleave to Him, her spirit one with His? . . . Happy is he, and holy too, to whom it has been given, here in this mortal life rarely or even once, for one brief moment only, to taste this kind of love! It is no merely human joy to lose oneself like this, so to be emptied of oneself as though one almost ceased to be at all; it is the bliss of heaven.[17]

Regrettably, Bernard sighs, the world drags one back from such bliss. His fleshly needs intervene, the "weakness of his fallen nature fails," and above all, "his brother's need calls on him to return." Bernard concludes that "alas, [he] has no choice but to come back, back to himself and to his own affairs; and in his grief he cries, 'O Lord, I am oppressed, undertake for me,' or yet again, 'O wretched man that I am, who shall deliver me from the body of this death.' "[18] While part of the reason for the brevity of those moments of bliss in the "fourth degree of love" appears to be the fallenness of the human condition, part of it also appears to be the sense of responsibility for the "brother's need," a sense that is grounded in that very love itself.

Still, Bernard thinks that "the command to love the Lord our God with all our heart and soul and strength will not be perfectly fulfilled until the mind no longer needs to think about the flesh, and the soul ceases having to maintain the body's life and powers."[19] Later, when this earthly existence has passed away, one "may hope to reach the fourth degree of love—or, rather, to be taken into it, for it is not attained by human effort but given by the power of God to whom He will. . . . [And] souls loosed from their bodies, we believe, will be immersed completely in that sea of endless light and bright eternity."[20]

A later medieval mystic, Catherine of Siena (1347–1380), was a Dominican nun. Her published prayers, correspondence, and account of her dialogue with God[21] throughout express this mystical spirit of union with God, while also passionately addressing the moral issues of her time. She was, in fact, born into a difficult world. The plague broke out in the year of her birth, shaking medieval society to its foundations. The church was fundamentally split, the papal seat itself residing, in semi-captivity, at Avignon. Political intrigue and violence raged in Catherine's native Italy.

Even discounting the exaggerations of her early biographers, the story of Catherine is remarkable. Her family was well off but by no means part of the political-economic elite. She was a woman in a male-dominated church and society. Her health, especially in later years, was fragile. She lived only thirty-three years. Yet by the time of her death she was a figure of enormous influence in church and society.

Her writings contain many directly moral teachings, and it would be tempting to detach these, as her relevant contribution to Christian ethics, from the "spiritual" writings. But that would miss the main point about the contribution of mysticism to Christian ethics. For it was precisely in her analysis of the spiritual life, expressed so passionately in her writings, that Catherine deals most directly with the moral will and the center of value. All love and all the fruits of love are grounded in the love of God. In her mystical ecstasy, Catherine reports that God says to her that "charity gives life to all the virtues, nor can any virtue exist without charity. In other words, virtue is attained only through love of me."[22] In one of her characteristic prayers, Catherine says you are love itself. So the soul who follows your Truth's teaching in love becomes through love another you. Dispossessed of her own will, she is so well clothed in yours that she neither seeks nor desires anything but what you seek and will for her.[23]

Self-will, which is always directed toward what is less than God, is displaced by God's will. This sense of total identification with God's will pervades all of her writings, to the point that she yearns for release from the distractions and impediments of this worldly life into the sea of God's life.

Love of God, after the Fall, is not a human possibility. But God, through the Word, Jesus Christ, has offered his great mercy to humanity. Christ, in Catherine's striking metaphor, is the bridge across the otherwise impassable flood of human sin. To neglect this bridge is to merit and receive eternal punishment. To violate the infinite love of God is an infinite sin for which no finite suffering is punishment enough. In her writings about divine punishment, Catherine is quite as hard-nosed as any medieval moralist. But the mercy of God opens up the way to union with God. That mercy is even available to those who accept it in a more conventional way, for their continuing sin is no longer infinite. They will have to work it out in purgatory. The mystical approach of total renunciation is the higher way leading directly to God.

It is clear on nearly every page of Catherine's writing that this mystical way is not an escape into isolated individualism. Her relationship with God is very personal, but her relationship with other people is integral to her relationship with God. Nor is loving service something that one does simply as a consequence of what one has received from God. In another of her prayers she writes that "the conformity between person and person is such that when they do not love each other they cut themselves off from their own nature."[24] We belong to one another because of what God has done. "You know," she portrays God as saying to her, "that every evil is grounded in selfish love of oneself. This love is a cloud that blots out the light of reason. It is in reason that the light of faith is held, and one cannot lose the one without losing the other."[25] In other words, she has echoed Augustine's view that we are constituted by what we love, and the love of self rather than the love of God is the essence of sin. We cannot truly love other people until we love them in God, for if we do not love through God our love is centered on sensual things and self.[26]

The mystical vision has very earthly effects in her biting criticism of greedy misers and "usurers who become cruel robbers" blotting out God's mercy from their minds. "How many evils come from this cursed sin of avarice!" she asks. "How many murders, thefts, and pillagings; how many unlawful profits and how much hard-heartedness and injustice toward others!" Avarice "kills the spirit and makes people slaves to wealth who care nothing for God's commandments. Such people love no one except for their own profit."[27] Her indictment of the greedy rich implies that they participate in systemic economic evils, for which isolated individual acts of charity are not a sufficient corrective:

> How can these wretched evil people share their possessions with the poor when they are already stealing from them? How can they rescue others from indecency when they are the ones who shoved them into it. . . . But if they will not share their possessions, how will they ever give their lives for the salvation of souls? How will they give affection if they are being eaten up by envy?[28]

Her specific advice to persons of wealth is not, however, quite as radical as this might prepare one to expect. Echoing Clement of Alexandria, she counsels the wealthy that "though they may possess the riches of the world, they must own them humbly, not with pride, as things lent to them rather [than] as their own."[29]

Her words directed toward political elites also have a sting to them. She writes of "others who are so bloated with the power in their hands that the standard they carry is injustice. They inflict their injustice on God and their neighbors and even on themselves."[30] Catherine was not reluctant to speak very directly to the most powerful rulers in Europe, as this passage from a letter to King Charles V of France attests:

> The second thing I am asking is that you uphold true holy justice. Let it not be adulterated by selfish love for yourself or by flattery or by human respect. And don't pretend not to see if your officials are inflicting injustice for money, denying the poor their rights. No, be a father to the poor as a dispenser of what God has given you. And see to it that any wrongs in your kingdom are punished, and virtue honored. For all this is the work of divine justice.[31]

Criticizing Charles for making war on fellow Christians and not directing his energies toward a crusade to recover the Holy Land, she begs him "to stop being the agent of so much evil and the obstacle to such a good."[32] The king's power is not contested, but he must remember that he possesses it only for a day and that he is God's steward in its exercise.

Catherine's credibility in directly challenging economic and political interests was grounded both in her mystical visions—which were obviously taken very seriously by her contemporaries as direct communications from God—and in her well-known history of directly and fearlessly ministering to the needs of victims of the plague and other loathsome outcasts.

Her contribution to Christian ethics (like that of Bernard and other Christian mystics) is primarily in the analysis of the moral will and its ultimate center of value. God is the center of life, and those things that are valued in place of God are the sources of distortion in the moral will. Does this more or less formal principle of religious ethics contribute anything substantive to moral judgment? In her frequent comments on "discernment," Catherine in effect is saying that, on the one hand, the pure love of God is what draws one into clarity of reason as well as joyous fulfillment—and that, on the other hand, self-love is responsible for our lack of clarity about moral issues. One of her letters to Pope Gregory XI makes this point strikingly. Do not, she writes, follow "the advice of those who love only their own life, honor, status, and pleasure—for their advice goes where their love is."[33]

That point is not devoid of substance; it provides an angle of analysis upon the moral life through careful examination of the fundamental motives of its agents, all grounded in the fundamental conviction that God is the source of all goodness and that God's love is the basis of mutual human caring. That at least has much to say about what is at stake, ultimately, in the moral life.

In a sense, the approach to moral judgment is basically intuitive. Love God, it seems to say, and your intuitions will not go far off course. Nevertheless, it must be noted that the actual intuitions and judgments of a Catherine or a Bernard were deeply influenced by other factors. Certainly the received biblical traditions and writings of earlier church leadership greatly affected their judgments. Certainly the broad outlines of medieval culture, now viewed as archaic, were by them given normative status. The organic conception of society, with its deep sense of mutual responsibility and caring, has a universal ring to it. But to challenge its medieval hierarchical forms would never have occurred to even these deepest medieval spirits. Power was a sacred trust, to them, but making kings and princes accountable to peasants as well as to God would have been equally unthinkable. The Crusades, now seriously questioned for a host of reasons, were actively encouraged by both Bernard and Catherine. The subservient role of women was taken for granted—though here the possibilities for leadership seized by a Hildegard or a Catherine and the respect they widely received from male contemporaries is worth pondering as we assess that age. Augustine's quite negative view of human sexuality continued to cast a long shadow through the medieval centuries.

7

THE CONFESSIONAL

Catherine of Siena expressed exactly the belief of medieval Christianity in her distinction between three kinds of Christians: Those who have eagerly put aside self-love in their full embrace of the love of God; those of "commonplace love" who embrace the mercy of God but never very perfectly; and the "wicked sinners" who are "damned in hate and despair."[1] Not many, practically speaking, could be in the first category, though that remained the norm for Christian life. Its practice by monks and nuns, lifted to spectacular heights in popular imagination by the saints, was a constant, visible reminder of the perfect way. Most people doubtless felt themselves to be somewhere in the second category, burdened by the responsibilities and cares of the world and susceptible to its allurements, but never with an easy conscience. Most people appear to have been deathly afraid of sinking into the third category of the out-and-out damned.

The fear was stoked by the rhetoric of the monastic movement, which often implied that a rather sizable majority of baptized Christians really were so self-centered as to be beyond the reach of salvation. The conception of God was not simply stern and judgmental, though one does not have to read very far into the literature of the monks to gain that impression. God is grace and mercy, but those who have neglected that grace and mercy to follow their own self-will are all the more worthy of God's righteous judgment.

But God has given the church the power to "loosen" and to "bind" (Matt. 18:18; John 20:23). Its sacraments have become means of grace, helping Christians along the way to heaven. Its saints contribute their prayers so that their more heroic goodness is registered in favor of ordinary Christians.

While ordinary Christians may sin and still return to grace, it is very important for them to confess their sin fully and accurately and for the church to prescribe appropriate penance—a punishment in this world substituting for the incomparably more severe punishment to be anticipated in the life to come.

The Development of Auricular Confession

It is not surprising, given the underlying view, that ordinary Christians should seek opportunity to confess their sins, accept their due penance, and be absolved by the church of their burden of guilt. In the early church this appears to have been a public exercise.[2] Later, private confession came into practice.

Even in the early centuries controversy developed over the extent to which Christians, having repented, should be received again into the full sacramental ministries of the church. On this matter, Tertullian had been especially strict, holding that the three most serious sins—idolatry, adultery, and homicide—could not be forgiven. The Council of Nicaea (A.D. 325), which had to deal with the possible restoration of followers of Arius, expressed a more lenient attitude. A few years earlier (c. A.D. 306), the Council of Elvira, an assembly of Spanish bishops, had developed a long list of canons defining the circumstances under which absolution could or could not be allowed.[3] Dozens of specific sins were listed, with a notation of penance required and whether or when the confessing sinner could be restored to Communion. In a number of instances the sin was considered so severe that the hapless sinner might not be restored even when death had become imminent. (For instance, Canon 7 states that "if a Christian completes penance for a sexual offense and then again commits fornication, he or she may not receive communion even when death approaches."[4]) What is interesting about these early efforts to codify morality for Christians is the way confession and penance are linked to the granting or withholding of the church's sacramental ministry—especially access to Communion. The ultimate sanction became increasingly clear and terrifying: denial of the sacrament carried with it the most severe risk of eternal damnation. Given the enormousness of the stakes, it is not surprising that ecclesial authorities found it increasingly necessary to be more and more specific about the different possible forms and degrees of sin, with a correspondingly refined cataloging of penalties.

It is also not surprising that a more elaborate system of confession and penance should develop. Under strict requirements like the canons of Elvira it was clear that one could not afford to confess too soon! Given the possibility of only one repentance and restoration for many of the more serious sins, one would not want to use up one's absolution if there were any possibility of slipping into further sin before one died. The logic of this seems to have consigned large numbers of Christians to "a permanent state of ecclesiastical delinquency."[5] Penance needed to be held in reserve until one was near death.

The easing up of so strict a system of church discipline seems to have developed out of the monastic movement in Ireland and Wales. The monastic discipline entailed spiritual direction of novices and monks by their superiors, and in those territories regular confession and absolution came to include local lay people as well.[6] What makes this so interesting in the development of Christian ethics is that as early as the sixth century penitential books came into being to help guide the confessor. The vigorous Celtic monastic missionary movements seem to have carried the practice of private confession and the books with them into other parts of western and southern Europe.[7] These manuals increasingly set the parameters for the church's discussion of ethics. The confessional is where the church confronted communicants with their moral responsibilities, the priests were the ones who did the confronting, and the manuals were the main source of guidance to the priests. Initially the books were resisted by ecclesial authorities; in time the need of the priests for such guidance and the lack of an alternative gave the manuals acceptability and very wide influence in the medieval church.

The books catalogued a wide variety of sins, carefully indicating the penance to be given for each. They include the kinds of questions the confessor was to ask. They make distinctions among the categories of penitents (e.g., bishop, priest, lay adult, child) and the penance appropriate. One does not find much theoretical discussion, nor is there even much care in citing the scriptural or patristic authority for the moral definitions and distinctions that are offered. In general, the penitential books relied upon "Sacred Scripture, canonical and monastic tradition, and their own spiritual judgment."[8]

The books, especially the earlier ones, could be fairly crude—possibly crude enough to justify the verdict of one Victorian-era commentator:

> The penitential literature is in truth a deplorable feature of the medieval Church. Evil deeds, the imagination of which may perhaps have dimly floated through our minds in our darkest moments, are here tabulated and reduced to a system. It is hard to see how anyone could busy himself with such literature and not be the worse for it.[9]

To sample some of this literature is at least to wonder what kind of Christians the authors were dealing with. For instance, the sixth-century Penitential of Finnian contains these provisions:

12. If one of the clerical order falls to the depths of ruin and begets a son and kills him, great is the crime of fornication with homicide, but it can be expiated through penance and mercy.

18. If any cleric or woman who practices magic misleads anyone by the magic, it is a monstrous sin.

19. If, however, such a person does not mislead anyone but gives [a potion] for the sake of wanton love to some one, he shall do penance for an entire year on an allowance of bread and water.[10]

The seventh-century Penitential of Cummean has an amusing, to modern ears, sequence of provisions for those guilty of gluttony:

6. He who suffers excessive distention of the stomach and the pain of satiety [shall do penance] for one day.

7. If he suffers to the point of vomiting, though he is not in a state of infirmity, for seven days.

8. If, however, he vomits the host [consecrated Communion bread], for forty days.

9. But if [he does this] by reason of infirmity, for seven days.

10. If he ejects it into the fire, he shall sing one hundred psalms.

11. If dogs lap up this vomit, he who has vomited shall do penance for one hundred days.[11]

The same manual notes that "he who sins with a beast shall do penance for a year" and "he who defiles his mother shall do penance for three years."[12] Even the more refined and influential seventh-century Penitential of Theodore includes such points in a list of 308 specific sins or cases requiring the decision of a confessor or bishop. Theodore's catalog includes items ranging from sexual offenses (much emphasized) to various kinds of perjury, idolatry, heresy, manslaughter, avarice and theft, gluttony and drunkenness, along with a number of provisions for the ordering of church life and worship.[13] The influence of earlier Christian thought on such listings is evident. But the penitentials go much further in specifying sins. Did they need to?

A major early study of the literature emphasized the need for such a disciplining influence in the life of a church largely made up of "uncultured barbarian" peoples far removed from the older centers of Christian life.

Crude and contradictory as were the Penitentials in many things, taken as a whole their influence cannot but have been salutary. They inculcated on the still barbarous populations lessons of charity and loving-kindness, of forgiveness of injuries and of helpfulness to the poor and the stranger as part of the discipline whereby the sinner could redeem his sins. Besides this, the very vagueness of the boundary between secular and spiritual matters enables them to instill ideas of order and decency and cleanliness and hygiene among the rude inhabitants of central and northern Europe.[14]

Notwithstanding the need for discipline, one still wonders how the penitentials could have specified such severe penalties as they did. Years of penance, long periods of fasting, and prolonged public mortification were prescribed for various offenses in many of the manuals. An eighth- or ninth-century Irish penitential requires anyone eating horsemeat to do penance for three and a half years.[15] The same penitential would punish even an unintended falsehood with a silent fast or a hundred blows to the hand. The eighth-century Burgundian penitential calls for seven years' penance—of which three should be on bread and water—for the sin of perjury.[16] And so on. Of course, in some cases the penalties appear to have been scandalously light. For instance, one is shocked to read in the fifth-century Penitential of Ciudad that "anyone who kills a Jew or a pagan shall do penance for forty days."[17] Even the seven years' penance prescribed by some of the manuals for killing may strike a modern reader as comparatively light. On the whole, however, the penances are very severe, sometimes shockingly so.

We may doubt that the really severe penalties were often actually prescribed or, if prescribed, that they were necessarily accepted. Nevertheless, the underlying reality was clear enough to the medieval mind. Punishment in this life, severe though it might seem, is much to be preferred to the eternal agonies of damnation. The ultimate sanction, to which the manuals had reference, is the power of the church to "bind" or "loose," to determine who would or would not attain everybody's goal of going to heaven.

Given the seriousness of the sanctions underlying the confessional system—that is, salvation or damnation—it is no wonder that there was a felt need for more uniform definitions of the forms and degrees of sin and for a corresponding uniformity of penance. Continued access to the sacraments necessary to salvation could not be allowed to hinge on the subjective intuitions of the different priest-confessors. The penitential manuals provided a certain uniformity of practice while also serving the needs of poorly educated priests.

Consequences of the Confessional System

It would be difficult to overstate the importance of the confessional system, with its penitential manuals, in the further development of the church's moral teaching. While the church's great ethical teachers could grapple with the deeper questions of theological ethics in their writings, the manuals had a more immediate, practical purpose. The latter were addressed to the pastoral situation of individual, very ordinary Christians. Not surprisingly, the moral issues surveyed in the manuals tended to be drawn from the common life. Common personal vices are analyzed in consummate detail; questions of systemic morality are seriously neglected. The tendency, therefore, is to emphasize individualism in ethics. The issues with which the church came to be preoccupied in its ethical teaching were those drawn from immediate pastoral experience. That is not all bad, of course. But it may have deflected attention from broader systemic questions, the answers to which were taken more for granted than examined by the penitentials.

Given the ultimate purpose of the manuals of guiding a system of confession, we should also not be surprised to find ethics there presented in negative terms: Ethics is not so much about the good to be embraced as it is about the evil to be avoided. The whole point is to keep reasonably clear of those sins that might place one's eternal life in jeopardy. A consequence of this is that moral rules are framed by the minimum requirements of morality. The rules define morality in terms of what it is to avoid, not what it is to work for in positive terms. In that sense, love is defined by what is against love, not by its creative possibilities. Such an ethic might appear to be far removed from the monastic context out of which it developed, not to say the more exalted quest of the mystics. But we must remember that monasticism and even mysticism had this deeply negative side as well. The monks were withdrawing from the evil world to be saved from its downward pull; the mystics sought to purify themselves of the pride that obstructs our access to God's mercy. Still, the monks and mystics had a more positive agenda; they were the "religious." They were devoted directly to God. Lay Christians had to be content with observing the minimums as scrupulously as possible, confessing their moral failures, serving penance, and receiving absolution and the sacraments of the church.

The confessional system, with its manuals specifying sins and penances, gave rise to another important tendency in medieval Christian ethics. Specific deeds and their consequences and remedies were increasingly objectified. A given (objective) penance satisfied the given (objective) offense. Sacramental remedies, administered by the church through its priesthood, achieved the intended good. Questions of motive, while not exactly ignored in the penitential manuals, came to have secondary importance. Morality, increasingly, was an objective transaction, the manuals serving as the rule books setting forth the objective requirements. The more seriously committed male and female "religious" had the higher vocation of more perfectly entering into communion with God. But even they, while aspiring to the perfect love of God, had adopted objective rules designed to enable that higher way. The theory underlying the objective rules was always that the rules were means to the higher end. The disciplines of fasting and devotion, the penalties assigned as penance for sins, the rituals of obedience were not understood—in theory—to be ends in themselves. Inevitably, however, the fact that they were perceived to be necessary means to the higher end of loving and serving God increasingly had the effect of transforming them into ends in themselves. The monastic movement had difficulty keeping this balance—even the great mystics experienced that difficulty.[18] For the vast majority of ordinary lay Christians, walking the narrow way in "sin haunted medieval Europe,"[19] the moral life must have seemed all the more a matter of objective requirements with objective consequences.The more objective the whole schema came to be, the more necessary it was to elaborate the different kinds of cases that might come before the confessor. The confessor's responsibility, then, was not to explore the overall state of the penitent Christian's moral health; it was to match specific offenses to the catalog of possible sins and to apply the prescribed penance.

In the penitential manuals (and in common practice) this moral objectivity came increasingly to be expressed through the practice of commutation. Commutation was the payment of money as a penalty or a payment in lieu of some other penalty. Obviously, commutation made life a good deal easier for persons of means. To be sure, there was a logic to commutation in some kinds of cases: as compensation to those whom one has injured materially or as a penance for the sins of greed or envy. But it came to be possible in some instances for rich people to buy their way out of more demanding penances. Since the ultimate issue was access to the sacramental means of salvation (or the number of years one might otherwise have to spend in purgatory), this meant that the church was accepting money in exchange for absolution.

As John McNeill and Helena Gamer note, however, "at this point the penitentials are related to the rise of indulgences and to the abuses of the indulgence system."[20] When the means to the end of salvation are so objectified and when these means are so clearly under the power of the church, the means can be bought and sold. That was not the purpose, of course, and one cannot charge that the system was wholly corrupt. But the possibility was there for the absolving authority (the church) to extend its indulgences for reasons not directly related to the sins of the penitent. The very objectivity of it all conferred great power on the confessional authority. That authority, having the power to "bind" or "loose," could use that power for all kinds of actual reasons. The church had, in the very objectivity of the system, enormous leverage. Thus, for example, Pope Urban II, in summoning all Christendom to the First Crusade in 1095, could promise full indulgence to all who responded.

At points in medieval history abuses appear to have been widespread and crude. There were also voices of protest and, at its best, the penitential system, manuals and all, made some contribution to the establishing and regularizing of Christian morality in Europe.

8

THE THOMISTIC SYNTHESIS

For a long time after the death of Augustine, Christian ethics had lived on borrowed intellectual capital. To be sure, the monastic movements and the great mystics exhibited great moral vitality. Ordinary people were also preoccupied with the myriad requirements of a confessional ethic that engaged the conscience of the whole of Christian civilization. Christian ethics was, in a real sense, everybody's business. But the intellectual basis for the church's moral teachings had been set by earlier thinkers, particularly by Augustine.

That basis included, in the most general sense, a philosophically principled belief in God, consistent with the major philosophical views of the ancient world. The Christian conception of God had successfully vanquished dualism, as represented in Gnosticism and Manichaeanism. It included a more or less sophisticated defense of the use of Hebrew and Christian scriptures. It included a love ethic centered in God and in response to God's grace, both of which were successfully defended by earlier Christian thinkers in opposition to crude pagan conceptions of deity. Augustine's analysis of the moral will, with its conception of pride as the essential sin, had become the basis of much of the church's moral discipline, along with its corresponding emphasis upon the virtue of humility. It had established a positive view of and relationship to the state, notwithstanding the collapse of the central Roman authority soon after the triumph of Constantinianism. Such theological, philosophical, and ethical beliefs were not without their internal tensions. But the intellectual accomplishments of early Christian thought had succeeded in laying the foundations for a remarkably unified theological/social/moral worldview among medieval Christians. That worldview was so broadly shared that there was little stimulus for bold, creative thinking.

Late Medieval Intellectual Renewal

Soon after the turn of the first millennium, a noticeable intellectual renewal brightened the medieval world. Some of the new currents rose out of the monastic movement and related schools. A few figures, like Peter Abelard (1079–1142), became restless with beliefs too long unexamined. The universities developed in the thirteenth century, becoming centers of inquiry and debate. The works of Aristotle, most of which were unknown to medieval Europe until the thirteenth century, were rediscovered (largely through contacts with the Muslim world), inspiring new questions and a new style of answering them.

How are we to account for this intellectual quickening? Why did the recovery of Aristotle's works have so great an influence? One could not say that the medieval worldview had collapsed, creating an intellectual and moral crisis comparable to the first centuries of the Christian era. The intellectual ferment of the early centuries was based, as we have seen, on the quest for an ordering, unifying principle in a deeply fragmented age.

The medieval problem was not that of holding the world together; there was no crisis of belief comparable to that confronting early Christian thought. If anything, the intellectual quickening of the late Middle Ages may have reflected more the felt need to reach beyond a complacency that had become tinged with corruption. The writings of Aristotle opened up a whole new world of possibilities. In part, Aristotle represented a new focus on the empirical world; in part he suggested new possibilities for the systematic ordering of all knowledge. The overall challenge was to a deepening of the intellectual life of medieval Europe. A number of first-rate thinkers emerged.

The Aristotelianism of Thomas Aquinas

Of these, Thomas Aquinas (1225–1274) was indisputably foremost. A Dominican monk of aristocratic parentage, Thomas benefited both from the intellectual disciplines of the order and from easy access to circles of influence and power. His life project was the creation of a synthesis of the "new" knowledge (Aristotle) with the inheritances of Augustine, monasticism, and the evolving conceptions of church and sacrament. Both in his articulation of the major theological currents of the late medieval world and in the vastness of his subsequent influence, Thomas Aquinas was the most important Christian thinker of the Middle Ages. In this achievement, the appropriation of the rediscovered Aristotle was very important. (Its importance, in his own opinion, is suggested by the fact that he persistently refers to Aristotle as "the Philosopher.")

Thomas Aquinas developed a basic conception of reality, a synthesis of Aristotle with traditional theology, that is fundamentally teleological. Every aspect of reality is to be considered in relation to its true end (*telos*),[1] the fulfillment of which is its created purpose in being. The "good" of every thing is the fulfillment of its *telos*, of its potentiality. All things, insofar as they have being or actuality, are good. Following Aristotle, Thomas argues the point as follows:

> The essence of goodness consists in this, that it is in some way desirable. Hence the Philosopher says: *Goodness is what all desire.* Now it is clear that a thing is desirable only in so far as it is perfect, for all desire their own perfection. But everything is perfect so far as it is actual. Therefore it is clear that a thing is perfect so far as it is being; for being is the actuality of every thing, as is clear from the foregoing. Hence it is clear that goodness and being are the same really.[2]

The argument is securely in the tradition of Augustine's insistence (against the Manichaeans) that there is no ultimate reality outside of God. Everything, insofar as it has being, is good; evil consists in nonbeing or in turning away from God, the source of being. But Thomas has given this an Aristotelian dimension by incorporating the specific end or *telos* of each being. "Evil," he writes, "consists . . . in the fact that a thing fails in goodness."[3] A being that is fully actual is characterized as "perfect" being—that is, a being that perfectly actualizes its created potentiality. And evil is not simply the absence of being or even an Augustinian turning away from the source of being; with Thomas it is in the imperfection of a being. Evil consists in a being not fulfilling its created *telos*.

This way of putting it allows for an analysis of beings that is, so to speak, pre-theological. One does not have to invoke divine revelation in order to analyze the *telos* of different aspects of the natural world, although it is in the juxtaposition of the natural with the supernatural that Thomas's synthesis becomes fully theological. Aristotle could make important contributions to ethics, fully acknowledged by Thomas, where a theologian less competent in moral philosophy than Aristotle might fail. Ultimately, however, the destiny of human beings is eternal, not temporal. Hence, no moral analysis neglecting the supernatural dimension will do justice to the final *telos* of people.

To understand this, we must note with Thomas that all things exist in hierarchical order. At the apex of the hierarchy of being is God, who is the first cause of all other things and in whom being and goodness are perfectly and completely realized. Beneath God are the angels, whose *telos* is fulfilled in their spiritual nature. Beneath the angels are human beings, who combine spiritual with corporeal natures. Beneath human beings are animals, with physical bodies capable of feeling and appetite. Then there is insentient vegetation, then inanimate matter.

Human beings are both biological and spiritual. As biological beings, they have a physical *telos* like that of the animals. As spiritual beings, they have an intellectual/spiritual *telos* like that of the angels. Ethics that is proper to human beings therefore contains both physical or corporeal and intellectual/spiritual elements. The corporeal and spiritual good of human beings requires the fulfillment of those corresponding ends. But since humanity possesses an eternal, and not only temporal end, the corporeal serves the eternal.

What is that eternal end for human beings? Following Aristotle again, Thomas speaks of "happiness" as the ultimate *telos*. Obviously, he does not mean this in the sense of simple pleasure any more than Aristotle did. After surveying and rejecting a series of traditional definitions of human happiness, Thomas concludes as follows:

> Accordingly, if man's ultimate happiness does not consist in external things, which are called goods of fortune; nor in goods of the body; nor in goods of the soul, as regards the sensitive part; nor as regards the intellectual part, in terms of the life of moral virtue; nor in terms of the intellectual virtues which are concerned with action, namely, art and prudence:—it remains for us to conclude that man's ultimate happiness consists in the contemplation of truth.[4]

But that ultimately means not universal truths about first principles or sciences dealing with things; it means "wisdom, based on consideration of divine things." Thus, happiness for human beings is found in contemplation of God.

Ultimate human happiness is therefore not possible in this life, for complete knowledge cannot be gained here. Moreover, human life is generally limited by evil. In a remarkable acknowledgment of the universality of human sin, Thomas writes that

> man cannot be wholly free from evils in this state of life, and not only from evils of the body, such as hunger, thirst, heat, cold and the like, but also from evils of the soul. For there is no one who at times is not disturbed by inordinate passions; who sometimes does not go beyond the mean, wherein virtue consists, either in excess or in deficiency;[5] who is not deceived in some thing or another; or who at least is not ignorant of what he would wish to know or does not feel doubtful about an opinion of which he would like to be certain.[6]

Therefore, he concludes, "man's ultimate happiness cannot be in this life." This two-sidedness of human good—the temporal and the eternal—is expounded by Thomas in two interesting ways.

Virtue, According to Thomas Aquinas

One way of viewing human good is found in his discussion of moral virtues. Following Aristotle, Thomas emphasizes that the moral life does not consist in acts alone. Human beings are rational moral agents. A moral will that expresses our rational character is directed to more than individual acts, taken in isolation. It is concerned with all potential acts of a particular kind. At the same time, the moral will does not exist simply in thinking about morality; the moral will decides and acts. With Aristotle, Thomas therefore emphasizes the importance of habit.[7] A habit is a disposition of the will. It is not something we acquire naturally, but it can become ingrained in us through our upbringing and through the pattern of our own choices and actions. Through repetition, certain kinds of actions become more automatic, though they remain acts of will and not involuntary natural forces determining the will. If we repeatedly indulge our appetites in disregard of reason, that does not mean that such habits have nothing to do with reason. It means that we have allowed our appetites to determine our reason and thence our will. Or we can develop habits through which our reason controls our appetites. Quoting Aristotle, Thomas observes that "choice is either intellect influenced by appetite or appetite influenced by intellect."[8] In either case, habitual choice includes both intellect and will. But typically, when appetite habitually determines the intellect and will, one is controlled by vice, whereas the opposite is more likely to express virtue.

In agreement with his contemporary Peter Lombard, Thomas defines virtue as "a good quality of the mind, by which we live righteously, of which no one can make bad use, which God works in us without us,"[9] although he promptly substitutes the word "habit" for the word "quality." Virtue, he continues, "is a habit which is always referred to good." We may say, then, that virtue is a habit or disposition of the will toward a good end. It is a disposition to fulfill our potential *telos*. Thomas notes that the ends toward which our choices and virtues are directed are themselves means to the ultimate end of happiness.[10] A virtue is, accordingly, a disposition of the will to choose means that are appropriate to that ultimate end.

Thomas identifies four principal or cardinal virtues: prudence, justice, temperance, and fortitude.[11] *Justice* is the virtue of a right ordering of relationships and distributions. *Temperance* is the virtue of controlling the passions inciting us to act against reason. *Fortitude* is the virtue of resisting the impulse to turn away caused by fear of toil or danger. *Prudence* is the first of all the virtues, for it is the formal principle whereby the will is ordered by reason. Justice, temperance, and fortitude are, in that sense, aspects of prudence.

These virtues are called "cardinal" because all of the other virtues known to philosophers fall under them. "For instance," he writes, "any virtue that causes good in reason's act of consideration may be called prudence; every virtue that causes the good of rectitude and the due in operations, be called justice; every virtue that curbs and represses the passions, be called temperance; and every virtue that strengthens the soul against any passions whatever, be called fortitude."[12]

These cardinal virtues, however, could be named by any reasonable philosopher, whether Christian or not. Thomas has, in fact, derived them from the classical tradition—especially through Aristotle and Cicero. They are suited to the ends of human existence that are accepted universally by reasonable persons. These virtues are "proportioned to human nature."[13] They do not pertain to the ultimate human *telos*, which is eternal happiness through the contemplation of God. Eternal happiness surpasses human nature; it can be obtained only through the power of God:

> because such happiness surpasses the power of human nature, man's natural principles, which enable him to act well according to his power, do not suffice to direct man to this same happiness. Hence it is necessary for man to receive from God some additional principles, by which he may be directed to supernatural happiness, even as he is directed to his connatural end by means of his natural principles.[14]

These additional principles "are not made known to us, save by divine revelation, contained in Holy Scripture." Thomas identifies these as the three theological virtues of faith, hope, and love (*caritas*), derived from 1 Corinthians 13. He speaks of the interrelationships of these three theological virtues in the following way:

> Now it is by faith that the intellect apprehends what it hopes for and loves. Hence, in the order of generation, faith must precede hope and charity. In like manner, a man loves a thing because he apprehends it as his good. Now from the very fact that a man hopes to be able to obtain some good from someone, he looks on the man in whom he hopes as a good of his own. Hence, for the very reason that a man bases his hopes in someone he proceeds to love him; so that in the order of generation, hope precedes charity as regards their respective acts. But in the order of perfection, charity precedes faith and hope, because both faith and hope are quickened by

charity, and receive from charity their full complement as virtues. For thus charity is the mother and the root of all the virtues, inasmuch as it is the form of them all.[15]

The virtues that are based upon our nature are developed through human action, but the theological virtues that enable us to achieve supernatural ends are dependent upon the action of God. They are infused in us by God. Infused virtue may in fact require us to go beyond the norms set by natural virtue. As an illustration of this, Thomas notes that the natural virtue of temperance requires only that in the consumption of food we do no harm to health or reason. But virtue infused by God requires more serious disciplining of the body to bring it into subjection.[16] Infused virtue does not set aside the natural virtues; it draws us beyond them toward our eternal happiness.

God's grace, in Thomas's reformulation, thus is not so much a restoration of humanity from its state of original sin (though that element is also present). It is a perfecting of our created nature as a means toward our supernatural end. Our natural self has not been totally distorted by original sin, but even so the infusion of God's grace with appropriate theological virtues is necessary to our ultimate end, eternal happiness with God. Thus, in his consideration of virtues, Thomas has provided both for natural virtue (summarized in the cardinal virtues) and for virtue that is dependent upon God's revelation and grace. The first "track" appropriates directly and fully the classical moral teachings, especially those of Aristotle. The second draws upon the theological tradition of Augustine and medieval practice, while shifting its focus through some redefinition.

Thomas on Moral Law

A second way of viewing human good is found in Thomas's reformulation of moral law. It is perhaps inevitable that even an end-directed ethic like Thomas's would also have to be stated in prescriptive form—for that had been the recognizable form of most moral teaching for many centuries. The general form of his ethic remains teleological, however. Law does not exist for its own sake but rather as means to natural and supernatural ends.

The ultimate form of law, for Thomas, is *eternal law*—understood to be the mind or reason of God. It is the "exemplar of the divine wisdom . . . moving all things to their due end."[17] We do not know eternal law as it is in itself, for it belongs to the essence of God. We do know eternal law through its effects in creation as *natural law*. All people are capable of knowing natural law, which is universal, whether or not they are Christian. Thus Aristotle and other philosophers, depending upon the clarity of their thought, are capable of understanding and dependably presenting and applying natural law. Since natural law does not direct us to our supernatural good, it is complemented by *divine law*. Divine law is a direct revelation of the reason of God, as in the codes of laws God gave to the Jews. Divine law is also a needed corrective for the sinfulness and weakness of human beings, among whom natural law is often distorted. (Again, however, Thomas does not view the Fall as necessarily obscuring the grasp of natural law by reasonable human beings.) Finally, human law exists as the specific application of natural law to the circumstances of earthly life. Human law is the enactment of law by civil authority.

Two things may be noted from this formulation. In the first place, it is a basis, in reason, for universal agreement—or at least dialogue—concerning moral principle. It does not rest upon special Christian revelation. In the second place, it establishes a basis for criticism of human law when the latter is in conflict with natural law. Given Thomas's overall bias for human authority, we should take special note of his discussion of such conflicts. After noting that human law is binding on the conscience, he acknowledges that such laws may be unjust in two ways:

> first, by being contrary to human good . . . either in respect of the end, as when an authority imposes on his subjects burdensome laws, conducive, not to the common good, but rather to his own cupidity or vainglory; or in respect of the author, as when a man makes a law that goes beyond the power committed to him; or in respect of the form, as when burdens are imposed unequally on the community, although with a view to the common good. Such are acts of violence rather than laws.[18]

Such unjust laws, he argues, are not binding upon the conscience— although he immediately adds that one should perhaps still obey them "to avoid scandal or disturbance." We have here, then, a version of the "higher law" doctrine already anticipated in the natural law teachings of the Stoics.

Of course, these laws are formal principles. The really interesting questions begin when we ask, in suitable detail, what natural law requires. Where does the content come from? In the vast elaborations of moral teaching in the *Summas*, Thomas reasons carefully, but the fundamental assumptions on which rest his reasoning are evidently drawn from his inherited culture and traditions.

We cannot follow all this in a survey of this kind, but we must note that his division between natural law and divine law, and the analogous division between the cardinal and theological virtues, raises an important question of perennial concern to Christian ethics: How can the ethic derived from what is supposed to be universal reason be truly binding if the good to which it aspires is a lesser good than our supernatural end? Thomas has noted in his discussion of the virtues that a purely natural version of a virtue (such as temperance) may have to be set aside—or made much more rigorous—for the sake of the supernatural end. Does this mean that the supernatural is really already a part of the natural law ethic and that the relative autonomy of the natural law ethic is more apparent than real?

The problem is dealt with, in a sense, by Thomas's portrayal of the natural law as the expression, in creation, of the eternal law. Natural law, if rightly understood, could not possibly be in conflict with eternal law, for the former is but an application of the latter. But how, then, can a philosopher (like Aristotle) with no insight into the supernatural end of humankind fully grasp the significance of the natural law that finds its true expression as a means to that end? The tension is there. But it remains true that, to Thomas, the ends of natural law, which can be grasped by natural reason, are still divinely appointed means to the more ultimate end even when that in itself cannot be grasped by natural reason alone.

The Emerging Social Ethic

Thomas's social ethic emphasizes, with Aristotle, that "man is by nature a social animal."[19] The fundamental end of society is the common good in which the good of each is the good of all. Society, like reality in general, is a hierarchical configuration of ends. All aspects of society—its institutions, functions, and roles—serve specified ends. In general, the architecture of society is of a community of mutual service in which every aspect serves every other. While the system of social roles is hierarchical, the end of those of highest rank is to serve those beneath them just as the *telos* of the lowest is to serve their superiors. The whole structure reflects natural humanity, as created by God. Thomas would have endorsed, possibly with enthusiasm, the lines of the archaic hymn: "The rich man in his castle, the poor man at his gate, God made them high and lowly, and ordered their estate." The ethic of mutual service activating this relieves it of its worst features. The overall conception is rather like that of Paul's metaphor for the church as the "body of Christ," in which each member serves every other. The troublesome point is that social roles are implicitly fixed by nature. We are what we are by inheritance. Practically speaking, that is of course a nearly exact description of the way things were in medieval society—and the way they had been from time immemorial. The only truly available place for upward social mobility was the priesthood and (ironically) monastic life. But preferment in priestly or monastic vocations generally reflected prior aristocratic upbringing; even when it did not the point was that one had theoretically moved out of the natural social hierarchy and into vocations pertaining to supernatural life.

The Thomistic Political Ethic

Thomas's view of politics is an excellent illustration of the hierarchical conception. The state, or political community, is like the family except that, unlike the family, it is a "perfect" society. By this Thomas means that the state, unlike the family, has at its own disposal all of the means necessary to the fulfillment of its appointed end—which is the common good. Part of the meaning of this is the use of coercive force to restrain evil: that is, "Since some are found to be dissolute and prone to vice and not easily amenable to words, it was necessary for such to be restrained from evil by force and fear, in order that, at least, they might desist from evil-doing, and leave others in peace, and that they themselves, by being habituated in this way, might be brought to do willingly what hitherto they did from fear, and thus become virtuous."[20] But Thomas's state is not simply coercive. Its broad vocation is to advance the common good of its people, in accordance with natural law and with ultimate accountability to God. The ruler's responsibility includes bringing the multitude into a unity of peace, directing the multitude to good action, providing a sufficient supply of what is necessary for good living, correcting whatever is wrong, and perfecting what can be improved.

This broad agenda for the state definitely includes, as far as possible, the suppression of vice and the inculcation of virtue among its people. But Thomas specifically disavows the effort to repress all vices. "Now human law," he writes, "is framed for the multitude of human beings, the majority of whom are not perfect in virtue. Therefore human laws do not forbid all vices, from which the virtuous abstain, but only the more grievous vices, from which it is possible for the majority to abstain; and chiefly those that are injurious to others, without the prohibition of which human society could not be maintained."[21] While this might appear, in one sense, to place the human law of the state in conflict with the higher natural law, it is itself a canon of natural law that the state must not attempt to do what cannot effectively be done.

The Doctrine of Just War

Thomas, like Augustine before him, considered war to be a sometimes necessary evil. Under some carefully delineated circumstances a ruler might be called upon to wage war. Thomas, adhering rather closely to Augustine's earlier formulation, states three conditions under which a war can be considered just: first, that it be waged under authority of the sovereign ("for it is not the business of a private individual to declare war"); second, that the cause be just ("those who are attacked, should be attacked because they deserve it on account of some fault"); third, that those who wage war should have a "rightful intention" ("so that they intend the advancement of good, or the avoidance of evil").[22] To this outline of conditions, Thomas adds that "those who wage war justly aim at peace, so they are not opposed to peace, except to [an] evil peace."

Thomas elsewhere appears to have anticipated the later principle of proportionality with the judgment that revolution against a tyrant should be undertaken only if the continuing submission to the tyrant were more harmful than the foreseeable damage from a revolution.[23] This does, however, also introduce the notion that revolution against a tyrant might be a legitimate form of justified war.

One of Thomas's most important additions to just war doctrine also appeared through the back door. In a passage dealing with the legitimacy of killing someone in self-defense, Thomas remarks that "nothing hinders one act from having two effects, only one of which is intended, while the other is beside the intention." In such an instance, he continues, it is the intended effect that counts morally. In the instance of self-defense, the act "may have two effects, one is the saving of one's life, the other is the slaying of the aggressor."[24] Since the saving of one's life is altogether lawful, the fact that while intending to do that one may also kill an aggressor does not render the deed unlawful unless "one uses more than necessary violence." (The latter would be unlawful, even when accompanied by good intention, "if it be out of proportion to the end.") While not developed by Thomas as a condition of the just war, this principle of "double effect" helped define, in succeeding centuries, the requirement that the means used in war may not be contrary to moral law.

Thomistic Economic Doctrine

Thomas had little to say on economic matters that would have offended the wealthy, beyond reminding them that their possessions were from God and urging them to be more generous. Property is in accord with natural law as regards its use: "Man has a natural dominion over external things, because by his reason and will, he is able to use them for his own profit, as they were made on his account."[25] Besides, we know by divine law that God gave dominion over things, for their use, to humankind (Psalm 8 and Genesis 1). But should ownership of things be individual or should things be held in common? Thomas's arguments against common ownership are essentially practical: Individuals are more likely to produce what they will be able to use; the conduct of human affairs is more orderly when each must care for his or her own property; private ownership is more conducive to peace, for "quarrels arise more frequently where there is no division of the things possessed."[26] Nevertheless, in the *use* of property "man ought to possess external things, not as his own, but as common, so that, to wit, he is ready to communicate them to others in their need."[27] The right of property is thus affirmed legally but relativized ethically. Later, it is even relativized legally. For Thomas considers it lawful to take the property of another when in dire need or imminent danger.[28]

In a section dealing with what we would today call business ethics, Thomas elaborates arguments against price gouging and cheating.[29] In this discussion he presupposes but does not precisely define a "fair price." He considers the selling of goods at a profit (without which there could be no tradesmen) to be in accord with moral law. Nevertheless, he subjects commercial activity to insult: "Trading, considered in itself, has a certain debasement attaching thereto, in so far as, by its very nature, it does not imply a virtuous or necessary end." Of greater interest is his argument against usury, which he defines as taking "payment for the use of money lent."[30] By requiring the borrower to repay more than the amount borrowed, the lender is charging for something nonexistent. Borrowed money can be consumed and should be repaid; when interest is charged it is money that could not be consumed. We can strain over the economic logic demonstrated here; of greater importance is the twofold fact that Thomas's rejection of usury helped to maintain in effect an important medieval barrier to banking while his allowing Christians to *pay* usury assured that the banking system would have to be developed by non-Christians.

Sex and Gender in Thomas Aquinas

Thomas presupposes and elaborates inherited medieval notions about sex. Sexual expression is not unlawful; indeed it is necessary for procreation. But it is not necessary to the procreation of humankind that all people participate in procreation. There are special moral dangers attached to sexual lust and, besides, marriage and family responsibilities can distract from higher callings. Accordingly, while not treating lawful marriage as in any way sinful, Thomas argues that virginity is preferable to marriage since "virginity is directed to the good of the soul in respect of the contemplative life, which consists in thinking on the things of God, whereas marriage is directed to the good of the body, namely the bodily increase of the human race."[31]

In his several discussions of the nature and role of women, Thomas weaves his way between affirming their full human dignity, on the one hand, and their subordination to men, on the other. Thus, we read that "the image of God, in its principal signification, namely the intellectual nature, is found both in man and in woman."[32] But we also read that "the good of order would have been wanting in the human family if some were not governed by others wiser than themselves. So by such a kind of subjection woman is naturally subject to man, because in man the discernment of reason predominates."[33] Thomas is sometimes interpreted as subscribing to Aristotle's characterization of woman as "a misbegotten male." He does cite that quotation and agrees with that in the sense that woman is "defective" in the "active power" associated with the male seed. At the same time, he affirms that "as regards universal human nature, woman is not misbegotten, but is included in nature's intention as directed to the work of generation."[34] His interpretation of the subjection of women to men is that it is not for the benefit of men (a kind of subjection resulting from sin) but it is the kind of subjection "whereby the superior makes use of his subjects for their own benefit and good."[35] Similar forms of subjection characterize Thomas's whole hierarchical conception of society.

The Thomistic Synthesis

In his classic *Social Teaching of the Christian Churches* (1911), Ernst Troeltsch interpreted Thomist ethic as the maximum expression of the idea of an "ecclesiastical unity of civilization."[36] That ethic was peculiarly able to illuminate every aspect of medieval life, sacred and secular, in accordance with its division between nature and supernature. It was able to provide theoretical justification for social hierarchies, locating ethical purpose for each social role in secular society in accordance with its divinely appointed natural end, but drawing the whole to focus on the supernatural ends appointed to human life. In respect to the latter, the church, with its treasury of merit and sacraments, provided the means of grace whereby the temporal life gained eternal meaning. While few could make the total commitments for the truly religious life of monasticism, the merits and prayers of the "religious" served the supernatural end of all Christians.

Sociologically speaking, the system made it possible for there to be a unity of civilization encompassing not only "ordinary" Christians whose faith was inevitably corrupted by the world but also those who sought the purer morality and spirituality of monastic life. What is interesting is that the impulse of the monastics to withdraw from the world, which might have broken medieval Christendom apart, instead was incorporated as a resource for the whole. The Aristotelian notion of ends, adopted by Thomas, and the complementary distinction between nature and supernature helped render this theoretically possible.

Troeltsch's interpretation of Thomas (along with the rest of Troeltsch's historical survey of Christian social teaching) reminds us of a more subtle point as we survey the history of Christian ethics. The institutional form of church, adopted in theory and practice, is an expression of the social ethic of the Christian community. Ecclesiology is an aspect of Christian ethics. The church institutionalizes the Christian community's understanding of God's purposes in and for the world. Thus, a purely sectarian conception of the life of the Christian community is likely to express some form of dualism between the realm of the redeemed and the fallen world. With variations, this is what Troeltsch referred to as the "sect-type." The concept of an ecclesiastical unity of civilization, such as that articulated by Thomas, presupposes the natural goodness or redeemability of the whole society. That, with variations, is what Troeltsch referred to as the "church-type."[37] The "church-type" does not define itself in opposition to society's structures of economic life, political power, and intellectual culture; it seeks to draw them into its ultimate sphere of meaning. The "sect-type" abandons those structures, seeking to cultivate the pure religious experience within its highly constricted communal existence.

9

LATE MEDIEVAL FORERUNNERS

The theology of Thomas Aquinas had portrayed church and state as the perfect societies by means of which the temporal and spiritual ends of human life are advanced. It was an intricately developed vision of an organic civilization in which temporal and spiritual realms were perfectly integrated, yet each preserved independence in its own sphere. In the centuries before and after Thomas there were, in fact, serious conflicts between temporal and spiritual authorities. The investiture controversies of the eleventh and twelfth centuries and the conflicts between popes and the kings of England and France in subsequent centuries were serious enough to scandalize Christendom.

There was room for scandal on both sides. Efforts by secular authorities to control episcopal appointments and even to determine papal elections threatened to diminish the church's integrity, independence, and universal character. The popes, for their part, had enormous leverage in a sacramental system that could be used for very secular ends. The fact that the church could provide or withhold access to sacramental means of grace and salvation created a corruptible form of power. A number of moral thinkers in the centuries following Thomas sought to address some of the resulting power questions, with important implications, in some cases, for subsequent history. In this chapter we shall briefly sketch the work of four of these thinkers.

Dante

Dante Alighieri (1265–1321) is chiefly known as the greatest medieval poet. He was, in fact, a serious thinker as well. His *Divine Comedy* might seem more the work of a moralist than an ethicist, if by that we mean that he was more engaged in criticism of contemporary life on the basis of the given moral assumptions of his period. The *Divine Comedy* is indeed a treasury of moral critique. The various levels of hell, purgatory, and heaven are carefully delineated in terms of the relative seriousness of sins and the relative merit of virtues. Some of his observations in that work represent penetrating moral thought—in particular, his portrayal of the punishments of hell as intrinsic to the sins of the damned. Sin, the poem suggests, is its own punishment, just as is virtue, in a sense, its own reward. That understanding of the meaning of moral judgment was not always true of the Middle Ages, where morality was often motivated by the desire to gain rewards and escape punishments having little to do with the morality itself.[1]

Special note must be made, however, of Dante's *De monarchia*.[2] In that Christian interpretation of the state, Dante sought to answer three questions: Is monarchy essential to the common good? Was the Roman Empire rightfully Roman? Is the monarch's authority derived directly from God or mediately through church authority? These questions were framed in response to the chaotic political situation in Europe in the early fourteenth century. The Holy Roman Empire was in disarray. The kingdoms of France and England were in ascendancy. The various Italian states were at each other's throats. Popes had, for some centuries, asserted the right to dominate the empire (such as it was) and the rising nation states (such as they were to be). Dante's tract was implicitly in support of Henry VII (who was crowned emperor in 1309), in opposition to the maximum claims of the popes, and in resistance to the rising tide of nationalism. These purposes achieved mixed results. Practically speaking, the Holy Roman Empire had no future, though Henry VII achieved modest results in Italy. The rising nation-states could not be resisted. Only in respect to papal claims was Dante in harmony with the movement of history. But his ideas remain interesting. In setting them forth, Dante relied substantially upon scripture and Thomist Aristotelianism, with much self-conscious use of syllogistic form.

In support of monarchy, Dante argues that the ruler is to the state what the mind is to the body or the father is to the household ("if we consider a home, the purpose of which is to train its members to live well, we see that there has to be one member who directs and rules"[3]). Moreover, since the worst obstacle to justice is human cupidity, the best form of government is the one that places a single ruler beyond the reach of cupidity—by giving him in advance everything he should want. Being already master of the whole realm, "the Monarch, then, can have no cause for cupidity (or, of all men, has the least cause for it . . .) and since cupidity alone perverts the judgment and compels justice, it follows that the Monarch is in a perfect—or at least the best possible—condition for governing."[4] It is also, he argues, superfluous to have more than one do what one can do alone: "if A alone is adequate for doing what A and B together can do, the introduction of B is unnecessary."[5] "A" here means the Monarch; "B" means anybody else participating in the decision making. A monarch is, moreover, best able to assure unity. Thus, "all concord depends upon the unity of wills; mankind is at its best in a state of concord; for as a man is at his best in body and soul when he is in a state of concord, the same is true of a house, a city and a kingdom, and of mankind as a whole." This unity of wills is, however, impossible "unless there is one will which dominates all others and holds them in unity, for the wills of mortals, influenced by their adolescent and seductive delights, are in need of a director."[6]

Such arguments anticipate the age of royal absolutism in the emerging nation-states. But Dante's purpose was to emphasize the importance of political unity at the universal level. All humankind is one political community. True unity and concord are not possible with a multiplicity of princes; there is need for "a prince over all, whose will guides and rules those of all." Here, we have a call for world government.

It should, he thinks, take the form of empire. "We notice," he writes, "that not only individual men but also certain whole peoples are born to rule, whilst others are born to be ruled and serve. . . . [N]ot only is it expedient for the latter to be ruled, it is actually just, even though they are forced to it."[7] The Roman Empire, he feels, clearly demonstrated its special capacities. Ideally, therefore, the empire of the world should come in some kind of recovery of the Roman Empire. He is extravagant in his praise for Rome. "Who will not acknowledge," he asks, "that the father of the Roman people, and therefore that people itself, was the noblest beneath the heavens."[8] Furthermore, the miraculous origins of Rome prove that it was the will of God for Rome to be the seat of the world's greatest empire: "The Roman Empire was brought to perfection with the aid of miracles, and was therefore willed by God."[9] Indeed, the fact that Rome won out in the intense competition of peoples for world domination proves that it did so "by divine decree."[10] In a final burst of enthusiasm, Dante exclaims, "From all of which it is plain that the Roman people triumphed over all its rivals in the competition for world empire; thus it triumphed by divine decree, thus it won the crown with divine assent; its victory was based upon right."[11]

Dante then asserts that the monarch's legitimate authority is derived directly from God; it is not conferred through church authority. The supreme pontiff is, to be sure, the "vicar of God." But that does not mean that he is God. God has done many things that the "vicar of God" cannot do, such as making the earth rise. The office of vicar, while unquestionably superior in respect to spiritual matters, does not apply to the temporal sphere where the law of nature governs. Indeed, he reminds his readers, the Roman Empire flourished when the church did not even exist.[12] Along the way, Dante disposes of a number of arguments derived from scripture before asserting that the divine law, as "enshrined in the Old and New Testaments," nowhere gives the church the right to confer authority upon the secular prince. "I have looked in vain," he writes, "within those shrines [of Old and New Testaments] for any command to priests in either the old or the new dispensation to take care of temporal affairs." Quite to the contrary, he finds, "the priests of the old dispensation were specifically excluded from temporal affairs by God's commandments to Moses; and those of the new dispensation by Christ's commands to his disciples."[13] Christ, after all, had said "my kingdom is not of this world." Thus, "two guides have been appointed for man to lead him to his twofold goal: there is the Supreme Pontiff who is to lead mankind to eternal life in accordance with revelation; and there is the Emperor who, in accordance with philosophical teaching, is to lead mankind to temporal happiness."[14]

The enduring weight of *De monarchia* is not in its romantic effort to recover the Roman Empire, nor even in its strongly argued preference for monarchial government—an idea that did come into its own in the three or four following centuries. Of greater importance was this medieval assertion of the case for universal political community—a kind of world government. Perhaps even more arresting was Dante's direct challenge to papal authority. Less than a decade before the writing of *De monarchia*, Pope Boniface VIII had issued his bull *Unam sanctam* asserting the supremacy of spiritual over temporal power:

> And we learn from the words of the Gospel that in this Church and in her power are two swords, the spiritual and the temporal. . . . Both are in the power of the Church, the spiritual sword and the material. . . . The one sword, then, should be under the other, and temporal authority subject to spiritual. . . . Furthermore we declare, state, define and pronounce that it is altogether necessary to salvation for every human creature to be subject to the Roman pontiff.[15]

In light of that pronouncement, how might Dante's words have been read: "Although I maintain that Peter's successor has the power to bind and loose in fulfillment of the office entrusted to Peter, it does not follow that he can bind and loose the decrees or laws of the Empire"?[16] So direct a challenge to so recent a papal decree would not have been possible had the papacy not already lost considerable prestige, with corresponding loss of fear of its available ecclesial sanctions. It was shortly to lose even more, with the removal of the papacy to Avignon, France, for most of the rest of the century and with the subsequent spectacle of two, then three rival claimants to the Holy See. These events had a profoundly demythologizing effect (to use a contemporary term) upon the claims of the popes.

Marsilius of Padua

Alan Gewirth is correct in speaking of Marsilius of Padua (1280?–1343?) as "one of the few truly revolutionary figures in the history of political philosophy."[17] A younger contemporary of Dante, Marsilius articulated an even more radical doctrine of the independence of temporal power from ecclesial control—indeed, his doctrine goes further by asserting the primacy of the temporal. But Marsilius's understanding of sovereignty was far removed from Dante's monarchism.

The state, to Marsilius, is a community banded together for the purpose of advancing the good life, since "men had to assemble together in order to attain what was beneficial through these arts and to avoid what was harmful."[18] The need for the state arises from the fact that there is contention within the community, leading to its disintegration. The state therefore had to establish a standard of justice and a guardian "to restrain excessive wrongdoers as well as other individuals both within and outside the state who disturb or attempt to oppress the community," as well as provide for other needs.[19] But the law is not simply the will of one or a few; it is the creation of the people. Here we have a very strong medieval restatement of the principle of popular sovereignty. The legislator, he writes, "is the people or the whole body of citizens, or the weightier part thereof, through its election or will expressed by words in the general assembly of the citizens."[20] This remains imperfect as a democratic concept, for women and slaves are excluded from citizenry, along with boys and aliens. But the conception remains broadly democratic. Marsilius's view of the sovereignty of citizens contains much that anticipates the great Enlightenment contract thinkers (Hobbes, Locke, Rousseau) and it voices ideas that are also quite ancient, owing much to the Stoics and Aristotle and to the Roman lawyers. And while his statement is put in fairly radical form, the concept of popular sovereignty was generally assumed throughout the Middle Ages. In defense of the authority of the whole community, Marsilius observes that people are more likely to obey laws they have had a hand in adopting. Against the view that most people are not competent, he protests that the general run of citizens are generally of sound reason. And while not everyone is capable of initiating good laws, the whole community is capable of recognizing and distinguishing good from bad proposals.[21]

In a distinction between legislative and executive functions, Marsilius allows for the latter authority to be exercised by a much smaller group, even by a monarch. But executive authority is finally accountable to the legislative—that is, to the whole community. The point is made clear in his statement that when rulers execute the law, "the entire community does it, since the rulers do it in accordance with the legal determination of the community, and, being few or only one in number, they can execute the legal provisions more easily."[22]

Dante had insisted upon the independence of temporal authority from the spiritual. Marsilius actually reverses the maximum papal claims by holding that the church should be subservient to political authority—not in its purely spiritual functioning but in its temporal aspects. The church, to Marsilius, is "the whole body of the faithful, who believe in and invoke the name of Christ, and all the parts of this whole body in every community, even the family."[23] Its proper business, as church, is spiritual matters, which have to do with such things as "contemplation of God, love of God and of one's neighbors, abstinence, mercy, meekness, prayer, offerings for piety or divine worship, hospitality, pilgrimage, castigation of one's own body, contempt for and flight from worldly and carnal pleasures."[24] Priests or bishops depart from the spiritual when they engage in temporal pursuits and when they seek exemption from regulation by temporal authority. Thus, Marsilius calls for control over all temporal aspects of the life of the church by the civil community.

Church government, according to Marsilius, should ultimately be in the hands of a general council. The general council, not the hierarchy, should deal with questions of faith and order within the church.[25] Such a general council is to be selected in an astonishingly democratic way: "Let all the notable provinces or communities of the world, in accordance with the determination of their human legislators whether one or many, and according to their proportion in quantity and quality of persons, elect faithful men, first priests and then non-priests, suitable persons of the most blameless lives and the greatest experience in divine law."[26] In case there might remain some ambiguity about the implications of this for papal claims, Marsilius writes that "when the Roman or any other bishop ascribes to himself plenitude of power over any ruler, community, or individual person, such a claim is inappropriate and wrong, and goes outside, or rather against, the divine Scriptures and human demonstrations."[27] And what should be done about those usurpations of authority? "Such claims on the part of the Roman or any other bishop must be completely stopped, through admonition and even through coercive power if necessary, by the human legislators or by the men who rule by their authority." Nor would Marsilius allow a pope or bishops to convene a general council. That, too, would be the responsibility of the "faithful legislator or the whole body of the believers," just as it would devolve upon the legislator to implement the council's decisions through coercive decrees.[28] Marsilius does believe there might be some point in having a chief bishop or overall head of the church. But the authority to establish such leadership should remain with the council and the faithful legislator. He suggests that the church's head should be appointed or dismissed by this faithful legislator, noting that when the secular realm is in infidel hands that responsibility must be taken by the general council. The authority of the church's head should be restricted to advising the faithful legislator when a council should be summoned, chairing the council and suggesting its agenda, and helping to implement its decisions.

So Marsilius, in addition to his radical understanding of the political order, proposed sweeping changes in the church's own structure of authority—changes bordering on anticlericalism. Was his work offered as a contribution to *Christian* political and ecclesial thought, or were his theological and scriptural points only a pious smokescreen for an essentially secular worldview? That is difficult to tell. Certainly the chaotic state of the church of the fourteenth century, with its corruptions and naked power struggles, contributed to cynicism. Then, too, Marsilius was deeply implicated in the political moves made by Ludwig of Bavaria as Holy Roman Emperor.[29] Given his sweeping condemnations of the papalist claims, it is certainly not surprising that he was excommunicated by Pope John XXII.

Still, the *Defensor pacis*, Marcilius's principal writing, does not dispute the importance of scripture, sacraments, and even priesthood. Marsilius's focus is on power, not upon the means of salvation, though in his relentless critique of papal claims, he inevitably had to confront the relationship between those claims and the spiritual sanctions available to give them force. He denied the authority of the hierarchy to excommunicate persons or place cities or nations under interdiction, which meant, ultimately, that he denied the objective efficacy of priestly decisions to offer or withhold the sacraments. He continued, thus, to consider penance important to salvation, but the internal contrition of the penitent is efficacious even without priestly absolution while priestly absolution is not efficacious without internal contrition. Marsilius's sacramental theories thus moved a long step toward subjectivism; but he had grasped the connection between an objective theory of sacraments and the political consequences implicit in a priesthood authorized to extend or withhold the sacraments to believers who consider those sacraments necessary to their salvation.

John Hus

Dante and Marsilius had offered revolutionary new conceptions of political authority to the late medieval world. Within two generations, John Wycliffe (1325?–1384) of England and John Hus (1372?–1415) of Bohemia were to offer even deeper challenges to ecclesial authority. Wycliffe was perhaps the more original and radical of the two. But Hus (whose essential ideas were largely derived from Wycliffe) had a more immediate and lasting effect on events. Both challenged the authority of the pope, though Wycliffe's characterization of Gregory XI as a "terrible devil" illustrates his greater gift for undiplomatic language.[30] Both insist upon the primacy of scripture over any other source of authority; both test the pretensions of pope and hierarchy against scripture and find them wanting. Hus writes: "Every Christian is expected to believe explicitly and implicitly all the truth which the Holy Spirit has put in Scripture, and in this way a man is not bound to believe the sayings of the saints which are apart from Scripture, nor should he believe papal bulls, except in so far as they speak out of Scripture. . . . [F]or both the pope and his curia make mistakes from ignorance of the truth."[31] Jesus Christ is himself the head of the church. The church contains both the predestined elect, who are really its members, and the reprobate who are not. Similarly, some outside the church are among the predestined—as was Saul of Tarsus prior to his experience on the road to Damascus. The government of the church need not be pope and cardinals; "others besides these may be vicars of the apostles."[32] The test of who truly are such vicars is whether they conform to Christ or live at variance with Christ.[33] Indeed, quite ordinary Christians should put their superiors to the test:

> Therefore, subjects living piously in Christ ought to pay heed to the life of the apostles and see to it whether their superiors live conformably to the apostles. For, if in their spiritual ministry they are out of accord with the apostles, if they are busy in exacting money, spurn evangelical poverty and incline to the world, nay, if they evidently sow offenses, then they know by their works that they have departed from the religion of Jesus Christ the Lord. Therefore, O ye who love Christ's law from the heart, first note their works and see if they incline to the world, second give heed to their commands, whether they savor of avarice or the gain of this world, and third consult holy Scripture whether they command in accordance with Christ's counsel. And in the light of this counsel believe them; or disbelieve them, if they command contrary to this counsel.[34]

"Inferiors" who do not critically examine their superiors in this way "would be in peril of eternal death, if they did not judge wisely about these things."

This kind of broadside (combined with his criticism of the ultimate ecclesial sanctions of excommunication and interdiction) evoked a severe response. The criticisms of corruption in the church, even in its hierarchy, had abundant precedent in the monastic movements of the Middle Ages. But Hus had not simply questioned the corrupt behavior of church leaders; he cast doubt on the legitimacy of their authority. Perhaps more to the point, Hus created a substantial following. A gifted preacher, Hus captivated a good deal of Bohemia with his preaching and writing, and the resulting movement was perceived to be a deadly threat to the unity of the church.

The rest of the story is a familiar though tragic chapter in church history. Summoned to the Council of Constance in 1414, he was subjected there to a dramatic trial. Notwithstanding his having been guaranteed safe conduct by the current Holy Roman Emperor Sigismund, he was condemned as a heretic in 1415 and burned at the stake. The irony is that the Council of Constance was itself largely the product of a reform movement devoted to overcome the scandal of three rival claimants to the papacy and to broadening the authority of general councils in the life of the church.

The Conciliar Movement

Marsilius's advocacy of the general council as supreme authority in the life of the church anticipated, and probably influenced, a strong movement in that direction in the late fourteenth and early fifteenth centuries. The immediate occasion was the crisis of the papacy. For nearly seventy years (1309–1377) the papacy was removed from Rome to Avignon, France, in a striking evidence of the rising power of French temporal power over a greatly weakened papal office. The papacy returned to Rome in 1377, the election of Pope Urban VI in 1378 led that same year to the election of a rival pope, Clement VII, by the same College of Cardinals. With Urban VI in Rome and Clement VII back in Avignon, the church now had two rival heads with fairly equal followings. In an effort to resolve the conflict, the Council of Pisa elected yet a third pope in 1409, so the church now had a three-way division.[35] This papal schism scandalized the church morally and theologically while immensely complicating its governance. Thinking Christians looked for a way out, and the conciliar movement developed as the most interesting possibility.

The movement acquired some theoretical foundation from such figures as Francisco Zabarella, Peter d'Ailly, Jean Gerson, and Nicholas of Cusa.[36] It is debatable how far the conciliarists were prepared to go in restructuring the church. But seen in political terms, they wished to emphasize the sovereignty of the whole body of the church and the accountability of pope and hierarchy to that body, at least to the extent of securing its consent. Efforts by the conciliarists at the Council of Constance and the later Council of Basel (1432) were only partially successful. They had succeeded in convening the Council of Constance apart from papal authority and in overcoming the papal schism. Moreover, that council had adopted the following decree, setting forth a strong statement of conciliar authority:

This holy Council of Constance . . . declares, first that it is lawfully assembled in the Holy Spirit, that it constitutes a General Council, representing the Catholic Church, and that therefore it has its authority immediately from Christ; and that all men, of every rank and condition, including the Pope himself, [are] bound to obey it in matters concerning the Faith, the abolition of the schism, and the reformation of the Church of God in its head and its members.[37]

The movement soon fizzled, however, for lack of a coherent plan for institutional reform and for want of serious support, now that the scandal of the papal schism was over. Troeltsch's epitaph on the movement's failure is worth pondering. The movement, he concluded, was destined to fail "since it could not even imagine in theory the abolition of the real root of the institutional conception in priesthood, sacrament and hierarchy." It "ultimately only issued in the victory of the hierarchy, which logically incorporates and centralizes the institutional idea." Nevertheless, wrote Troeltsch, "the ideas which had once been set in motion remained effective, and did their part to undermine the Catholic conception of the Church."[38] They also did their part to prepare the postmedieval world for constitutional and democratic forms of government, but that would not come for several more centuries.

Niccolò Machiavelli

One may wonder whether it is appropriate to include Machiavelli (1469–1527) in an introductory history of Christian ethics. Was he authentically Christian? Was there even a shred of ethics to be found in his work? We cannot linger over the ongoing debates concerning whether his writing had serious moral intent or whether, indeed, his most important work, *The Prince*, was actually satire. (We may be skeptical about both.) In any case, his work is important as an illustration of the disintegration of the medieval moral vision and for its remarkable grasp of the sources of political power.

The Prince is not a finished philosophical essay on sovereignty and justice. It is written as advice to rulers on how to gain and exercise power in a highly competitive political environment. Two points emerge overall: It is not possible to gain or exercise political power without substantial popular support, and anything that influences the will of people is translatable into either support or opposition. Cutting through medieval assumptions about legitimate authority, Machiavelli is interested in what will gain and maintain sufficient popular support to rule effectively. Machiavelli is quite aware that in the real world many rulers have lost their thrones despite being, in the medieval sense, legitimate authorities; he is even more aware of the many rulers who have gained power despite their lack of traditional legitimacy. The former are ruined without much sympathy being wasted upon them; the latter find that their astuteness is rewarded quickly enough by an aura of legitimacy.

So Machiavelli, noting that fear is a more dependable motivation than love, urges the prince to cultivate a healthy fear among his competitors and subjects. People are, he writes, "less careful how they offend him who makes himself loved than him who makes himself feared."[39] Love is vulnerable to "every whisper of private interest," while fear of punishment "never relaxes its grasp." Indeed, Machiavelli argues that even cruelty may, in the long run, be the most merciful course, noting that "he who quells disorder by a very few signal examples will in the end be more merciful than he who from too great leniency permits things to take their course and so to result in rapine and bloodshed; for these hurt the whole State, whereas the severities of the Prince injure individuals only." Nevertheless, he continues, "a Prince should inspire fear in such a fashion that if he does not win love he may escape hate."[40]

His discussion of the prince's own morality and religion illustrates perfectly his grasp of how political power derives from influence over the will of subjects. One must, he writes, become skillful in deceit. "Men are so simple, and governed so absolutely by their present needs, that he who wishes to deceive will never fail in finding willing dupes."[41] Above all, the prince must *appear* to be moral and religious. It is not necessary that he *have* all the good qualities, "but it is most essential that he should *seem* to have them."[42] Indeed, it may be dangerous to seek to observe all the moral qualities too resolutely, while it is still important to appear to do so. Thus, he concludes, "it is well to seem merciful, faithful, humane, religious, and upright, and also to be so; but the mind should remain so balanced that were it needful not to be so, you should be able and know how to change to the contrary." Machiavelli's celebrated passage on religion continues in precisely this spirit:

> A Prince should therefore be very careful that nothing ever escapes his lips which is not replete with the five qualities above named, so that to see and hear him, one would think him the embodiment of mercy, good faith, integrity, humanity, and religion. And there is no virtue which it is more necessary for him to seem to possess than this last; because men in general judge rather by the eye than by the hand, for every one can see but few can touch. Every one sees what you seem, but few know what you are, and these few dare not oppose themselves to the opinion of the many who have the majesty of the State to back them up.[43]

This remarkable passage, alongside others of like vein throughout the book, warrants further comment. Note the rather low estimate of human nature that Machiavelli seems to hold. For instance, "the vulgar are always taken by appearances and by results, and the world is made up of the vulgar," or "if all men were good, this would not be good advice, but since they are dishonest and do not keep faith with you, you, in return, need not keep faith with them." In itself, this estimate of human nature is no break from typical medieval theological literature, grounded as it was in Augustine's doctrine of original sin and in the monastic portrayals of the nonreligious life of common people. Nor, for that matter, did Machiavelli invent cruelty for supposedly lofty ends. That, after all, is partly why alleged heretics like John Hus were publicly condemned to the stake. Nevertheless, Machiavelli was unique in the utter frankness with which he counseled rulers to manipulate the weaknesses of the multitude.

Even apart from the low estimate of human nature, such passages make an important point about political power. If such power does depend upon public support, *anything* that potentially influences people is translatable into power. Power, thus, cannot be reduced to any one set of values—not even economic gain or bodily fear, important as these are in Machiavelli's analysis. In that respect, Machiavelli is much more cautious than some modern political theorists in observing the nuances and variations in influence. What "works" politically with one person or population may not with another.

Nevertheless, with Machiavelli we have come a long way from the political thought of Augustine or the great medieval thinkers. Medieval thought, following Augustine, clearly affirmed political authority as a part of God's purposes. A dose of Machiavelli might have led more than one to ask again whether the Constantinian revolution was such an unmixed blessing for Christian ethics! Or perhaps it would have come as a reminder that politics is an inescapable aspect of human society and that every analysis of power must be accompanied by ethical analysis and moral discipline.

PART IV

The Era of Reformation and Enlightenment

The great intellectual synthesis of Thomas Aquinas may have appeared to signal the drawing together of medieval Christendom in a unified cultural vision, shared by all. In fact, the late medieval world was turbulent. The Crusades had begun to shatter Europe's insularity—a process quickened by intrepid explorers and traders like Marco Polo and Vasco da Gama. Commercial activity soon followed, with the development of great trading companies like the Fuggers of Belgium and the British East India Company. Settled patterns of economic feudalism gave way to greater economic freedom. Thomas's own intellectual achievement, far from constraining further thought, actually stimulated it by demonstrating the independence of reason. Humanism, stimulated in part by the continuing recovery of classical culture, expressed itself in the arts and philosophy. Europe's checkerboard of small, feudal principalities began to be consolidated into larger nation-states whose rulers exhibited increasing independence and absolutism.

The unity of the universal church, for which Thomas had provided elaborate theological rationale, broke under the weight of moral corruption and a lack of responsiveness to movements of reform. While the Protestant Reformation of the sixteenth century appeared as a vast theological and ecclesial revolution, the continuities it preserved with important theological and moral emphases of the early church were also impressive. The Reformation did, however, shatter the vision of a universal church uniting Christendom. It also played an important role in shaping and defining the modern world.

10

THE REFORMERS: LUTHER AND CALVIN

The Protestant Reformation burst on the scene in the early sixteenth century, breaking the medieval world apart and recasting the religious and political map of Europe. It was, beyond question, a decisive moment in Western church history. Energies flowing from the Reformation were to affect the character of the spread of Christianity to other continents while fundamentally shaping the culture of much of Europe and North America.

Still, in reading the works of the major Reformers, one is struck by the immensity of their indebtedness to prior Christian thought—especially that of Augustine.

Therein lies a curious paradox, for Augustine had also shaped the thought of the medieval Christianity that developed over the course of a thousand years. It may be a question of which Augustine! Benjamin Warfield may have been shrewd in this assessment: "the Reformation, inwardly considered, was just the ultimate triumph of Augustine's doctrine of grace over Augustine's doctrine of the church."[1] For that doctrine of grace was indeed the hallmark of the Reformation. And, in the thought of the great Reformers, it did indeed do battle with an ecclesiology in which grace had largely assumed objective sacramental form. We must not oversimplify. But the recovery of Augustine's doctrine of grace was basic to the Christian ethics of the foremost Reformation thinkers, notably Luther and Calvin.

Luther

Most of Luther's theological agenda was anticipated by Augustine (and the apostle Paul), and most of his program of reform was prefigured in the writings and activities of Wycliffe and Hus. But Martin Luther (1483–1546), unlike Wycliffe and Hus, found the times ripe for revolutionary change. The posting of his Ninety-five Theses was a public invitation to debate abuses in the system of papal indulgences and related issues. While this was not an altogether routine event, nobody could have anticipated its sweeping consequences. Luther was soon caught up in a vast tide of change. His was a formidable theological mind, and his subsequent writings articulated the deeper implications of his challenge to the system of indulgences while also responding to some of the practical consequences.

Christian Liberty

If Christian ethics includes consideration of both motivations and actions, Luther's ethics emphasizes the former much more than the latter. His classic treatise "Concerning Christian Liberty," in fact, proclaims the freedom of the Christian from the objective constraints of life based upon external "works." We are not saved by such works nor by the laws that command them; we are saved by faith. The Christian, he writes, "is free from all things." Such a person "needs no works in order to be justified and saved, but receives these gifts in abundance from faith alone."[2] An ethic based upon obedience to external commandments would likely be motivated by self-seeking. In any event, it would be futile, since none of us is capable of fulfilling the law without the empowerment of grace given to us only through faith. Echoing the words of Paul's letter to the Romans, which had a profound impact upon his thought, Luther argues that "the word of God cannot be received and honored by any works, but by faith alone."[3]

The primary question addressed by Christian ethics, thus, ought not to be the consideration of "works" or moral precepts; rather it should be consideration of the moral will itself. We are not good because of the good things we do; the things we do are good because we are good. Thus, he writes,

True, then, are these two sayings: "Good works do not make a good man, but a good man does good works"; "Bad works do not make a bad man, but a bad man does bad works." Thus it is always necessary that the substance or person should be good before any good works can be done, and that good works should follow and proceed from a good person.[4]

In understanding this point, Luther might have agreed with an analogy drawn from educational experience: We do not become educated by virtue of receiving good grades; we receive good grades as an effect of becoming educated. Education itself—which occurs within us—is primary; evaluation by our teachers is secondary. While bad grades may goad us into greater effort, what really counts is our love of truth and our faith in the possibility of knowledge.

Luther, like Paul, has here insisted upon freedom from enslavement to external precepts and laws.

But also like Paul, Luther immediately writes that those who are justified by faith will in fact respond gratefully and lovingly, thereby fulfilling the true intent of the law. "We do not," he continues, "reject good works; nay, we embrace them and teach them in the highest degree. It is not on their own account that we condemn them, but on account of this impious addition to them and the perverse notion of seeking justification by them." In a moving passage, Luther writes of the moral fruit borne out of justification by faith:

> Thus from faith flow forth love and joy in the Lord, and from love a cheerful, willing, free spirit, disposed to serve our neighbor voluntarily, without taking any account of gratitude or ingratitude, praise or blame, gain or loss. Its object is not to lay men under obligations, nor does it distinguish between friends and enemies, or look to gratitude or ingratitude, but most freely and willingly spends itself and its goods, whether it loses them through ingratitude, or gains goodwill. For thus did its Father, distributing all things to all men abundantly and freely, making His sun to rise upon the just and unjust.[5]

The radical morality to which this leads is suggested by a further comment: "We give this rule: the good things which we have from God ought to flow from one to another and become common to all, so that every one of us may, as it were, put on his neighbor, and so behave towards him as if he were himself in his place."[6] Such a morality cannot, however, be detached from its source: "This is true love and the genuine truth of Christian life. But only there is it true and genuine where there is true and genuine faith."[7] We cannot truly and genuinely "put on" our neighbors—translated in modern idiom, we cannot be a genuine community—apart from this grounding in the gracious love of God. But those who are thus grounded will, by necessity, *be* a loving, sharing community.

What then comes of moral laws and precepts? In one sense they are, of course, cut off at the root. Obedience to laws and precepts no longer "counts" as moral good. It is possible to obey any and all injunctions, no matter their source and authority, while remaining a quite wicked person—if, that is, one's *reason* for obeying them is not a response to God's gracious love. In that sense, with Luther there is no longer an objective content to morality. Still, Luther takes pains to avoid the impression that moral law no longer counts for anything. At one point in his argument he suggests that the law retains its validity as a reminder of our utter inability to generate moral goodness from within ourselves:

> Now when a man has through the precepts been taught his own impotence, and become anxious by what means he may satisfy the law—for the law must be satisfied, so that no jot or tittle of it may pass away, otherwise he must be hopelessly condemned—then, being truly humbled and brought to nothing in his own eyes, he finds in himself no resource for justification and salvation.[8]

Thus convinced of one's own powerlessness, one is brought to the "promises of God," which are grounded in the grace of God and display the glory of God. Through faith in the promises, one receives the gift of salvation and the capacity to love from the heart and not as external conformity to law.

Such persons devote themselves to serving others, doing whatever is necessary in the life of the world. Christian vocation, with Luther, thus departs sharply from the medieval conception. The latter, in accordance with the monastic ideal, understood vocation to mean a special calling to be a seeker after union with God or a priest in the church. The majority of humankind, notwithstanding the economic and social necessity of their daily work, were not understood to have a "calling" to pursue it. To Luther, however, there is no greater dignity or spiritual worth attached to priestly office than to the ordinary work of the world. Any form of work that is essential to human well-being is a fitting response to God's gracious love; it is a "calling" in the fullest sense of the word.

While Christian vocation is thus liberated, in Luther, from clericalism, it remains largely captive to medieval notions of occupational destiny. At points, Luther implies some freedom of decision making so that Christians might freely choose, out of love, to match their capabilities with areas of greatest need. More typically, however, he assumes the hereditary given-ness of most callings. A son could be expected to do what his father had done, whether as a peasant farmer, butcher, baker, craftsman, soldier, or nobleman. A daughter was expected, even more, to be what her mother had been, a homemaker, childbearer, and nurturer of the young. Calling, to Luther, thus became more a matter of the attitude of loving service brought to given tasks than a matter of choosing what those tasks would be. Of course, the economic structure of Luther's world would have made a thorough-going conception of vocational choice and mobility almost totally irrelevant. That economic structure, essentially fixed for a thousand years, was based almost exclusively on hereditary destiny.

The main exception to this, the one point where vocational and status mobility existed to some degree, was in the priesthood and monastic orders. Here, it had long been accepted in principle that any Christian, intent upon pursuing the hard way of the cross, might move away from his father's or her mother's place in life to enter another institutional world.[9] Luther's challenge to a clerical definition of vocation, while it did not in itself challenge the hierarchical medieval economic structure, implicitly recognized that vocation might ultimately represent choosing and not only reflect one's spirit in accepting.

The "Two Kingdoms" of Martin Luther

Where are persons to be found who exhibit such faith and love, such devotion to the well-being of others? Luther's view of human nature is not optimistic. "Few believe," he writes, "and still fewer live a Christian life."[10] Accordingly, in a formulation reminiscent of Augustine, Luther holds that "all who are not Christians belong to the kingdom of the world and are under the law."[11] Those who thus belong to the "kingdom of the world" have been provided by God with "a different government outside the Christian estate and God's kingdom." They have been "subjected . . . to the sword, so that, even though they would do so, they cannot practice their wickedness." He continues, "if it were not so, seeing that the whole world is evil and that among thousands there is scarcely one true Christian, men would devour one another, and no one could preserve wife and child, support himself and serve God; and thus the world would be reduced to chaos."[12]

So Luther argues that it is romantic nonsense for Christians to think of governing the world directly in accordance with the precepts of love:

First take heed and fill the world with real Christians before ruling it in a Christian and evangelical manner. This you will never accomplish; for the world and the masses are and always will be unChristian, although they are all baptized and are nominally Christian.[13]

To Luther, this kind of romantic thinking is not harmless innocence: if put into effect it threatens the very foundations of social living. Evil in this world must be restrained. It is no act of love to fail to resist evil; it is to invite wickedness and injustice promising massive suffering, death, and destruction.

How, then, are we to deal with the clear gospel word to love and not to resist evil?

Luther did not seek to evade the message of the Sermon on the Mount and, as we have seen, love is at the very center of his ethic. But he made two important distinctions. First, he distinguished between personal self-defense, which he rejected as contrary to Christian love, and the defense of others, which he considered to be an expression of that same love. A Christian, he writes, "should be so disposed that he will suffer every evil and injustice, not avenge himself nor bring suit in court, and in nothing make use of secular power and law for himself." When we forcibly defend ourselves we are behaving in a self-centered, unloving way. When we defend others, however, a Christian "may and should seek vengeance, justice, protection and help, and do what he can toward this."[14] Thereby, "you govern yourself according to love and suffer no injustice for your neighbor's sake."[15] Sometimes, of course, self-defense is inextricably linked with the protection of others, in which case it is entirely to be approved.

The other distinction follows from this: Love can be expressed in negative, indirect ways as well as in a positive, direct manner. The first is known among interpreters of Luther as his doctrine of the "strange work of love": It is strange because it is not at all what it appears to be. It appears to be against love, for it involves physical force, even to the point of killing. But in fact it is love. It is prompted, not by ill will toward the evildoer, but by love of the evildoer's potential victims. Thus, in his counsel to secular rulers, Luther sought to justify military action in defense of their subjects. In a justified war, he writes, "it is a Christian act and an act of love confidently to kill, rob, and pillage the enemy"—though he promptly follows this with admonitions to offer mercy to those who surrender and not to harm the innocent.[16]

Luther applied this doctrine in response to the rebellion of the Swabian peasants in 1524–25, the social causes of which he appeared to have understood not at all. In his famous diatribe "Against the Robbing and Murdering Hordes of Peasants," Luther detailed what he took to be the sins of the peasants in their disobedience to properly constituted rulers, especially warning against their rebellion as a prelude to anarchy:

> For rebellion is not simple murder, but is like a great fire, which attacks and lays waste a whole land. Thus rebellion brings with it a land full of murder and bloodshed, makes widows and orphans, and turns everything upside down, like the greatest disaster. Therefore let everyone who can smite, slay, and stab, secretly or openly, remembering that nothing can be more poisonous, hurtful, or devilish than a rebel. It is just as when one must kill a mad dog; if you do not strike him, he will strike you, and a whole land with you.[17]

The "hard book against the peasants" evoked much criticism. Luther quickly issued clarifications and modifications. But the essay remains as a vivid expression of his underlying conception of a fallen humanity requiring the stern governance of the kingdom of the world. At the same time, Luther remembers the kingdom of God, wherein love reigns among the faithful, however few they may be. The latter kingdom cannot be brought into being by secular power; the former cannot rule *without* that power:

> For this reason these two kingdoms must be sharply distinguished and both be permitted to remain; the one to produce piety, the other to bring about external peace and prevent evil deeds; neither is sufficient in the world without the other. For no one can become pious before God by means of the secular government, without Christ's spiritual rule.[18]

How radical is the dualism of the "two kingdoms"? So many of Luther's writings were forged in the heat of some crisis or controversy that one must be cautious in taking them simply at face value. Clearly he understood his doctrine of love to have temporal consequences: we are to share worldly possessions, seeking the temporal well-being of others. And, the diatribe against the peasants notwithstanding, he clearly counseled rulers to be merciful and to have due regard for the spiritual well-being of their subjects. But the separation between the temporal and the spiritual remains sharply delineated in Luther's writing. In the writing against the peasants, he contended that baptism does not provide a basis for compulsory socialization of goods; nor does it provide bodily or material freedom, but only freedom of soul. The essential point is applied to priests and bishops as well as to peasants. Such clerical leaders are reminded that they are no better than other Christians and that they should not employ secular means to enforce spiritual ends. "Therefore," he writes, "they should not impose any law or decree on others without their will and consent; their rule consists in nothing else than in dealing with God's Word, leading Christians by it and overcoming heresy by its means.

On the other hand, he reminds rulers that they have no jurisdiction over spiritual matters: "where temporal power presumes to prescribe laws for the soul, it encroaches upon God's government and only misleads and destroys the souls."[19] Even heresy is not to be controlled by the sword, for "heresy is a spiritual matter, which no iron can strike, no fire burn, no water drown."[20]

While Luther did not maintain a strict consistency in his two kingdoms doctrine, it would be difficult to imagine a more complete break from medieval assumptions than his dualism represents. Even at the height of the medieval controversies between secular and religious authority, neither side could have conceived of a world in which secular authority was not used to enforce orthodox doctrinal teaching or one in which religious authority had no temporal power.

Calvin: Ethics and the Sovereignty of God

At first glance, John Calvin (1509–1564) was simply the great systematizer of Luther. Converted to Protestantism from a humanistic form of Catholicism while still in his early twenties, Calvin adopted Luther's main ideas as his own. Above all, Christian life was understood to be a life of faith and faithfulness in response to God's grace. Salvation is entirely the gift of God's grace; in no respect is it the effect of human "works." Moral effort is response to grace, essential but not independently initiated. Moral law manifests the righteousness of God, but it also reveals the utter frustration of humanity mired in sin. As with Luther, Christian ethics is not so much about objective good and evil to be done as it is about the response of the human subject to what God has already done.

Moreover, Calvin—also with Luther—stresses the importance of vocation. We are "called" by God to a morally responsive life and our "calling" is by no means limited to the then-traditional conception of priestly or monastic vocation. To Calvin, as to Luther, the calling can be expressed as fully in secular pursuits. Even Calvin's celebrated doctrine of predestination is largely shared with Luther, both of the Reformers being indebted to Augustine at that point.

Through his *Institutes of the Christian Religion*, published in several successively enlarged editions beginning in 1536, Calvin gave intellectual force and systematic detail to ideas Luther had expressed in the heat of battle. But to say no more would understate the originality of Calvin's own ethic.[21]

Calvin's theological ethic is grounded in the sovereignty of God, whose ineffable majesty transcends all human thought while impacting upon creaturely existence at every point. To Calvin, God's will is everything; human creativity for its own sake is nothing. The whole point of ethics is to respond to God, to worship God, to glorify God, to do the will of God; it is all absolutely God-centered. Some interpreters of Calvin, impressed by that, contend that Calvin's God is more majesty than love. Ernst Troeltsch, for instance, holds that "the predominant idea in the Calvinistic conception of God is not love, but majesty, holiness, sovereign power, and grace" and that the point of biblical religion is the creation of "a community in which the glory of God will be realized."[22] But there is a paradox in Calvin's portrait of God. Humankind, utterly fallen and sinful as it is, can give God no gift on its own terms. But God, whose majestic will is everything, freely chooses to express that will by reaching down to fallen humanity with saving love. Without that gracious love humankind is utterly lost. But with it there comes into existence a new possibility. So God is both majestic and loving and, indeed, the majesty of God is most fully, most characteristically expressed through love.

But the paradox deepens with Calvin's doctrine of election. God chooses whom to give this salvation; indeed, from all time God has, in the ineffable mystery of the divine will, known who will receive the gift and who will not. Those who do are, through grace, empowered to respond to the divine love and devote their lives wholeheartedly to the glory of God, inheriting eternal life. Those who do not will remain mired in the quicksands of sin, destined to eternal damnation. But is it not an appalling indictment against God that some should have been chosen for damnation while others are elected to salvation? From the first publication of his work, Calvin's critics argued that point—as it well may be argued. But to understand Calvin we need to recognize that his God is not arbitrary but loving. The love of God is *everything* to Calvin; human effort is *nothing*. The observable fact, buttressed amply by scripture, is that some respond to God while others do not. If God's love is everything, then the reason why some do and others do not respond is to be found in God, not in humanity. Then is God less than humane? No, for all *deserve* damnation. The reason why some are chosen and others are not remains a mystery of God's inscrutable will. But Calvin suggests that without contrast between salvation and damnation the awesome glory of God, and even the depth of the love of God, would remain unrevealed.

The paradox reaches to the question of human freedom as well. For if God has known from all eternity who will and who will not be saved, and if human effort is utterly contingent upon the workings of God's grace or the absence of God's grace in the life of the sinner, then what has become of human freedom? If human beings do not have moral freedom—freedom to choose between good and evil—then how can anybody either be praised or blamed for their actions? If we are bound to do what we do, then why should we be concerned about doing good and not doing evil? In short, does not the loss of freedom lead to moral complacency?

In an extended discussion of the moral will,[23] Calvin explores classical philosophical writings and some Patristic writings (which he finds, on the whole, to be ambiguous). But his most serious conversation is with Augustine, whose views are closest to his own. With Augustine he affirms that we do will, for good or evil. There is therefore no excuse for sin. But also with Augustine he insists that apart from God's grace we are bound or enslaved to evil.[24] That is, apart from grace, our *desire* is evil; we *want* evil, therefore we *will* evil. We do not *want* good; therefore we cannot *will* good. In a characteristic formulation, Calvin seeks to distinguish between necessity and compulsion. "The chief point of this distinction," he writes,

> must be that man, as he was corrupted by the Fall, sinned willingly, not unwillingly or by compulsion; by the most eager inclination of his heart, not by forced compulsion; by the prompting of his own lust, not by compulsion

117

from without. Yet so depraved is his nature that he can be moved or impelled only to evil. But if this is true, then it is clearly expressed that man is surely subject to the necessity of sinning.[25]

En route to making this point, Calvin notes the philosophical controversy among Plato, Aristotle, and others over the question whether knowledge of good and evil determines the will to do good. Here Calvin distinguishes between general knowledge of the good, which he holds possible even for humanity in its natural state, and the application of this knowledge to one's own circumstances. Citing Aristotle and Themistius, he notes that "the intellect is very rarely deceived in general definition or in the essence of the thing; but that it is illusory when it goes farther, that is, applies the principle to particular cases."[26] We may understand that murder and adultery are evil, in general; but we forget all about that when we contemplate the death of our enemy or our own adultery. "The light of nature is extinguished," he writes, when one "enters upon this abyss."[27] We are, indeed, "like an animal [who] follows the inclination of his nature, without reason, without deliberation."[28] The only way out of this box is by God's intervention to convert the will from evil to good. This is "wholly God's doing."[29] It is not even a matter of the will's cooperative response to the work of God, for the will cannot even be activated apart from that grace. The will has been liberated, now, from bondage to sin, exchanging this for service to God wherein lies its salvation. Thus, while all are sinners, "it is through God's mercy [alone] that not all remain in wickedness. . . . Therefore, though all of us are by nature suffering from the same disease, only those whom it pleases the Lord to touch with his healing hand will get well. The others, whom he, in his righteous judgment, passes over, waste away in their own rottenness until they are consumed."[30]

In later editions of his *Institutes* Calvin was forced to struggle with criticisms of this entirely God-centered conception of the moral will. Thus, in answer to the objection that if sin is necessary it is not sin while if it is not necessary it is avoidable, Calvin replies that sin does not come from our nature but from the corruption of nature whereby "Adam willingly bound himself over to the devil's tyranny." All humanity, according to Calvin, is "deservedly held guilty of this rebellion."[31] Similarly, in response to the charge that reward and punishment lose their meaning, Calvin argues that "they are justly inflicted upon us, from whom the guilt of sin takes its source. [For what] difference does it make whether we sin out of free or servile judgment, provided it is by voluntary desire—especially since man is proved a sinner because he is under the bondage of sin."[32]

What then are the uses of scriptural law? Calvin speaks of three uses of the law: As an evidence to us of our moral powerlessness apart from the grace of God, as an external constraint upon the behavior of the wicked, and as a teaching tool for the believers (so they may "learn more thoroughly each day the nature of the Lord's will to which they aspire, and to confirm them in their understanding of it"[33]). Each of these three functions of the law, however, must still be seen in light of the fundamental truth that only God's grace renders moral goodness possible. Even when the wicked obey the law, it is out of fear of punishment, not by virtue of their desire to be and do good. The latter occurs only through God's grace.

Calvin here challenges the medieval distinction between mortal and venial sins. If, he writes, "venial sin is desire without deliberate assent, which does not long remain in the heart," how can this be understood to be less than a fundamental violation of the commandment to love God with our whole heart, mind, and soul? For has not the mind, "laid low by the crafty devices of unbelief," begun to look elsewhere and to receive temptations from such fleeting impulses? "Unless," he writes, "all the powers of the soul are intent on loving God, we have already abandoned obedience to the law. For the enemies who rise up in our conscience against his Kingdom and hinder his decrees prove that God's throne is not firmly established therein."[34] Every sin, thus, is a deadly sin, a manifestation of the fundamental rebellion of humanity against God contained in the Fall. In that sense, no distinction can be made among sins: all are "mortal" in the traditional sense.

Nevertheless, the acceptance of the three uses of law makes it possible for Calvin to move beyond the general consideration of our fallenness and our dependence upon grace to discuss the particularities of sin and goodness. As long as we remember that the fundamental issue of the moral life is our condition of sinfulness and our utter dependence upon God's grace, it is possible to discuss specific problems of the moral life, including, for example, matters related to family life, or economics, or politics. In every one of these areas, however, the fundamental issue is how we may through God's grace glorify God in obedience to God's will.

All of this points to a deeper level of paradox in the psychology of the believer, often noted by bemused readers of Calvin: How could people, knowing that they have been predestined either for salvation or damnation, summon the moral energy to do good and to struggle against evil? If the basic issue has already been settled, whether I shall be saved or damned, whether I shall be good or evil in the final analysis—that is, if I can neither add nor detract from the way in which the basic issue has been settled—then what is the point in my bestirring myself morally? The question has a certain logical force.

The traditional reply is a bit subtle. It begins with the reminder that, while the issue is indeed settled, if I am among the elect I will in fact live, through God's grace, to the glory of God. Moral complacency, on the other hand, is evidence that I may not be among the elect. I cannot have sure knowledge of my election to salvation or damnation, but as a Calvinist I will eagerly celebrate whatever evidences of salvation I see at work in my life while I am bound to be concerned, even anxious, about evidences to the contrary.

It may oversimplify Calvin and the Calvinists to say that the moral activism generated by his point of view derives from this anxiety, but the psychological possibility is certainly there. On the other hand, the positive side of the ethic—the glorification of God—helps account for the moral vigor of Calvinism. If God is all in all, then the whole purpose of human existence is transformed from every form of self-seeking into a radical endeavor to bring every aspect of human existence into conformity with the divine will.

Vocation and Stewardship

Thus, two of the distinctive Reformation doctrines gain special impetus from Calvin's thought. Vocation, as with Luther, is liberated from medieval ecclesiology. It no longer is limited to a monastic or priestly "calling." But, here unlike Luther, vocation is also liberated from the medieval forms of social organization. It can be much more radical: A Christian, responding through God's grace to the gift of salvation, is impelled to seek the glory of God anywhere and everywhere. No aspect of human existence is, theoretically, insulated from the question whether it serves or impedes the realization of God's sovereign will. Calvin himself does have a sense of propriety about actions in certain spheres, as we shall see below—what is a proper vocation for some may not be for others. But Calvin's way of framing the fundamental issue of Christian ethics invites a more sweeping attack upon the evils of this world, wherever they may be found, conceding very little to the constraints of tradition and the power of evil.

In any event, all of us have a calling, and our various callings commit us to duties fitted to our situation and possibilities. Our commitment to our calling helps keep our life steady, preserving us from the "great restlessness" with which "human nature flames."[35] In a characteristic passage, Calvin speaks of the calling in this way:

> [God] has appointed duties for every man in his particular way of life. And that no one may thoughtlessly transgress his limits, he has named these various kinds of living "callings." Therefore each individual has his own kind of living assigned to him by the Lord as a sort of sentry post so that he may not heedlessly wander about throughout life. . . . It is enough if we know that the Lord's calling is in everything the beginning and foundation of well-doing.

And if there is anyone who will not direct himself to it, he will never hold to the straight path in his duties. . . . [E]ach man will bear and swallow the discomforts, vexations, weariness, and anxieties in his way of life, when he has been persuaded that the burden was laid upon him by God. From this will arise also a singular consolation: that no task will be so sordid and base, provided you obey your calling in it, that it will not shine and be reckoned very precious in God's sight.[36]

Similarly the doctrine of stewardship emphasizes that all property is held in trust for God, to be used to the glory of God. Calvin upheld the idea of private property against the sectarian communist movements of the early Reformation era. But property cannot be held for one's own selfish ends. Can a Christian, then, much enjoy property on Calvinist terms? Again a paradox: God's gifts in the material world are created not only for utility, "but also for delight and good cheer." Thus, he writes,

the purpose of clothing, apart from necessity, was comeliness and decency. In grasses, trees, and fruits, apart from their various uses, there is beauty of appearance and pleasantness of odor. . . . Has the Lord clothed the flowers with the great beauty that greets our eyes, the sweetness of smell that is wafted upon our nostrils, and yet will it be unlawful for our eyes to be affected by that beauty, or our sense of smell by the sweetness of that odor? . . . Did he not, in short, render many things attractive to us, apart from their necessary use?[37]

Nevertheless, we must resist inordinate material desire "which, unless it is kept in order, overflows without measure."[38] We resist it, first, by the quality of our thanksgiving to God the giver;[39] second, by bearing poverty "peaceably and patiently, as well as [bearing] abundance moderately";[40] and third, by remembering that "all those things were so given to us by the kindness of God, and so destined for our benefit, that they are, as it were, entrusted to us, and we must one day render account of them."[41]

This last point is the fundamental one for Calvin. Again, Calvin does not disapprove of private property. But we hold it as stewards. In our stewardship, he writes, we do well to "remember by whom such reckoning is required: namely, him who has greatly commended abstinence, sobriety, frugality, and moderation, and has also abominated excess, pride, ostentation, and vanity; who approves no other distribution of good things than one joined with love; who has already condemned with his own lips all delights that draw man's spirit away from chastity and purity, or befog his mind."[42] So, while we may indeed enjoy the gifts of God, we are stewards of those gifts and we had better not enjoy them too much. We must avoid ostentation. We should avoid overindulgence. We should use our gifts as a facility for love.

The combination of the doctrines of vocation and stewardship in Calvin provide a religious basis for a very active economic life, while at the same time severely restricting the extent to which selfishness can be its goal. Taken literally, Calvin was no ascetic, as that term is generally applied. But in light of the awful accountability we have before God for our calling and for our use of the material resources committed to our care, it is little wonder that Calvinists often seemed to prefer the security of an ascetic manner of life to the risks of self-indulgence.

The Political Order

Calvin's *Institutes* concludes with a lengthy treatise on civil government. Faithful to the Augustinian tradition, he stipulates the important distinction between civil and spiritual government. Comparing the two with the distinction between body and soul, Calvin argues that "Christ's spiritual Kingdom and the civil jurisdiction are things completely distinct."[43] Against any form of Christian anarchism, he insists that there is an important place for civil government in the divine order. We must not, he writes, "consider the whole nature of government a thing polluted, which has nothing to do with Christian men." He continues:

> That is what, indeed, certain fanatics who delight in unbridled license shout and boast: after we have died through Christ to the elements of this world [Col. 2:20], are transported to God's Kingdom, and sit among heavenly beings, it is a thing unworthy of us and set far beneath our excellence to be occupied with those vile and worldly cares which have to do with business foreign to a Christian man. . . . But as we have just now pointed out that this kind of government is distinct from that spiritual and inward Kingdom of Christ, so we must know that they are not at variance.[44]

Those who deny the importance of the civil government forget the depth of human evil. What do we expect evil people to do, Calvin asks, "if they see that their depravity can go scot-free—when no power can force them to cease from doing evil"?[45] So "civil government has as its appointed end, so long as we live among men, to cherish and protect the outward worship of God, to defend sound doctrine of piety and the position of the church, to adjust our life to the society of men, to form our social behavior to civil righteousness, to reconcile us with one another, and to promote general peace and tranquillity."[46]

Given the necessity of civil government, the role of the magistrate is approved by the Lord as a calling with dignity and honor. Such persons, indeed, "have a mandate from God, have been invested with divine authority, and are wholly God's representatives, in a manner, acting as his viceregents."[47]

Of course, this also means that the magistrates have a solemn obligation to *act* as "vicars of God." Their calling is "to represent in themselves to men some image of divine providence, protection, goodness, benevolence, and justice." And if they commit faults, this is not only injury to those whom they have been called to serve, but it is also "insulting toward God himself, whose most holy judgments they defile."[48]

Calvin is aware that many rulers do not conform to such an ideal. Some, indeed, have become tyrants. Sometimes tyranny is a just form of punishment, a kind of divine retribution upon a sinful community; sometimes its harshness is necessary to the governance of a community that is unready for more benign forms of government. ("Divine providence has," he writes, "wisely arranged that various countries should be ruled by various kinds of government."[49]) Christians, recognizing the commandments of scripture and the judgments of God, are bound to respect the authority of even the unjust ruler.[50] The vindication of the right should normally be left to God. The unjust ruler must be obeyed, just as children and wives remain bound to obey harsh and undutiful parents and husbands. Nevertheless, Calvin goes further than Luther or most medieval political thought in justifying rebellion against unjust rulers. While acknowledging that the vindication of right should remain with God, Calvin notes that God sometimes uses people for that purpose. This is not the proper role of private persons; it may be that of intermediate magistrates, like the ephors of ancient Sparta or the Roman tribunes.

With this background, and with his deeply pessimistic account of human sinfulness, we are not surprised to discover that Calvin accepted the occasional need for rulers to use physical violence, up to and including war. An important part of the vocation of the king is to restrain evildoers. If rulers fail to do so, in order to "keep their hands clean of blood, while abandoned men wickedly range about with slaughter and massacre, they will become guilty of the greatest impiety."[51] This principle applies equally to the restraint of evildoers within the kingdom and to the defense of the realm against foreign invaders. Thus, Calvin can be counted among the Christian thinkers who recognize the difficulty of drawing a moral line between the police powers of the state and the defense of a just international order. He puts it succinctly:

Indeed, if [rulers] rightly punish those robbers whose harmful acts have affected only a few, will they allow a whole country to be afflicted and devastated by robberies with impunity? For it makes no difference whether it be a king or the lowest of the common folk who invades a foreign country in which he has no right, and harries it as an enemy. All such must, equally, be considered as robbers and punished accordingly. Therefore, both natural equity and the nature of the office dictate that princes must be armed not only to restrain the misdeeds of private individuals by judicial punishment, but also to defend by war the dominions entrusted to their safekeeping, if at any time they are under enemy attack.[52]

Calvin's position was developed in opposition to the pacifism of Anabaptists, whose views he feared as a prelude to anarchy. In response to their claim that the New Testament provided no justification for war, he offered a three-fold answer: first, that the reasons that originally justified war are still present; second, that the purpose of the apostles was not to establish a civil government but rather the spiritual realm of Christ; and third, that soldiers asking how they might be saved, in Luke 3:14, were not told to abandon military service but only to behave fairly and be content with their wages.

In these views, Calvin follows Augustine closely. He also reflects Augustine's view that the police and war-making power of the magistrate must be exercised sparingly and dispassionately. While Calvin does not develop a refined version of just war doctrine, the rudiments are there: a justification of war only in those instances where it is a necessary defense against aggression and a requirement that "everything else ought to be tried before recourse is had to arms."[53]

The "Protestant Ethic," Democracy, and Capitalism

Since the appearance of Max Weber's famous book *The Protestant Ethic and the Spirit of Capitalism*, the term "Protestant ethic" has been employed loosely to refer to a compulsive attitude toward work, a judgmental attitude toward those who are unable to earn their own way in life, and an ascetic attitude toward pleasures and wasteful consumption of material goods. The term, as popularly used, hardly does justice to the views of either Weber or the Reformers. But there does seem to be a striking correlation between the ethic of the Reformers and the emerging economic and political culture of predominantly Protestant countries. It is especially interesting that modern capitalism and modern democracy developed first in such countries. Is there a causal connection?

Max Weber never argued that point, although he did note that the peculiar form of capitalism encountered especially in Anglo-Saxon countries most heavily influenced by Calvinism owes much to the Protestant ethic. The doctrine of vocation helps account for the single-minded activism of many entrepreneurs in such countries, and the doctrine of stewardship helps account for readiness to defer consumption while amassing capital for further investment in productive enterprises.

Similarly, it can be argued that the Protestant ethic helped shape the democratic political ideologies that proved so influential in many of the same countries. Both Luther and Calvin strongly supported existing ruling authorities; neither can be counted a true democrat. Nevertheless, the assertion of the transcendent sovereignty of God and the relativizing of any ruler's exclusive access to knowledge of the will of God, combined with a strikingly individualistic emphasis upon the faith relationship of each person before God, doubtless contributed at least indirectly to ideas of popular sovereignty. The covenantal religious conceptions of the Calvinists likewise contributed—at least indirectly—to the covenantal theories of civil society.[54] In these social conceptions, human beings cannot be regarded only as subjects of the state; they are also *members* of the state.

The political and economic ideologies of the Enlightenment era, which followed shortly upon the Reformation and in the countries where the Reformation was most influential, were largely expressed in secular form. But it is a nice question whether those ideas would have been as successful in the absence of the Reformation, or even whether they would have taken the same form.

We must also ask whether the capitalist and democratic revolutions of the early modern era are of a piece with each other. Clearly both express a kind of individualism. But there may be as much tension between capitalism and democracy as there is affinity. For, to the extent that democracy is a covenant of mutual self-rule, it may be weakened by the independence of economic power from the effective jurisdiction of that covenant.

Obviously, such questions were remote from the life experience of the Reformers, although their articulations of Christian ethics were to have immense influence in the shaping of subsequent secular as well as religious history.

11

CATHOLIC HUMANISM
AND COUNTER-REFORMATION

Did the Protestant Reformation overshoot its mark? Clearly, the late medieval Church had yielded to corruption at many points. Some of these, such as the sale of indulgences to which Luther reacted, were truly egregious. The scandal was felt among thoughtful, morally sensitive Christians throughout Europe. But not all agreed with the Reformers' theological diagnosis, and not all were prepared to join the Reformation in dividing the church.

Catholic Humanism

Some deeply principled intellectual leaders, such as Desiderius Erasmus of Rotterdam (1466–1536) and Sir Thomas More of England (1478–1535), sought a different kind of reform. They agreed with the Reformers on the need to end the obvious corruptions and abuses of power, and they shared a reaction against the intellectual rigidities of scholasticism. Moreover, they also embraced the recovery of scriptural authority and the need to call the church back to its primitive roots. But they reacted against the dangers of a new Reformation theological dogmatism, and they were appalled by the prospect of the disintegration of the Catholic church.

Erasmus of Rotterdam

An older contemporary of Luther, Erasmus best exemplified the spirit of the northern European Renaissance and a new Catholic humanism.

While Erasmus's humanism remained deeply committed to Christian faith, it sought to enrich the understanding of that faith with values and insights drawn from universal human experience. Steeped in classical languages and literature, equally at home in several European lands, Erasmus sought to liberate Christian thought from provincialism and dogmatism. His writing was learned, tolerant, and witty. His program for conquering pretense, superstition, and corruption was to expose them to the weapons of irony and satire. For example, he had the following to say about monks:

> I cannot . . . see how any life could be more gloomy than the life of these monks if I did not assist them in many ways. Though most people detest these men so much that accidentally meeting one is considered to be bad luck, the monks themselves believe that they are magnificent creatures. One of their chief beliefs is that to be illiterate is to be of a high state of sanctity, and so they make sure that they are not able to read. . . . According to them . . . they are setting an apostolic example for us by their filthiness, their ignorance, their bawdiness, and their insolence. . . . Members of [some] orders shrink from the mere touch of money as if it were poison. They do not, however, retreat from the touch of wine or of women. . . . Many of them work so hard at protocol and at traditional fastidiousness that they think one heaven hardly a suitable reward for their labors; never recalling, however, that the time will come when Christ will demand a reckoning of that which he has prescribed, namely charity, and that he will hold their deeds of little account.[1]

In a similar vein, he took after the theologians:

> In how many volumes do these writers give instruction about restitution, confession, vows, scandal, and innumerable other matters? And though they examine minutely each single topic and so define each as if they mistrusted the abilities of all the other writers, indeed even as if they mistrusted the goodness of Christ, while they set forth precisely how He ought to reward or punish each deed, yet they fail to agree among themselves, nor do they often explain anything clearly if they are more closely consulted. . . . Moreover, . . . how many have the time to read such volumes? Who can carry around with him Aquinas' *Secundae secunda*? And yet it is important for all to live a good life, the path to which Christ intended to be accessible to all, not by way of a difficult labyrinth of argument but by a sincere faith and by an unfeigned charity which a confident hope accompanies.[2]

In this same writing, Erasmus acknowledges the significance of the work of theologians and lawyers, but he appeals for less pretense and complexity, more directness and simplicity: "Rather, we must strive to render this art as simple as possible and accessible to all. Let our aim be not to appear learned but to lead as many as possible to a Christian life."[3] Not bad advice, this, for Christian ethics!

In his voluminous writings, Erasmus has occasion to comment on a wide variety of subjects. His writings on peace are especially compelling, breathing as they do the spirit of a deeply humane, cultivated, and international man. In one long, eloquent sentence he marvels at the utter irrationality of war:

> If without [peace] nothing is flourishing, nothing safe, nothing pure or holy, nothing pleasant to mortals, or grateful to the Supreme Being; if, on the contrary, war is one vast ocean, rushing on mankind, of all the united plagues and pestilences in nature; if, at its deadly approach, every blossom of happiness is instantly blasted, every thing that was improving gradually degenerates and dwindles away to nothing, every thing that was firmly supported totters on its foundation, every thing that was formed for long duration comes to a speedy end, and every thing that was sweet by nature is turned into bitterness; if war is so unhallowed that it becomes the deadliest bane of piety and religion; if there is nothing more calamitous to mortals, and more detestable to heaven, I ask, how in the name of God, can I believe those beings to be rational creatures; how can I believe them to be otherwise than stark mad; who, with such a waste of treasure, with so ardent a zeal, with so great an effort, with so many arts, so much anxiety, and so much danger, endeavour to drive [peace] away from them, and purchase endless misery and mischief at a price so high?[4]

He accepts some wars as "just and necessary"[5] (being purely defensive); he bitterly criticizes wars between Christians and the readiness of clerics and bishops to summon the faithful to war, and then to display its bloody trophies. War, he argues at length, is utterly inconsistent with the spirit of Christ.

Erasmus grieves over the spirit of the times as much as Luther—perhaps even more so. He offers this lament in a letter to a friend in which he indicates why he wrote his *Enchiridion*, a work calling the Christians of his time back to a life of basic piety:

> I saw that the mass of Christians had been corrupted not only in their feelings but also in their opinions. I carefully considered that very many of those who profess to be shepherds and teachers abused the titles of Christ for their own advantage, to say nothing whatsoever in the meanwhile about those at whose command and prohibition human affairs are sent scurrying in all directions, and at whose vices, although they are public, one is scarcely permitted to groan. . . . Who, truly pious, does not see and lament over this age, the most corrupt by far? When did tyranny, when did avarice ever hold sway

more widely or with more impunity? When was more attention ever paid to ceremonies? When has injustice abounded more freely? When has charity grown so cold? What is asserted, what is read, what is heard, what is proposed except that which savors of ambition and greed?[6]

Erasmus's program for the overcoming of institutional abuses was essentially to wait them out, never allowing oneself to become captive either to the institutional constraints of a narrow-minded church or to the waste of energy in struggling against those constraints.

While Erasmus may have made no distinctive theoretical contributions to the history of Christian ethics, he does provide a fascinating counterpoint to Luther's *sola fide, sola gratia*. For Erasmus, God's grace is not so much the divine response to utter human depravity as it is divine assistance to a humanity that has not been totally corrupted by the Fall. Erasmus paid close attention to Luther, obviously attracted by much of the Reformer's program. In the end, he challenged Luther directly in his *Diatribe de libero arbitrio*, in which he carefully dissected the implications of Luther's doctrine of election: If grace is everything and human effort is nothing, have we not abandoned freedom of the will altogether? And, if so, have we not abandoned ethics? Even if, for the sake of argument, it were true that everything we do is by necessity and not by free choice, Erasmus wonders about the practical effects upon the faithful of publishing such a doctrine. "What weakling," he wonders, "will be able to bear the endless and wearisome warfare against his flesh? What evildoer will take pains to correct his life?"—if he knows, all the while, that what he will finally decide to do is determined all along anyway. And in a particularly telling question, Erasmus asks, "Who will be able to bring himself to love God with all his heart when He created hell seething with eternal torments in order to punish his own misdeeds in his victims as though he took delight in human torments?" He adds, "For that is how most people will interpret them."[7]

Against so sweeping a doctrine of grace, Erasmus is concerned to defend an essentially ethical understanding of Christianity. In theological terms, he asks whether Luther has surrendered to a new form of Manichaeanism. And he counterposes an understanding of grace that preserves some freedom of the will while enhancing and encouraging its acting toward the good. Luther responded with his own attack on free will, *De servo arbitrio*, an essentially Augustinian account of the bondage of the will, either to sin or to grace.

The controversy between Erasmus and Luther cut deeper than the conflicts over institutional church reform. Their differences mirrored Erasmus's more optimistic and Luther's more pessimistic account of human nature—and with it, differences over the capacities and limitations of universal human reason.

Thomas More

Erasmus's friend Thomas More likewise exemplified the humanist intellectual spirit of the northern European Renaissance. More provides a heroic,
though not unambiguous chapter in this history of Christian ethics. While he
also subjected ecclesial corruption and abuse to wit and satire, More paid with
his life for his loyalty to papal authority and his resistance to King Henry
VIII's effort to make himself head of an independent church of England. Still,
as Henry's chancellor, he had earlier been responsible for the execution of
Protestant heretics. Altogether, his life remains a fascinating drama.

Some of his ideas are equally fascinating in the ongoing history of
Christian ethics. His famous work, *Utopia*, was written both to satirize the
irrationality of contemporary economics, politics, and criminal justice and
to venture possibilities for social reconstruction. The word *utopia* literally
means "nowhere," and his use of the word has brought it into the language
to signify the imaging of nonexistent institutions or societies as a way of
challenging the adequacy of existing ones. There is enough whimsical tenta-
tiveness in More's style to lead us to be cautious in taking it too literally, and
he himself cautions that he "cannot agree and consent to all things" in
Utopia.[8] But *Utopia* is not just creative fiction. The book contains shrewd criticism, and certain themes are developed seriously. The literary device enables
More to explore radical ideas without inhibition, while evading much of the
criticism that a straight exposition of those ideas would have drawn.

And radical ideas there are. At several points the book portrays the
Utopians as having a communist form of social-economic organization: "all
things being there common, every man hath abundance of everything."[9]
Only Utopia can legitimately be described as a "commonwealth," he writes:
"For in other places they speak still of the commonwealth, but every man
procureth his own private wealth. Here where nothing is private, the
common affairs be earnestly looked upon."[10] In Utopia people have no need
to starve in the presence of wealth; they need not fear sickness or old age.
Since all work productively, sharing equally in the fruits of their labor, none
need work more than six hours per day. Allowing eight hours for sleep, the
Utopians have up to ten hours per day for reading and other creative leisure
activities. They live together in communelike settings, with common meals
of higher quality than any could provide for themselves. But marriages are
monogamous and very stable. The picture is as appealing as it is radical:

> There [in Utopia] where all things be common to every man, it is not to be
> doubted that any man shall lack anything necessary for his private uses, so that
> the common storehouses and barns be sufficiently stored. For there nothing is dis-
> tributed after a niggish sort, neither there is any poor man or beggar. And though

no man has anything, yet every man is rich. For what can be more rich, than to live joyfully and merrily, without all grief and pensiveness; not caring for his own living, nor vexed or troubled with his wife's importunate complaints, nor dreading poverty to his son, nor sorrowing for his daughter's dowry.[11]

In Utopia, gold and silver and fine apparel are looked upon as childish. Symbols of wealth and status are replaced by wholesome utility. Economics has been turned on its head.

So has religion, one might suppose. For the priests are married and—could this be a respectable sixteenth-century Catholic intellectual?—even women can be priests ("for that kind is not excluded from priesthood, howbeit few be chosen, and none but widows and old women"[12]). Politics is not entirely turned on its head, though the monarch is elected (for life) and the political hierarchy is constitutional and generally accountable.

In part 1 of *Utopia*, where ideas are expressed independently of the description of a fictional society, More attacks the harsh criminal justice system of his day. He is especially critical of the use of capital punishment for crimes less than murder. "For simple theft," he writes, "is not so great an offence, that it ought to be punished with death."[13] To hang thieves is not only an outrage against justice, it fails in its avowed purpose of preventing theft. He notes that there is not any punishment "so horrible, that it can keep them from stealing, which have no other craft, whereby to get their living."[14] Therefore, it would be far more sensible to attack thievery by removing its causes, which he finds to be primarily economic.

In sum, More's views, to the extent they are seriously advanced, are a remarkable anticipation of nineteenth- and twentieth-century political liberalism and economic socialism. But to what extent are they authentically Christian?

More takes pains to relate Christianity to his mythical kingdom of Utopia, noting the enthusiasm with which the Utopians receive the gospel upon its presentation by European visitors. The Utopians, in fact, find Christian ideas a confirmation of their existing social practices.

More's Christianity, like that of Erasmus, is a primarily ethical expression of universal truth. It is specifically tolerant of other religions, to the extent they reflect similar moral values. Those values, as expressed by the Utopians, affirm happiness. The Utopians "define virtue to be a life ordered according to nature, and that we be hereunto ordained of God."[15] The principles of ethics and religion represent a joining of philosophy and religion. They include belief "that the soul is immortal, and by the bountiful goodness of God ordained to felicity. That to our virtues and good deeds rewards be appointed after this life, and to our evil deeds, punishments." While these principles are primarily religious, yet "they should be believed and granted by proofs of reason."[16]

In contrast with Reformation thought, *Utopia* can only be described as optimistic. It is worlds apart from the Reformation/Augustinian doctrine of the Fall, with its profound abyss of human sinfulness. Its humanism is attractive and orderly, its values positive, its future hopeful. It does not invoke the radical cure of grace; its humanity is capable through reason and imagination to create an attractive new world. But *Utopia* is not "utopian" in the sense that it has no grasp of the sinful, antisocial aspects of human existence. Part of the appeal of the fanciful land is its realism in making institutional provision for antisocial behavior (this is also convenient, for convicted criminals are available as bondsmen to do society's dirty work). Likewise, though More is sharply critical of war, the necessity of military provisions is also accepted in Utopia—though the Utopians, functioning with their own version of just war doctrine, shrewdly bribe assassins to kill the enemy's ruler as an alternative to full-scale combat in which multitudes will be killed. War itself is not to be undertaken except as a distinct last resort.

Is the thought of Catholic humanists like Erasmus and More so far outside the mainstream of Reformation-era Christian ethics that we can safely ignore it? I do not think so. For one thing, its humanism is an important connecting link between an era of theological ferment and the secularization of humanistic ethics in the modern world and twentieth-century liberal Christian ethics. This Catholic humanism managed to reach back to some of the deeply humane values in earlier chapters in the history of Christian ethics.

Counter-Reformation and the Council of Trent

The Counter-Reformation of the Roman Catholic Church involved both internal renewal and external defense against Protestant ideas and influences. The rapid rise of the Protestant movement, with its splitting of the church and its restructuring of the map of Europe, must have had a shock effect on the mainstream of Catholicism not unlike that experienced by Roman Christians of Augustine's time when barbarians swept into Rome. The shock led many to deeper commitments to the church and a determination to cleanse it of corruption. The Spanish renewal movement and the emergence of the Society of Jesus under the leadership of Ignatius Loyola reflect this commitment. The summoning of the Council of Trent (1545–1563) became the focal point for the church's defense against Protestant ideas.

The Council of Trent reasserted the importance of "works" alongside "faith" in the salvation of the faithful, though it also accepted with Luther that "justification" is not by human works or human nature "apart from the divine grace through Jesus Christ."[17] It insisted upon the importance of tradition alongside scripture, noting that scripture itself is the product of the church and therefore subject to interpretation by the church. It repeated the listing of seven sacraments, against the Protestant numbering of two or three. It even reaffirmed the church's right to grant indulgences, though not in the gross form against which Luther had reacted. The flavor of the Council's thinking is revealed in some of the statements or propositions it specifically *rejected*:

- That the free will of man, moved and aroused by God, does not co-operate at all by responding to the awakening call of God, so as to dispose and prepare itself for the acquisition of the grace of justification, but it does nothing at all, like some inanimate thing, and is completely passive.

- That man's free will has been wholly lost and destroyed after Adam's sin.

- That all works before justification, for whatever reason they were done, are in truth sins and deserve the hatred of God, or that the more strongly a man strives to dispose himself to receive Grace, the more grievously he sins.

- That a man reborn and justified is bound by faith to believe that he is assuredly in the number of the predestinate.

- That a man once justified can no more sin, nor can he lose the grace. . . .

- That justification once received is not preserved and even increased in the sight of God through good works, but that these same works are only fruits and signs of justification, not causes of its increase.

- That penance is not truly and properly a sacrament in the Catholic Church, instituted for the faithful by Christ our Lord, for their reconciliation to God whenever they fall into sin after baptism.

- That sacramental confession was neither instituted by divine authority, nor is it necessary to salvation by divine authority. . . . [18]

Obviously, the Council fathers had been reading their Luther and Calvin!— although some of the propositions thus anathematized are distorted forms of Reformation teaching.

From the standpoint of the history of Christian ethics, the Council's most important points of emphasis were those reasserting the freedom of the will, the necessity of auricular confession, and the power of the church, through its priesthood, to give absolution. The church's reassertion of its power to grant absolution was implicitly a reaffirmation of its authority over all moral matters, including the power to confer indulgences remitting the penitential penalties required of sinners. Nevertheless, while the church's power to confer indulgences was thus reaffirmed, the Council made clear that abuses, such as the sale of indulgences, must be avoided. Bishops should "prohibit, as scandals and sources of offense to the faithful, things which pander to curiosity and superstition or which savor of base lucre."[19] On the whole, the Council of Trent reacted to the Reformation by defending medieval Catholic doctrine, moral theology, and sacramental practice vigorously, seeking meanwhile new levels of commitment and integrity.

The Controversy Over Probabilism

The Counter-Reformation era also witnessed important developments in Catholic moral theology. Among these, the debate over probabilism was most important. Essentially, the controversy concerned the question of moral judgment in doubtful or uncertain cases. The issue is present in any ethical theory that acknowledges any degree of uncertainty in moral judgment. It is particularly important to an ethical viewpoint buttressed by severe religious sanctions. We have already seen the importance to the development of Catholic moral theology of the confessional manuals guiding the moral prescriptions of priest confessors. In the Counter-Reformation's reaffirmation of the whole confessional/sacramental system, the question of how to deal with uncertainty and the possibility of priestly error returned in a new form.

A Spanish Dominican, Bartolomeo de Medina, addressed this question in a 1577 commentary on Thomas Aquinas with the famous formulation that "if an opinion [on a moral question] is probable, . . . it is permissible to adopt it, even if the opposite is more probable."[20] An opinion is probable if it is "stated by wise men and confirmed by very good arguments." The word "probable" in this context is equivalent to "arguable" or "demonstrable." Medina meant that it is permissible to adopt a moral viewpoint if a serious, not frivolous or irrational, case could be made for it—and if some acknowledged authorities in moral theology were persuaded by it. For instance, Medina might have argued that Christians may become pacifists, even though the mainstream of Christian moral tradition considers the "just war" viewpoint to be a better representation of Christian morality. For, although pacifism is a minority viewpoint with less weighty arguments in its favor (at least as seen by the majority), it is still a viewpoint for which serious arguments can be given and it has been adopted by serious thinkers.

The principle of probabilism was embraced and developed by other thinkers, such as the great Spanish Jesuit theologian Francisco de Suarez

(1548–1619). It also provoked outrage among many thinkers (ultimately including the French thinker Blaise Pascal [1623–1662]), who considered it an invitation to moral subjectivism and license. Indeed, probabilism implicitly elevates freedom and subjective judgment on doubtful questions. In effect, it declares that the church can teach as certain only what it clearly *knows* to be certain. When in doubt, the informed conscience must be free to follow its own judgment—provided it has the authority of serious reasons and thinkers to back it up. Some opponents of probabilism countered with "probabiliorism," a principle asserting that one must rely upon the *most* probable (or weighty) of the alternative views. Still others argued that if competing moral viewpoints had approximately equal arguments and authorities in their favor, then (but only then) one might be free to choose either. That was known as "equiprobabilism." Still others were persuaded by "tutiorism," which held that one should follow the law or principle that appears safest in respect to the salvation of one's soul.

The debates over probabilism, in their original linguistic form, have an unreal quality to modern ears. But the issue was real enough: How much latitude should be granted in the moral life to conscience and judgment over against objective law and authority? It was a replaying, in that era, of the perennial struggle between subjective and objective aspects of moral authority. It is interesting that the Counter-Reformation era in Roman Catholicism presented a climate in which that debate could be joined—even if it was not fully resolved.

It is also interesting that even those who opted for the more subjective principles of probabilism found it necessary to express those principles in legal form. That is to say that even the probabilists located their freedom within boundaries set by objective law, not in interpersonal or religious relationships. Thus, even the probabilists confirmed in their own way the Counter-Reformation's reassertions of objective morality.

The Jesuits and Suarez

The Society of Jesus was a particularly creative force in the development of moral theology during the Counter-Reformation period. While the Jesuits produced a number of notable moral theologians, we may note especially their founder, Ignatius Loyola, and the Spaniard Francisco de Suarez.

Loyola's writings might not impress all readers as a creative expression of moral theology, for he took pains to insist that the Jesuits commit themselves to absolute obedience to the pope and their superiors in the order. Thus, he writes:

> Let us with the utmost pains strain every nerve of our strength to exhibit this virtue of obedience, firstly to the Highest Pontiff, then to the Superiors of the Society; so that in all things, to which obedience can be extended with charity, we may be most ready to obey his voice, just as if it issued from Christ our Lord . . . , by rejecting with a kind of blind obedience all opposing opinion or judgement of our own; and that in all things which are ordained by the Superior where it can be clearly held that any kind of sin intervenes.[21]

For those who may not have gotten the point, Loyola continues: "And let each one persuade himself that they that live under obedience ought to allow themselves to be borne and ruled by divine providence working through their Superiors exactly as if they were a corpse which suffers itself to be borne and handled in any way whatsoever; or just as an old man's stick which serves him who holds it in his hand whenever and for whatever purpose he wishes to use it."[22] Of course, Loyola here prescribed the commitment of those freely choosing to become Jesuits. In this, he sought to create a force of indubitable moral integrity in face of the vast corruptions that had invaded church and society. An escape hatch was provided for those instances where Jesuits could not obey ecclesial authority without sin, though the burden of proof must remain against any form of disobedience.

That the rule of the Jesuits did not inhibit creative moral thought is illustrated by the work of Suarez. Certainly he was no "corpse suffering itself to be borne"! We have noted above his acceptance of probabilism. In his political thought, Suarez developed serious arguments against monarchical absolutism, anticipating the debates over the divine right of kings. While accepting monarchy itself—possibly even preferring it—Suarez insists that the source of the power to rule resides in the community as a whole. "In the nature of things," he writes, "all men are born free; so that, consequently, no person has political jurisdiction over another person, even as no person has dominion over another; nor is there any reason why such power should in the nature of things, be attributed to certain persons over certain other persons, rather than *vice versa*."[23] In giving man dominion over living creatures, God did not say, "Let us make man that he may have dominion over man."[24] So political power "resides, by the sole force of natural law, in the whole body of mankind." The ruler may not properly be deprived of his power, however, unless he becomes a tyrant, in which case he may be deposed by the kingdom.

Suarez's view of the "just war" lies in the Augustinian-Thomistic tradition, to which he brought further refinements. War itself is not intrinsically evil; if waged defensively, it may even be a moral necessity. In face of aggression, states could not be "maintained in peace" if denied the right of resistance. "This kind of warfare," he writes, "is allowed by natural law;

and even by the law of the Gospel, which derogates in no way from natural law, and contains no new divine commands save those regarding faith and the Sacraments."[25] A just war is not opposed to peace but only to an *unjust* peace—"for it is more truly a means of attaining peace that is real and secure."[26] A just war is not even necessarily opposed to love of enemies, "for whoever wages war honorably hates, not individuals, but the actions which he justly punishes."[27]

War, thus, may be justly waged under some circumstances. Suarez groups his version of the just war criteria under three headings: "First, the war must be waged by a legitimate power; secondly, the cause itself and the reason must be just; thirdly, the method of its conduct must be proper, and due proportion must be observed at its beginning, during its prosecution and after victory."[28] The basis of the criteria is Suarez's conclusion that while war is not intrinsically evil, "on account of the many misfortunes which it brings in its train, it is one of those undertakings that are often carried on in evil fashion." Therefore, he concludes, war "requires many justifying circumstances to make it righteous."[29]

The writings of Counter-Reformation thinkers like Suarez carry the mainstream of Catholic moral thought to a much greater degree than those of Catholic humanists like Erasmus and More. The former, still decisively influenced by medieval moral theology, especially in its Thomist form, were destined to shape the course of Catholic thought until well into the twentieth century. The latter anticipate strong currents of Catholic moral thought following the Second Vatican Council.

12

THE RADICAL REFORMATION

Did the Protestant Reformation go far enough? If Catholic humanists and the Counter-Reformation thought it overshot the mark, many radical movements and sects were influenced by the Reformation but convinced it did not address the deeper religious and moral problems of the age. Of course, Luther and Calvin were not even the first to challenge medieval conventions in moral thought and ecclesial practice—the Lollards, Hussites, and sundry "heretical" sects had long since appeared on the European scene. But the substantial character of the Reformation and its sweeping political success provided opportunity and precedent for other movements, some of them much more radical in their moral commitments and social proposals and programs than the Lutherans and Calvinists. The revolt of the Swabian peasants, to which Luther had responded so intemperately in 1525, illustrated the social radicalism that found opportunity in the Reformation, although that revolt was itself quickly snuffed out. Figures like Andreas Karlstadt and Thomas Müntzer, both originally attracted by Luther, began to proclaim a more radical gospel and to advocate sweeping socioeconomic and political reforms. Their key theological emphasis was upon the inward spirit, and manifestation of the life of the spirit was taken by them to be the primary evidence of salvation. Müntzer advocated armed rebellion and participated in the Peasants' Revolt. Believing the time was ripe for world transformation, Müntzer urged his former parishioners to "begin to fight the fight of the Lord! It is high time! . . . All of Germany, France, and Switzerland has been awakened. The Master wants to start the game."[1]

"Even if there are only three of you who trust God," he continued, "you need not fear a hundred thousand. At them! At them! The time is now. . . . Have no consideration for the misery of the ungodly. They will beg and whine like children. Do not be merciful."[2] In the end, Müntzer himself was tortured and beheaded.

The Anabaptists

Continental radicalism was more enduringly represented by Anabaptists, who insisted, in the words of John Denck, "all who truly fear God must renounce the world." And while it is necessary to live in the world, Christians "ought always to be prepared for struggle and ready for adversity as sojourners upon the earth."[3] Taking scripture absolutely at face value, the Anabaptists found there a sufficient guidebook to salvation and the moral life. In their emphasis upon scriptural authority, they were in broad agreement with Luther and the contemporary Swiss reformer Ulrich Zwingli, and a number of their leaders were first influenced by the great Reformers. But they became convinced that Luther and Zwingli had not gone far enough in emphasizing the moral teachings of the Gospels and in restricting the church to those prepared to make a full commitment to those teachings. They reacted vehemently against what they perceived to be the substitution of "grace" for "works."

In several writings, Anabaptists also took on the question of free will, insisting that God's desire is for the salvation of all and that all can, if they will, respond to God. In language reminiscent of Erasmus's *Diatribe de libero arbitrio*, published five years earlier, the Dutch Anabaptist Melchior Hofmann wrote that "they blaspheme God grievously who lay it to him that he wishes sin, does and effects the same in man." People who hold God responsible for sin "make the most high and eternal God into a devil and Satan and insult the high, praiseworthy good as evil, and the eternal light as darkness." But "God is none other than eternal good, and from him nothing but good comes."[4]

The Anabaptists insisted upon believers' baptism. The implication of the latter was more than liturgical. It reflected the conviction that no one is a Christian except by conscious choice. Moreover, it represented a direct challenge to the theological legitimacy of churches—Lutheran and Reformed included—which presumed to include whole populations. Such churches included many who did not meet the first test of Christian discipleship—their total commitment to Christ and his way. The Schleitheim Confession of 1527, an influential declaration of Anabaptist principles, called upon Christians to live carefully disciplined moral lives in a church made up of baptized believers. Such Christians should not engage in violence or coercion, although the Confession recognized the need for government in a sinful, fallen world.

While the Anabaptists were thus committed to pacifism, they also recognized the need for internal discipline within the life of their own religious communities. In lieu of more physical forms of coercion, they elaborated the "ban" as a form of social control. As explained by Menno Simons, the ban was grounded in Paul's admonition that Christians should not associate with notorious sinners (1 Cor. 5:11). Menno writes, "Since the Scripture admonishes and commands that we shall not associate with such, nor eat with them, nor greet them, nor receive them into our houses . . . and then if somebody should say, I will associate with them, I will eat with them, I will greet them in the Lord, and receive them into my house—he would plainly prove that he did not fear the commandment and admonition of the Lord, but that he despised it, rejected the Holy Spirit, and that he trusted, honored, and followed his own opinion rather than the Word of God."[5] The ban applied to everybody. One should shun even one's own spouse or children if, in the judgment of the community of faith, their behavior warranted banning. The purpose of the ban is, however, to reform the sinner. And while he states the purposes of the ban in very severe language, Menno Simons insists that it must be "a work of divine love and not of perverse, unmerciful, heathenish cruelty." So people who are under the ban should still receive love and "necessary services."[6]

Anabaptists were generally committed to peaceful behavior, taking the love commandment and other biblical moral injunctions seriously and at face value. They should have posed little physical threat to the rest of society. But it was a cruel age, and the radical character of their moral and spiritual challenge was met by stern repression from Catholics and Protestants alike. For instance, the official sentence pronounced by an Austrian court upon Michael Sattler, one of the formulators of the Schleitheim Confession, was as follows:"Judgment is passed that Michael Sattler shall be delivered to the executioner, who shall lead him to the place of execution and cut out his tongue, then forge him fast to a wagon and thereon with red-hot tongs twice tear pieces from his body; and after he has been brought outside the gate, he shall be plied five times more in the same manner (and then burned to ashes as a heretic)."[7] A favorite method of executing condemned Anabaptists was by drowning, thus cruelly mimicking their rite of baptism. But, notwithstanding considerable persecution, the movement expanded rapidly, spreading to various parts of Europe and, ultimately, North America. In the modern world, the various Baptist and Mennonite churches trace their origins to this movement.

The Quakers

The Society of Friends (or Quakers) was founded by George Fox (1624–1691) in mid-seventeenth-century England. Broadly influenced by Protestantism, the Quakers tempered scriptural authority by the conviction that God has given every person an "inner light" which, if followed, will lead to truth. The movement was carefully disciplined, but the doctrine of inner light had important other consequences for the Quakers' approach to Christian ethics: The Friends were much more tolerant of other churches and sects—or even other religions, since all people are understood to have the inner light. The method of arriving at moral truth was basically intuitive: we can trust the inner light to lead us to truth. The Society, while emphasizing the integrity of each of its members in their individual apprehension of the "light," was also social. The sharing of perceptions on a question continued until there was a "sense of the meeting," a consensus embracing the integrity of each of the members. The Society also mistrusted the forms, institutions, and trappings of the established churches, preferring the simplicity of the gathered meeting. Consequently, it generally eschewed a professional clergy.

The Quakers were radical enough in such matters to have to face persecution in a generally intolerant era. But their own tolerance and integrity helped protect the Quakers from the worst forms of persecution. The movement's most prized convert, William Penn (1644–1718), was able to secure a royal grant in the new world for what became the Commonwealth of Pennsylvania, a haven for the Friends and other dissenters.

Moral truth, for the Quakers, included a rejection of war. The early *Rules of Discipline* included the "weighty concern" that "our ancient and honourable testimony against being concerned in bearing arms, or fighting, may be maintained; it being a doctrine and testimony agreeable to the nature and design of the Christian religion, and to the universal love and grace of God." So the Friends were enjoined to be united in love "not only one unto another, but to the whole creation of God" and "by our patience and peaceable behaviour to show, that we walk in obedience to the example and precepts of our Lord and Master, who hath commanded us to love our enemies, and to do good even to them that hate us."[8] Quaker pacifism and tolerance produced, in the experimental colony of Pennsylvania, a strikingly more peaceful accommodation with the Native Americans.

The Friends were also known for their rejection of slavery. The *Rules of Discipline* stated flatly that "it is the sense of this meeting, that the importing of Negroes from their native country and relations by friends, is not a commendable nor allowed practice, and is therefore censured by this meeting." The *Rules* note with appreciation the success by some of the Friends in the American colonies in lessening the practice of slavery.[9] Quakers were destined in fact to play a leading role in the eighteenth- and nineteenth-century American abolition movement.

A striking feature in early Quaker writings on moral issues is their intuitive, commonsense character. William Penn's moral maxims, contained in his *Fruits of Solitude*, are noteworthy for their lack of specific scriptural buttressing. Many of these could have been composed by a Stoic, in the manner of Marcus Aurelius's *Meditations*, an observation that could hardly have offended a Quaker who believed the inner light to be universally available.[10] To illustrate:

18. . . . we have nothing that we can call our own; no, not our selves: For we are all but Tenants, and at Will too, of the great Lord of our selves, and the rest of this great Farm, the World that we live upon.
28. Such is now become our Delicacy, that we will not eat ordinary Meat, nor drink small, pall'd Liquor; we must have the best, and the best cook'd for our Bodies, while our Souls feed on empty or corrupted things.
50. Frugality is good if Liberality be join'd with it. The first is leaving off superfluous Expences; the last bestowing them to the Benefit of others that need.
57. Love Labor: For if thou dost not want it for Food, thou mayest for Physick. It is wholesom for thy Body, and good for thy Mind.
73. Excess in Apparel is another costly Folly. The very Trimming of the vain World would cloath all the naked ones.
80. If love be not thy chiefest Motive, thou wilt soon grow weary of a Married State, and stray from thy Promise, to search out thy Pleasures in forbidden Places.
88. Covetousness is the greatest of Monsters, as well as the Root of all Evil.

Not surprisingly, when Penn does quote scripture, it is to quote from the epistle of James: "Pure Religion and undefiled before God the Father, is this, to visit the Fatherless and the Widows in their Affliction, and to keep our selves unspotted from the World." He writes in selection 472, "Amuse not thy self with the numerous Opinions of the World, nor value thy self upon verbal Orthodoxy, Philosophy, or thy Skill in Tongues, or Knowledge of the Fathers. . . . But in this rejoyce, That thou knowest God, that is the Lord, who exerciseth loving Kindness, and Judgment, and Righteousness in the Earth."

English "Levellers" and "Diggers"

Yet another form of radical religio-political movement in the seventeenth century was presented by the English "Levellers" and "Diggers." The Levellers movement was short-lived—essentially only from 1646 to 1649 during the English civil war. While short-lived, the movement exerted great long-run influence in British and American political history. Inspired by figures like John Lilburne, William Walwyn, and Richard Overton, the Levellers derived their name from their egalitarian political program. The movement can be characterized as religious only in the broad sense that it grew out of the Calvinist-Puritan seedbed of seventeenth-century England and in the occasional theological and biblical argumentation of some of its pamphleteers. In the main, the Levellers justified their political views through natural law arguments, obviously deriving these more from Stoic than from Aristotelian/Thomistic sources.

The Levellers' main political objective was that of making power accountable to common people through increasing the power of Parliament over against the Crown and reforming the basis of parliamentary elections so that all could participate equally in them. Such ideas were, of course, far ahead of their time. The most dramatic moment in the brief history of the Leveller movement was the great debate within Cromwell's army at Putney Church in October and November, 1647. The debate centered on the question whether voting for Parliament should be open to every man (at that point in history women suffrage was beyond the comprehension even of "levellers") or restricted to those holding a property interest in society. The latter view was stated at length by Henry Ireton, clearly representing Cromwell himself. Ireton raised the specter of the undermining of property rights, with all things held in common, if voting power were given to those not propertied—a specter disavowed by the Levellers, whose agenda was political, not economic. In the debate, Colonel Thomas Rainsborough stated the Leveller argument eloquently:

> Really I think that the poorest he that is in England hath a life to live as the greatest he; and therefore truly, sir, I think it's clear, that every man that is to live under a government ought first by his own consent to put himself under that government; and I do think that the poorest man in England is not at all bound in a strict sense to that government that he hath not had a voice to put himself under.[11]

In response to Ireton's further argument that those lacking a (property) interest in the community would comprehend the whole interest of the kingdom, Rainsborough insisted that what was at stake for every man was his possible loss of "that which God and nature hath given him."[12]

The Leveller case was, at the same time, a remarkable new surfacing of ancient Stoic rationalism and popular sovereignty and an anticipation of contract political theory, which was shortly to emerge.[13] John Wildman made the position even more succinctly, also in the Putney debates:

Every person in England hath as clear a right to elect his representative as the greatest person in England. I conceive that's the undeniable maxim of government: that all government is in the free consent of the people. If then upon that account, there is no person that is under a just government, or hath justly his own, unless he by his own free consent be put under that government. This he cannot be unless he be consenting to it.[14]

If the Levellers disavowed any intention to make all property common, that was exactly the purpose of the more radical Diggers of the same period. The Diggers derived their name from their resistance to efforts to deprive the common people of access to the common lands by nobility who sought to enclose the land and make it into private property. Inspired by Gerrard Winstanley, the movement explicitly sought greater economic equality and communal sharing. A Digger manifesto of 1649 protested the enslavement of part of humanity by the "Teachers and Rulers," especially singling out the enclosures of land that deprived common people of access to the "Common Treasury" of Earth. "And the Earth, which was made to be a Common Storehouse for all, is bought and sold and kept within the hands of a few, whereby the Great Creator is mightily dishonoured, as if He were a respecter of persons, delighting in the comfortable livelihood of some, and rejoicing in the miserable poverty and straits of others."[15] The same pamphlet, anticipating the theme of liberation theology a few hundred years yet to come, utilized the exodus analogy with repeated words, "Let Israel go free."

Winstanley himself excoriated the "cheaters" who "have cozened the plain-hearted of their Creation Birth-rights, and have possessed themselves in the Earth, and call it theirs, and not the others, and so have brought in that poverty and misery which lies upon many men."[16] Winstanley's own utopian vision of the future is distinctly communistic:

The Earth is to be planted and the fruits reaped and carried into Barns and Storehouses by the assistance of every family. If any man or family want corn or other provisions, they may go to the Storehouses and fetch without money. If they want a horse to ride, go into the fields in Summer, or to the Common Stables in Winter, and receive one from the Keepers, and when your journey is performed, bring him where you had him, without money. If any want food or victuals, they may either go to the butchers' shops and receive what they want without money, or else go to the flocks of sheep or herds of cattle, and take and kill what meat is needful for their families, without buying and selling. The reason why all the riches of the Earth are a Common Stock is this: Because the Earth and the labors thereupon are managed by common assistance of every family, without buying and selling.[17]

Winstanley's ethic was grounded in a kind of Christian mysticism, though his argumentation was frequently expressed in natural law terms. His mystical references to the inner light by which he was guided have led more than one critic to look for a connection between his ideas and those of the seventeenth-century Quakers. Indeed, the similarities are striking, including his tendency toward pacifism and his reasoned condemnation of capital punishment. On the whole, however, his writing is more communistic and less pacifistic than most of the Friends', and his theological rhetoric more given to flights of symbolic fancy.

Neither the Levellers nor the Diggers lasted long as religio-social movements, but both illustrate the persisting impulse to organize life in accordance with reason and theological vision. And both were destined to exert influences far beyond the middle of the seventeenth century.

PART V

Eighteenth- and Nineteenth-Century Rationalism and Evangelicalism

Medieval Christianity passed important legacies on to the later church. Nevertheless, its sought-after unity of Christianity and civilization could not be sustained, and its synergistic hierarchies in church and society dissolved before the intersecting forces of Renaissance, Reformation, and Enlightenment. The church was to address new questions with different resources.

The eighteenth and nineteenth centuries were a turbulent, creative era— a fitting prelude to the even more turbulent twentieth century. For Europeans, the nineteenth century climaxed a period of worldwide exploration and discovery. The "New World" of the Americas excited the imagination and whetted the appetite of Europeans for conquest and colonization. Empires came into being on a world scale—no longer restricted to contiguous territories. Trade grew ever more important and with it new forms of economic exchange, above all the corporation. The Industrial Revolution began, energized by hydraulic and steam power. Peasants were driven from the land, congregating in the emerging industrial towns and cities to seek employment in the new factories. Economics came into being as a more distinct field of study, grounded primarily in the analysis of market forces. Protest movements and ideologies, ranging from utopian experiments to the "scientific socialism" of Marx and Engels, challenged the sway of the new capitalism and sought to overcome its oppressions. Chattel slavery, an assumed reality in much of recorded history, reached new levels of dehumanization in the African slave trade and the plantation system. Racism, often a reality throughout recorded human history, found systematic expression—in large measure in the effort to justify slavery. Nineteenth-century struggles over slavery, culminating in the American Civil War, deeply affected the consciousness and institutional life of the church.

The revolutionary political movements of the Reformation era took on secular form and gained important victories in the British American colonies and France. The American Revolution demonstrated the workability of contract political theories and democratic political institutions. The French Revolution, with its much more sweeping social agenda, shook Europe to its foundations, although it was less successful in the short run in establishing enduring institutions. Its anticlericalism and its attempts to create a wholly secularized society evoked strongly reactionary currents in European churches.

Modern science, essentially a product of the Enlightenment, made major strides during the eighteenth and nineteenth centuries. Earlier accomplishments in astronomy and physics were followed during this period by great advances in chemistry and biology. The scientific discoveries were themselves important, partly as an advance in human knowledge, partly as support for the rapidly developing technologies of the Industrial Revolution. Perhaps even more important were the changes wrought by scientific method in the way people looked at their world. Systematic empirical research required radical reexamination of human nature, factual history, and the materials and traditions upon which theology and Christian ethics were based. Sir Isaac Newton's comprehensive scientific theories established a basis for equally comprehensive secular philosophies and ideologies. The new era, optimistically referred to as the Enlightenment, offered further challenges to the intellectual and spiritual dominance of Christian theology while also influencing the direction of Christian ethics. Thinkers as diverse as Hobbes, Locke, Hume, Kant, Rousseau, Hegel, Marx, and Nietzsche put a secular stamp on the moral thought of the eighteenth and nineteenth centuries and beyond.

13

RATIONALISM AND REVIVAL
IN THE EIGHTEENTH CENTURY

The development and increasing prestige of science and reason in the postmedieval world began to impact upon Christian ethics more seriously in the eighteenth century, especially in England and France. Religious claims based upon revelation were increasingly subjected to rational criticism. In the previous century, writers like Thomas Hobbes and John Locke had grounded their ethical thought on analysis of human nature. While Locke (more than Hobbes) understood himself to be a Christian and, indeed, often alluded to scripture or Christian symbolism, his serious writings do not depend upon Christian faith or tradition for their validity. Thus, the second of his *Two Treatises on Government* develops a covenantal or contractual theory of the state that rests upon ancient Stoic conceptions of sovereignty. Ultimately, each of us is free and independent. But we are vulnerable in our independence to the like independence of others. Hence, we form the political covenant for the purpose of protecting our natural rights, "life, liberty, and property." And we are therefore morally bound to obey the dictates of the state because we have, by becoming a part of it, agreed to abide by that covenant. All of which can be said without reference to God, Christ, sin, redemption, grace, or any other theological idea. Ultimately, this new confidence in reason evoked explicit criticism of Christian theology by such writers as Voltaire and Thomas Paine, both of whom subscribed to a deistic natural religion.

Among Christian thinkers, the Age of Reason stimulated efforts to portray Christian ethics as an expression of natural reason—or at least as being consistent with natural reason. In some respects, this marked a return to the problem faced by the second- and third-century Alexandrians: how to express Christian faith in harmony with the intellectual culture of the day without, at the same time, abandoning what is essential to that faith. Some of the Christian writings of the period resemble those of Clement of Alexandria to a remarkable degree.

Bishop Joseph Butler

The best illustration of this point is Joseph Butler (1692–1752), a bishop of the Church of England. In the sharpest possible contrast to the passionate, sometimes dogmatic rhetoric of seventeenth-century radical reformers and Calvinists, Butler's moral writing is cool and even detached. He was not a deist—indeed, his most important work, *The Analogy of Religion*, is largely an attempt to defend Christianity against deism. Nevertheless, he was rationalist through and through. His agenda was not unlike that of Clement of Alexandria; he wished to demonstrate the reasonableness of Christianity and to present Christianity in reasonable terms. Christianity, to Butler, is both an expression of natural religion and a new dispensation depending upon revelation. Both are, however, treated in thoroughly rationalist fashion. He writes,

> But the importance of Christianity will more distinctly appear, by considering it more distinctly: first, as a republication, and external institution, of natural or essential religion, adapted to the present circumstances of mankind, and intended to promote natural piety and virtue: and secondly, as containing an account of a dispensation of things not discoverable by reason, in consequence of which, several distinct precepts are enjoined us. For though natural religion is the foundation and principal part of Christianity, it is not in any sense the whole of it.[1]

Revelation lends fresh authority to natural religion; without it, Butler doubts that humanity would have been capable of arriving at natural religion on its own. But revelation also draws us toward Christ and the Holy Spirit, opening those specific relationships to us. Just as "God is the Governor of the world, upon the evidence of reason," so "Christ is the Mediator between God and man, and the Holy Ghost our Guide and Sanctifier, upon the evidence of revelation."[2]

Butler's fundamental definition of Christianity, whether natural or revealed, is moral. We are in fact free to accept or reject either natural or revealed religion: "The light of reason does not, any more than that of revelation, force men to submit to its authority; both admonish them of what they ought to do and avoid, together with the consequences of each; and after this, leave them at full liberty to act just as they please, till the appointed time of judgment."[3] And while Butler speaks of original sin and the consequent "ruin" of humanity, that "ruin" is not so great in his mind as to deprive human beings of the freedom to choose good or evil.

Nor, when Butler elaborates his conception of Christian ethics, is that dependent upon the special claims of revealed religion. The ground principle with Butler is *benevolence*. This he understands to have the same relationship to society that self-love has to individuals. Both are positive dispositions in created human nature, the one serving to preserve and enhance the individual, the other to advance the needs and interests of society. Moreover, Butler sees no serious conflict between self-love and benevolence. He writes that "though benevolence and self-love are different; though the former tends most directly to public good, and the latter to private: yet they are so perfectly coincident that the greatest satisfactions to ourselves depend upon our having benevolence in a due degree; and that self-love is one chief security of our right behaviour towards society."[4] He adds that "we can scarce promote one without the other" and that this "is equally a proof that we were made for both." He concludes that "we were made for society, and to promote the happiness of it, as we were intended to take care of our own life, and health, and private good."[5]

The emerging understanding of human nature, in both its individual and social dimensions, is neither negative nor complicated. We are what we are by creation. Our created nature is fundamentally good, so that when we act best in accordance with self-love and benevolence our own best interests and those of society are fulfilled. We do not have a fundamental drive toward evil; when we act with "ungoverned passions" it is on the basis of mistaken means employed toward good ends. Thus, "there is no such thing as love of injustice, oppression, treachery, ingratitude, but only eager desires after such and such external goods; which, according to a very ancient observation, the most abandoned would choose to obtain by innocent means." Thus, "the principles and passions in the mind of man, which are distinct both from self-love and benevolence, primarily and most directly lead to right behaviour with regard to others as well as himself, and only secondarily and accidentally to what is evil."[6] Sin becomes "a manifest negligence in men of their real happiness or interest in the present world, when that interest is inconsistent with a present gratification; for the sake of which they negligently, nay even knowingly, are the authors and instruments of their own misery and ruin."[7]

Conscience, then, is our inner guide to save us from such misery and ruin. In part, it is the natural sense of "shame" that identifies shameful deeds. In part, it is "the rule of right, and obligations to follow it," as Paul said.[8] This conscience seeks to govern our whole self, so that individual drives or instincts do not lead us to ruin. Again, he affirms that all of our "several passions" are naturally good, but they must also be "naturally subordinate to the one superior principle of reflection or conscience."[9] Again, there is no real conflict between conscience and self-love: "they always lead us the same way." Therefore, Butler can write, "duty and interest are perfectly coincident; for the most part in this world, but entirely and every instance if we take in the future, and the whole; this being implied in the notion of a good and perfect administration of things."[10]

Butler's discussion of virtue is consistent with this optimistic account of human nature and reason. Benevolence is the primary virtue, expressing as it does the coincidence of personal and social well-being. In the expression of benevolence, however, prudence is also an important virtue. For prudence not only correctly measures actions against consequences but it also correctly apportions benevolent actions to the deserving or undeserving among other persons. Prudence requires that we not neglect due regard for our own interest or happiness nor fail to care adequately for others.[11]

Butler does not develop a substantial social ethic. Far from carefully considering the wider horizons of political or economic responsibility, he offers a reason why our benevolent love of neighbor is more appropriately expressed in interpersonal relationships. The universe is much too large to be the object of benevolence among limited human beings; even humankind is too great. So also one's own country is too broad an object for the common run of people, since "common men do not consider their actions as affecting the whole community of which they are members." What is needed for most people is a more immediate "object of benevolence." Therefore, he writes, "the scripture, not being a book of theory and speculation, but a plain rule of life for mankind, has with the utmost propriety put the principle of virtue upon the love of our neighbour; which is that part of the universe, that part of mankind, that part of our country, which comes under our immediate notice, acquaintance, and influence, and with which we have to do."[12]

Butler's version of Christian ethics thus aspires to reasonableness and benevolence among human beings whose nature, if anything, predisposes them to reasonableness and benevolence. Notwithstanding his affirmation of the need for special revelation and his occasional citations of scripture, the specific contribution of Christianity to this ethic is more one of confirmation. On the whole, it was a comfortable message addressed to comfortable people.

Evangelical Revival

If it can be said that the reasonable optimism of a Joseph Butler fit the spirit of the times, it must be added immediately that that could only have applied to the educated, well-to-do classes. For them, the dominant yearning must have been for social peace and order after a turbulent century of interreligious conflict and civil war. What was called for was a return to the ordinary decencies and civilities of people influenced by the Enlightenment and a desire for a return to normalcy. The church, for such people, was indistinguishable from other institutions of polite society, as theology was from natural reason.

But that does not supply an adequate picture of the times. The England in which Bishop Butler wrote was torn apart by class divisions and deeply corrupted in its social life. Large numbers of people had lost the protections of the medieval feudal order without gaining the freedoms and affluence of a new industrial age. While ostensibly members of the established Church of England, they were in fact also deprived of its ministry and effectively scorned by its more respectable communicants. Moreover, the rationalism of the times effectively denied cultural approval for emotional outlet. Crime became a more serious problem, with severe, even inhuman punishments (such as hanging for petty theft) devised in a futile attempt to bring it under control.

A major evangelical revival developed in the midst of this unpromising cultural situation. Its preachers, notably John and Charles Wesley and George Whitefield, emphasized the doctrines of grace and justification. Each individual, no matter how low in the social structure, was given to understand that he or she was important to God; each was given opportunity for emotional expression; each was encouraged—even required—to acquire great personal self-discipline; each was provided opportunity to engage in works of charity and compassion. At first, this revival was in the context—though on the fringes—of the established church; ultimately, it resulted in the founding of separate denominations. The individual pietism thus engendered was expressed among various Continental religious groups, such as the Moravians, and in North America it was manifested in the first Great Awakening.

John Wesley

While not the original spark for the English evangelical revival, John Wesley (1703–1791) became its natural leader, theologian, moral teacher, and organizer. Over a long lifetime—more than fifty years of which were devoted to leadership of the Methodist movement—Wesley contributed both theological and practical insight to Christian ethics. Several of his foundational theological convictions are especially pertinent.

Of these, his peculiar juxtaposition of the doctrines of justification and sanctification is noteworthy. Justification occurs with the sinner's recognition both of his or her unworthiness and of the free gift of God's grace. To be justified is to be received as a child of God in the boundless love of God, despite that unworthiness. To this typically Protestant point of emphasis, Wesley appended his own doctrine of "assurance." As "justified" sinners we need be in no doubt as to our salvation. We can accept our assurance of that. With Wesley, then, there was no further need for continued preoccupation with the question of one's salvation, no need for anxious daily review of the evidences of salvation in one's own life. Nevertheless, justification and assurance were but the beginning. Received as a sinner, one was nonetheless expected to continue in the process of being made holy. This process of sanctification was understood by Wesley to last a lifetime. Here indeed Christians must hold themselves to account—while, in their religious societies, holding one another to account.

Wesley's emphasis on sanctification was expressed in his doctrine of "Christian Perfection." We are to strive toward perfection; indeed, we are to expect to be made perfect in this life. By this, Wesley did not mean abstract or moralistic perfection, measured against a catalogue of vices to be avoided and virtues to be cultivated. The word itself may indeed have been poorly chosen, precisely because it carries such a connotation. Wesley also carefully notes that he does not mean perfection in knowledge or reasoning nor even that Christians can ever be free from temptation. What he meant, rather, was perfection in love—becoming a wholly loving person, no longer enslaved to animosities or self-centeredness. In an early tract, he expressed it in this way:

> Whether he lie down or rise up, God is in all his thoughts; he walks with God continually, having the loving eye of his soul fixed on Him, and everywhere "seeing Him that is invisible." And loving God, he "loves his neighbor as himself," he loves every man as his own soul. He loves his enemies, yea, and the enemies of God. And if it be not in his power to "do good to them that hate" him, yet he ceases not to pray for them. . . . Love has purified his heart from envy, malice, wrath, and every unkind temper. . . . [H]is one desire is the one design of his life, namely, "to do not his own will, but the will of Him that sent him."[13]

Elsewhere Wesley speaks of Christian perfection as "love filling the heart, expelling pride, anger, desire, self-will; rejoicing evermore, praying without ceasing, and in everything giving thanks."[14]

153

The doctrine of perfection proved troublesome to Wesley and the Methodists, as attested by the number of defenses and clarifications of the doctrine that issued from his pen through the years. In a 1764 writing he summarized his clarifications by reasserting that "there is such a thing as perfection, for it is again and again mentioned in Scripture"; that it is not the same thing as justification; that it can occur during one's lifetime, that is, before death; that it is not absolute since "absolute perfection belongs not to man nor to angels but to God alone"; that it does not make us infallible; that it involves "salvation from sin," whether or not that means sinlessness; that its essence is perfect love; that it is amenable to further improvement; that it can be lost.[15]

It could be argued that the plain meaning of the word "perfection" has somehow been lost amid the concessions and clarifications. Wesley himself seemed to sense this. His reluctance to abandon the doctrine of Christian perfection was evidently based on his belief (1) that justification, in the Reformation sense, is not enough if it does not lead to the transformation of life, (2) that the grace we receive in Jesus Christ is sufficient to enable a total transformation, and (3) that love is the essence of this new life in Christ.

In the course of his long life and active leadership of the Methodist movement, Wesley had occasion to write or comment on a wide variety of moral problems. On the whole, his writing and preaching is more directed toward personal moral questions than broader social issues. His Methodist societies were organized into "classes" of a dozen or so members, with exacting moral disciplines and processes of examination. They were expected to act always to the glory of God, to avoid luxurious or conspicuous consumption, to engage in charitable works such as visiting the sick and imprisoned and caring for the needy, to avoid spiritually harmful recreations and entertainments.

In a famous sermon, "The Use of Money," Wesley affirms money in the present state of fallen human nature—while noting that its use would be superseded if we were in a state of innocence or, like the early church in Jerusalem, "filled with the Holy Ghost." But since we are not living in that kind of world, we must seek and use money responsibly. His three-point summary of that is that we should (1) gain all we can, (2) save all we can, and (3) give all we can. The first of these expresses a forthright call for economic activity: we are to be active, productive people. We are not to shy away from economic gain. At the same time, Wesley warns against some gainful pursuits that are injurious to one's own physical or spiritual health or to the public good. The second point, on saving, warns against waste and over-indulgence. The third, on giving, emphasizes that we are but stewards of God's wealth. Wesley notes, somewhat ruefully, that his Methodists were better on the first two points than on the third. He also reflects upon the paradox that the emphasis upon hard work and saving helped many

Methodists to rise out of poverty into affluence or wealth—which had, then, the effect of making them less spiritually alive. "I fear," he wrote, that

> wherever riches have increased, the essence of religion has decreased in the same proportion. Therefore I do not see how it is possible, in the nature of things, for any revival of true religion to continue long. For religion must necessarily produce both industry and frugality, and these cannot but produce riches. But as riches increase, so will pride, anger, and love of the world in all its branches. . . . Is there no way to prevent this—this continual decay of pure religion?[16]

Wesley, who may thus be cited in support of a highly individualistic conception of economic ethics, did struggle to understand the vast economic forces that were gripping the England of the early Industrial Revolution. In his "Thoughts on the Present Scarcity of Provision" he provides a vivid portrait of poverty as he had personally experienced it:

> I have known those who could afford to eat a little coarse food once every other day. I have known one in London (and one that a few years before had all the conveniences of life) picking up from a dunghill stinking sprats, and carrying them home for herself and her children. I have known another gathering the bones which the dogs had left in the streets, and making broth of them, to prolong a wretched life! I have heard a third artlessly declare, "Indeed I was very faint, and so weak I could hardly walk, until my dog, finding nothing at home, went out and brought in a good sort of bone, which I took out of his mouth, and made a pure dinner!"[17]

He ponders why this could be "in a land flowing as it were, with milk and honey! abounding with all the necessaries, the conveniences, the superfluities of life!"[18] He ventures a number of conjectures about the structural economic problems that might lie behind the scarcity and high cost of food. Among these were his concern over the diversion of grain to the production of distilled gin, the breeding of horses as a substitute for cattle and sheep, and the growing of oats for horses rather than for people—all instances of the diversion of food resources from necessity to luxury. Overall, his economic analysis may have been superficial. Clearly it was grounded in a deep concern for the plight of poor people.

He also anticipated a great deal of subsequent Christian debate over poverty by insisting that poor people are not, themselves, to be blamed for their plight. In his *Journal* he records a visit to poor people, finding them "half-starved both with cold and hunger." Nevertheless, he "found not one of them unemployed, who was able to crawl about the room." He explodes:

"So wickedly, devilishly false is that common objection, 'They are poor, only because they are idle.' "[19]

Wesley's opposition to slavery and the African slave trade was unremitting. In his *A Serious Address to the People of England,* he wrote that "I would to God it may never be found more! that we may never more steal and sell our brethren like beasts; never murder them by thousands and tens of thousands! . . . Never was anything such a reproach to England since it was a nation, as the having any hand in this execrable traffic."[20] In his pamphlet "Thoughts on Slavery," Wesley disputed the claim that slavery was authorized by law. How, he asks, "can law, human law, change the nature of things? . . . Notwithstanding ten thousand laws, right is right, and wrong is wrong still."[21] Slavery was, he contended, contrary to every principle of natural justice:

> Where is the justice of inflicting the severest evils on those that have done us no wrong? of depriving those that never injured us in word or deed, of every comfort of life? of tearing them from their native country, and depriving them of liberty itself, to which an Angolan has the same natural right as an Englishman, and on which he sets as high a value? Yea, where is the justice of taking away the lives of innocent, inoffensive men; murdering thousands of them in their own land, by the hands of their own countrymen; many thousands, year after year, on shipboard, and then casting them like dung into the sea; and tens of thousands in that cruel slavery to which they are so unjustly reduced?[22]

It is worth noting that one of Wesley's last writings, as a very old man, was a letter to William Wilberforce, who led the British movement to outlaw the slave trade, encouraging him in that continuing struggle: "Go on," he wrote, "in the name of God and in the power of His might, till even American slavery (the vilest that ever saw the sun) shall vanish away before it."[23]

Wesley was not a political theorist, although he also had occasion to write on political subjects. His "Calm Address to Our American Colonies," published at the outset of the American Revolution, called for an end to rebellion and questioned the moral credentials of democracy: "No governments under heaven are so despotic as the republican; no subjects are governed in so arbitrary a manner as those of a commonwealth."[24] In another writing he asserts that "there is most liberty of all, civil and religious, under a limited monarchy; there is usually less under an aristocracy, and least of all under a democracy."[25] It is noteworthy that the criterion employed here by which to judge forms of government is liberty; ironically, it is for the sake of human rights that Wesley opposes democracy. His loyalty to monarchy, though hardly open to question, had clearly been informed by the struggles of the preceding century, both in his support of the ordering function of a limited monarchy and in his support for political rights within that order.

Wesley could not have been classified as a pacifist, but he contributed one of the finest pieces on the ironies and follies of war known to Christian literature:

> Here are forty thousand men gathered together on this plain. What are they going to do? See, there are thirty or forty thousand more at a little distance. And these are going to shoot them through the head or body, to stab them, or split their skulls, and send most of their souls into everlasting fire, as fast as they possibly can. Why so? What harm have they done to them? O none at all! They do not so much as know them. But a man, who is King of France, has a quarrel with another man, who is King of England. So these Frenchmen are to kill as many of these Englishmen as they can, to prove the King of France is in the right. Now, what an argument is this! What a method of proof! What an amazing way of deciding controversies! . . . [W]hat farther proof do we need of the utter degeneracy of all nations from the plainest principles of reason and virtue?[26]

Wesley considered war to be a prime illustration of original sin. Surely, he writes, "all our declamations on the strength of human reason, and the eminence of our virtues, are no more than the cant and jargon of pride and ignorance, so long as there is such a thing as war in the world."[27] Some among his followers resisted military conscription, while others participated. Wesley did not enjoin either course of action, nor do we have from his pen a Methodist version of just war theory.

Overall, the contrast between the ethic of the cool Anglican bishop Joseph Butler and the evangelical leader John Wesley could scarcely have been more striking. The two actually met when Wesley, still in his thirties, ventured to preach in Butler's Bristol diocese. Butler chided Wesley and his Methodists for their emotionalism and special claims: "Sir," he declared, "the pretending to extraordinary revelations and gifts of the Holy Ghost is a horrid thing, a very horrid thing."[28] Their theological differences had ecclesiastical ramifications as well. Butler refused to grant Wesley permission to preach in the Bristol area; Wesley declined to accept his authority.

Jonathan Edwards

If the eighteenth century was capable of drawing its rationalistic and evangelical elements into a profound synthesis, it was not to be through a Butler or a Wesley so much as it was through a theological genius in colonial America. A contemporary of Butler and Wesley, Jonathan Edwards

(1703–1758) was the preeminent Christian thinker of colonial America, though his work was read on both sides of the Atlantic and his influence continues to the present day. Edwards was one of the leading figures in the American version of eighteenth-century revival, the Great Awakening. His sermons from that period, such as the colorful "Sinners in the Hands of an Angry God," may continue to bemuse students of American literature; his theological writings endure for weightier reasons.

Deeply read in Enlightenment thought as well as in the theological classics, Edwards accepted the rational unity of being as central to theology and ethics. In this, his thought was akin to the Newtonian conception of the universe. His universe, like that of Newton, is unified and comprehensible. Every aspect of it affects every other. In sharp contradiction to the deists, however, his universe is not a clock left to run on its own, for it must be empowered throughout by God. Also in contrast to the deists, his humanity is not simply a rational being. Humanity thinks, but it also feels and wills. The "affections," or feelings and will, are to Edwards the mainspring of our being. It is in the analysis of the affections, as they relate to being, that Edwards grounds his Christian ethics. In this, he is at home with the evangelicals on both sides of the Atlantic. (If he had chanced upon the lines from a 1740 Charles Wesley hymn, "God is love! I know, I feel," he would have heartily agreed.)

In his principal writing on ethics, *The Nature of True Virtue*, Edwards argues that virtue does not consist in our love of particular beings—even other people, as such. Rather, "it consists in benevolence to Being in general." Abstractly considered, "Being in general" refers to "the great system of universal existence."[29] He argues, "no exercise of love, or kind affection to any one particular Being, that is but a small part of this whole, has anything of the nature of true virtue."[30] Love of some aspect of being, whether that be an object of beauty, another human being, a whole nation, can in fact stand over against our love of being in general. These lesser objects of love represent "private affections" which "will set a person *against* general existence, and make him an enemy to it."[31] Does he have Bishop Butler in mind when he concludes that self-interest is not a high enough principle, even when balanced with benevolence toward others? He writes,

> As it is with *selfishness*, or when a man is governed by a regard to his own private interest, independent of regard to the public good, such a temper disposes a man to act the part of an enemy to the public. As in every case wherein his private interest seems to clash with the public; or in all those cases wherein such things are presented to his view that suit his personal appetites or private inclinations but are inconsistent with the good of the public. On which account a selfish, contracted, narrow spirit is generally abhorred, and

is esteemed base and sordid. But if a man's affection takes in half a dozen more, and his regards extend so far beyond his own single person as to take in his children and family; or if it reaches further still, to a larger circle, but falls infinitely short of the universal system, and is exclusive of Being in general, his private affection exposes him to the same thing, viz. to pursue the interest of its particular object in *opposition* to general existence.[32]

As theologian, Edwards does not leave the object of the "affections" on the plane of "Being in general" or "general existence." He is speaking about God, who is "infinitely the greatest Being."[33] Therefore, he writes, "unless we will be atheists, we must allow that true virtue does primarily and most essentially consist in a supreme love to God, and that where this is wanting there can be no true virtue."[34] Therefore, "a truly virtuous mind, being as it were under the sovereign dominion of *love to God*, does above all things seek the *glory of God*, and makes *this* his supreme, governing, and ultimate end."[35]

Edwards thus aligns himself with those who consider ethics to be intrinsically a theological subject. Efforts to account for the moral life without reference to God—or "Being in general"—fall short:

> Hence it appears that those *schemes* of religion or moral philosophy, which, however well in some respects they may treat of benevolence to *mankind* and other virtues depending on it, yet have not a supreme regard to God, and love to him, laid in the *foundation*, and all other virtues handled in a *connection* with this, and in *subordination* to this, are not true schemes of philosophy, but are fundamentally and essentially defective. It may be asserted in general, that nothing is of the nature of true virtue, in which God is not the *first* and the *last*; or which, with regard to their exercises in general, have not their first foundation and source in apprehensions of God's supreme dignity and glory, and in answerable esteem and love of him, and have not respect to God as the supreme end.[36]

Edwards's soteriology—or doctrine of salvation—is not unlike the Calvinist/evangelical stream in which he stood. It is through the atoning grace of Jesus Christ that our "affections" are transformed and our whole being enabled to respond to God, who is at the heart of "Being in general."

Notwithstanding his theological grounding of ethics, however, Edwards acknowledges that the private affections of natural humanity do contain something of an analogy to "true virtue." They do "tend to the good of the world of mankind" and they also "tend several ways to restrain vice, and prevent many acts of wickedness."[37] On the one hand, the moral life, lived on the level of the "private affections," does not in itself draw one toward that theological foundation of "true virtue." True virtue, on the other hand,

159

does lead one to benevolence toward all aspects of existence seen, as they are, as they exist in relation to God. Thus, true virtue contains the objects of the "private virtues," but no longer just as objects in themselves.

In light of this, Edwards can preach the importance of charity and benevolence as consequences of the central affection by which Christians live— even affirming that our charitable works are a necessary expression of our faith. He concludes,

> Christ, by his redemption, has brought us into a more near relation one to another, hath made us children of God, children in the same family. We are all brethren, having God for our common Father; which is much more than to be brethren in any other family. He hath made us all one body; therefore we ought to be united, and subserve one another's good, and bear one another's burdens, as is the case with the members of the same natural body. . . . Apply these things to yourselves; and inquire, whether you do not lie under guilt on account of the neglect of this duty, in withholding that charity which God requires of you towards the needy?[38]

14

NINETEENTH-CENTURY PHILOSOPHICAL
AND CHRISTIAN ETHICS

Western ethics in the nineteenth century was dominated by philosophical, not theological, thinkers. That century witnessed a ferment of moral thought, with seminal—though very diverse—contributions from such minds as Kant, Hegel, Schopenhauer, Bentham, Mill, Marx, and Nietzsche. A potpourri of secondary figures, such as Claude-Henri de Rouvroy Saint-Simon, Charles Fourier, and Auguste Comte, can be added—along with scientists like Darwin, whose work had important ramifications for ethics. Some of the philosophers and scientists would have been comfortable with the designation Christian; few of them depended in any conscious way upon Christian scripture or tradition; a few were explicitly anti-Christian. These thinkers, and the many by whom they were influenced, were decisive in shaping the public discussion of ethical themes. Their cultural weight continues to register in the twentieth century.

The work of Christian ethics was much less influential during this period. It could even be argued that during the nineteenth century, for the first time since Augustine, dominant thought on moral questions was not carried out in a theological context. Nevertheless, there were self-consciously Christian thinkers and movements of some importance during that century. Their work needs to be seen in relation to secular thought, sometimes in its reaction against those currents, sometimes in its endeavor to translate secular thought into theological terms. Before turning to the specifically Christian thinkers, therefore, we need a brief reminder of the moral ideas jostling for attention in that century.

Formative Ideas in Nineteenth-Century Moral Philosophy

While *Immanuel Kant* (1724–1804) lived most of his life in the eighteenth century, his writing was, in a sense, the foundational work for nineteenth-century moral thought. Kant argues that the morality of an act is not derived from its end or goal but from its motivation. The only thing that can be said to be morally good (without further qualification) is the good will. To will the good is to will in accordance with universal law. Kant's "categorical imperative" calls for us always to act in such a way that the basis (or "maxim") of our action could become universal law. Any other basis for action is an expression of a "pathological will," by which Kant means a will moved by feeling. Such a will is not autonomous; it does not move itself. Thus, "when one's own happiness is made the determining ground of the will, the result is the direct opposite of the principle of morality."[1] To put this differently: for an act to be moral, it must not be determined from outside the self. It must represent one's own decision, grounded, first of all, in one's determination to be moral. Thus, with Kant, the moral life is above all life based on duty. We are to do our duty regardless of the unpleasantness of the results. Kant's ethic, therefore, is diametrically opposed to the pleasure principle of hedonism as it is, also, to doing good *in order to* receive an earthly or an eternal reward. The question of what *is* in accordance with universal moral law must be addressed by reason and experience. Kant is convinced that one canon of universal moral law is that one ought never to tell a lie. Another is that we should always treat other persons as ends in themselves, and not exploit them merely as "means" to other purposes.

Kant's underlying philosophy is germane to theology—and theological ethics—in a more basic way. In the *Critique of Pure Reason* he demonstrates the impossibility of certain knowledge of any aspect of the external world. Reality is presented to us only in the forms that can be mediated through the mind. We cannot know any "thing in itself." Thus, we can neither prove nor disprove the existence of God or any other religious meaning—though Kant regards the existence of God and of life after death as necessary to make sense out of the moral life.

Georg W. F. Hegel (1770–1831) developed a moral philosophy around the self-actualizing will. Beginning with pure will and abstract right, Hegel describes the moral life as the unfolding process whereby both come into actual existence. The will is internal; it is subjective; it is the "I" that is empty of any actual content. In itself it is neither moral nor immoral. Abstract right is moral principle not yet embodied in actual existence. When I will in accordance with abstract right I bring it into existence and at the same time become myself a person. In doing so, I cannot treat other persons as less than the moral will that I am without disintegrating my own personhood.

Thus, Hegel is resolutely opposed to slavery or, in principle, exploitation of any kind. Hegel, on this basis, affirms the moral character of marriage as a covenant of moral equals in which both partners actualize themselves at a higher level of existence. His conception of criminal law requires that criminals submit to punishment as a condition of reassuming the moral dignity destroyed by their violation of the law. Hegel understands the state to be the highest form of self-actualization. It is not that we subordinate ourselves to the state; it is that we collectively find therein our freedom to act in world history. The latter, Hegel understands as the sublime self-actualization of God as Absolute Spirit.

These ideas, which were to resonate in the nineteenth century (and the twentieth) in all sorts of ways, are developed in dialectical form. In contrast with the long-honored Aristotelian logic, based on the importance of consistency, Hegel's dialectical logic contrasts opposing truths in the development of a more inclusive truth. Thus, particular contradictions may not be mutually exclusive; each may be true, in its limited way, while both point toward a higher truth. Even this higher truth, in turn, is limited in the same way and must be synthesized with its own contradiction. Hegel sees all aspects of human moral existence working their way forward in dialectical fashion as that existence embodies more and more the reality of Absolute Spirit.

In contrast with the moral idealism of Kant and Hegel, *Arthur Schopenhauer* (1788–1860) presented the nineteenth century with a profoundly pessimistic view of the moral will. The will, to Schopenhauer, is but a particular expression of the "will to live" of all life. It is "without knowledge, and is merely a blind incessant impulse."[2] Its basis is nothing more than "need, deficiency, and thus pain."[3] Happiness, therefore, is merely negative; it is only the relief of want or pain: "the satisfaction or the pleasing can never be more than the deliverance from a want."[4] Apart from the endless treadmill of needs and wants and their satisfaction, human life is emptiness, ennui. (An evidence of this, in Schopenhauer's mind, is the fact that people find satisfaction in playing cards, an intrinsically meaningless activity, to relieve their boredom.) In face of this pessimistic account of human nature, Schopenhauer offers asceticism as the way out: extinguishing, as far as possible, the involvement of the will in the cycles of need and satisfaction—recognizing that ultimately he is calling for an end to life. Justice, to Schopenhauer, lies in fellow-feeling in the midst of this great sea of human misery.

Karl Marx (1818–1883) is well known as the author of scientific socialism, understood by him and by his collaborator Friedrich Engels to be a scientific description of social reality, not a new system of moral philosophy. Drawing important ideas from Hegel, Marx nevertheless saw that idealistic philosophy as reality turned on its head. It is not abstract right and moral will that are actualizing themselves through history; it is concrete history, grounded ultimately in economic forms that are reflected in abstract thought and social institutions. Marx understood human beings to be creative and social. He affirmed (with Hegel) that we actualize our humanity through our work. Similarly, we enter into concrete social relationships through what we do with and for others. Our humanity has been "alienated" from us, however, through previous epochs of human history. Each epoch has involved a different characteristic form of exploitation, with one socioeconomic class typically dominating another. In contemporary (nineteenth-century) society, the intrinsic activity of self-actualization has been replaced by work for the extrinsic reward of money, the fetish which has replaced the true human essence.[5] Religion is the distorted lens through which we view ourselves; it is our alienated self-consciousness. Religion as "the opium of the people" is a narcotic deadening the pain of alienated existence. But "the abolition of religion as the *illusory* happiness of men, is a demand for their *real happiness.*"[6] Since Marx did not consider alienation to be a consequence of human moral failure, per se, but rather of objective socioeconomic forces and relationships, his call was not for moral reform but rather for social revolution. He and Engels explicitly contrasted this agenda with the myriad forms of "utopian" socialism in nineteenth-century Europe and North America.

The Utilitarians *Jeremy Bentham* (1748–1832) and *John Stuart Mill* (1806–1873) represented a nineteenth-century revival of the ancient moral philosophy of hedonism, with this important difference: The Utilitarians understood the pleasure principle primarily in social, not individual, terms. The good to which all moral beings aspire is indeed pleasure, or happiness (and the corresponding avoidance of pain). But as a moral objective, this principle must be expressed as the maximizing of happiness for all, not simply for oneself. As Mill put it, the utilitarian standard "is not the agent's own greatest happiness, but the greatest amount of happiness altogether."[7] Mill understood the motive of the moral will itself to be the quest for happiness, thus introducing a possible contradiction between that personal objective and the larger utilitarian principle of the greatest good for the largest number of people (which might not include oneself!). But he attempted to bridge this possible conflict by asserting that those who have the widest experience of life will choose the nobler pleasures associated with seeking the good of others. "Better," he wrote, "to be Socrates dissatisfied than a fool satisfied."[8] Whether or not the utilitarian moral theory finally held together, Mill and the other Utilitarians distinguished themselves with a wide variety of progressive campaigns for human rights. These included the emancipation of women and equality of franchise. Mill's essay "On Liberty" was a brilliant presentation of the case for freedom of expression.

Friedrich Nietzsche (1844–1900) reacted vigorously against the "slave ethics" he associated with Christianity. "All truly noble morality," he wrote, "grows out of triumphant self-affirmation."[9] Christian ethics, with its glorification of humility and tender, other-regarding sentiments, is precisely contrary to this self-affirmation. "The church fights passion with excision in every sense: its practice, its 'cure,' is *castratism*. It never asks: 'how can one spiritualize, beautify, deify a craving?' . . . But an attack on the roots of passion means an attack on the roots of life: the practice of the church is *hostile to life*."[10] What then is the good? "Everything," he writes, "that heightens the feeling of power in man, the will to power, power itself." And what is bad? "Everything that is born of weakness." So Nietzsche preaches "not contentedness but more power; not peace but war; not virtue but fitness." The most harmful thing is "active pity for all the failures and all the weak: Christianity."[11] Nietzsche's philosophy dovetailed rather well with the Social Darwinism of the late nineteenth century, which drew social ethical conclusions from Charles Darwin's theories concerning the "survival of the fittest" in biological evolution. And it must be said that his troubled and troubling thoughts anticipated some of the darkest chapters in the history of the twentieth century.

Nineteenth-Century Christian Ethics

Again, it cannot be said that Christian ethics dominated Western thinking during this century. We can even question the extent to which Christian ethics provided a substantial dialogue or debating partner for the philosophical alternatives. The latter were presented too articulately; broader cultural forces continued to gnaw at the settled assumptions and conventions of Christian traditions in both their Catholic and Protestant forms.

This does not mean that the church itself was altogether on the defensive. The nineteenth century was a great era of Christian expansion, with missions bursting across the face of Africa and Asia and with new Christian denominations springing forth to conquer the American frontier for the church. Nor does it mean that there were no Christian moral thinkers worthy of note. Four of these deserve special mention.

Friedrich Schleiermacher

Friedrich Schleiermacher (1768–1834) possessed a systematic mind not unlike his two fellow Germans Kant and Hegel. He was versed, moreover, in the same stream of philosophical and scientific thought. But his work was devoted to systematic theology, not to the creation of a philosophical system. His ethics, in particular, helps to illustrate the difference—and along with it, his own distinction between Christian ethics and systematic theology.

Schleiermacher's theology and ethics are both grounded, ultimately, in his conception of God-consciousness. It is God-consciousness to which scripture and church bear witness; it is Jesus' God-consciousness that lends revelatory power to his life and which, shared with his disciples and subsequent Christians, is the basis of redemption. Theology and ethics are distinct from philosophy in that the former are uniquely Christian, not derived from rational principles per se—though they may be explicated in relation to such principles. The God-consciousness of Christians is not derived from rational reflection but from concrete historical experience. Similarly, while Christian ethics is an expression of Christian faith, it is not derived from dogmatic theology. The latter is an intellectual expression of a prior reality. Christian ethics, like dogmatic theology, arises from that reality itself—not from ideas about it. "Christian faith is indeed assumed, but only in the form of the primordial consciousness, not dogmatic [intellectual] development. It is assumed that there was a Christian life before there was Christian ethics."[12] That Christian life has its basis in Christ. "Therefore," he argues, "the existence of a special Christian ethics stands or falls with the superhuman conception of the person of Christ."[13] "Superhuman" here does not abolish the humanity of Jesus; it refers to Christ's own openness to the reality of God, which transcends the human. This God-consciousness of Jesus is taken, by Christians (and thus by Christian ethics), to be real. It is in the spreading of this consciousness—one might almost say the *infection* of this consciousness in the lives of others—that Christian faith and Christian ethics are made reality in human history.

For this reason, Schleiermacher does not take the direction suggested by Kant's categorical imperative. One could argue that Schleiermacher's God-consciousness leads to the same result, for it defines moral action in relation to the universal (God). But Schleiermacher's moral self is grounded in a particular outlook, with historical and cultural experience lying behind it. Kant's is an abstract expression of human freedom seeking to express itself through duty to what the mind can know about universal law.[14] With Kant, the abstract possibility of the moral will might be realized in any culture, in any historical epoch in which rational beings (regardless of the particularities of culture, time, and place) live in accordance with duty. With Schleiermacher, the moral will is not a universal absolute; it is an emergent in actual history. Thus, Schleiermacher also anticipates some later tendencies in Christian ethics by referring to it with indicative rather than imperative language. Christian ethics is not so much a matter of what we "ought" to do (as Kant would have it); it is a *description* of what Christians in fact do in consequence of their being Christian. The focal point is *virtue*, "an inner disposition that comes to light through action." It is not *duty*, which has to do with "something external."[15] Relating this point to Paul's notion of freedom from the law, Schleiermacher remarks, astutely, that "law is given where it is presupposed that the content of the law would not be followed if the law were not given." But living in the reality of Christian faith, the law has become irrelevant among people who will live the Christian life because that is who they are: "Wherever the Spirit is and wherever human beings develop for themselves the fruit of the Spirit, there is no longer any connection with law. For such persons the law no longer exists."[16]

How do we know all this? In one sense, the reality precedes our knowing anything about it and our knowledge is but a reflection upon that reality. But Schleiermacher also speaks of scripture as the church's fundamental record. He carefully distances his view of the authority of scripture from any kind of literalism. Long before the full development of critical biblical scholarship he can write that

> if we consider how the general cosmopolitan circumstances of the Christian church have changed drastically from what they were in the New Testament period, it seems self-evident that we can no longer make use of many prescriptions, and for many situations in our lives we find no prescription in Scripture. Contemporary non-Christians who live among Christian people stand in a totally inverse relationship from that of the first century. And as for the political relationships, there are absolutely no prescriptions. . . . [It is therefore] the task of Christian ethics to refine its approach to Scripture and indeed more precisely than has been customary.[17]

So, he suggests, "we must here employ an interpretation like the judicial where laws from an earlier time must often be applied to situations arising in the present." So, he concludes, "the main point is that one correctly determine the circumstances either by right principles or by analogy with other circumstances addressed by prescriptions in Scripture."[18]

He is, however, painfully clear that church authority must not be imposed as a substitute. He is sharply critical of the Roman Catholic Church, with its top-down conceptions of authority and its pretensions to infallibility. The Protestant Reformation abolished "the distinction between those-who-command and those-who-obey in the church" and established "an equality of all under Christ and the divine Word."[19] In Protestantism, he writes, "we know nothing of obedience to the church, for this is the place of our common obedience to Christ himself."[20]

Nevertheless, with Schleiermacher, the church is also a principal focal point for Christian ethics. Christian ethics, in fact, would be unthinkable without reference to the church. It "is indeed limited solely to that which proceeds from the Christian spirit within the Christian church."[21] While Christian ethics is grounded in "the fact of revelation," it has validity "only for the community of the church."[22] For it is "through Christ and by his own testimony and the corresponding testimony of Christians from the earliest period onward [that] an active power has entered the Christian church."[23] That power, "designated the divine Spirit," is "the moral capacity that is at the same time effective in the Christian church."[24]

We thus have with Schleiermacher a version of Christian ethics that strongly emphasizes the fact of Christ's consciousness of God, through which the divine Spirit is set loose in the Christian church and in accordance with which individual Christians have taken on the Christian life. It is an ethic that emphasizes the given character of Christians and of the church of which they are inescapably a part. Ethics is what they express in their lives and what they seek to do in the world.

Søren Kierkegaard

The strange, often enigmatic, but undeniably brilliant Danish theologian/ philosopher Søren Kierkegaard (1813–1855) betrays the influence of both Kant and Hegel, though with his own unique twist. With Kant he affirms the centrality of freedom of the will and, to a point, the understanding that ethics lies in the decision to live in accordance with universal law. With Hegel he understands actualization of the self to lie in its moral life. He has, nevertheless, the strongest possible objections to what he takes to be a substitution of moral philosophy for concrete moral existence.

The main burden of Kierkegaard's struggle is the actualization of the self in existence. His gifted polemical pen is directed against the dishonesties of human culture, whereby people drift along with the social tide without themselves making clear moral decisions. To profess beliefs, such as belief in Christianity, without bringing them into existence in one's actual life is worse than not to profess them in the first place. In his first great work, *Either/Or*, he stresses the distinction between aesthetic and ethical existence. The aesthetic self lives only in the immediacies surrounding it, essentially only a product of forces outside itself—there are echoes here of Kant's rejection of the "pathological will." The ethical self makes clear, honest decisions. He writes that "the choice itself is decisive for the content of the personality, through the choice the personality immerses itself in the thing chosen, and when it does not choose it withers away in consumption."[25] Not to choose is, ultimately, to have others choose for one, and thereby to lose one's self. Kierkegaard suggests that the content of the choice—the thing chosen—is secondary to the fact of choice itself. Better to choose wrongly than not to choose at all. Not to choose is to surrender one's personhood. To choose, even though wrongly, is to open oneself to the possibilities of correction. He writes,

He who would define his life task ethically [rather than aesthetically] has ordinarily not so considerable a selection to choose from; on the other hand, the act of choice has far more importance for him. . . . [I]n making a choice it is not so much a question of choosing the right as of the energy, the earnestness, the pathos with which one chooses. Thereby the personality announces its inner infinity, and thereby, in turn, the personality is consolidated. Therefore, even if a man were to choose the wrong, he will nevertheless discover, precisely by reason of the energy with which he chose, that he had chosen the wrong. For the choice being made with the whole inwardness of his personality, his nature is purified and he himself brought into immediate relation to the eternal Power whose omnipresence interpenetrates the whole of existence.[26]

"This transfiguration," he adds, "is never attained by that man who chooses merely aesthetically."

But there is a higher stage than either the aesthetic or the ethical: the religious. In a discussion of the "teleological suspension of the ethical," Kierkegaard contemplates the possibility of a religious ground to set aside even the clear dictates of morality. Employing the Old Testament story of Abraham's aborted sacrifice of Isaac, Kierkegaard notes that Abraham is prepared to kill his own son, not for the sake of some higher ethical good—some greater approximation to the universal—which we all might applaud, but in response to God that is beyond the ethical. From a purely ethical standpoint we are appalled by such an unthinkable deed. But in a way that is itself the measure of the authenticity of the act: It cannot have been contemplated for any reason other than faith. And thus, Kierkegaard reports—really against Kant—that "faith is precisely this paradox, that the individual as the particular is higher than the universal, is justified over against it, is not subordinate but superior." But this is only because "the universal becomes the individual who as the particular is superior to the universal, *inasmuch as the individual as the particular stands in an absolute relation to the absolute.*"[27]

Language such as this is not easily deciphered! But has not Kierkegaard here made a classic Hegelian move? The individual at a purely aesthetic level cannot be affirmed because he or she lives only in immediate experience in which choice (and therefore personhood) is missing. The contradiction to this, the ethical person, chooses all right, but the choice is for the universal in which the person as individual is lost. But in the higher "synthesis," the religious person, as individual, becomes higher than the universal through his or her relation to the religious absolute. And yet, it is not accurate in Kierkegaardian terms to treat this as a higher level of ethics, for it is a suspension of the ethical. He sees it both as risk and temptation. Such faith cannot be explicated, or "mediated" as Kierkegaard would say, by reason. He writes that "to him who follows the narrow way of faith no one can give counsel, him no one can understand. Faith is a miracle, and yet no man is excluded from it; for that in which all human life is unified is passion, and faith is a passion."[28]

Toward the end of his life Kierkegaard engaged in a sharp, even brutal polemic against "Christendom." His *Attack Upon Christendom* was a ruthless exposure of the hypocrisies of church leadership and religious culture. The essence of the attack was his claim that the church was utterly unfaithful to New Testament Christianity, which is the only real Christianity. New Testament Christianity calls upon Christians to take up their cross, to be self-sacrificial, to take no thought of their own temporal well-being in their obedience to Christ. The church rather exists as a system of temporal benefits which, while mouthing the message of the New Testament, is exactly the contrary. He writes: "So the way has now become a different one, not that of the New Testament: in humiliation, hated, forsaken, persecuted, condemned to suffer in this world—no, the way is: admired, acclaimed, crowned with garlands, accorded the accolade of knighthood as the reward of a brilliant career."[29] The state, by making Christianity official, has in fact greatly hindered real Christianity. Its one thousand clergy—whom he refers to as state officials—depend upon a truncated Christianity for their economic existence. So "the State employs 1000 officials who, under the name of preaching Christianity . . . are pecuniarily interested in: (a) having men call themselves Christians (the bigger the flock of sheep the better), assume the name of being Christians; and (b) in having it stop there, so that they do not learn to know what Christianity truly is."[30] Christianity, "which came into the world as the truth men die for, has now become the truth upon which they live, with family and steady promotion."[31] "Christendom" represents, "not Christianity but a prodigious illusion." In order to introduce real Christianity the illusion would first have to be done away with, even though this might first appear to be an attack on Christianity itself.[32] So, he concludes, "nothing is more dangerous to true Christianity, nothing more contrary to its nature, than to get men to assume lightmindedly the name of Christian, to teach them to think meanly of what it is to be a Christian, as if it were something one is as a matter of course."[33]

While the situation to which Kierkegaard immediately referred, the established state church of Denmark, was somewhat unique, it would be a mistake to take his "attack upon Christendom" as only a criticism of the hypocrisies and self-contradictions of the church and its leadership in that setting. For all churches, even the most sectarian, have systems of reward and penalty which can appeal to non-Christian or even un-Christian motives. Kierkegaard has drawn attention to a more universal dilemma: For Christianity to exist in the social world it must have identifiable institutional structure and continuity and it must be able to influence political, economic, and social decisions and policies—and these institutions and policies invariably offer rewards quite apart from simple, self-sacrificial love. But to offer such rewards is to turn away from the central call of the gospel, which is to this life of simple, self-sacrificial love. Kierkegaard's response to this dilemma is to insist upon the latter and to treat the institutional accoutrements of "Christendom" as impediments the church must shed if it is to exist as New Testament Christianity.

In the end, however, it is a mistake to treat Kierkegaard systematically, as though his work were fully rational and consistent. As we have seen, his emphasis upon the radical particularity of the self in its faith decision precludes ultimate reliance upon abstract concepts about the self and the faith. The "scandal" of particularity in the work of Kierkegaard is the recognition that rational concepts cannot ultimately be trusted and that seemingly inconsistent "particulars" can be embraced simultaneously. That is a scandal in face of the mind's insistence upon consistency, but Kierkegaard considers it more faithful to the ultimate truth. Since the dominant minds of the nineteenth century were, on the whole, very committed to rationalism in one form or another, it is not surprising that the greatest influence of Kierkegaard had to await a quite different cultural climate in the twentieth century.

Frederick Denison Maurice

F. D. Maurice (1805–1872) is of special interest in a survey of this kind because of his explicit interest in relating Christianity to social problems. In his *The Kingdom of Christ*, Maurice voices the frustration of the churchman who encounters "one of our awful manufacturing districts." The first impression he will have is of "the sense of his own utter inadequacy to deal with the mass of evil which he meets there." Nevertheless, the churchman "is there, and he knows that there is One who cares for this mass of living beings infinitely more than he does."[34] Maurice is clear that things can be done. He does not accept the more sweeping conceptions of original sin that consider improvements in the human condition problematic. The "Kingdom of Christ" is not simply a premillennial perfection that must await the second coming of Christ. Maurice "cannot conceive a darker or more dreadful vision than this."[35] Rather, he wishes to proclaim that this reality is already present in human history:

If it be meant by outward and visible, that Christ's dominion will not be merely over the heart and spirit of man, over that which directly connects him with God and the unseen world, but over all his human relations, his earthly associations, over the policy of rulers, over nature and over art, then, I say, this is as much the truth now as it ever can be in any future period. This dominion has been asserting itself, has been making itself felt, for these eighteen centuries.[36]

His quarrel with those who speak of the second coming is "with a system which has tended to prevent men from acknowledging it; to make them think lightly of their present responsibilities, to give them a fantastic habit of speaking respecting the course of God's providence in the world, as if it signified nothing now, but was only leading to something hereafter."[37]

So, this nineteenth-century Anglican theologian recognized the presence of massive social evil and affirmed the responsibility and capacity of Christians to act effectively in dealing with it. What are they to do?

Maurice is hesitant about secular measures designed to reach people through changes in external circumstances. While, for instance, he is appreciative of the English reformer Robert Owen and the French utopian Henri de Saint-Simon, Maurice faults them for abandoning religious faith. Without the spiritual principle, every reform is empty.[38] The point is all the clearer, he feels, in the case of Benthamite utilitarianism, with its empty mathematical formula of the greatest good for the largest number. (The latter he continued to criticize thirty years later, noting that there is an intrinsic contradiction between that formula and the moral will of the individuals who are supposed to implement it.[39]) And he is deeply critical of Rousseau and the endeavor of the French Revolution to reconstitute society on universal lines utterly ignoring the unique aspects of national histories. He is even skeptical about democracy and the ideas of universal suffrage that were exciting the Utilitarians and others during this period. And he would not have Christians investing themselves in parties.

His own prescriptions are not very sweeping. For the churchman it comes down to what can be done in his parish. He writes:

> a churchman, such as I have supposed, would be both compelled by his circumstances, and urged by his principles, to change these convictions into action, by enlisting all the wealthier inhabitants of his parish in different services and occupations for the benefit of their inferiors. I am unwilling to enlarge upon this subject; first, because my practical ignorance makes me unfit to offer any suggestions upon it; and, secondly, because I am certain that our English political wisdom, guided by Catholic feeling, is already doing much in many parts of this land, in the accomplishment of such a design.[40]

Far superior, he feels, "than all societies constructed upon a party model" is one that "is held together by sacramental bonds, and is moving under the direction of an appointed pastor."[41]

Still, this same F. D. Maurice is known to history as the leading figure in the Christian socialism movement of Victorian England! How are we to understand the apparent contradiction between his mild, even parochial designs for change, and his plunging into the turbulent waters of nineteenth-century socialism?

In part, it is a question of definition. "Socialism" to Maurice did not mean the utopian schemes of an Owen or a Saint-Simon, much less the scientific socialism of his contemporaries Marx and Engels. It did not entail public ownership of the means of production and public systems of distribution. Rather, his socialism was an expression of economic cooperation, rather vaguely developed. Some, indeed, in the Christian socialist movement were unhappy about his lack of deeper ideological grounding. Why, then, use the name "socialist"? In part, it was because he and the other Christian socialists were genuinely critical of the laissez-faire versions of political economy that had gained ascendancy with the Industrial Revolution. He evidently wished to take head-on the criticisms of those who dismissed any movement in behalf of working people as socialistic.[42] He remarked that his desire was to engage the "unsocial Christians and the unchristian Socialists."[43] It is evident, then, that for Maurice socialism meant simply a cooperative spirit for addressing the economic and social problem within the kingdom of Christ.

An interesting historical footnote on the movement is supplied by no less a source than Marx and Engels's *Communist Manifesto*, where it is said that "Christian Socialism is but the holy water with which the priest consecrates the heart-burnings of the aristocrat." Maurice would not at all have accepted the structural conceptions of Marxism; his failure to deal substantively with questions of structure and power is not to his credit. He may, however, have perceived a more transcendent dimension of real socialism that the "unChristian" socialists were unable to grasp.

Albrecht Ritschl

Arguably one of the two greatest systematic theologians of the nineteenth century (along with Schleiermacher), Albrecht Ritschl (1822–1889) was indebted to both scriptural and philosophical sources in the grounding of his ethics. In his use of scripture, Ritschl was clearly influenced by the nineteenth-century beginnings of modern biblical scholarship. That more scientific and critical approach to scripture will not allow him to use simple proof-texts to establish theological or ethical viewpoints, and it leads him to be critical of traditional methods of exegesis. The full account of that is beyond our purposes here, but it is interesting to note his own summary of how the theologian or Christian ethicist should use the Bible:

> Now exegesis itself, certainly, deals with many particular passages in such a way as to reduce the cognate symbolical expressions they contain to one conception of the greatest possible clearness. For in part exegesis must view the particular in the light of its relationship to everything which resembles it, in part it has to fill up the chasm between our way of thinking and the Israelites' symbolical manner of speech, in part its task is to clear away false ideas forced upon certain Biblical symbols by exegetical tradition.[44]

Each passage should be developed in relation to "the religious ideas furnished by Biblical Theology." But even that is not sufficient. For the truth of a particular point to be clear, it must be understood through a systematic theology in which it can be related to the whole. This frank acknowledgment of the human and cultural limitations of the biblical canon is as noteworthy as the affirmation of the Bible as a deposit of the fundamental theological ideas upon which theology depends.

Ritschl considered the kingdom or sovereignty of God to be the fundamental principle on the basis of which all other aspects of Christian theology should be interpreted. He accepted the writings of the Old Testament and of the apostle Paul as important (the first as preface to the New Testament, the second for its disavowal of legalism). But the heart of the New Testament is in Jesus himself and the teachings of Jesus contained in the Gospel narratives. The idea of the Christian religion "is reached by an orderly reproduction of the thought of Christ and the apostles."[45] The center of the thought of Christ and the apostles is the kingdom of God.

What is the character of that kingdom? In contrast to the Old Testament, where the kingdom is defined as a national commonwealth, the New Testament Christian "Kingdom of God is represented as the common end of God and the elect community, in such a way that it rises above the national limits of nationality and becomes the moral society of nations."[46] Christianity thus "shows itself to be the perfect moral religion." In a characteristic passage Ritschl writes that

> Christ made the universal moral Kingdom of God His end, and thus He came to know and decide for that kind of redemption which He achieved through the maintenance of fidelity in His calling and of His blessed fellowship with God through suffering unto death.[47]

Ritschl criticizes previous Protestant theology for overemphasizing the redemptive aspect of the faith "while injustice is done to the ethical interpretation of Christianity through the idea of the Kingdom of God."[48]

For Ritschl, the foundation metaphors for the kingdom of God are the "Fatherhood of God and the brotherhood of man." The former is Jesus' own characteristic revelation of God, while the latter is a consequence of our being children of God. Accepted by God as his children, we are redeemed. But this is not just a new spiritual state of being. It is our incorporation into the kingdom. God's grace, in that kingdom, enables us to participate through loving relationships with others.

> The Christian designation of God as our Father, it is true, comprises also the notion of His Lordship over the Kingdom of God. For under that title we pray to God that His Kingdom may come. Now, love to one's fellow-men is a deduction from the highest principle which dominates all moral action, namely, regard to the Kingdom of God. Therefore the impulse to such love stands also in relation to the idea of God as Father.[49]

In the Kingdom of God, he concludes, every human being is understood to be "worth more than the whole world."[50]

Taking the ethic as a whole, we may have here, in Ritschl, a theological replay of Kant's conception of the intrinsic worth of the human persons in the Kantian "kingdom of ends."[51] Certainly the general tenor of Ritschl's ideas about the intrinsic worth and freedom of moral beings at least illustrates the enormous influence Kant's views cast upon the nineteenth century. In any event, Ritschl's kingdom of God is a kingdom of love, defined by mutual respect for the inestimable worth of every person and protected by institutions of family and state.[52] These ideas, loosely gathered under the catchphrase "Fatherhood of God and brotherhood of man," were destined to play a very important role in the social gospel movement and other manifestations of liberal Protestantism in the final decades of the nineteenth century and the first half of the twentieth.

One important intellectual conduit for Ritschl's ideas was the German scholar Adolf Harnack (1851–1930). Harnack summarized the meaning of Christianity, contained in Jesus' teaching, as: "Firstly, the kingdom of God and its coming. Secondly, God the Father and the infinite value of the human soul. Thirdly, the higher righteousness and the commandment of love."[53] Such ideas were to find expression in the preeminent voice of the American social gospel movement, Walter Rauschenbusch, whose work we will consider in a later chapter.

There is an irony in the work of Ritschl and Harnack that we must pause to note. The ethic of both was dominated by the teachings of the historical Jesus, especially the teaching about the kingdom of God. At the same time, both played an important role in the development of critical use of scripture.

But biblical criticism was shortly to undermine confidence in the historicity of the portrait of Jesus presupposed in their ethic. Specific words and events attributed to Jesus were more and more subject to criticism, especially to the criticism that they were an interpretation by the early church or even that they were a culturally determined intrepretation by theologians like Ritschl and Harnack![54]

Leo Tolstoy

The kingdom of God was also the dominant moral theme in the writing of the great Russian novelist Leo Tolstoy (1828–1910). But his use of the term is very different from that of a Ritschl or a Harnack. Tolstoy was neither a professional theologian nor a New Testament scholar, though he was a Russian Orthodox Christian whose ideas on Christian love can be claimed by the Orthodox as a legitimate expression of the meaning of love in that tradition. His earlier life, during which he became a world-famous novelist, was not even—as he would later say—Christian. In his spiritual autobiography,[55] Tolstoy speaks of a deep spiritual crisis, in which he experienced the emptiness of life despite his world renown. His moment of illumination came upon rereading the Sermon on the Mount. There, encountering the words "Do not resist one who is evil" (Matt. 5:39), Tolstoy suddenly realized that the radical demand of the gospel meant exactly what it said and that the positive ethic of Jesus is the only possible way of incorporating the Christian gospel into actual existence. The commandment should be fully, precisely, and literally obeyed. Resistance to evil implies compromise with evil, but Christians must live entirely—without compromise—on the positive plane of love.

In a denunciation of the church that might be considered extreme even by Kierkegaard, Tolstoy asserts that "the churches have not only never united, but have always been one of the chief causes of the disunion of men, of the hatred of one another, of wars, slaughters, inquisitions, nights of St. Bartholomew, and so forth, and the churches never serve as mediators between men and God. . . . [T]hey put up dead forms in the place of God."[56] We must choose between the Sermon on the Mount and the Council of Nicaea, the former representing the pure gospel of Jesus, the latter the distortions of the church.

The teachings of Jesus represent, to Tolstoy, the liberation of humanity from the brute force of animal nature—with its violence and self-centeredness—to "the consciousness of a filial relation to God."[57] Tolstoy believes in the ideal and possibility of human moral perfection. He writes:

Christ's teaching differs from previous teachings in that it guides men, not by external rules, but by the internal consciousness of the possibility of attaining divine perfection. And in man's soul there are not moderated rules of justice and of philanthropy, but the ideal of the complete, infinite, divine perfection. Only the striving after this perfection deflects the direction of man's life from the animal condition toward the divine, to the extent to which this is impossible in this life. . . . To lower the demands of the ideal means not only to diminish the possibility of perfection, but to destroy the ideal itself.[58]

This ideal of perfection will become the basis of human social life. "The time will come, and is already at hand, when the Christian foundations of life, equality, brotherhood of men, community of possession, non-resistance to evil, will become as natural and as simple as the foundations of the family, the social, and the political life now appear to us."[59]

Tolstoy identifies coercive human institutions as the major constraint upon the bursting forth of the new consciousness of love and its capacity to govern human life. The state, with its coercive instruments of armies, police, and prisons, is the basic impediment. If the state and the instruments of coercion can be abolished, the new reality of love in the kingdom of God will be free to burst forth.

Tolstoy, therefore, specifically rejects any use of the state by Christians to reach moral ends. He acknowledges that "the defenders of the social concept of life generally try to mix up the concept of power, that is, of violence, with that of spiritual influence," but he argues that "this admixture is quite impossible."[60] A spiritual influence must coincide with a person's very desires, but coercive power is imposed upon people contrary to their desires. How, he asks, can we expect people to be drawn into a society of love by coercion? It is a self-contradiction. Violence "does not protect humanity, but, on the contrary, deprives humanity of the one possibility of a true protection through the establishment and diffusion of the Christian public opinion as regards the existing order of life."[61] Thus, "only with the abolition of violence will Christian public opinion cease to be corrupt, and receive the possibility of an unimpeded diffusion, and men will not direct their strength toward what they do not need, but toward the one spiritual force which moves them."[62]

One of Tolstoy's happy discoveries, in the responses of a worldwide readership of his *My Religion*, was that the New England Quakers and others had long preached and practiced what he had discovered for himself in the reading of the Sermon on the Mount. He found this further evidence of the sweeping force of the new social consciousness in the world. Tolstoy cannot be charged with ignoring evil nor with assuming that nonviolent techniques will always be successful. Nor can he be credited with pioneering the methods of nonviolent resistance that were to become so important as a method of peaceful social change in the twentieth century, although his writing was to play a part in the development of such methods. His work is also noteworthy as a powerful expression of Christian pacifism and anarchism.

Ernst Troeltsch: Preface to Twentieth-Century Christian Ethics

Reference has been made from time to time, in the present volume, to Ernst Troeltsch's seminal work, *The Social Teaching of the Christian Churches*.[63] In writing that massive history of Christian social ethics, Troeltsch did more than chronicle the development of ideas and institutions; he laid the foundations for twentieth-century social ethics and sociology of religion.

Ernst Troeltsch (1865–1923) was drawn into that study as he grappled with the tension between the Marxist interpretation of religion and the dogmatic claims of Christian theology. The former treated religion as the effect of deeper socioeconomic forces in human history; the latter regarded the object of faith as a "given" that is more the cause than the effect of such forces. In a brief autobiographical sketch, Troeltsch recounts his developing interest:

> The problem was now stated something like this: to what extent are the appearance, the development, the modification, and the modern impasse of Christianity sociologically conditioned, and to what extent is Christianity itself an actively formative sociological principle? . . . [N]o one who had grasped this problem could any longer think of the history of Christianity purely in terms of the history of dogma or the history of ideas. This time I dropped every programmatic preparation and instead of merely getting ready to, I actually plowed into an indescribably laborious task. The invitation to review a miserable book by Nathusius on *The Social Task of the Evangelical Church* made me conscious of my ignorance, and ours, about these matters, and instead of writing a review I wrote a book of nearly a thousand pages.[64]

Troeltsch's monumental work, while not ultimately resolving the tension, explored the interaction between fundamental Christian ideas and the social-political-economic forces of succeeding epochs of Western history. The study helped illuminate the power of religious ideas in shaping history; it also illustrated the immense influence of historical forces in the shaping of religious ideas and institutions. Like his famous sociological collaborator, Max Weber, Troeltsch was interested in the way historical forces were limited and shaped by dominant religious conceptions and, in reverse, by the way those forces helped determine which religious conceptions would prove dominant.

Troeltsch's study makes one important point very clearly: The very structure of the church is itself an interpretation of Christian teaching. The church teaches by what it is, not only by what it says. Christian ideas have taken three recurrent forms through Christian history, in his view. (1) The "Church-type" conceives of an ecclesiastical unity of all civilization as the logical outcome of Christian faith. Its vision of Christianity is of an all-encompassing civilization, formed by the faith, in which every aspect of life would gain Christian interpretation and sanctification. Individual Christians would be born into the faith, conducted by the faith through life, and ushered through the portals of death by the faith. That view of Christian organization is best exemplified, in his view, by the medieval church. (2) The "Sect-type" understands the Christian community as the much more limited company of those truly committed Christians who are prepared to pay the full price of discipleship. The world outside this community is, in this view, essentially fallen. The Christian community must strive to redeem as many as possible from their fallenness while serving as a witness to the gospel, a light shining in the darkness. (3) Mysticism, which views all human institutions (including churches and sects) as fairly superficial expressions of faith, regards faith experience as a direct, intense encounter with God.

In light of Troeltsch's work, it is clear that the church, as social teacher, is not simply a "given." The church that does the teaching is also a part of the message being taught.

The three types are not understood by Troeltsch as being perfectly expressed anywhere in history, but they are recurring tendencies, and by understanding them we can better appreciate the complexity of actual Christian teaching and institutional life.

Troeltsch's work proved to be extraordinarily influential in twentieth-century sociology of religion, which endlessly refined and applied his typology. But it was even more important in the development of Christian social ethics. Most of the Christian moral thinkers we will consider later in this volume were greatly influenced by Troeltsch's work.

15

NINETEENTH-CENTURY SLAVERY AND FEMINIST CONTROVERSIES

Special note should be taken in a history of Christian ethics of two significant controversies of the nineteenth century. The slavery controversy began earlier than the nineteenth century and its legacy of racism continued later. But slavery itself was essentially resolved as an issue in Christian ethics during that century. The feminist controversy began, as a major issue, during that period, though its resolution has had to come later.

Both controversies point to significant issues; both relate to the oppression and lower status of large numbers of people. From that standpoint, the human dimensions are compelling. However, both struggles also involve very deep theoretical issues in the development of Christian ethics. In the first place, both raise the question of Christian use of scripture. Prima facie, a case can be made, from scripture, that slavery is wholly acceptable to Christians, as an institution, if it is not in fact a part of God's providence. During the nineteenth-century controversy substantial numbers of Christians took exactly that position. A similar case can be made for the subordination of women, with various proof-texts marshaled to buttress the point. In both cases, the prima facie scriptural witness enjoyed many centuries of support from practice and tradition. The interesting thing is that challenges to slavery and the subordination of women had, at the same time, to question a literalist interpretation of scripture—and it had to be done in a theological context in which scripture was taken very seriously. In effect, the Christian abolitionists and feminists had to distinguish between what scripture "says" (in the proof-texts) and what it "means" (in its central core of meaning). That is a very important methodological move, especially in predominantly

Protestant Christian cultures where scripture enjoyed almost exclusive authority in matters of faith and morals. To be sure, the nineteenth century was also the seedbed of modern critical biblical scholarship. The debates over slavery show little evidence of being influenced by that, and while some of the feminist spokespersons addressed biblical issues in a fairly sophisticated way, critical biblical scholarship was hardly the source of the feminist movement. It may be the case that the contradiction between the plainer words of scripture and the growing moral sensitivities of the time had as much influence on the development of biblical scholarship as the other way around. In any event, these two great controversies led to greater sophistication in the use of the Bible as moral authority.

The Church Struggle Over Slavery

We have already noticed the rejection of slavery by Quakers, as early as the seventeenth century, and by the eighteenth-century Wesleyans. The Quaker leader John Woolman (1720–1772) became convinced that it was utterly wrong to hold these "fellow creatures" as slaves and sought, with considerable success, to persuade his fellow Quakers to refrain from buying slaves. Long before the development of the abolitionist movement, Woolman set the tone for a quiet and effective Quaker witness on the subject. Woolman's journals reveal the progressive development of his conscience on the subject, concluding that the easy rationalizations concerning slaveholding could have no weight before "that awful Being who respecteth not persons nor colors."[1]

That had also been a clear issue to John Wesley, who had, almost in his dying breath, referred to American slavery as "the vilest that ever saw the sun." Wesley's encouragement of the movement to ban the slave trade helped set the tone for antislavery policies by early American Methodism—even after the break between American and British Methodism occasioned by the Revolutionary War and despite the fact that the major development of Methodism was in the South. The Methodist Conference of 1780 held that "slavery is contrary to the laws of God, man, and nature, and hurtful to society; contrary to the dictates of conscience and pure religion" and required its preachers to pledge to free any slaves they might hold.[2] The Conference of 1784—which formally organized American Methodism—adopted a declaration on slavery stating that "we view it as contrary to the golden law of God, on which hang all the law and the prophets, and the inalienable rights of mankind, as well as every principle of the Revolution, to hold in the deepest abasement . . . so many souls that are all capable of the image of God." Acknowledging their duty to find "some effectual method to extirpate this abomination from among us," the conference required all Methodist slaveholders to emancipate their slaves within one year and held that thereafter slaveholders could not become members.[3]

These remarkable statements paralleled to some extent the views of other religious bodies and even such political leaders as Jefferson and Washington. Such antislavery sentiment might have prevailed had not economics intervened. But the invention of the cotton gin, the development of vast cotton-growing plantations in the South, and the reciprocal development of textile production in Britain and New England vastly increased the real dependency of both America and Britain upon the slave labor supply. During the early decades of the nineteenth century the churches grew very rapidly in the American South. But, despite the earlier pronouncements against slavery, the winning of the South for Christ did not mean the winning of the South for the antislavery cause. Instead, it meant the incorporation within the churches of ever-increasing numbers of people who were first economically, then morally committed to slavery as an institution. The stage was set for a great church struggle over this issue. The issue was joined especially in the 1830s and 1840s, when the abolitionist movement confronted Christian proslavery sentiment most directly.

In one sense, the proslavery Christians had the stronger arguments— if one accepted their proof-texting method of arriving at biblical moral teaching. They could, and did, refer to the classic New Testament texts (e.g., "Slaves, obey in everything those who are your earthly masters, not with eyeservice, as men-pleasers, but in singleness of heart, fearing the Lord"; Col. 3:22). Such texts were preached, with equal fervor, to plantation slaves and to northern abolitionists. Biblical statements and precedents about slavery itself were supplemented by a more problematical effort to gain biblical sanction for racism. The Genesis story of Noah's curse upon Ham was invoked as evidence of God's curse upon Africans to become thenceforth the hewers of wood and drawers of water. So God had both ordained slavery as an institution and determined who, racially speaking, the slaves should be.

Proslavery tracts and speeches also emphasized that slavery was best for the slaves and that it was, in any case, a good deal better than the exploitation of wage labor in the North and in England. One apologist asks, rhetorically, "Have our slaves then . . . been wronged, in being raised, through the institution of slavery, to a condition of moral, intellectual, and civil improvement, and to a state of protection, comfort, and happiness never elsewhere . . . known?"[4] Another compares the care given slaves with that provided free laborers:

Employers of free laborers, like the riders of hired horses, try to get the most possible work out of them for the least hire. They boast of the low rates at which they procure labor, and still hold up their heads in society, uncensured and unreproved. No slaveholder was ever so brutal as to boast of the low wages he paid his slaves, to pride himself on feeding and clothing them badly, neglecting the young, the aged, the sick, and infirm.[5]

Occasionally, even, there would be a tacit acknowledgment that the sheer economic interests of the Christian slaveholders had something to do with their moral fervor in defense of the system. William A. Booth, a southern Methodist layperson, interpreted the conflict between North and South in his church as the North's opposition "to a certain species of property held throughout the whole South, upon which the greater portion of its wealth is based." The magnitude of the conflict was related to the fact that "the love of property is deep."[6]

The abolitionist side of the controversy did not concede the authority of scripture to those apologists, but it took the biblical law of love, not the proof-texts, to be the true expression of the Bible on the subject of slavery. A leading Presbyterian abolitionist exclaimed that

> the whole Bible is opposed to slavery. The sacred volume is one grand scheme of benevolence. Beams of love and mercy emanate from every page, while the voice of justice denounces the oppressor, and speaks to his awful doom.[7]

Charles G. Finney, whose evangelical revival corresponded almost exactly to the period of the controversy over slavery, understood the abolitionist implications of Christian evangelicalism. He understood slavery to be sin. "We will speak of it," he wrote in 1836, "and bear our testimony against it, and pray over it, and complain of it to God and man.—Heaven shall know and the world shall know, and hell shall know, that we protest against the sin and will continue to rebuke it, till it is broken up."[8]

Impatient with the reluctance of many mainline Christian denominations to deal forthrightly with the slavery question, groups of antislavery Christians broke away from those churches to form new, explicitly antislavery denominations. This development is of interest, not only to church institutional history, but as evidence that many Christians were giving the issue *status confessionis*. That is, being wrong on the issue was not simply a sin or error, it was to be outside the faith. The new Wesleyan Methodist Connection asserted, for instance, that "the practice of endorsing the Christian character of slaveholders by fellowshipping them as Christians and treating them in any way as the children of God, is giving the most direct encouragement and support to slavery."[9] The Free Presbyterians similarly held that "no person holding slaves, or advocating the rightful-ness of slaveholding, can be a member of this body."[10] The "Comeouter" movement, encouraged by the abolitionist leadership, developed as a way of sharpening this total withdrawal of recognition of Christians supporting slavery. Individuals as well as groups were encouraged to leave, or "come out" of, churches perceived as soft on the slavery question in as public a way as possible. One illustration of this is a public letter by a Henry C. Wright explaining why he was leaving his Massachusetts congregation:

> I am deeply and sorrowfully impressed with the belief that by your opposi-tion to the Anti-Slavery enterprise, and by your silence in regard to the wrongs of the slave and the guilt of the slaveholder, you, as a church, are doing more to make our holy religion the scorn and execration of mankind than all that Jew, or Heathen, or Infidel, ever did or can do. While you thus continue by your silence or otherwise to sustain this system of wrong and outrage—I cannot regard you as a christian church: and I DO HEREBY RENOUNCE YOU AS A CHRISTIAN CHURCH.[11]

The ethical reasoning underlying the antislavery Christian movement was biblical, in the general sense referred to above. It also invoked other strands of moral thought. One notes, for instance, the easy incorporation of the Enlightenment doctrine of inalienable rights and "every principle of the Revolution" into the Methodist Conference declaration of 1784. It is remarkable that even the evangelical Charles G. Finney drew, for his moral reasoning, from utilitarian views. He writes that "you should regard your neighbor's happiness according to its real value, and the happiness of all mankind, according to the relative importance of each one's individual hap-piness, and the happiness of the whole, as much above your own, as the aggregate amount of theirs is more valuable than yours, is right in itself."[12] And his appeal to the "reasonableness and utility of benevolence" as "the exercise of the same regard to, and desire for their happiness, as we have for our own"[13] seems to display the fingerprints not only of utilitarianism but of Joseph Butler's rationalism.

Voices of the oppressed also came to the surface in the slavery contro-versy. Some of this was in the schisms caused by racism in the northern churches, as when the African Methodist Episcopal Church and the African Methodist Episcopal Zion Church broke away from the Methodist Episcopal Church.

One of the great voices of the slaves themselves was that of the former slave Frederick Douglass (1817–1895). Douglass was not, of course, a theologian or spokesperson for the church. Nor was he restrained in his criticisms of churches and church leaders for temporizing with the institution of slavery.

Nevertheless, he had a deeply formative involvement with the church. His great appeal as an abolitionist lecturer, writer, and editor was essentially an ethical one. Like many others in the antislavery movement, his fundamental ethic represented a mixture of theological, rational, and practical values. An address in England in 1848 contrasts the Christianity that was identified with slavery with the Christianity that called slavery under judgment:

> I love the religion of our blessed Savior. I love that religion that comes from above, in the "wisdom of God, which is first pure, then peaceable, gentle, and easy to be entreated, full of mercy and good fruits, without partiality and without hypocrisy." . . . I love that religion that is based upon the glorious principle, of love to God and love to man; which makes its followers do unto others as they themselves would be done by. If you demand liberty to yourself, it says, grant it to your neighbors. If you claim a right to think for yourself, it says, allow your neighbors the same right. If you claim to act for yourself, it says, allow your neighbors the same right. It is because I love this religion that I hate the slaveholding, the woman-whipping, the mind darkening, the soul-destroying religion that exists in the southern states of America. It is because I regard the one as good, and pure, and holy, that I cannot but regard the other as bad, corrupt, and wicked.[14]

Slavery is, he concludes, "a system of wrong, so blinding to all around, so hardening to the heart, so corrupting to the morals, so deleterious to religion, so sapping to all the principles of justice in its immediate vicinity, that the community surrounding it lacks the moral stamina necessary to its removal." He appeals to the British to help in eliminating that system for "no one nation is equal to its removal. It requires the humanity of Christianity, the morality of the world to remove it."[15]

Initially Douglass was convinced that moral appeal was the best way to deal with the slave system, although even in his earliest years as lecturer and writer he could voice scathing criticism of the U.S. political system for its support of slavery. Later, in the years just before the American Civil War, Douglass abandoned hope in peaceful efforts to influence change. In a defense of John Brown, he wrote in 1859 that "he has attacked slavery with the weapons precisely adapted to bring it to the death. Moral considerations have long since been exhausted upon slaveholders. It is in vain to reason with them." He concludes that "slavery is a system of brute force. It shields itself behind *might*, rather than right. It must be met with its own weapons."[16] During the war, Douglass played a substantial role in recruiting African-American soldiers and as an occasional consultant with President Lincoln.

Frederick Douglass was noteworthy in at least two other respects. He saw the connections between the slavery issue and a number of other issues, including especially the equal status of women, which he supported with vigor and insight. And, unlike some within the antislavery movement, Douglass made a connection between that movement and respect for the full equality of persons regardless of color. He sought both freedom and equality.

The slavery controversy culminated in the secession of the southern states and the American Civil War—the most murderous conflict during the century between the Napoleonic wars and World War I. The controversy had, in more ways than one, prepared the way for the national division and war. The slavery controversy led to north/south division in several of the mainline denominations, a fact illustrating not only the depth of the moral disagreement but also providing important precedent for the political division and war yet to come.[17] Moreover, it contributed to the prevailing sense in both North and South that this was a cause worthy of resort to arms.

The war itself brought the debate over slavery to an end. For the first time in more than eighteen hundred years it was possible to say that this was now essentially a closed issue. The racist underpinning of much of the defense of American slavery continued with substantial theological support well into the twentieth century, for the debate had been about freedom, not about equality or unity in human relationships.

The Feminist Movement

The nineteenth-century feminist movement also had important precedents in the history of Christian ethics, as we have seen. The biblical legacy included passages easily interpreted in support of the equality of women along with accounts of women whose faith and contributions were exemplary. Christian history, as we have seen, also recorded the lives of women saints and martyrs whose active leadership was acknowledged freely. Even the political history of Christian nations had included examples of outstanding women leaders, ranging from the French Joan of Arc to Queen Elizabeth I of England.

Nevertheless, the overwhelming weight of Western Christian history was against, not for, the equality of women in home, church, and society. The same scriptures that supported slavery also admonished women to remain in their place, respecting the governance of men.

The origin of the nineteenth-century American feminist movement was closely related to abolitionism, although some public discussion began as early as the 1790s. Some of the earliest feminist leaders, such as Angelina and Sarah Grimké, Elizabeth Cady Stanton, Susan B. Anthony, and Lucretia Mott, were deeply involved in antislavery activity, and the abolitionist leaders William Lloyd Garrison and Frederick Douglass were outspoken supporters of the feminist cause. For women, experience in the antislavery movement helped sharpen skills in public leadership while also giving a clearer sense of the importance of human rights and institutional power. In a later time, it might be said to have "radicalized" them.

Indeed, events in 1839 and 1840 had exactly this radicalizing effect. In 1840 a split occurred within the American Anti-Slavery Society that helped precipitate more intentional efforts at organization of the feminist movement. Nearly a decade later, in 1848, feminism attained both organizational and ideological focus at the Seneca Falls Convention. That meeting and its declaration were followed by subsequent conventions and public statements contributing to a growing national debate.

The Seneca Falls Declaration itself provided the keynote of the feminist movement by outlining the "repeated injuries and usurpations on the part of man toward woman, having in direct object the establishment of an absolute tyranny over her."[18] The list of injuries included the following points:

> He has never permitted her to exercise her inalienable right to the elective franchise.
>
> He has compelled her to submit to laws, in the formation of which she had no voice.
>
> He has withheld from her rights which are given to the most ignorant and degraded men—both natives and foreigners.
>
> He has made her, if married, in the eye of the law, civilly dead.
>
> He has taken from her all right in property, even to the wages she earns.
>
> He has made her, morally, an irresponsible being. . . . In the covenant of marriage, she is compelled to promise obedience to her husband, he becoming, to all intents and purposes, her master.
>
> He allows her in Church, as well as State, but a subordinate position, claiming Apostolic authority for her exclusion from the ministry, and, with some exceptions, from any public participation in the affairs of the Church.[19]

The document, which had been drafted basically by Elizabeth Cady Stanton, was patterned after the U.S. Declaration of Independence, not only in its form but in the moral grounding of its appeal to equality. For it refers to "the laws of nature and of nature's God" and holds "these truths to be self-evident: that all men and women are created equal; that they are endowed by their Creator with certain inalienable rights."[20]

The feminist movement could not ground its position wholly on these Enlightenment (and originally Stoic) ideas, however. For one thing, many if not most of the feminists were fundamentally Christian in their own religious commitments. For another, the main weight of opposition they confronted was religious. Their principal opponents appear to have been male clergy, and the main ground of opposition was drawn from scripture. Even if not influenced by the Bible themselves (though most were), the feminists could scarcely have avoided dealing with the charge that their movement was unbiblical.

One of the most articulate spokespersons for the movement at this point was Lucretia Mott, herself a minister in the Society of Friends. Her refutation of clergymen in 1854 at a Woman's Rights Convention in Philadelphia has become a classic in the movement's history.[21] Women have been subordinated, she argued, not by Christianity but by "priest-craft" by whom "the pulpit has been prostituted [and] the Bible has been ill-used." Reform after reform has been resisted by use of biblical passages taken out of context. "Instead of taking the truths of the Bible in corroboration of the right, the practice has been to turn over its pages to find example and authority for the wrong, for the existing abuses of society." It is important to see the different constructions that can be placed upon biblical passages as well as to check the translations carefully. When one does this, she continued, one sees that "it is not so Apostolic to make the wife subject to the husband as many have supposed." Still, she does "not want to dwell too much upon Scripture authority" because "we too often bind ourselves by authorities rather than by truth."

Other feminist leaders sought to ground their views in the teaching and example of Jesus. In an 1867 book, Mary Dodge replied to a clergy critic:

> What gospel is this? Honor and dignity and happiness [for women] consist not in truth, integrity, self-sacrifice, self-command, benevolence, communion with God, and likeness to Christ, but in marriage and motherhood and house-keeping! Where is the warrant for such affirmations? Not surely in the words of the Master. Christ propounded no such doctrines. . . . He looked upon woman, he treated woman, as a human being. Nothing that he ever said could be construed into a concession of her inferiority to man.[22]

The Methodist feminist and temperance leader Frances Willard echoed that theme in concluding that "no utterance of his [Jesus] marks a woman as ineligible to any position in the church he came to found; but his gracious words and deeds, his impartation of his purposes and plans to women, his stern reproofs to men who did them wrong, his chosen companionships, and the tenor of his whole life and teaching, all point out precisely the opposite conclusion."[23] The year Willard published those words (1888) she had the distinction of being one of the first women elected to the General Conference of the Methodist Episcopal Church—and the frustration of being refused a seat in that body.

Such feminist leaders disputed the selective literalism of their clerical opponents while also drawing upon biblical criticism in their own exegesis of scriptural passages. Frances P. Cobbe's exegesis of the household codes in the New Testament books of Ephesians and Colossians is representative. Cobbe notes the inconsistency of those who take those codes literally to reinforce the submission of women while no longer applying it to slavery and political despotism. "In our day, men habitually set aside this apostolic teaching, so far as it concerns masters and slaves, despots and subjects, as adapted only to a past epoch." Therefore, she exclaims, "I am at a loss to see by what right, having done so, they can claim for it authority, when it happens to refer to husbands and wives."[24] Frances Willard carefully demonstrated that the Bible itself contains many contradictions and cannot therefore be applied literally. To get at the whole truth of the Bible she urged that "we need women commentators to bring out the woman's side of the book; we need the stereoscopic view of truth in general, which can only be had when woman's eye and man's eye together shall discern the perspective of the Bible's full-orbed revelation."[25]

Elizabeth Cady Stanton's *The Woman's Bible* project was based on the more radical notion that the Bible is so riddled with problems for women that it must be supplemented in a more enlightened age. Expressing her own skepticism about the exegetical efforts by her sisters, Stanton declared that "whatever the Bible may be made to do in Hebrew or Greek, in plain English it does not exalt and dignify woman."[26] Therefore, in her judgment, "the Bible cannot be accepted or rejected as a whole, its teachings are varied and its lessons differ widely from each other."[27] We should accept the general principles of "love, charity, liberty, justice and equality for all the human family" to be found in the Bible and other holy books, while rejecting the "false sentiments and vicious characters bound up in the same volume."

The Woman's Bible aroused a storm of criticism, even within the movement. In defense of her work, Stanton wrote that "my heart's desire is to lift women out of all these dangerous and degrading superstitions and to this end will I labor my remaining days on earth."[28]

A different kind of critique, anticipating the twentieth-century "Womanist" movement expressing the double-sided experience of oppression by black women, was offered the movement by Sojourner Truth, the former slave. In her celebrated impromptu speech "Ain't I a Woman?" she responded to derogatory comments by white male clergy at an 1851 woman's convention in Akron, Ohio:

> That man over there says that women need to be helped into carriages, and lifted over ditches, and to have the best place everywhere. Nobody ever helps me into carriages, or over mud-puddles, or gives me any best place! And ain't

I a woman? Look at me! Look at my arm! I have ploughed and planted, and gathered into barns, and no man could head me! And ain't I a woman? I could work as much and eat as much as a man—when I could get it—and bear the lash as well! And ain't I a woman? I have borne thirteen children, and seen them most all sold off to slavery, and when I cried out with my mother's grief, none but Jesus heard me! And ain't I a woman? . . . Then that little man in black there, he says women can't have as much rights as men, 'cause Christ wasn't a woman! Where did your Christ come from? . . . From God and a woman! Man had nothing to do with Him. If the first woman God ever made was strong enough to turn the world upside down all alone, these women together ought to be able to turn it back, and get it right side up again! And now they is asking to do it, the men better let them.[29]

The feminist movement of the nineteenth century fell short of achieving many of its immediate goals. It failed to achieve, within the nineteenth century, the right to vote, the right to equal participation in the ministry of the church (at least most churches), and equality within the family. It did register notable achievements in opening the doors of education and some professions and its momentum accomplished equality of suffrage within two decades of the twentieth century. Along with the antislavery cause, with which it was frequently allied, it helped Christian ethics grapple more seriously with the moral implications of biblical literalism and with the centrality of issues of social power.

PART VI

Christian Ethics in the Twentieth Century

At the beginning of the twentieth century, an obscure religious journal expressed the optimistic triumphalism of the time by changing its name to *The Christian Century*. Whatever else one might say, as this century draws to a close it is very difficult to call it that! Nevertheless, in retrospect most of us would declare this a most extraordinary period in world history.

But has the twentieth century really been as unusual as we like to think? Has not the church, in every era, thought of its own times as peculiarly fraught with crisis, danger, and opportunity? Is it not empty conceit to regard one's own century in these terms, simply because this is when and where we live and the terrain is more familiar to us than any other? Will the erosion of time efface the details and this century merge into all the rest?

Obviously, I do not know. Certainly we know our own time best of all, which makes it both easier and more difficult to write about. It is easier, because we know the details better. It is more difficult, because we have a less clear sense of which details are most important. We know the personalities, the movements, the problems more immediately. But time has not yet sorted them all out.

Nevertheless, have these not been extraordinary years? When before has the world's population increased by four times? What previous era has witnessed such remarkable inventions and discoveries: the airplane, radio, television, penicillin, fiber-optic communications, nuclear energy, space travel, the computer, heart transplants, genetic science and technologies. Wonder of wonders! All within the life span of many people now living, whose world was transformed from one of horse-and-buggy transportation to jet travel, from the printed page to instantaneous world-wide television news, from dreaded diseases to wonder drugs. The scientific and technological wonders, taken in isolation, seem to justify the bursts of optimism that greeted this century.

But the twentieth century has also been extraordinary in its calamities. Less than a generation had passed before the world was engulfed in the first world war, with appalling carnage made possible by harnessing technology to weaponry. Then, but a single generation later, humankind suffered another world war on an even more devastating scale. In the midst of this, for the first time, whole cities were leveled by aerial bombardment including, at war's end, the use of atomic bombs. Six million Jews were systematically killed in the ultimate expression of demonic racism. Medical advances were mocked by the sudden emergence of AIDS, reminding us that the consequences of our ignorance can still be deadly. Agricultural advances and miracles of economic production were mocked by the continued existence of utter destitution and want in the lives of hundreds of millions of people. Technology was mocked by environmental disasters threatening, as never before, the health of the natural world upon which all life on this planet depends. Vast cities developed in all parts of the world, partly the fruit of technical advances but even more largely the result of rapid population growth and the inability of people to find employment on the land. In most parts of the world, urbanization brought not only increased opportunity but also a whole new series of intractable problems, including homelessness, crime, and drug addiction.

Slavery had been set aside in the previous century, at least for the most part and in principle. Racial oppression continued in even the most advanced societies. Woman's suffrage was soon adopted in several countries, the fruit of the nineteenth-century feminist movement, and there were other notable improvements in the social, political, and economic condition of women, but the lower status of women continued stubbornly. The lot of workers in industrial countries improved dramatically, but the struggle for workers' rights achieved no final resolution. Marxism gained dramatic victories in Russia, China, Eastern Europe, and other parts of the world. But those victories were tarnished by accompanying oppression and economic failures. Toward the end of the century communism had collapsed after seven decades of rule in the Soviet Union and had either fallen or was in crisis in its other strongholds.

The century witnessed important movements in support of human rights. The feminist movement continued into the century and achieved significant rebirth in the 1970s. The civil rights movement won important victories over racial discrimination and segregation in the United States. Similar struggles in India and South Africa and elsewhere achieved considerable success. Following World War II a series of revolutions achieved decolonization and independence throughout Africa and Asia.

What of Christian ethics in this turbulent century?

We cannot be the final judges of this, but a later time may record that this was also a remarkably fruitful period. The work of theology and ethics gained creative new focus in the thought of a number of theologians and Christian ethicists. As the century wore on, the company of classical thinkers was augmented by theologians writing out of the experiences of oppression in the formerly colonial territories as well as Europe and North America. It was a time of discovery of the possibilities of "social Christianity" by major Christian bodies, including the ecumenical movement, which arose largely in response to the great moral questions.

Summarizing these developments in the ongoing history of Christian ethics, we will, without apology, devote more attention to the twentieth century than to earlier periods. Even so, the number of thinkers and writings is so great that we must continue to be very selective.

16

THE SOCIAL GOSPEL MOVEMENT

As we have seen, there really has never been a time when Christians had nothing to say about moral questions. One way or another, ethics has always been a part of the Christian message. But that part of the message gained striking new emphasis among North American and European Christians in the late nineteenth and early twentieth centuries. In this chapter we shall summarize the Protestant developments; in the next, the new emphasis as expressed in Roman Catholic teaching.

The Social Gospel in America

The American social gospel movement, as it came to be called, began at the end of the Civil War, gained momentum in Protestant church circles in the following decades, and continued until the beginning of World War I (though with much ongoing influence in the decades following that historical watershed). Some of its intensity derived from the earlier anti-slavery movement, the temperance movement, and feminism. But the major focus of the social gospel was upon social problems growing out of industrialization. The Civil War itself had quickened the pace of the Industrial Revolution in the North, as industries grew up overnight to supply the Union war machine. Unlike the South, which was devastated, the North was stimulated economically. The following years were a time of rapid expansion: new factories were developed to manufacture new products, railways were built spanning the continent, trade expanded. Wave after wave of new immigrants came to America to provide cheap labor.

It was a time of growing prosperity for many, and some became fabulously wealthy during what historians have called the Gilded Age. But many people—especially those concentrated in the working-class sections of the industrial cities—were caught in the backwash. For them, industrialization meant backbreaking toil, long working hours, child labor, exploitation of women, adulterated food, periods of unemployment, vulnerability to industrial accidents and disease, little educational opportunity, inadequate medical attention, and general impoverishment. Efforts to unionize the workers were resisted by industrial employers, often with the brutal assistance of the state.

The plight of this army of immigrants, workers, and poor people touched the conscience of a growing number of Christians in the mainline denominations. Their response was influenced by a number of intellectual developments at the same time, such as Darwinian theories of evolution—with spin-offs in the social sciences emphasizing social progress, the prestige of Henry George's Single Tax movement, and the growing influence of Ritschlian theology—with a focus upon the teachings of Jesus and the kingdom of God, interpreted as the redemption of society. They reacted vigorously against conservative quietism and individualism, insisting that Christian faith is about social relationships and institutions as well.

The social gospel was expressed by three overlapping but distinct strategies. A more conservative strategy was to meet the needs of poor people and immigrants directly, with settlement houses (like Jane Addams's Hull House in Chicago) that developed various educational and economic programs. This more conservative approach did not interpret the problem in structural or political terms so much as in individual human terms, though people like Jane Addams were enlisted from time to time in support of specific reforms. The various ventures of hands-on problem solving were not usually developed by churches and denominations as such, though they might find support from the organized church. Nevertheless, the motives underlying them were specifically Christian.

A second strategy could be called radical in the sense that it did interpret the problems in structural terms and called for sweeping societal change. The social gospel radicals were typically socialist in self-understanding, though their socialism was not generally defined in Marxian terms. (It was more generally influenced by Henry George or British Fabianism.) Radicals like George D. Herron and W. D. P. Bliss thought of socialism as a necessary consequence of serious Christian morality; to them it represented the next stage in human development, identified with the progressive movement of

God in history. The Society of Christian Socialists was founded in 1889 "to show that the aim of Socialism is embraced in the aim of Christianity [and] to awaken members of Christian churches to the fact that the teachings of Jesus Christ lead directly to some specific form or forms of Socialism."[1] The socialist wing of the social gospel movement aimed scathing critiques at capitalism, the "profit motive," the social consequences of greed.

The third, and dominant, strategy was more reformist. While a number of its major figures could also be described as socialist, their objectives were meliorist, their style gradualist. They were sharply critical of the abuses of the Gilded Age. They supported the rights of workers and a more equal distribution of wealth and income. But they were more inclined to urge business leaders to use their power and wealth to advance social aims than to incite workers to overturn the business system.

Washington Gladden (1836–1918), a Congregationalist minister and social gospel leader, illustrated the more moderate stance of such reformers. In a typical book, his 1886 volume *Applied Christianity*, Gladden decries the growing gulf between employers and their workers, while listing "ominous signs of the times": "The hundreds of thousands of unemployed laborers, vainly asking for work; the rapid increase of pauperism, indicated by the fact that during the last Winter, in the chief cities of this rich commonwealth, nearly one tenth of the population sought charitable aid from the infirmary director or the benevolent societies; the strikes and lock-outs reported every day in the newspapers; the sudden and alarming growth of the more violent types of socialism."[2] Gladden specifically approves the great increase in wealth, attributing this to the influence of Christianity. At the same time he criticizes the great chasm between the handful of wealthy people and the masses of poor people, an inequitable condition he largely attributes to speculation in stocks and commodities. He is specifically critical of socialism —outlining several objections to it, including the flaws in Marx's labor theory of value and the practical problem that "the attempt to regulate the social and industrial life of a great nation like ours by a centralized bureaucracy would break down under its own weight."[3] He is not even willing to see the state used overmuch: "To urge a distribution among the poor, by the power of the state, of the goods of the rich, would be a blunder. . . . No one who clearly apprehends the drift of Christian teaching on the subject would ever think of such a thing."[4] He continues: "All that intelligent Christians will ask the state to do . . . is to provide for the general welfare, as it now does, by taxation; to protect all classes in the exercise of their rights; to strike down those foes that now clutch our industries by the throat, and then to leave the natural laws of trade and the motives of humanity and good-will to effect a more equitable distribution."[5] Gladden put great store in the possibilities of cooperation. First, employers must stop thinking of labor simply as a commodity. It is that, all right, in economic terms. But labor also represents thinking, feeling human beings, whose cooperation must be enlisted if industry is to prosper and social health is to be restored. To that end, Gladden supported labor organization—a quite remarkable view for a leading minister of his generation. As early as 1876 he had written concerning unions:

> They have a perfect right to deliberate together concerning the wages they are receiving, and to unite in refusing to work unless their wages are increased. The law gives to capital an immense advantage in permitting its consolidation in great centralized corporations; and neither law nor justice can forbid laborers to combine, in order to protect themselves against the encroachments of capital, so long as they abstain from the use of violence, and rely upon reason and moral influence.[6]

This statement is noteworthy as one of the first by a mainline Christian leader to recognize the importance of economic power in industrial relations.

Walter Rauschenbusch

The major strands of the social gospel came together in the thought of Walter Rauschenbusch (1861–1918). Shaped by his German-American pietist upbringing and an excellent bicultural (German and American) theological education, Rauschenbusch was plunged into social Christianity through an eleven-year ministry in the slums of New York City and early contact with significant figures in the social gospel movement.[7] He became a professor of church history at Rochester Theological Seminary in 1897, where he served until his death in 1918. During those years his writings brought the social gospel fully into the mainstream of American Protestant theology and church life. Bringing his studies in church history to bear, Rauschenbusch was able to ground the movement solidly in mainstream Christian tradition, demonstrating that issues of social justice were no recent invention of a few overzealous reformers. Even the apocalyptic hope of the primitive church was for the inauguration of a kingdom of God embodying "the hope of social perfection . . . a political hope . . . in antagonism to the existing political situation."[8] To this historical sense, Rauschenbusch also brought a gift for systematic thought. His final book, *A Theology for the Social Gospel*, brought greater coherence to the movement's main theological themes.

Impressive as Rauschenbusch's intellectual gifts undoubtedly were, the great popularity of his work may have owed as much to his extraordinary gifts as a writer. He was able to draw a very large audience directly into the sufferings and tragedies of masses of poor people in the crowded cities. His writing also conveyed something of his own deep spirituality, and his work can still be read among the devotional classics.

Rauschenbusch's theology was in the familiar Ritschlian vein, centering on the kingdom of God as anticipated by the Old Testament prophets and as focused upon in the life and teachings of Jesus. His *A Theology for the Social Gospel* grounds the theme in Christ. "The fundamental first step in the salvation of mankind," he wrote, "was the achievement of the personality of Jesus. Within him the Kingdom of God got its first foothold in humanity."[9] Rauschenbusch reacted strongly against a Christology treating Christ as an "effortless inheritance." Jesus was a very real human being. "His temptations and struggles were not stage-combats. At every point of his life he had to see his way through the tangle of moral questions which invited to errors and misjudgments; his clarity of judgment was an achievement." Throughout his life, and not only in the desert, Christ "had to re-affirm his unity with the will of God and make all aims subservient to the Kingdom of God."[10] The personality of Jesus became "a new type in humanity." It "became the primal cell of a new social organization."

Rauschenbusch seeks to liberate the idea of salvation from the excessive individualism of much traditional piety. In this, he clearly is reacting against the individualistic revivalism of much nineteenth-century American Christianity. But Rauschenbusch retained a recognition of the importance of sin in the drama of salvation:

> When we undertook to define the nature of sin, we accepted the old definition, that sin is selfishness and rebellion against God, but we insisted on putting humanity into the picture. The definition of sin as selfishness gets its reality and shaping force only when we see humanity as a great solidarity and God indwelling in it. In the same way the terms and definitions of salvation get more realistic significance and ethical reach when we see the internal crises of the individual in connection with the social forces that play upon him or go out from him.[11]

"If sin is selfishness," he continues, "salvation must be a change which turns a man from self to God and humanity. His sinfulness consisted in a selfish attitude, in which he was at the centre of the universe, and God and all his fellowmen were means to serve his pleasures, increase his wealth, and set off his egotisms."[12]

Rauschenbusch's essay "The Kingdom of Evil" seeks to rescue the doctrine of original sin from literal conceptions of its beginning. "Theological teaching on the first origin of sin ought not to obscure the active sources of sin in later generations and in present-day life, by which sin is quickened and increased."[13] Just as God's kingdom of love and righteousness enters into social structures and relationships, so evil is perpetuated by social tradition and "social idealizations of evil." The "combinations for evil" in society "add enormously to the power of sin." So theology should not be so preoccupied by the psychology of sin and regeneration that it neglects the social. "Would (theology) stray from its field," he asks, "if it utilized sociological terms and results in order to interpret the sin and redemption of these super-personal entities in human life?"[14]

Rauschenbusch's understanding of the atonement seeks to connect "the idea of reconciliation and the idea of the Kingdom of God," beginning with "the solidarity between God and Christ" and proceeding "to the solidarity between God and mankind."[15] The death of Jesus on the cross affects humanity, first by its "conclusive demonstration of the power of sin in humanity," then by its "supreme revelation of love." The cross illuminates the reality and consequences of evil; at the same time, it brings evil into the sharpest contrast with the attractive power of love.[16] The cross, thus, "is the monumental fact telling of grace and inviting repentance and humility."[17] Rauschenbusch also understands this atonement as a reinforcement of prophetic religion—which he contrasts in many of his writings with priestly religion, as in the following:

> The priest is the religious professional. He performs religious functions which others are not allowed to perform. It is therefore to his interest to deny the right of free access to God, and to interpose himself and his ceremonial between the common man and God. He has an interest in representing God as remote, liable to anger, jealous of his rights, and quick to punish, because this gives importance to the ritual methods of placating God which the priest alone can handle. . . . The prophet [by contrast] becomes a prophet by some personal experience of God, which henceforth is the dominant reality of his life. . . . As a result of his own experience he usually becomes the constitutional enemy of priestly religion, the scorner of sacrificial and ritual doings, a voice of doubt about the doctrines and the literature which shelter the priest. . . . His highest desire is to have all men share what he has experienced.[18]

The church, in keeping with this contrast, has its sole legitimate purpose in the advancement of the kingdom of God. When it becomes in itself the end rather than a means to the end, it is in fact the enemy of the kingdom.

In all of his writings Rauschenbusch seeks to translate theological understandings of the kingdom of God into analysis of actual social relationships, structures, and problems. He nicely formulates what may have been the central insight of the whole social gospel movement: a new recognition of the systemic character of both good and evil. Humanity is not simply a collection of individuals; it is bound together relationally and structurally. The relationships and structures can either enable or impede the actual realization of God's loving purposes.

Rauschenbusch's book *Christianizing the Social Order*,[19] his most systematic attempt at social analysis, formulates the point as he contrasts the character of unchristian and Christian forms of social order:

> An unchristian social order can be known by the fact that it makes good men do bad things. It tempts, defeats, drains, and degrades, and leaves men stunted, cowed, and shamed in their manhood. A Christian social order makes bad men do good things. It sets high aims, steadies the vagrant impulses of the weak, trains the powers of the young, and is felt by all as an uplifting force which leaves them with the consciousness of a broader and nobler humanity as their years go on.[20]

Social gospel writers, Rauschenbusch included, have sometimes been criticized for believing that goodness and sinfulness are environmentally determined. That charge may be close to the mark with some of those writers. But Rauschenbusch's conception of a Christian versus unchristian social order is subtler. The social order puts limits on what we can or cannot do. A good person is forced to do bad things by social constraints, just as a bad person may be forced to do good things.

What, in light of this, was Rauschenbusch's assessment of society?

He writes that there are a number of points where society, relatively speaking, has been "Christianized" and a number of other spheres in which society remains unchristian. Rauschenbusch's point is not that some institutions are now perfect embodiments of the kingdom of God, but rather that some parts of the social order have been decisively and positively influenced in their very structure by the power of the kingdom. Here, for example, he lists the family. With all of its imperfections—which he acknowledges—the family is no longer quite the despotic institution it once was:

> The history of the family tells of a slow decrease of despotism and exploitation. Gradually wives were no longer bought outright. The right of divorce was hedged about. The wife gained an assured legal status and some property rights. When polygamy ceased and adultery was considered a crime in man as well as in woman, the basis was laid for equality between man and wife. But only within the last hundred years has woman risen toward acknowledged equality with swift and decisive steps. . . . The present agitation for woman's suffrage is one of the final steps of this ascent. The suffrage will abolish one of the last remnants of patriarchal autocracy by giving woman a direct relation to the political organism of society.[21]

Rauschenbusch notes, with alarm, that economic forces threaten to disintegrate this more Christianized family: "Unless these destructive forces are checked in this generation, the institution of the family will have been christianized only to perish like a flower in full bloom bitten by frost." Such a family cannot survive unless the rest of society is also Christianized.[22]

Rauschenbusch also finds the church, education, and democratic government to be spheres in which the social order has become relatively Christianized —in each case through the broadening egalitarianism in which mutual respect and social solidarity are possible. But these institutional structures are also threatened by the remaining unchristian aspects of the social order.

By that, he principally refers to economic life. Rauschenbusch is biting in his criticism of the laissez-faire organization of capitalistic economics and by the culture of greed that supports and is fostered by it.

> Our business life is the seat and source of our present troubles. . . . It is in commerce and industry that we encounter the great collective inhumanities that shame our Christian feeling, such as child labor and the bloody total of industrial accidents. Here we find the friction between great classes of men which makes whole communities hot with smoldering hate or sets them ablaze with lawlessness. To commerce and industry we are learning to trace the foul stream of sex prostitution, poverty, and political corruption. Just as an epidemic of typhoid fever would call for an analysis of the water supply, so these chronic conditions call for a moral analysis of the economic order and justify the presumption that it is fundamentally unchristian.[23]

Business life is thus "the unregenerate section of our social order."

In his critique of business life, Rauschenbusch aligns himself basically with the Christian socialist wing of the social gospel. His socialism is not uncritical. He has no illusions that socialism will perfect human nature, and he is specifically critical of unchristian forms of socialism. Nevertheless, he can write that "the modern socialist movement is really the first intelligent, concerted, and continuous effort to reshape society in accordance with the laws of social development." By contrast, capitalism "would have been thought intolerable and immoral in times past."[24] Socialism is, he thinks, the logical outcome of the labor movement. As such, it represents the overcoming of class antagonism—an idea doubtless influenced by, though not attributed to, Karl Marx. Socialism

> proposes to abolish the division of industrial society into two classes and to close the fatal chasm which has separated the employing class from the working class since the introduction of power machinery. It proposes to restore the

independence of the workingman by making him once more the owner of his tools and to give him the full proceeds of his production instead of a wage determined by his poverty. . . . [I]t proposes to give to the whole body of workers the ownership of these vast instruments of production and to distribute among them all the entire proceeds of their common labor. There would then be no capitalistic class opposed to the working class; there would be a single class which would unite the qualities of both.[25]

Rauschenbusch warned against the party spirit expressed intensely in socialist parties and the possibility of "narrow and jealous orthodoxy" springing up within the party.[26] Socialism is right "in emphasizing the economic basis of human society."[27] But that must, at last, be recognized only as the scaffolding. Jesus is also right in emphasizing society's spiritual ends. And if socialism seems a threat to overall production, Christianity can help us remember that "the spiritual values of human life are set above all economic aids to life as the real end to be sought."[28] Those spiritual values will be greatly enhanced by the achievement of social equality, which socialism will help us attain. In balance, Rauschenbusch finds, "we may safely trust that Socialism will slough off its objectionable elements as it matures. Those qualities against which the spirit of genuine Christianity justly protests are not of the essence of Socialism."[29]

While Rauschenbusch's major concern is thus with economic life, he had occasion to comment on other issues and problems. An illustration from his haunting "Prayers of the Social Awakening" on the subject of war contains these words:

O Lord, since first the blood of Abel cried to thee from the ground that drank it, this earth of thine has been defiled with the blood of man shed by his brother's hand, and the centuries sob with the ceaseless horror of war. Ever the pride of the kings and the covetousness of the strong has driven peaceful nations to slaughters. Ever the songs of the past and the pomp of armies have been used to inflame the passions of the people. . . . Grant us a quiet and steadfast mind when our own nation clamors for vengeance or aggression. Strengthen our sense of justice and our regard for the equal worth of other peoples and races.[30]

That prayer was a grim, but unknowing, anticipation of the "war to end all wars." For Rauschenbusch the great tragedy of World War I was compounded by the fact that it pitted the countries most dear to him against each other. The war also effectively broke the momentum of the social gospel movement, although the legacies of that movement have continued to have enormous influence throughout the twentieth century.

The Social Gospel in the Life of the Church

In the early decades, the social gospel movement was carried along by individual prophetic spirits and reform-minded organizations. It was often a gadfly to the churches, sometimes appreciated, more often not. As the movement gathered momentum around the turn of the century it became a more official part of the life of the church. One important evidence of this was the adoption of the Social Creed by the General Conference of the Methodist Episcopal Church in 1908. The same year, the Federal Council of Churches was formed by mainline denominations, under leadership greatly influenced by the social gospel. The Federal Council promptly adopted the Social Creed as its own. The Creed was fairly brief, almost exclusively devoted to economics. In its Methodist form it held that the church should stand

> For equal rights and complete justice for all men in all stations of life.
>
> For the principle of conciliation and arbitration in industrial dissensions.
>
> For the protection of the worker from dangerous machinery, occupational diseases, injuries, and mortality.
>
> For the abolition of child labor.
>
> For such regulation of the conditions of labor for women as shall safeguard the physical and moral health of the community.
>
> For the suppression of the "sweating system."
>
> For the gradual and reasonable reduction of the hours of labor to the lowest practical point, with work for all; and for that degree of leisure for all which is the condition of the highest human life.
>
> For a release from employment one day in seven.
>
> For a living wage in every industry.
>
> For the highest wage that each industry can afford, and for the most equitable division of the products of industry that can ultimately be devised.
>
> For the recognition of the Golden Rule and the mind of Christ as the supreme law of society and the sure remedy for all social ills.[31]

The General Conference sought to "summon all our ministry . . . to patient study of these problems, and to fearless but judicious preaching of the teachings of Jesus in their significance for the moral interest of modern society."[32] And all members were urged to "seek that kingdom in which God's will shall be done on earth as it is in heaven."

This statement became the model for a number of denominational statements. It touches the most important themes of the social gospel movement, including the invoking of the teachings of Jesus and the kingdom of God.

As a characteristic statement of official social Christianity, the Social Creed is as noteworthy for what it does not say as for what it does. How could it have ignored the racial problem in an era when the Jim Crow system of segregation was tightening throughout the South, almost in the very year when progressive racial leadership was founding the National Association for the Advancement of Colored People? How could it have ignored questions of war and peace, only six years before the beginning of the catastrophe of World War I? Why did it overlook the question of women's suffrage, just as the suffrage movement was commencing its final drive?

These are fair questions. But the Social Creed at least established the precedent that churches should have such statements. And the Social Creed was destined to broaden through the years to encompass a variety of other important issues long after the social gospel movement, as such, had faded.

The Social Gospel in Song

A fair test of the centrality of any doctrinal or moral emphasis in the church is the degree to which it can be incorporated in liturgy and hymnody. Various liturgical materials, including prayers and creeds and hymns, were strongly influenced by the movement. This included the "Korean Creed," with its brotherhood of man and fatherhood of God emphasis, and the effort in some denominations to establish "Kingdomtide" as one of the seasons in the liturgical year alongside Advent, Christmas, Epiphany, Lent, Easter, and Pentecost. It also included a number of poignant hymns, some written by social gospel leaders. For example, the haunting lines of Frank Mason North's 1903 hymn:

> Where cross the crowded ways of life,
>> where sound the cries of race and clan,
> above the noise of selfish strife,
>> we hear your voice, O Son of man.
> In haunts of wretchedness and need,
>> on shadowed thresholds dark with fears,
> from paths where hide the lures of greed,
>> we catch the vision of your tears.

Or the lines in John Haynes Holmes's 1913 hymn "The Voice of God Is Calling":

> I hear my people crying in cot and mine and slum;
>> No field or mart is silent, No city street is dumb.
> I see my people falling in darkness and despair.
>> Whom shall I send to shatter the fetters which they bear?

Or John Oxenham's 1913 hymn "In Christ There Is No East or West," with its "Join hands, then, brothers of the faith, What e'er your race may be. Who serves my Father as a son is surely kin to me."

Such hymns drew the passion of the movement into the lifeblood of the church, its worship.

Social Christianity in Europe

The social gospel was primarily an American phenomenon, but a parallel movement on a smaller scale also developed among European Protestants. The leading figures in the movement there in the late nineteenth and early twentieth century were Johann Christoph Blumhardt (1805–1880), his son Christoph Friedrich Blumhardt (1842–1919), and Leonhard Ragaz (1868–1945).

The Blumhardts attracted first notice through a spiritual movement in southern Germany. The elder Blumhardt was the catalyst for a kind of "great awakening" in 1842 in the small village where he was a Reformed pastor. His son, coincidentally born in that year, became a prominent mass evangelist and faith healer. Neither Blumhardt could be described as an academic theologian or a practical social reformer. But, on the foundation of a deep spirituality, they articulated a vision of the kingdom of God on earth with new power and urgency.

So Blumhardt[33] writes that the struggle to defeat evil "originally was an earthly one, not, as we Christians think, a heavenly one." Or rather, "it was the heavenly coming to reality upon earth; and to that extent was earthly."[34] Eternal life should be manifested on earth, not just in heaven. "We want to shine so brightly that heaven itself will become jealous of us." The true homeland that Christians seek is "of an earth cleansed of sin and death."[35] God cares about those who die; Blumhardt also believes in eternal life in heaven. Nevertheless, he argues, "it is to discard the whole meaning of the Bible if one argues, 'We have nothing to expect on earth; it must be abandoned as the home of man.' "[36] In one of his sermons he asks pointedly, "which is biblical: our going to God in death, or God's coming to us in life?"[37] Nor should Christians think of the kingdom of God as simply designed for their own happiness. Such love of self destroys our fellowship with God, whom we should rather honor with fidelity and hard work.

Blumhardt did not think of this in simple individualistic terms, either. God's kingdom is social and political as well. "Through revelation," he writes, "enlightenment also must come into politics."[38] He applies this specifically to the question of war and peace: "There is absolutely no justification for war; and we can dare to trust his [God's] almighty arm even when that seems a very risky thing to do.... We need no swords or cannon.

We should live and let live."[39] He complains that in this dog-eat-dog war-like world "things go according to particular rules of animal life, and the life of the Spirit is not to be found."[40] Even anarchy would, he thinks, be better. Humanity is on earth "to make progress" and people must actively seek to bring it about. "Thus, everyone who wants peace must undertake peace, must be a man of peace."[41]

The major emphasis of the Blumhardt message, however, concerns economic justice. That message is essentially socialist. In a passage reminiscent of Rauschenbusch's "Christianizing the social order" theme, Blumhardt cites the hard-won but now generally accepted social achievements of representative government and the abolition of slavery. In their time, these achievements were hard won and "genuinely new ways of looking at things." He considers the new aims of socialism to be that kind of advance. He asks:

> And now, when Socialism sets up the goal that every person have an equal right *to bread*, that matters of ownership be so arranged that neither money nor property but the life of man become the highest value, why should that be seen as a reprehensible, revolutionary demand? It is clear to me that it lies within the Spirit of Jesus Christ, that the course of these events leads toward his goal, and that there is bound to be revolution until that goal is reached. Resistance will be of no avail, because it is God's will that all men in every respect should be regarded equal.[42]

The socialist movement itself he considers to be "like a fiery sign from heaven warning of the coming judgment."[43] The judgment is that "greed is the root of all evil!" Blumhardt believes that his generation "is perishing in its acquiring of money and its desire for money."[44]

Blumhardt, accordingly, gave his personal backing to democratic socialism, even in its secular forms. Plunging into politics, he was elected to the Wurttemberg legislature, where he experienced some disillusionment with party politics. While continuing to espouse the ideals of socialism, he warned that "the attempt to carry my idea of God into earthly things cannot take root at a time when men are filled with the hope that they and they alone can create a blissful humanity. Now they first have to run aground on the rock of earthly things, in order to grasp the higher things."[45]

Blumhardt expresses the same criticism of Christendom and church we have already encountered in Kierkegaard and Rauschenbusch. The righteousness of God can scarcely still get a hearing within the churches today, he writes, because of its legalism, its superstition, and its bad habits.[46] When we "*enculturate* Christianity and even bring it to power . . . it is no longer what Jesus had in mind."[47] God, revealed in Jesus Christ, transcends our small-minded efforts to domesticate the Spirit. But God's kingdom, which is surely coming, is the source of real life.

The Blumhardts exerted great influence on the more visible social gospel leadership of the Swiss Reformed pastor and theological professor Leonhard Ragaz. Also specifically influenced by Ritschl, Ragaz's own theology likewise emphasized the theme of the kingdom of God. From the 1890s on, Ragaz was deeply committed to religious socialism—a commitment that he maintained until his death in 1945. And as his response to the great world wars of his lifetime, Ragaz strongly affirmed the dream of collective international security through institutions like the League of Nations.

In a characteristic passage in a 1908 sermon, Ragaz summarized the themes that were central to the social gospel on both sides of the Atlantic:

> If God is the Father, if he is the God of love, then we his children are brothers, mankind is a family, and the law of solidarity that is based on a unifying God and on the law of service that forms the kernel of the gospel should rule among us. In politics, trade, and industry, solidarity, mutual effort, and service should replace bitter war. These, too, must be freed from hatred, from service to Mammon, and from egoism and must become a service to God—and thus also a service to man.[48]

Nevertheless, Ragaz was clear that social change is not simply effected by institutional manipulation. "Genuine change will come about not by a change of society alone," he wrote in 1906; "a radical renewal of the spirit is also required." So "social change and religious reform need each other."[49] But under some circumstances "bread becomes spirit." The "battle for bread" is presently an "unspeakable burden" for humanity. When this burden is lifted, "then greatness and loveliness, sublimity and spirituality will sprout like the green corn that has long been yearning for the sun."[50] He exclaimed, "Oh how freely we would be able to breathe if Mammonism no longer pressed us down!"

Ragaz was unapologetic in his support for socialism since, he wrote, "I am convinced that socialism in its basic goals provides the direction that will lead us out of capitalism to the next higher level in historical development."[51] Still, he does not want that support to be misunderstood as an identification of the teachings of Christ with any particular social arrangement, even socialism. Those teachings are the standard, and "the first requirement is that an economic order *serve* man and not rule over him." By that standard "capitalism stands condemned."

> Its economic *telos* is, as we have seen, purely mechanical and impersonal: it centers on the increase of capital. The person, who according to the gospel

and also according to Kant should never be treated simply as a means but always as a being of intrinsic value, is used simply as a means to greater profit. ... Man is debased in the very place that should be the creative center of his moral self: at his work place.[52]

Ragaz's life spanned the development of socialism from the democratic socialism typical in pre–World War I Europe, through the Russian Revolution of 1917 and the increasing dominance of Bolshevism over international socialism in the Third International. Through those decades, Ragaz's commitment to the socialist ideal remained firm, but he reacted vigorously against Bolshevism and violent revolution. Socialism must come through struggle and even revolution, but if it seeks power through violence it will destroy its essential character. Socialism must choose, he writes, between viewing itself as "an absolute and despotic power or as a democratic one, either as an authoritarian coercive force or as a power of freedom."[53] If socialism allows itself to focus only upon outward conditions, neglecting education and the feelings of people, then it "will easily end up in despotism and absolutism."[54] But such a socialism will fail, "just as each kingdom of violence has fallen." Socialism must bring two things together: "a powerful sense of community and a passionate consciousness of freedom ... freedom in community and community in freedom."[55] Writing on behalf of Swiss socialists in 1919, Ragaz explained why they would not join the Third International:

> We reject the element of violence. This is self-evident from what we have said before. We consider the watchword of the "dictatorship of the proletariat" to be deceitful. We detest the militarism, the dogmatic fanaticism, and the lack of freedom and breadth implicit in Bolshevism.[56]

Both the American and European versions of the social gospel thus emphasized the kingdom of God; both were influenced by socialism; both were committed to political democracy and, whether pacifist or not, to peace; both understood the transcendence of God but also the direct involvement of God in human history; both were suspicious of the church or "Christendom," viewing ecclesiastical institutions not as ends in themselves but as instruments in support of the kingdom. Both had been influenced in important ways by the thought of Albrecht Ritschl. It is worth noting that Ragaz and Rauschenbusch had a direct personal relationship, beginning in 1907, and that Rauschenbusch's *Christianity and the Social Crisis* was translated into German by Ragaz's wife.

17

THE SOCIAL ENCYCLICALS

During the period generally corresponding to the American and European Protestant social gospel movements, an important series of papal social encyclicals developed within Roman Catholicism. The first of these, *Rerum novarum*, by Pope Leo XIII, was published in 1891. *Rerum novarum* is sometimes erroneously treated as the first of the papal encyclicals, despite the fact that such pronouncements, addressed to the whole church, had been written for centuries before 1891. *Rerum novarum* was, however, ground breaking in the way it addressed modern social problems.

To understand why, we must remember that Roman Catholicism had been on the defensive for more than a century. It had witnessed the collapse of European Christendom, with the irreparable breach with Protestantism and the rise of secular states in many European countries. The Italian papal states had shrunk in size to the minuscule Vatican City. Its fundamental social theory, still largely derived from Thomas Aquinas, was organic and hierarchical, but the mood if not the reality of the times was egalitarian and democratic. It had suffered a very rude awakening in the French Revolution of 1789, with the latter's deep-seated anticlericalism and even thinly masked atheism. It had been powerless before the cataclysm of the Napoleonic wars. Even countries still predominantly Catholic in Europe and Latin America were increasingly out of control. Its fundamental economic doctrine, which was communitarian but also hierarchical, was challenged by the new doctrines of laissez-faire and the new realities of commerce and industry. The *Communist Manifesto* had been published in 1847, with its explicit linking of socialism to antireligion. North American forms of democracy and religious disestablishment were interpreted—and rejected —in light of the French Revolution. In face of these forces, the church's reaction was mainly defensive. Pope Pius IX published the *Syllabus of Errors* in 1864 condemning a series of propositions of modern democratic values, including religious liberty. During that same pontificate the First Vatican Council defined the doctrine of papal infallibility.

Pope Leo XIII's Encyclical *Rerum novarum*

Rerum novarum was significant as a first effort to address the new economic situation with an eye, not just to the preservation of authority, but to the well-being of workers and the achievement of the common good. The encyclical was not egalitarian, either in its conception of authority or social rewards. But it condemns the exploitation of workers for inadequate wages and inappropriate and damaging forms of work for children and women (the latter point being mixed, of course, with the pope's conservative view of the limited role of women). Leo expounded a theory of the "just wage," which specified that the worker should receive enough "to enable him to maintain himself, his wife, and his children in reasonable comfort."[1] This family theory of the just wage was grounded in the natural law doctrine of the responsibility of the father (paterfamilias) to provide for those naturally under his care. While the pope made no effort to reconcile the just wage to the market realities of wage determination, he did assert that wage as the responsibility of the Christian employer. The pope is aware that sometimes workers have no choice but to settle for less than a just wage because employers have the economic power to pay them less. But "if through necessity or fear of a worse evil, the workman accepts harder conditions because an employer or contractor will give him no better, he is the victim of force and injustice."[2]

Leo is reluctant to approve unions. Many workmen's associations "are in the hands of invisible leaders, and are managed on principles far from compatible with Christianity and the public well-being."[3] Nevertheless, he does approve of workmen's associations organized with "special and principal attention to piety and morality."[4] The pope's vision for such associations is to foster cooperation among workers and between workers and employers. He does not explore the need for and possibilities of collective bargaining where the united strength of the workers' associations might provide greater bargaining power over against the corporate economic power of employers.

In *Rerum novarum*, Leo gave special emphasis to the concept of the "common good." He urges all citizens to "contribute to that common good in which individuals share so profitably," while recognizing that the contributions of different people will be unique to them.[5] The civil society as a whole also "exists for the common good, and, therefore, is concerned with the interests of all in general, and with the individual interests in their due place and proportion."[6]

Since the end of the state is to secure the common good, Leo views it as a positive institution and not merely (in the Lutheran sense) a "dyke against sin." Its duty is "to make sure that the laws and institutions, the general character and administration of the commonwealth, shall be such as to produce of themselves public well-being and private prosperity."[7] The state's "gift of authority" is not merely human. It is divine in origin, "a participation of the highest of all sovereignties." It should therefore "be exercised as the power of God is exercised—with a fatherly solicitude which not only guides the whole but reaches to details as well."[8]

Rerum novarum states the principle, later elaborated by Pope Pius XI as the principle of "subsidiarity," that the state should undertake to solve only those problems which cannot be dealt with effectively by lower, more immediate levels of social organization. He admonishes the state to show restraint: "Let the State watch over these [private] societies of citizens united together in the exercise of their right; but let it not thrust itself into their peculiar concerns and their organization, for things move and live by the soul within them, and they may be killed by the grasp of a hand from without."[9]

Nevertheless, Leo is also very clear that "whenever the general interest of any particular class suffers, or is threatened with, evils which can in no other way be met, the public authority must step in to meet them."[10] Moreover, he argues that "the poor and helpless have a claim to special consideration" by the public authority. "The richer population have many ways of protecting themselves, and stand less in need of help from the State; those who are badly off have no resources of their own to fall back upon, and must chiefly rely upon the assistance of the State." So wage earners "should be specially cared for and protected by the commonwealth."[11] How far should the state go? In this earliest version of papal teaching of the principle of subsidiarity, Leo lays it down that "the limits must be determined by the nature of the occasion which calls for the law's interference—the principle being this, that the law must not undertake more, nor go further, than is required for the remedy of the evil or the removal of the danger."[12]

Leo specifically rejected socialism. Its effort to do away with paternal authority is contrary to nature. Its effort to overcome inequality overlooks the natural origin and social advantages of human differences. Its proposal of socializing all goods would invite a host of moral and practical problems. Socialism "would open the door to envy, to evil speaking, and to quarreling; the sources of wealth would themselves run dry, for no one would have any interest in exerting his talents or his industry; and that ideal equality of which so much is said would, in reality, be the leveling down of all to the same condition of misery and dishonor."[13]

The main basis of Leo's rejection of socialism lies, however, in his view of the natural right of property. Property does not exist by virtue of social convention; it is inherent in the nature of human economic activity. In a doctrine of property highly reminiscent of John Locke's *Two Treatises on Government*, Leo argues that property is established by labor: "Now, when man thus spends the industry of his mind and the strength of his body in procuring the fruits of nature, by that act he makes his own that portion of nature's field which he cultivates—that portion on which he leaves, as it were, the impress of his own personality; and it cannot but be just that he should possess that portion as his own, and should have a right to keep it without molestation."[14] Socialists, by proposing to transfer property to the community at large, "strike at the interests of every wage earner, for they deprive him of the liberty of disposing of his wages, and thus of all hope and possibility of increasing his stock and of bettering his condition in life."[15] Leo also finds property to be "one of the chief points of distinction between man and the animal creation."[16] Human beings, unlike beasts, can think beyond the moment. Property rights lend substance to long-run purposes and plans.

Rerum novarum helped stimulate a great increase in Catholic social activity, including Catholic workmen's associations and, overall, a more positive attitude toward labor. In the United States, where millions of exploited industrial workers were immigrants from Catholic countries, the encyclical provided ammunition for those supporting the labor movement. In Europe, workers' associations and Catholic political parties took on great significance. The encyclical also stimulated an important series of similar messages by popes of the twentieth century.

The Encyclicals of Pope Pius XI

Three encyclical letters by Pope Pius XI were especially important. *Quadragesimo anno* was written in 1931 to commemorate the fortieth anniversary of *Rerum novarum*, and it explored similar themes. It is most notable for its formulation of the doctrine of subsidiarity, already anticipated by the earlier encyclical. The term "subsidiarity" refers to the positive role of the state as a help (*subsidium*).[17] In essence, the principle is designed to illuminate the question of when the state or other large-scale institutions should interfere in the private or smaller-scale sphere. *Quadragesimo anno* acknowledges that "much that was formerly done by small bodies can nowadays be accomplished by large organizations." Nevertheless, in his statement of the principle of subsidiarity, Pius XI writes that it is a fundamental principle of social philosophy, fixed and unchangeable, that one should not withdraw from individuals and commit to the community what they can accomplish by their own enterprise and industry. So, too, it is an injustice and at the same time a grave evil and a disturbance of right order, to transfer to the larger and higher collectivity functions which can be performed and provided for by lesser and subordinate bodies.[18]

In other respects, this encyclical followed in the train of *Rerum novarum*: In its rejection of socialism, in its affirmation of a hierarchical ordering of society, in its positive appreciation for the moral value of labor and its relationship to property, in its support for the "just wage" (defined, as Leo had done, by the income needed to support the workingman and his family at a level befitting his station), in its affirmation of worker associations. In defining the just wage, Pius XI introduced the caveat that an employer cannot be expected to pay so high a wage that the business would be ruined.

The encyclical specifically rejected the use of economic power in labor relations, either through strikes or lockouts, stipulating instead that "if the contending parties cannot come to an agreement, public authority intervenes."[19] Thus, Pius XI disavows a balance-of-power model. "Just as the unity of human society cannot be built upon 'class' conflict, so the proper ordering of economic affairs cannot be left to the free play of rugged competition."[20] But Pius does not think that competition, as such, is as important an economic reality as it had been when *Rerum novarum* was written forty years earlier. Now, as a result of the unrestrained competition of the past, "immense power and despotic economic domination is concentrated in the hands of a few."[21] The concentration of economic power has led to struggle for control of the economy, efforts to control the state, and international conflict.

Written during the depths of the world economic depression of the 1930s, *Quadragesimo anno* spoke eloquently of the effects of unemployment: "Now unemployment, particularly if widespread and of long duration, as We have been forced to experience it during Our Pontificate, is a dreadful scourge; it causes misery and temptation to the laborer, ruins the prosperity of nations, and endangers public order, peace and tranquillity in the world order."[22]

Quadragesimo anno's rejection of socialism was informed by an intervening period of forty years of socialist development, the principal event in which was the Russian Revolution of 1917. Pius XI vigorously indicted communism:

Now communism teaches and pursues a twofold aim: merciless class warfare and the complete abolition of private ownership. This it does, not in secret and by hidden methods, but openly, frankly, and by every means, even the most violent. To obtain these ends, it shrinks from nothing and fears nothing, and when it comes to power, it shows itself cruel and inhuman, in a manner unbelievable and monstrous. Witness to this are the tragic ruins and destruction which communism has left throughout the vast reaches of Eastern Europe and Asia. Moreover, the antagonism and open hostility it has shown Holy Church and even God Himself, are, alas! well proven by facts and known to all.[23]

Pius continued to reject the more moderate forms of democratic socialism, but in more conciliatory tones: "It would seem as if socialism were afraid of its own principles and of the conclusion drawn therefrom by the communists, and in consequence were moving toward the truth which Christian tradition has always held in respect; for it cannot be denied that its programs often strikingly approach the just demands of Christian social reformers."[24]

In his 1937 encyclical *Divini redemptoris*, Pius XI returned to the theme of communism and socialism, with even more forceful and detailed rejection: "Communism is intrinsically wrong, and no one who would save Christian civilization may collaborate with it in any undertaking whatsoever."[25] The faithful, he believes, need to be warned against its trickery and hypocrisy. The reality is not as positive as the propaganda. "Where Communism has been able to assert its power—and here We are thinking with special affection of the people of Russia and Mexico—it has striven by every possible means, as its champions openly boast, to destroy Christian civilization and the Christian religion by banishing every remembrance of them from the hearts of men, especially of the young."[26] Communism, he writes, "is by its nature anti-religious."[27] But it "will not be able to achieve its objectives even in the merely economic sphere."[28]

The overall tone of Pius's writings on socialism and communism is thus sharply polemical. The latter encyclical also asserts, however, that communism would have had no opportunity had political and economic leaders not neglected the church's teachings. In both encyclicals, Pius condemns laissez-faire capitalism with its competitive individualism and argues the case for Christian social justice as an alternative to communism and socialism. In one memorable quotation, Pius asserts that "the wage-earner is not to receive as alms what is his due in justice. And let no one attempt with trifling charitable donations to exempt himself from the great duties imposed by justice."[29] In another, he writes that "the rich should not place their happiness in things of earth nor spend their best efforts in the acquisition of them."[30]

Papal Teaching on Sexuality

Pius XI was the first pope of the modern era to devote a major encyclical to sexual relationships. In his 1930 encyclical *Casti connubii* he responded to early twentieth-century ideas of free love and companionate marriage, to the development of contraceptive techniques for birth control, and to the feminist movement. This encyclical, like his others, was grounded in an interpretation of Thomistic natural law doctrine. The morality of our exercise of natural functions, such as sexual intercourse, is determined by the created natural end or purpose of such functions. Similarly, human social roles are fixed by their natural ends, which Christian morality must respect and uphold. The proper end of sexual intercourse, fixed by nature, is the begetting of children. Anything that impedes this or frustrates this end is therefore intrinsically immoral. He makes the point explicitly, even memorably clear in respect to artificial forms of birth control:

> But no reason, however grave, may be put forward by which anything intrinsically against nature may become conformable to nature and morally good. Since, therefore, the conjugal act is destined primarily by nature for the begetting of children, those who in exercising it deliberately frustrate its natural power and purpose sin against nature and commit a deed which is shameful and intrinsically vicious.[31]

This is not to say, he continues, that a married couple may not engage in sexual intercourse at times when procreation is naturally impossible, for the pope recognizes that "there are also secondary ends, such as mutual aid, the cultivating of mutual love, and the quieting of concupiscence which husband and wife are not forbidden to consider as long as they are subordinated to the primary end and so long as the intrinsic nature of the act is preserved."[32]

Abortion is explicitly disallowed, even in tragic instances where this may be necessary to preserve the life of the mother in childbirth. He asks, "however much we may pity the mother whose health and even life is gravely imperiled in the performance of the duty allotted to her by nature, nevertheless what could ever be a sufficient reason for excusing in any way the direct murder of the innocent?"[33] He calls upon rulers to do their duty in framing laws to protect the innocent, remembering that if they do not do so God will avenge their innocent blood.

In respect to the status and role of women, Pius XI wished to resist the early twentieth-century movement for the social independence of women. Such modern teaching is

> not the true emancipation of woman, nor that rational and exalted liberty which belongs to the noble office of a Christian woman and wife; it is rather the debasing of the womanly character and the dignity of motherhood, and indeed of the whole family, as a result of which the husband suffers the loss of his wife, the children of their mother, and the home and the whole family of an ever watchful guardian. More than this, this false liberty and unnatural equality with the husband is to the detriment of the woman herself, for if the

woman descends from her truly regal throne to which she has been raised within the walls of the home by means of the Gospel, she will soon be reduced to the old state of slavery (if not in appearance, certainly in reality) and become as amongst the pagans the mere instrument of man.[34]

Based upon a sacramental conception of marriage, the pope continues the church's long-standing disapproval of divorce. Under unusual circumstances separation is morally permitted; but divorce, never. The indissolubility of marriage applies not only to marriages that are sacramentally joined by the church, but also those that are "natural." Those who remarry, after divorce, commit adultery.

Prior to the pontificate of John XXIII (1958–1963), whose teaching will be noted in a later chapter, the popes struggled to preserve an organic understanding of society in face of the pressures of modernity. Following the lead of *Rerum novarum*, Catholic teaching resisted the competitive individualism of laissez-faire economic theories and practices and sought to formulate an understanding of workers' rights and the common good in terms relevant to the new industrial age. The papal teachings on economic, social, political, and sexual matters were grounded in their interpretation of Thomistic natural law ethics. The power of the state was affirmed, provided it did not interfere with the workings of subordinate natural forms of society unless necessary for the common good. In all spheres, the natural legitimacy of social hierarchy was affirmed.

18

FORMATIVE CHRISTIAN MORAL THINKERS

In studying the thought of previous centuries, one occasionally comes across the writings of a once-popular author whose work no longer attracts the slightest notice. This is not simply evidence that *sic transit gloria mundi*. It also means that we cannot always form accurate judgments of which contemporary voices are singular enough to endure. It may be especially difficult for us to decide who among twentieth-century Christian moral thinkers to include in a history of this kind. It is not that there has been too little writing of high quality; quite the opposite. During the period following World War I, Christian ethics has blossomed as never before. This may prove, in time, to have been one of the great ages for such thought. Our problem is to select from the scores, even hundreds of significant voices, those whose ideas have opened particularly fruitful ways of exploring the moral implications of Christian faith. We will do so in this chapter, not by attempting a full exploration of the thought of a few selected thinkers, but by focusing on the pivotal ideas. We will leave to a later chapter the developments in the various forms of liberation theology.

The Christian Realism of Reinhold Niebuhr

Reinhold Niebuhr (1892–1971), while best known for his emphasis on original sin and realism about power politics, was greatly influenced by the social gospel movement. His first great book, *Moral Man and Immoral Society*,[1] in fact combined the idealism of the social gospel with a certain hardheaded realism. His thesis was that individuals in face-to-face settings can manifest a high level of morality that is belied by the immorality of the larger groups and institutions in which they participate. The distinction between the individual and collective forms of morality, in his view, "justifies and necessitates political policies which a purely individualistic ethic must always find embarrassing."[2] This is not quite the way Rauschenbusch would have put it. But is this realism about power not implicit in Rauschenbusch's comment that a "Christianized" social order is one in which bad people are *forced* to do good things? And did not the social gospel leaders constantly emphasize the collective immoralities that a more individualistic gospel is always prone to overlook?

On the basis of such a distinction, Niebuhr also contrasted love and justice. Love, defined in his various writings as selfless regard for the other, is the purest expression of the Christian ethic. But, to Niebuhr, the claims of justice precede those of love and must be satisfied before it is possible to talk about love. Love without justice is sentimental. In fact, it is not really love at all, although it may have the appearance of love. Justice is the tolerable but imperfect accommodation of life to life, with protection of basic human rights and liberties. It is characterized by balances of power, whether at the intimate levels of family life or in international relations. While the higher expressions of love are an expression of grace and Christian faith, justice can be understood and fought for in more universally accepted forms—though Christian faith also provides resources helping one to overcome that egoism in one's life that diminishes the commitment to justice.

Niebuhr's realism is grounded in a deeper appreciation of the truth of the Christian doctrine of original sin, and Niebuhr more than most writers in the history of Christian ethics is able to draw important social ethical conclusions from that doctrine. Original sin, to him, is not attributable to the sexual transmission of human life or to other superficial or mythological explanations. Nor does the universality of original sin mean that humanity lacks the freedom of moral decision making and action. Niebuhr agrees that without some moral freedom there could be, in principle, no moral life. Nevertheless, the doctrine of original sin points to the universality of human decision for sin. How could that be so? Niebuhr describes sin in the paradox that it is inevitable but not necessary. How could something be inevitable that is not necessary?

In his important work *The Nature and Destiny of Man*,[3] Niebuhr explains the paradox in these words:

> The temptation to sin lies . . . in the human situation itself. This situation is that man as spirit transcends the temporal and natural process in which he is involved and also transcends himself. Thus his freedom is the basis of his creativity but it is also his temptation. Since he is involved in the contingen-

cies and necessities of the natural process on the one hand and since, on the other, he stands outside of them and foresees their caprices and perils, he is anxious. In his anxiety he seeks to transmute his finiteness into infinity, his weakness into strength, his dependence into independence.[4]

The self is inevitably self-centered because it can see no other way to protect itself from destruction. It can contemplate a universe and infinite time, but it also recognizes its own finitude. It therefore, inevitably, centers that universe in upon itself. "It seeks to find its life and thereby loses it."[5] Its need is to subject itself to God in faith and trust. Lacking such faith and trust, it is self-centered: inevitably in sin.

This understanding of original sin as *hubris*, or pride and self-centeredness, is recognizably Augustinian in origin. Niebuhr supplies a distinctly contemporary way of understanding it.

Niebuhr's view does not require him to treat self-centeredness as total; life itself presupposes some dependency upon a center outside the self. Nevertheless, sin is sufficiently universal that we can presuppose it to be an important factor in the life of every person.

Niebuhr draws important ethical consequences from this. Structures of justice, sufficient to protect the helpless members of the community, are urgently commended. In an intriguing discussion of the case for political democracy, Niebuhr relates this to the fact of sin as well as to the goodness he also finds in human nature: "Man's capacity for justice makes democracy possible," he writes, "but man's inclination to injustice makes democracy necessary."[6] Such a grounding for participative democracy and protected civil rights is deeper, he believes, than sentimental utopian versions of human nature on the one hand or pessimistic views of total human sinfulness on the other. The first do not make a convincing case for the necessity of democracy—if human nature can be so much trusted, why is universal participation in power so important? The second do not help us understand the possibility of such participation. Such pessimism, indeed, generally contributes to support for strong rulers who are not accountable to the governed; but then, if such rulers are needed to condition the unmitigated evil of people, who is to rein in the evil of the rulers themselves?

In balance, Niebuhr's discussion provides theological support for the legitimacy of democratic government. Such government, while imperfect in this imperfect world, at least translates Christian insight into supportable institutional form. Niebuhr does not apply this insight directly to the economic sphere, and the true implications of his economic ethic remain in sharp dispute. Nevertheless, it is noteworthy that his *The Children of Light and the Children of Darkness* takes pains to detach the case for democracy, which he regards as universally compelling, from the case for bourgeois capitalism, which he then treated as an ephemeral chapter in human history. Bourgeois individualism, he felt, grasps neither the depth of human sin nor the extent of human need for community.

Niebuhr's realism about sin also contributed to one of the striking critiques of pacifism in the history of Christian ethics. In his essay "Why the Christian Church Is Not Pacifist," Niebuhr distinguishes between two forms of Christian pacifism.[7] The one, which acknowledges the higher norm of the law of love but which has no illusions about the power of human sinfulness, is a useful witness and reminder that we must not allow warfare to be accepted too easily—"lest we accept the warfare of the world as normative, lest we become callous to the horror of war, and lest we forget the ambiguity of our own actions and motives."[8] Niebuhr believes that even this form of pacifism cannot become the dominant Christian response to war without settling too readily for injustice as the price for preventing the anarchy of war.

But his most serious quarrel is with the second form of pacifism, which regards living by the law of love to be a simple possibility in human history. This he finds to be a form of heresy, not because of its conclusion but because of its premise. To speak thus of the law of love is to dismiss the reality of sin; it is to treat grace as the enablement of moral success, not as the forgiveness of our guilt. He poses the issue in this way: "The question is whether the grace of Christ is primarily a power of righteousness which so heals the sinful heart that henceforth it is able to fulfil the law of love; or whether it is primarily the assurance of divine mercy for a persistent sinfulness which man never overcomes completely."[9] The first of these leads, Niebuhr thinks, to new forms of self-righteousness. The second enables us to act with assurance amid the tragedies and ambiguities of history. The first is akin to Renaissance doctrines of human perfectibility. The second recognizes that no perfection completely frees humanity from the reality of sinfulness.

But Niebuhr regards the "heretical" form of pacifism as having very dangerous political consequences as well. Harboring, as it does, the illusion that the tyrant can be persuaded by nonviolent love to abandon tyranny or the illusion that one's own nonviolent form of resistance is an expression of the higher love, heretical pacifism greatly compounds the injustices and tragedies of history.

The essay was written during the early months of World War II, after Hitler had subdued Europe but before the full furies of the war had been unleashed. The situation invited a Christian theologian and moralist to ask the question of Christian participation in war in a new, deeper perspective. It also sharpened in Niebuhr's mind the enormous, though still relative, stake Christians have in the preservation of tolerable forms of justice and creative forms of democracy.

Covenant and Creation to Karl Barth

This century's most important theologian—in the eyes of many—Karl Barth (1886–1968) also made highly significant contributions to Christian ethics. Barth insists that Christian ethics is not a subspecies of ethics in general. We do not think generally about ethics, as philosophers like Kant or Hegel might do, and then decide how to fit Christian ethics in. Rather, to Barth, ethics is defined by God's grace as shown through Jesus Christ.[10] In Jesus Christ it is revealed that God has chosen (elected) us from all eternity. So "we cannot avoid the free decision of His love in which God has actually put Himself into this relationship, turning towards man in all the compassion of His being, actually associating Himself with man in all the faithfulness of His being."[11] The election of God is also the "command" of God. It is the command to be what, by grace, God has chosen us to be. Though a command, it is a command that humanity can, in its freedom, choose to obey or disobey. But the decision to obey is the decision for life—the decision "to be." That decision is to be, in our existence, a part of God's covenant. So to acknowledge our real being, in response to God's grace, is to be responsible in the only possible sense of that word. It is also to live in freedom—that is, in freedom from every human source of power or enthrallment. No longer is one under the control of any agency or power; now one's whole life is a life in grace.

What is the content of this, in ethical terms? One cannot ask such a question, as far as Barth is concerned, if one is imposing upon God's grace and covenant some ethical categories derived from some other source. But one can answer in general terms that the content is supplied by grace itself. That is, in general terms, Christian ethics is existing in grace. What does that mean? Certainly it means at least that one lives through the acceptance of being affirmed by God and invited into fellowship by God. It means that one is not substituting for this some form of acceptance based upon some other notion of the good; one is not under the control of economic force, political realities, cultural pressures. This freedom is not necessarily the freedom to do—for what we are able to do is certainly affected by these things. But it is the freedom to *be*: to *be* what, through God's grace, we *are*. While such freedom might appear less than a substantial answer to the detailed questions normally treated by ethics, it is always relevant to economics, politics, and culture that here are people who cannot be counted upon to be and do what is contrary to their being and doing as Christians living under grace.

But, through his doctrine of creation, Barth does supply more detailed, substantive response. Barth writes of "creation as the external basis of the covenant" and of "covenant as the internal basis of creation."[12] What makes the covenant possible, in the "internal" sense, is simply "the free love of

God." That is its meaning. What makes it possible from an "external" standpoint is the whole objective, tangible created universe apart from which covenant would have no form. He writes thus about the creation:

> Creation is the external—and only the external—basis of the covenant. It can be said that it makes it technically possible; that it prepares and establishes the sphere in which the institution and history of the covenant takes place; that it makes possible the subject which is to be God's partner in this history, in short the nature which the grace of God is to adopt and to which it is to turn in this history.[13]

Just as God "could not be satisfied with the eternal covenant as such"—that is, without actual beings with whom to enter into covenant—so it was necessary to create, giving "existence and being" to the creature.[14] But creation is still only the "external" basis of the covenant; it is not the covenant itself.

So Barth has here supplied an answer to one of the central questions of ethics: What is the moral significance of the natural world, our physical bodies, economic life, political structures, visible institutions? His answer is both negative and positive. Negatively, none of these things is meaningful and good simply in and of itself. But positively, all of these things matter because God's covenant of grace and love *depends* upon them. And along with such general observations, Barth has here supplied a criterion for *judging* all of the tangible aspects of created existence: How well, or badly, do they serve as the "external basis of the covenant"?

Barth scrupulously avoids the natural law approach to Christian ethics. The tangible structures of creation do not in and of themselves disclose their own moral meaning. But there are still morally significant patterns in creation. Perhaps the best illustration of this in Barth's thought is his lengthy discussion of man and woman.[15] He finds the created distinction between male and female to be, in the created natural order, a special ground for covenant. To be human is to accept and embrace that one is male or female; it is also to accept that one must be completed in one's being through one's relationship with the complementing gender. Barth does not mean that one must necessarily marry or have sexual intercourse; such completion of the self is possible in the fellowship of men and women. He is also clear that sexual expression, engaged in simply for its own sake, is a distortion of this created complementarity. It is reversing the order, making the basis of covenant into its meaning. He likewise speaks of the "malady called homosexuality" as "the physical, psychological and social sickness, the phenomenon of perversion, decadence and decay, which can emerge when man refuses to admit the validity of the divine command in the sense in which we are now considering it."[16] So, while Barth disavows a natural law approach to Christian ethics, his application of the doctrine of creation allows him to draw very definite inferences from the observed structure of things in the natural world.

Some of this takes conservative directions. It is worth mentioning that he refuses to conclude from the distinction between the sexes that either is superior to the other. Moreover, his discussion of economic and political questions—and his practical treatment of such issues during his lifetime—was generally on the radical side. He had been influenced by Christoph Blumhardt and Leonhard Ragaz, and he displayed socialist leanings throughout his life.[17]

Barth was not a pacifist. He wrote that "the church must not preach pacifism" and that "it is not commissioned to proclaim that war is absolutely avoidable."[18] But he remained deeply troubled by the tragedy of war and the tendency of war to carry people along, even Christians, in waves of hysteria. So he could write these memorable lines: "All affirmative answers to the question [of war] are wrong if they do not start with the assumption that the inflexible negative of pacifism has almost infinite arguments in its favour and is almost overpoweringly strong."[19] He does not supply us with a version of the traditional just war criteria, though plainly Barth wishes the church to place a serious burden of proof against war: "the many ways of avoiding war which now exist in practice should be honestly applied until they are all exhausted."[20] But then Christians can be placed in a situation of having "to yield something which must not be betrayed, which is necessarily more important to them than the preservation of life itself, and which is thus more important than the preservation of the lives of those who unfortunately are trying to take it from them."[21] Such a war, though still tragic, "cannot be shirked for the sake of a worthless peace."[22]

Consistent with this discussion, Barth affirms the theological legitimacy of the state: "The state which Christian ethics can and must affirm, which it has to proclaim as the political order willed and established by God, is not in itself and as such the mythological beast of the jungle. . . . According to the Christian understanding, it is no part of the normal task of the state to wage war; its normal task is to fashion peace in such a way that life is served and war kept at bay." War becomes necessary only when the state has failed to "rightly pursue its normal task."[23]

Barth's view of the relationship between church and state emphasizes the positive theological grounding and limitations of each, their distinctiveness, and their interdependency.[24] The church is the assembly of the faithful, called into being by the Word, Jesus Christ. The state is the people of a region or territory who are bound together by a common government whose laws are binding upon all. Both reflect God's purposes, but in limited ways. The church exists as a promise of God's greater purpose, the city of

God come down from heaven to earth and embracing all. Even that conception of the church is further limited by recognition that Christians and their churches are often faithless, given over to idolatry and pride, scarcely fit representatives of Christ to humanity. The state exists as a part of the providence of God, giving "an external, relative, and provisional embodiment 'in the world that is not yet redeemed,' in which it is valid and effective even when the temporal order is based on the most imperfect and clouded knowledge of Jesus Christ or on no such knowledge at all."[25] Barth can refer to the state even as "an instrument of divine grace."[26] But the civil community, as such, has no knowledge of ultimate meaning; "it is blind to the whence and whether of human existence."[27] It preserves the space in which civility is preserved and in which the church can proclaim its message. But Barth strenuously opposes efforts by the church in the political arena "to fight for its claim to be given public recognition."

Barth was one of the first theologians to see clearly the profound challenge of German Nazism to the fundamental character of both church and state. Nazism had turned the state into a fraudulent church while depriving the real church of its authentic independent existence. Barth was the principal theological mind in the formulation of the Barmen Declaration of the German "Confessing Church" movement in 1934, a prophetic statement challenging the fundamental assumptions of Nazism.

Dietrich Bonhoeffer

In a life tragically ended by the rulers of Nazi Germany at almost the very end of World War II, Dietrich Bonhoeffer (1906–1945) made significant though tantalizingly incomplete contributions to Christian ethics. In an early book, Bonhoeffer responded to the tendency in some Lutheran theological circles to draw the wrong conclusion from the priority of grace to law in Luther (and Paul). Grace is central, all right, but grace is not to be equated with moral permissiveness and complacency. Grace is not just accepting that one is accepted. Such complacency is "cheap grace." And "the word of cheap grace has been the ruin of more Christians than any commandment of works."[28] It is not just that "cheap grace" is a failure to act out the implications of grace. "Cheap grace" betrays unbelief. Faith and obedience are not separate things, the one following the other; they really are different sides of the same thing. Thus, he writes with emphasis, "*Only he who believes is obedient, and only he who is obedient believes.* . . . For faith is only real when there is obedience, never without it, and faith only becomes faith in the act of obedience."[29] So "cheap grace" is no grace at all, just as obedience to moral law in the absence of grace is not Christian morality.

In his posthumously published *Ethics*, Bonhoeffer developed a distinction between the "ultimate" and the "penultimate" which, in common with Barth's distinction between creation and covenant, helps clarify what is morally at stake in the objective world. The ultimate, to Bonhoeffer, is the justification of the sinner by grace through faith. The penultimate is everything that helps make that possible. The penultimate aids or impedes the work of God's grace, which is the ultimate. He explains it in these words:

> What is this penultimate? It is everything that precedes the ultimate, everything that precedes the justification of the sinner by grace alone, everything which is to be regarded as leading up to the last thing when the last thing has been found. . . . For the sake of the ultimate the penultimate must be preserved. Any arbitrary destruction of the penultimate will do serious injury to the ultimate. If, for example, a human life is deprived of the conditions which are proper to it, then the justification of such a life by grace and faith, if it is not rendered impossible, is at least seriously impeded.[30]

So here we have, so to speak, a spiritual rationale for the importance of dealing with material problems. We can understand why hunger and oppression, disease and war matter. It is not because the material conditions to which they refer are themselves "ultimate." It is rather because such conditions impede the life in grace that is intended by God. So "the hungry man needs bread and the homeless man needs a roof; the dispossessed need justice and the lonely need fellowship; the undisciplined need order and the slave needs freedom." For "to allow the hungry man to remain hungry would be blasphemy against God and one's neighbour, for what is nearest to God is precisely the need of one's neighbor."[31] In an allusion to Isaiah 40, Bonhoeffer speaks of our dealing responsibly with the penultimate as "preparing the way." Giving bread to the hungry may not be the same thing as proclaiming God's grace to them. Bonhoeffer is as clear about that as he is that "to have received bread is not the same as to have faith." Yet there is a relationship. To experience persistent, gnawing hunger—especially in the presence of people who could do something about it if they would—is to have greater difficulty in experiencing grace. So, if "the coming of grace is the ultimate," then the penultimate is "the preparing of the way."[32]

Paul Tillich

Initially prominent in the 1920s for his support of religious socialism, a cause to which he gave his own unique twist, Paul Tillich (1886–1965) was forced by the rise of Nazism to leave his native Germany. Resettling in the United States, he launched a new academic career and became one of the world's leading theologians. Tillich's systematic theology is difficult to summarize briefly, but he made two highly significant contributions to twentieth-century ethics (in addition to his earlier espousal of religious socialism).

The first of these was his articulation of what he called the "Protestant principle." According to this principle, no absolute claim can be made for relative realities. As he put it,

> The Protestant principle, in name derived from the protest of the "protestants" against decisions of the Catholic majority, contains the divine and human protest against any absolute claim made for a relative reality, even if this claim is made by a Protestant church. The Protestant principle is the judge of every religious and cultural reality, including the religion and culture which calls itself "Protestant."[33]

Applied to Christian ethics, the implication is that the cultural expression of moral values and rules cannot be absolutized. The transcendence of God prohibits us from making idols of any moral claims. All such judgments are relative, subject to criticism, open to amendment. Similarly, honest doubt about the faith and intellectual uncertainty about particular moral claims must be honored, not simply as an accommodation to our sinfulness but as an expression of our devotion to God.

In an interesting twist on the Reformation doctrine of justification by faith, Tillich writes that this doctrine "refers not only to the religious-ethical but also to the religious-intellectual life. Not only he who is in sin, but also he who is in doubt is justified through faith."[34] Tillich wishes to remind us that we can no more reach God through "the work of right thinking or . . . a sacrifice of the intellect" than we can be saved by works of the moral law.[35] The point is clearly pertinent to the question of authority in the moral life. Simple obedience to an extrinsic (or, as Tillich would say, heteronomous) moral authority, such as public opinion or even one's church, is not to be morally authentic unless it is also an expression of honest conviction. Tillich's conclusion might appear highly individualistic; it has a certain affinity with Kant's understanding of the autonomous moral will. But Tillich understands that our individual moral self is not autonomous: Our being is grounded in God, apart from whom we are alienated from the true source of our being. Honest questioning of extrinsic moral authority, thus, brings us closer to the ground of our being than does dishonest acquiescence to moral authorities. Moreover, Tillich believed that a whole culture can be "theonomous." By this he meant that the value and symbol system of a culture can be an integrated expression of the honest faith shared by a whole people. In such a culture, "authority" is not intrinsic; it is internalized deeply by everybody. Thus, it would be a mistake to treat Tillich's "Protestant principle" as a simple expression of Enlightenment individualism, although it shares with that a critical attitude toward all intellectual dishonesty and unthinking conformity.

The critical principle means that Christian revelation cannot be turned into absolutes. Christian ethics, rather, points toward something it can never fully encompass. As Tillich has put it: "The final revelation does not give us absolute ethics, absolute doctrines, or an absolute ideal of personal and communal life. It gives us examples which point to that which is absolute; but the examples are not absolute in themselves."[36]

In an extended essay on the relationships of love, power, and justice,[37] Tillich has explored the sense in which love and justice are not contrasting but mutually defining terms. Justice is not something that must be satisfied before we can talk about love. Love is not a higher way than justice. They are aspects of the same reality. Tillich's discussion of these terms is grounded in ontology: love is the drive toward the reunion of separated beings, while justice is the form this takes. "Love," he writes,

> does not do more than justice demands, but love is the ultimate principle of justice. Love reunites; justice preserves what is to be united. It is the form in which and through which love performs its work. Justice in its ultimate meaning is creative justice, and creative justice is the form of reuniting love.[38]

Justice is guided by equality, a term Tillich differentiates carefully, by freedom, and by respect for personhood. But justice transcends mechanical structures through "creative justice," which is the endeavor to serve the deeper interests of love. The concept of "creative justice" prefigures, in an interesting way, much late twentieth-century discussion of "affirmative action," though it also suggests that latter term should not be detached from love.

Tillich's formulation of these relationships, while developed abstractly in more philosophical language, suggests that a Christian ethical grounding for justice can receive its most profound expression in grace and love—not in a more general theory of natural justice.

Tillich has made another significant contribution to twentieth-century Christian ethics by exploring theological polarities.[39] Polarities are mutually contradictory opposites that are yet complementary and necessary to each other. Thus, he writes of "individualization" and "participation," the first referring to the particular selfhood, the latter to its universal context. Thus, also, he considers "dynamics" and "form" and, as a third polarity, "freedom" and "destiny." This third polarity suggests a way of getting beyond the old dispute over freedom of the will and determinism.

227

Tillich's discussion of the polarities is an important reminder that many apparently opposite values or principles in ethics are complementary and not mutually exclusive.

H. Richard Niebuhr

It hardly seems equitable, in a summary of a handful of formative twentieth-century Christian ethicists, to include two from the same family! But H. Richard Niebuhr (1894–1962), brother of Reinhold Niebuhr, has to be included. While he was not as prolific a writer as his brother, each of H. R. Niebuhr's books made a distinctive contribution. Three of his typologies have been especially influential.

The first of these is developed in his book *Christ and Culture*,[40] a study that displays not only the great influence of Ernst Troeltsch's *Social Teachings* but also Niebuhr's own creative genius. The book addresses the different typical forms in which major Christian thinkers have understood the relationship between Christian faith and the social-cultural world. While acknowledging considerable overlapping of these "types" and all the difficulties of classification, Niebuhr finds five major forms of understanding that relationship. He illustrates each with three or four typical thinkers, illustrating how each type appeared in the ethical thought of different periods of Christian history. Type one is "Christ against culture." Thinkers, such as Tertullian and Tolstoy, who represent this view stress the radical antagonism between Christian faith and the corrupt, fallen world. The latter can scarcely be reformed. Those who are truly Christian must be totally committed. Their cultural strategy is essentially the cultivation of the pure moral life in the community of faith, seeking by their example and by the conversion of others to draw as many people as possible away from the corruptions of the world.

Type two, the "Christ of culture," is at the opposite extreme. It depicts Christian ethics as little more than an expression of the highest values generally shared in a world that is capable of goodness and reason in its common life. Type three, "Christ above culture," distinguishes between the generally shared natural law basis of ethics and the higher realm of revealed Christian truth that is ultimately necessary for salvation. Type four, "Christ and culture in paradox," distinguishes between the corrupt, fallen world and the pure gospel. The fall is complete enough that the world will not be redeemed before the consummation of history. But we all share in its sinful state; from that there is no place of withdrawal. Christians are called to act responsibly in that world, mitigating its evils and creating space within which the gospel can also be at work. Type five, "Christ the transformer of culture," calls for the transformation of culture in accordance with Christian understanding.

Niebuhr believed that each of the types represents an aspect of valid Christian understanding, though he clearly regarded the last three as most authentic and, of these, probably preferred type five.

The second of his typologies is contained in his book *Radical Monotheism and Western Culture*.[41] In this volume, Niebuhr analyzed the "centers of value" upon which the faith and moral commitments of all people are grounded. Niebuhr insists that all people have some value point of reference (or center of value) upon which all their other values are based. He finds three typical forms of center of value: (1) polytheism, the disintegrated holding of numerous values at once, presupposing a centering upon oneself; (2) henotheism, the centering of value in the "tribe" or group; and (3) radical monotheism, which identifies the center of value with the center of all being. Polytheism is the least integrative, most unstable of the centers of value—though not the least common. Henotheism is a higher form of morality, although it is still a limited center. Henotheism can represent one's own family, one's racial or ethnic group, one's nation, one's social class, or any other human grouping. In a striking insight, Niebuhr notes that it can even represent humanity as a whole—thus humanism is a form of henotheism. Only radical monotheism is capable of uniting and integrating all values and aspects of experience. Even humanism, as possibly the highest form of henotheism, cannot impute value to the nonhuman aspects of creation except as these are useful to human beings. But Niebuhr insists that all of creation has value, not just the human.

This typology is an elegant reminder of two points: First, every human being is a worshiping self—the only difference in human beings is in their choice of gods to worship. It is not that some people are religious and others are not. All are religious, but their gods vary. Second, ethics is ultimately religious or theological. Ethics ultimately is grounded in questions of value, and questions of value are ultimately grounded in the chosen center of value (translate: in the deity one chooses to worship). Any ethical theory neglecting that point must remain superficial, whatever help it offers in clarifying other kinds of moral concepts.

The third typology is outlined in a sketchy way in a posthumously published volume, *The Responsible Self*.[42] Here Niebuhr writes of three types of approach to ethics: (1) man-as-maker, which understands the moral life as the creation of value, as selecting good means for the accomplishment of good ends; (2) man-the-citizen, living under law, which understands the moral life as right living in obedience to the right moral principles; and (3) moral responsibility, which understands the moral life as responding in a fitting way to God as one confronts moral problems. Niebuhr's own ethic is an expression of the third of these. The "responsible self" is the person who responds to God, valuing all things as they are valued by God.

229

The Situation Ethics Debate and the Question of Principles

Several Christian ethicists, mostly American, contributed to a fascinating and in some respects clarifying debate in the 1960s over what was loosely called "situation ethics." In a book by that title,[43] Joseph Fletcher gave popular expression to an ethic of intuition based upon love. Moral principles can be helpful as "rules of thumb," but there are no intrinsically binding moral norms other than the general norm of love. Love decides "then and there," in the situation, what is the most loving thing to do. The work did not draw heavily upon theological resources other than the broad commitment to Christian love. In a similar, more theologically cast work, Paul Lehmann wrote of ethics in a "Christian context."[44] His "contextual ethics" had a double meaning: on the one hand "context" referred, as with Fletcher, to the situation confronted. But on the other hand it referred to the theological context. The two are joined in his formula that Christians are to do what God is doing—"to act in every situation in accordance with what it has been given to me to be."[45] Our knowledge of what we are to do is also intuitive. It is given to us through faith. It is a matter of discernment, of insight.

One of the sharpest critics of situational or contextual ethics was Paul Ramsey. His criticisms are all the more interesting when seen in light of his first significant book, *Basic Christian Ethics*, in which he affirmed key viewpoints of the later situation ethics movement. Note, for instance, the following passage, which might have been written by Fletcher himself:

> Christian love takes on the aspect of a quite indeterminate norm when compared with any and all forms of legalistic social ethic. The Christian man is lord of all and subject to none of the rule-morality. Set free on account of his so great responsibility, he must therefore be constantly engaged in "building up" an adequate social ethic realistically adjusted, not to precedents in law or existing conventions of society, but to concrete and changing neighbor need. Searching for a social policy Christian love may make *use* of, say, the ethical insights summed up in the so-called "natural law," but its *base* of operations never shifts over onto the ground of the rational moral law.[46]

But Ramsey's early exploration of the meaning of love *(agape)* was to develop into a way of combining the foundation of Christian ethics with the application of principles.

In a volume largely devoted to the ensuing debate over "situation ethics,"[47] Paul Ramsey offered both critical and constructive responses. In a critical vein, he pointed to the inconclusiveness of an ethic devoid of principles or rules. How are we to know what real love is, on the basis of which we are to act? How are we to adjudicate between contradictory claims, both supposedly grounded in "love" or "what God is doing in history"? Ramsey notes that among the illustrations offered by Fletcher, quite contradictory interpretations of "love" are implied. Ramsey's critique is all the more interesting because his own first important work, more than a decade earlier, had utilized the general principle of love (*agape*) in similar situational fashion.

But it is Ramsey's own effort to ground moral principle that is most interesting. Following a lead suggested in a nontheological context by the American philosopher John Rawls, Ramsey distinguished between what he called "act agapism," or acts directly motivated by Christian love, and "rule agapism," referring to rules that themselves embody love. This is interesting because it is an attempt to ground moral rules in something other than natural law. A love-embodying rule is not one to be delineated by rational reflection upon general human moral experience; it is a rule determined by its relationship to love. Ramsey's point is that rules can embody or frustrate love, just as individual acts can. Extending the point further, Ramsey notes that "rules of practice" can also be expressions of love. A rule of practice is a set of rules determining a sphere of human activity—or, one might say, an institution. Thus, the institution of marriage might be spoken of as a rule of practice that, as a rule, embodies love. One of the problems with situation ethics is that its concentration upon individual acts can lead to a weakening of rules of practice and, ironically, thereby to a weakening of love. At the least, when contemplating the breaking of a love-embodying rule or practice, one must consider the long-run consequences of weakening that rule or practice.

Ramsey's consideration of the just war tradition is an important illustration of his own application of principles and rules.[48] Addressed primarily to the circumstances of the nuclear balance of terror in the Cold War, Ramsey's study was an important Protestant application of traditional just war criteria. In that volume he found it possible to reduce the traditional criteria essentially to two: the principle of discrimination and the principle of proportion. The first of these rules out some kinds of acts (such as the direct killing of innocent people or the use of torture) as intrinsically immoral. To do these things is *always* and by definition wrong. The second of these principles requires us to weigh the good to be achieved through military action against the evil one must anticipate. If actions that do not violate the principle of discrimination nevertheless would result in more evil than good, then the principle of proportion rules them out as well.

Ramsey generally found it possible to justify military actions by the United States on the basis of his reading of the just war criteria—such as his strong support for the Vietnam War. Nevertheless, he did raise serious questions about U.S. strategic doctrine that targeted cities in the Soviet

Union. While he did not disapprove nuclear weapons per se, he did insist that they be directed only against the military forces of the adversary.

Walter G. Muelder and L. Harold DeWolf, following the lead of the philosopher Edgar S. Brightman, explored the possibilities of the latter's moral law system in Christian ethics.[49] Brightman's moral laws are themselves an elaboration of the Kantian concept of the moral will. The formal principles of consistency and coherence are therefore of central importance. To have moral integrity is to choose values that are, at some basic level, consistent and, more than that, mutually supportive. Recognizing that perfection is rarely attainable and that every possible decision may entail some evil, this moral law system emphasizes the "best possible."

Muelder's own contributions to twentieth-century Christian ethics include a much more explicit drawing upon the empirical sciences in Christian moral thought. In a finely tuned treatment of Christian social ethics,[50] he notes that there can never be closure since knowledge is always in process of further development. Social ethics is always at the intersection between empirical and normative disciplines. The sciences cannot be the source of our values, but neither can theology or moral philosophy be a substitute for sources of factual information. Christian ethics necessarily involves both. Therefore, writes Muelder, "my concern is for emergent coherence."[51] "Emergent," here, means always in process of emerging. For neither our science nor our theology is ever finally complete.

DeWolf contributes a broadened, less individualistic understanding of Christian love. He notes that most theories of love are too individualistic. That is as true for altruistic conceptions, such as the total self-giving agape emphasized by Anders Nygren,[52] as it is for the "benevolence" of Bishop Butler or even the *caritas* of Augustine. Love, in such conceptions, is what we give from ourselves to others—whether or not expecting anything in return. But DeWolf regards the more authentic Christian understanding of love to be summarized in the New Testament term *koinonia*, or "commonness," we have with one another. To love, in that sense, is to share, to see together, to act together. Love is more "we" than "I." Christian love, as he puts it, is "the desire to participate with another in a community of shared experience," and it includes "those treasures" from God that we share with one another.[53]

John C. Bennett's work in ethics has also been relevant to the question of whether moral principles are legitimate and useful tools for Christian moral thought. In natural law fashion, he argues that "there is a moral order in the world that can be known with varying degrees of clarity apart from revelation." Moreover, "the knowledge of this moral order is not as a matter of fact universal but it has a much broader basis than the Christian faith."[54] Building on a concept from the early twentieth-century ecumenical movement,[55] Bennett believes that "middle axioms" can be especially useful. "Middle axioms" are not as formal as universal principles nor as specific as particular programs. They are, in J. H. Oldham's characterization, "an attempt to define the directions in which, in a particular state of society, Christian faith must express itself. They are not binding for all time, but are provisional definitions of the type of behavior required of Christians at a given period and in given circumstances."[56] Bennett's own elaboration of the "middle axiom" is developed in a variety of works on politics, economics, and international relations over several decades. The hallmark of his work is recognition that ethical commentary on problems in these spheres must be rooted in historical circumstance and also be a distillation of principle. Bennett's work is thus in contrast with "situation ethics," though it shares with the situationalists the understanding that our principles are always provisional and that the particularities of situations must be addressed pragmatically.

The present writer has also sought to develop a basis for principled decision making while respecting the complexities and uncertainties of the historical situations.[57] I have sought to clarify the moral "presumptions" on the basis of which Christians can act in faithfulness to the implications of the gospel. A presumption is a norm or value or belief on the basis of which one will act unless sufficient evidence can be shown that one should not. The Christian just war tradition illustrates the approach: War, with all of its evils, is presumed to be wrong unless the burden of proof can be borne (in relation to the traditional criteria) that under this or that exceptional circumstance it is necessary in order to avoid still greater evils (as seen in light of the Christian gospel of love and justice). Similarly, a Christian presumption against marital separation or divorce can be affirmed—with the burden of proof being placed against the breakup of a marriage. A variety of "presumptions" have been elaborated in this work, such as a presumption in favor of the goodness of the created world, the value of each person's life, the unity of humankind, and human equality—along with the "negative" presumptions of human limitation and sinfulness. Such presumptions, interpreted through their theological points of reference, have been offered as a way of uniting the insights of the situationalists with those of more principled approaches to Christian ethics.

John Howard Yoder and the "Politics of Jesus"

The Christian pacifist tradition gained unusually articulate interpretation in the twentieth century through the work of John Howard Yoder.[58] Greatly influenced both by his Mennonite background and his contact with Karl Barth, Yoder's expression of pacifism sought to avoid illusions of human perfectibility, the irrelevance of sectarian detachment (with its own temptations toward self-righteousness), and moral complicity with war.

Jesus, according to Yoder, was politically relevant. Had he not been relevant, he would have made no enemies and there would have been no reason to have him crucified. He was a threat, not because he sought to become an earthly ruler—a political force in the usual sense—and not because he represented a military challenge. He was a threat because his gospel of love, peace, and justice made people less governable. Attracted to Jesus, people would no longer cooperate with systems of injustice. So Jesus had to be stopped.

But Jesus, for his part, totally renounced violent methods. It was not given to him to seek to control the course of events in that way. Even in the end, he submitted to the agony and humiliation of the cross rather than act in ways that would be inconsistent with God's way of love. Was the crucifixion, then, one more evidence of the impotence of God's way of love? Yoder's response is that the resurrection of Christ was God's final answer to that question. Through the resurrection God gave the victory to Jesus and the way of love and made permanently clear that that way of obedience is the only faithful response of humanity to the injustices and dilemmas of history. Specifically, this means that Christians must disavow efforts to control the course of history. Our responsibility is to be faithful, not successful. Success is God's business; obedience is ours. Indeed, to seek success on any other basis than the way of Jesus is to accomplish failure instead. Sometimes the way of obedience to love is promptly effective; sometimes it is not. Sometimes it yields only another cross. But in the long run, God has spoken decisively through the resurrection about what will finally happen. So Yoder refers the question of historical effectiveness to an eschatological dimension. But even in the short run this does not mean that Christians should not attempt to be effective. Resistance to injustice and evil, pursued in loving and nonviolent ways, remains the permanent assignment of Christians.

Thus, in contrast to Tolstoy, Yoder's Christian pacifism is not predicated on an overly optimistic view of human nature. Evil is not simply a reflection of coercive institutions. We cannot be sure that goodness and justice will flourish if only such institutions can be done away with. Even then, sin will still be a threatening reality. But Yoder believes that sin cannot be destroyed by sin. Only God, using the faithfulness of loving people, can ultimately destroy sin.

Yoder thus places a high premium on the company of faithful Christians. Influenced by this, a number of other Christian ethicists and theologians—such as Stanley Hauerwas and James William McClendon[59]—have structured Christian ethics around the reality of a more faithful church. The church must be a believing church, responding to the Christian "story" and making that story their own story. Such Christians are identified by their character, not by calculating decisions. Their real message is what they are, in response to the Christian story. They must act in history and they must bear witness to the Christian story. But they do not attempt to "control" history. And their primary focus is upon the church, not upon society at large.

Bernard Haring

Most of the formative moral thinkers considered in this chapter have been Protestants of one kind or another. But Roman Catholicism has also produced seminal work. In this century, Catholic moral thought has resonated through papal encyclicals and the notable contributions of the Second Vatican Council. Obviously, the evolving form of such declarations owes much to the careful work of individual theologians.

There is probably no Catholic moral theologian in the twentieth century whose work has been more influential in this regard than Bernard Haring. He is particularly important at the watershed between a dominantly natural law approach to Christian ethical teaching and an approach structured more directly around Christ and gospel.

The fundamental purpose of moral theology, Haring announces, "is not concerned first with decision-making or with discrete acts." Rather, "its basic task and purpose is to gain the right vision, to assess the main perspectives, and to present those truths and values which should bear upon decisions to be made before God."[60] The basic perspective is not autonomous from the church's fundamental theological perspective. Christian ethics cannot establish, "by way of a rational procedure, an ethics for all people."[61] Martin Luther, he writes, was rightly opposed to "a natural law theory which presented practically a closed system of an autonomous human reason."[62] To the extent natural law can be employed by Christian ethics it "must be explored, above all, in the light of Holy Scripture. There, it is presented as a part of the Good News of salvation."[63]

That good news, to Haring, is the good news of the covenant—of God's loving relationship with humanity as encountered in Jesus Christ. The essence of the covenant is love; its character is freedom. "Fidelity to Christ and to the people of the covenant creates a sphere of freedom in which we can live creatively in dialogue and mutuality."[64] The relationship between love and freedom suggests to Haring that no ethic of law, natural or otherwise, can convey the essence of the covenant. Law defines minimum behaviors; love creatively transcends all such standards. "One of the most uncreative approaches in the Church is to stress fidelity to certain negative commandments to such an extent that fidelity to Christ and his great affirmative commandments of justice, love and mercy is seriously neglected."[65]

This does not mean to Haring that love is a substitute for justice. Justice, for Haring, is also defined by love, for it exists ultimately to serve love. Expressed in the relationship between law and love, he writes that "as love implies obedience, so it implies law, and love and law are essentially and mutually interchangeable."[66] But legal obedience alone is not yet love:

> External laws are no more than universal regulations and therefore basically only minimum requirements. Universal rules cannot in fact even prescribe what is highest and best, since the best is not universal and cannot be demanded from men universally. On the contrary, love by its very nature strives for the highest and best and seeks the most perfect manifestation of its ideals in action.[67]

In summary, "since the minimum requirements are basic for the fulfillment of the law of love, love may never violate or ignore the law. At the same time one who truly loves may not remain at the lowest level of obedience and be satisfied with the bare legal minimum."[68] That point is underscored practically as Haring emphasizes that charity cannot be a substitute for justice. For example, an employer may not substitute almsgiving for the payment of inadequate wages. First, before giving the alms, the employer "must restore the amount to the worker who earned it, as a recompense for the work itself, and not as alms or other form of gratuity."[69]

Bernard Haring's practical conclusions are within the mainstream of twentieth-century Catholic social teaching, sometimes deviating modestly in a more progressive direction, sometimes (surprisingly) with a more conservative bent. It is his great shift from the scholastic natural law tradition to the more flexible and theologically grounded scriptural and christological orientation that marks his significance. His faithful allegiance to the church is clear throughout the work, along with a sometimes eloquent pastoral touch. Occasionally he will express sadness over the church's rigidities, as when he writes that "I suffer with the Church when I see parts of her enslaved by dead traditions in contradiction with our faith in a living God who works with his people at all times."[70] Still, it is within the Church that "our Lord calls us to be faithful to him, the Lord of history, and to the best of all traditions."[71]

Toward the end of the twentieth century, a number of creative Roman Catholic moral theologians—some directly influenced by Haring—have had to bear the burden of faithful and creative thought in a context that is not always receptive. Figures like Charles Curran, Richard McCormick, Edward Schillebeeckx, Hans Küng, and Leonardo Boff, who, in different ways, reflect the greatness of the Catholic tradition in a new era, have not always been well understood by the church authorities to whom they were accountable.

19

THE VATICAN II WATERSHED

Moral theologians like Bernard Haring and John Courtney Murray exerted great influence in Roman Catholic moral theology after the middle of the twentieth century. Haring, as we have seen, helped change the church's focus from primary reliance on the Thomistic natural law tradition to a scriptural and christological orientation. Murray, though still largely committed to the natural law basis, helped the church rethink its positions on church-state relations and religious liberty, thus also encouraging a more ecumenical stance. These thinkers, and a number of others, helped pave the way for the Second Vatican Council, an event that marked a sea change in Catholic moral teaching.

The Encyclicals of Pope John XXIII

The figure who was primarily responsible for that Council was, however, Pope John XXIII. John was not, himself, a notable moral theologian. And, elected as an elderly man, he served as pope for only five years (1958–1963). Nevertheless, no pope for at least a century had as profound an effect on the church and its moral theology as this one. During his brief pontificate, John issued two influential encyclicals and summoned the Second Vatican Council. His encyclical *Mater et magistra*, commemorating the seventieth anniversary of *Rerum novarum*, built upon the earlier tradition. Thus, for instance, it reaffirmed the doctrine of subsidiarity and the right of private ownership. At the same time, it turned these doctrines toward more egalitarian outcomes. For instance, he writes that "it is not enough to assert that the right to own private property and the means of production is inherent in human nature. We must also insist on the extension of this right in practice to all classes of citizens."[1] "Now," he continues, "is the time to insist on a more widespread distribution of property. . . . It will not be difficult for the body politic, by the adoption of various techniques of proved efficiency, to pursue an economic and social policy which facilitates the widest possible distribution of private property in terms of durable consumer goods, houses, land, tools and equipment . . . and shares in medium and large business concerns."[2] Moreover, John proceeds to affirm a strong public sector in the economy through "state and public ownership of productive goods."[3] This is made necessary by the demands of the "common good," a phrase repeatedly invoked by the encyclical. Public ownership should observe the limitations of subsidiarity—not extending "beyond what is clearly required by considerations of the common good properly understood, and even then there must be safeguards."[4]

Mater et magistra remains substantially within the natural law tradition. In dealing with population matters, it reaffirms the earlier twentieth-century doctrine that "certain ways and means" are excluded in view of the "inviolable and immutable laws of God." The solution to the population problem "is not to be found in expedients which offend against the divinely established moral order."[5] Like its immediate predecessors, the encyclical also appeals to the principle of subsidiarity, according to which "public authority must encourage and assist private enterprise, entrusting to it, wherever possible, the continuation of economic development."[6]

John XXIII's 1963 encyclical *Pacem in terris* was timely on two counts: It was written at one of those moments in the Cold War when consciousness of the threat of thermonuclear war was especially high and when the world was especially receptive to leadership in peacemaking. And it was published in the midst of the Second Vatican Council.

The letter is a lengthy plea for peace and a new world order. It asserted that "men's common interests make it imperative that at long last a worldwide community of nations be established"—a note that is hardly struck in the earlier encyclicals. Moreover, it develops the broader implications of the principle of subsidiarity. True enough, that principle asserts the importance of dealing with problems on the most feasible immediate level. But it notes that when problems cannot be solved locally or nationally the principle requires that we turn to universal levels of human community. While the language of section 137 of the document is somewhat convoluted, its point is that worldwide problems demand worldwide solutions:

> Today the universal common good presents us with problems which are world-wide in their dimensions; problems, therefore, which cannot be solved except by a public authority with power, organization and means co-extensive with these problems, and with a world-wide sphere of activity. Consequently the moral order itself demands the establishment of some such general form of public authority.[7]

This is not exactly a call for world government. But it is close enough to represent a remarkable reapplication of the doctrine of subsidiarity. That doctrine had always held that higher levels of power and authority should be utilized when necessary, but the implication generally was that problems should be dealt with locally or privately when possible. Now, Pope John XXIII has called attention to problems at the highest possible level of human community, that is, at the global level. And here, he has noted, there are scarcely any institutions at all to deal with those problems. New, global forms of authority are needed. To some extent, not specified in the encyclical, the nation state system itself must now be transcended. For, "the shape and structure of the political life in the modern world, and the influence exercised by public authority in all the nations of the world are unequal to the task of promoting the common good of all peoples."[8]

Not surprisingly, the encyclical goes on to express "our earnest wish that the United Nations Organization may be able progressively to adapt its structure and methods of operation to the magnitude and nobility of its task."[9] Equally to be expected is the document's call for a "cessation to the arms race" and its insistent plea that "nuclear weapons must be banned."[10]

Pacem in terris represents a departure at two or three other points. In its discussion of political authority, the encyclical, in effect, calls for civil disobedience when laws are passed "in contravention of the moral order, and hence of the divine will." Such laws and decrees "can have no binding force in conscience."[11] Moreover, John issues here the most explicit defense of democratic political structures to date, grounding this in the natural law principle of human dignity. By virtue of human dignity, he writes, it is "unquestionably" the right of all people "to take an active part in government," though, he acknowledges, "their degree of participation will necessarily depend on the stage of development reached by the political community of which they are members."[12] Here we have something of a reversal of the old principle of "thesis/hypothesis," according to which the democratic principle of freedom of religion is to be tolerated by the state only when political conditions make it impossible to control the open expression of error. John has argued, in this broader context, that the denial of democracy is to be allowed only when political conditions make its achievement yet impossible.

Pacem in terris, finally, expresses a version of what later came to be known as the "preferential option for the poor." John writes that "considerations of justice and equity can at times demand that those in power pay more attention to the weaker members of society, since these are at a disadvantage when it comes to defending their own rights and asserting their legitimate interests."[13]

The Second Vatican Council

Notwithstanding the great significance of these encyclicals, the larger impact of John's pontificate was in the calling of Vatican II. The Council, which lasted from 1962 to 1965, became a common focus for church renewal and an ecumenical event of surpassing importance. A number of its lengthy decrees were landmarks in the development of twentieth-century Roman Catholic moral teaching.

The "Pastoral Constitution on the Church in the Modern World" *(Gaudium et spes)* was the most important of these. This ambitious document sought to address the profound contradictions in the existence of twentieth-century humanity:

> Never has the human race enjoyed such an abundance of wealth, resources and economic power, and yet a huge proportion of the world's citizens are still tormented by hunger and poverty, while countless numbers suffer from total illiteracy. Never before has man had so keen an understanding of freedom, yet at the same time, new forms of social and psychological slavery make their appearance. Although the world of today has a very vivid awareness of its unity and of how one man depends on another in needful solidarity, it is most grievously torn into opposing camps by conflicting forces.[14]

In such a world, humanity is recalled to its true dignity in the recognition of the claims of God upon it. Indeed, "the recognition of God is in no way hostile to man's dignity, since this dignity is rooted and perfected in God."[15] Still, the fulfillment and expression of that dignity demands freedom. "Only in freedom can man direct himself toward goodness."[16] But in the exercise of that freedom, humanity stands in need of God's grace "since man's freedom has been damaged by sin." Freedom is given social context as well in the observation that "freedom is often crippled when a man encounters extreme poverty, just as it withers when he indulges in too many of life's comforts and imprisons himself in a kind of splendid isolation."[17] The document asserts the importance of full opportunity for "the largest possible number of citizens to participate in public affairs with genuine freedom." So, through *Gaudium et spes*, Vatican II continued the Catholic transition from a preference for political authoritarianism to solid support for democracy.

The document also calls for greater equality. Equality is grounded in the "rational soul" of all humans (thus repeating the old Stoic argument), the image of God, and redemption through Christ.[18] Equality is applied to economics in the call to each country "to remove as quickly as possible the immense economic inequalities which now exist and in many cases are growing and which are connected with individual and social discrimination."[19] As counterpoint to this theme, however, *Gaudium et spes* also repeats the recognition of private property as necessary "to the expression of personality."[20] And, when "the common good requires expropriation, compensation must be reckoned in equity after all the circumstances have been weighed."[21]

The document picks up the theme of *Pacem in terris* by noting that ultimately there is need at the global level for "the establishment of some universal public authority acknowledged as such by all and endowed with the power to safeguard on the behalf of all, security, regard for justice, and respect for rights." Meanwhile "the highest existing international centres must devote themselves vigorously to the pursuit of better means for obtaining common security. . . . [And] everyone must labour to put an end at last to the arms race."[22]

Taken as a whole, *Gaudium et spes* is a call to the whole church to respond creatively and decisively to the world's problems. It notes that the church, as a universal institution, has immense resources and points of contact with suffering people and their problems and differences of culture. The popular subtitle, "Pastoral Constitution on the Church in the Modern World," itself suggests the deeper point. To speak of this kind of document as "pastoral" is to think of it as an expression of the church's ministry of caring. Christians who were more prone to think of "pastoral" caring in terms of the individualistic relationship between a "pastor" and persons with spiritual problems could find here a whole new dimension of understanding. This suggests that individual and social aspects of human existence cannot so easily be separated if the church is to minister to whole persons in their actual social context.

In addition to *Gaudium et spes*, Vatican II issued a torrent of new teaching on religious liberty and the relationships between Roman Catholicism and other Christian communions and world religions. The Declaration on Religious Freedom (*Dignitatis humanae*) represented the work of a generation of theological scholars seeking to reverse the Roman Catholic Church's general stance on that subject—a position that had long been an embarrassment to the church in democratic countries. Echoing Pope John XXIII's reversal of the older "thesis/hypothesis" view, the Declaration sought a principled basis for affirming religious liberty as the norm. In general, that basis was asserted to have "its foundation in the very dignity of the human person, as this dignity is known through the revealed Word of God and by reason itself."[23] This dignity also means that people must seek the truth and live by it "once it is known." But this is not possible unless they have "psychological freedom" and "immunity from external coercion." So the right of freedom of religion is from our "very nature."[24] The document further argues, on the basis of the social dimension of human nature, that external social expression of religious freedom cannot be denied "except when the just requirements of public order do not so require."[25]

The *Declaration on Religious Freedom* did continue Catholic claims to be the "one true religion." ("God himself has made known to mankind the way in which men are to serve Him, and thus be saved in Christ and come to blessedness. We believe that this one true religion subsists in the catholic and apostolic Church."[26]) That claim has traditionally been the sticking point in affirming religious liberty. It is possible to accept religious liberty as necessary to the expression of human dignity while at the same time wishing to protect the innocent from exposure to error. If the truth has been identified objectively, it remains difficult to protect anybody's right to preach error. But it is at this point that the Council's Declaration on Non-Christian Religions (*Nostra aetate*) further undergirds support for tolerance and religious freedom. Here we read that "the Catholic Church rejects nothing which is true and holy in these religions. She looks with sincere respect upon those ways of conduct and of life, those rules and teachings which, though differing in many particulars from what she holds and sets forth, nevertheless often reflect a ray of that Truth which enlightens all men."[27] The document then calls for dialogue and collaboration, wherever possible. The implication here is that the church also has things to learn, from the other religions, about God's relationship with humanity. The import of this document for the question of religious freedom is that freedom can more easily been seen as protecting authentic witness to the truth in unexpected quarters.

The Encyclicals of Pope Paul VI

Paul VI, who became pope upon John XXIII's death in 1963, continued in office until his own death in 1978. It fell to his papacy to consolidate the work of the Second Vatican Council while continuing the legacy of the illustrious John. His own significant encyclicals included *Populorum progressio* (1967), *Humanae vitae* (1968), and *Octagesimo adveniens* (1971).

Populorum was primarily addressed to problems of the international order and, in particular, issues related to the social and economic development of poorer countries. Grounded in the now-typical concept of the "common good," this encyclical like most of its twentieth-century predecessors insisted that humanity is social as well as individual by nature. The document warned against "revolutionary uprisings" which might "engender new injustices, introduce new inequities and bring new disasters."[28] But it also called upon public authorities to provide serious leadership in addressing social injustices. Even in respect to too-rapid population growth, Paul affirmed "that public authorities can intervene in this matter, within the bounds of their competence."[29] The principles of free trade are not adequate to the needs for development. Echoing John XXIII's call for new global institutions, Paul commented that "international collaboration among the nations of the world certainly calls for institutions that will promote, co-ordinate and direct it, until a new juridical order is firmly established and fully ratified."[30] "Men are," he remarked, "growing more anxious to establish closer ties of brotherhood."[31]

Octagesimo adveniens, commemorating the eightieth anniversary of Leo's *Rerum novarum*, continued to warn against revolutionary panaceas. Still, it condemned "flagrant inequalities" among the nations. This encyclical also marked the first major papal emphasis on "the preferential respect due to the poor."[32] And, in a distinct departure from much previous papal teaching, *Octagesimo* expressed a guarded openness to some forms of socialism—with warnings against undemocratic or atheistic socialist ideologies. This encyclical, while noting the need for equality for women, hastened to add that "we do not have in mind that false equality which would be in contradiction with woman's proper role, which is of such capital importance, at the heart of the family as well as within society." Legislation should concentrate on protecting woman's "proper vocation" while also "recognizing her independence as a person, and her equal rights to participate in cultural, economic, social and political life."[33]

Many Catholics had expected Paul VI to abandon the church's total rejection of artificial contraception, especially after a specially appointed papal commission of experts had urged him to do so. His encyclical *Humanae vitae* did in fact give some emphasis to the importance of conjugal love and its implication of "responsible parenthood."[34] And he specifically affirmed the rhythm method of birth control for which "God has wisely disposed natural laws and rhythms of fecundity."[35] Nevertheless, the encyclical reasserted Pius XI's prohibition of artificial contraception. The church must, he wrote, call people "back to the observance of the norms of the natural law, as interpreted by its constant doctrine, . . . that each and every marriage act must remain open to the transmission of life."[36] The pope also feared that the acceptance of artificial birth control might lead to "conjugal infidelity and the general lowering of morality."[37] Paul advised rulers to translate this moral teaching into public law: "Do not allow the morality of your peoples to be degraded; do not permit that by legal means practices contrary to the natural and divine law be introduced into that fundamental cell, the family."[38] Sterilization and abortion are similarly to be rejected, though abortion occurring as the indirect effect of "those therapeutic means truly necessary to cure diseases of the organism" is not to be considered illicit.[39]

The Encyclicals of Pope John Paul II

Pope John Paul II, whose reign began in 1978, has written a series of important encyclicals, the most noteworthy of which are *Laborem exercens* (1981), *Sollicitudo rei socialis* (1987), and *Centesimus annus* (1991). In writings obviously colored by the pope's previous decades of living in Marxist Poland, John Paul emphasized the importance of religious freedom while also criticizing ideological atheism. In response to liberation theology, which had become a major development among Roman Catholic thinkers, he warned against dangers in uncritical appropriation of Marxist forms of analysis. At the same time, in his early *Laborem*, the pope implicitly addressed themes drawn from the early Marx by emphasizing the moral nature of work itself. "The primary basis of the value of work," he wrote, "is man himself, who is its subject."[40] While rejecting the Marxist doctrine of class struggle, he nevertheless insisted upon "the principle of the priority of labor over capital."[41] Capital is the means, while "labor is always a primary efficient cause."[42] The pope therefore warned against treating labor solely on the basis of its economic function. *Laborem* continued the long-standing papal support for private property. Nevertheless, it affirmed as long-standing Christian tradition that "the right to private property is subordinated to the right to common use, to the fact that goods are meant for everyone."[43] The encyclical even ventures that "one cannot exclude the socialization, in suitable conditions, of certain means of production."[44] In respect to this, however, John Paul warns against socialist elites. While ostensibly acting in behalf of the whole society, this class of governmental managers may in fact control the economy for its own narrow and selfish ends.

Sollicitudo rei socialis addressed and elaborated on the same developmental themes as Paul VI's *Populorum*. John Paul reasserted the commitment to the "preferential option for the poor," the general principle of equality, the right to private property conditioned by public good, the primacy of the spiritual over the material. The pope also sought to interpret Christian social doctrine in a way transcending the ideological conflict between capitalism and communism:

The Church's social doctrine *is not* a "third way" between *liberal capitalism* and *Marxist collectivism*, nor even a possible alternative to other solutions less radically opposed to one another: rather, it constitutes a *category of its own*. Nor is it an *ideology*, but rather the *accurate formulation* of the results of a careful reflection on the complex realities of human existence, in society and in the international order, in the light of faith and of the Church's tradition. Its main aim is to *interpret* these realities, determining their conformity with or divergence from the lines of the Gospel teaching on man and his vocation . . . [and] its aim is thus *to guide* Christian behaviour.[45]

The pope underscored this with an insistence that human liberation must be more than economic. Its "cultural, transcendent and religious dimensions" are primary. "Human beings are totally free only when they are completely *themselves*, in the fullness of their rights and duties."[46] The main point of authentic liberation, he argues, is freedom from sin. Social structures can be produced by sin, but they do not have moral reality in themselves. Sin, even personal sin, is always at the base of social evil.

John Paul II observed the centennial of *Rerum novarum* with the publication of yet another important encyclical, *Centesimus annus*. This document, arriving as it did in the midst of the collapse of Soviet and Eastern European Marxism, was promptly interpreted by some as a papal recommitment to capitalism. The encyclical does refer to "the failure of Marxism to contribute to a humane and better society."[47] And it refers to "the inefficiency of the economic system [of communism], which is not to be considered simply as a technical problem, but rather a consequence of the violation of the human rights to private initiative, to ownership of property and to freedom in the economic sector."[48] Nevertheless, the encyclical continues earlier papal warnings about consumerism in free-market societies. When the free market is touted as a better way to "achieve a greater satisfaction of material human needs than Communism, while equally excluding spiritual values," then such an ideology "agrees with Marxism, in the sense that it totally reduces man to the sphere of economics and the satisfaction of material needs."[49]

Moreover, John Paul insists that "it is unacceptable to say that the defeat of so-called 'Real Socialism' leaves capitalism as the only model of economic organization."[50] It remains important for the state to play a significant role in regulating as well as enabling the functioning of market mechanisms. And the state is needed to defend the "collective goods" without which society cannot function. The pope notes that

there are collective and qualitative needs which cannot be satisfied by market mechanisms. There are important human needs which escape its logic. There are goods which by their very nature cannot and must not be bought or sold.[51]

The Post–Vatican II Catholic Church

In summary, the social encyclicals of Popes Paul VI and John Paul II are intentionally in continuity with earlier papal teaching. Nevertheless, Vatican II had represented an important watershed. In the succeeding decades, encyclicals have been grounded more deeply in theological teaching, with much less emphasis on the earlier Thomistic natural law tradition and with greater emphasis on the Bible. They have expressed a much deeper and principled commitment to democracy and civil freedoms and a much less defensive stance toward socialism. The more recent statements have given special emphasis to the "preferential option for the poor" and to the justifiable restiveness of oppressed peoples. On issues related to the status and role of women and to human sexuality in general, papal statements remain fairly conservative. But even here, the fundamental equality of women is given some affirmation.

Roman Catholic teaching remains an expression of the church's hierarchy. But the Second Vatican Council has also unleashed a vast flow of energy from millions of progressive Catholics, lay as well as clergy, the world over. The Vatican felt it necessary to restrict creative teachers and scholars, like Hans Küng, Charles Curran, and Leonardo Boff, in order to preserve its conception of the purity of the faith and the church's teaching office (magisterium). Some practical ethical and ecclesiastical issues mark the conflicts between such scholars and the church's hierarchy as much more than academic. Should women be ordained as priests? Should priests necessarily be committed to a life of celibacy? Should divorce be permitted under some circumstances? Toward century's end, large numbers of Roman Catholic laity and theologians could no longer affirm the positions taken by the church's hierarchy. The practical needs of the church (for more clergy) and the actual behavior of large numbers of Roman Catholics increasingly placed the Vatican under pressure to revise its positions. Worldwide, the percentages of Roman Catholic couples utilizing contraceptive means of birth control was scarcely distinguishable from those of the general population, and studies have even shown widespread use of abortion by Catholic women in many countries. Serious conflict between the church's official teaching and the practice of its members suggests that in time the church must either modify those teachings or express them more convincingly. That is true in any religious community whose members deviate substantially from its moral teachings; it is all the more true of a religious community considering its official teachings to be binding on the will of the faithful.

The latter point ultimately raises the question of papal authority. One of the principal points of dispute between the Vatican and such moral theologians as Charles Curran centered exactly at the point of the character and authority of the "magisterium"—the church's "teaching office." Is that function ultimately centered in bishops and pope or is it more broadly shared with the priests, theologians, and teachers of the church? To what extent is deviation permissible without dissolving the essential character of the church? Every church must confront such questions at some point, for every church has some shared commitments and many points where disagreement is acceptable. Roman Catholicism, by virtue of its size, its worldwide extension, and its centered hierarchy, inevitably confronts such questions in more acute form than most religious bodies.

Notwithstanding some defensiveness and a good deal of internal struggle, Roman Catholicism seemed toward the end of the twentieth century to be irrevocably committed to a more ecumenical stance, a greater commitment to civil democracy, and an identification with the social-economic plight of the world's poor. Its later social teachings also placed it in a position to enter into serious dialogue over the institutional shape of a new world order.

20

LIBERATION THEOLOGY

If the social gospel movement represented the cutting edge of early twentieth-century social Christianity, liberation theology played that part toward the century's end. It is doubtful whether liberation theology was consciously influenced by figures like Walter Rauschenbusch and Leonhard Ragaz. And there are many dissimilarities between the two movements. But there are striking resemblances as well. Both are in conscious rebellion against religious otherworldliness. Both reject individualistic interpretations of the faith. Both emphasize the moral importance of social structures as embodying or obstructing social justice. Both criticize oppressive power structures, often identifying them with economic interests. Both have socialist tendencies—though many of the leaders in each of the movements could not be described as socialists without serious qualification.

Latin American Liberation Theology

When the term "liberation theology" burst on the world scene in the 1970s, it was first as an expression of Latin American social Christianity. Gustavo Gutiérrez, whose book *A Theology of Liberation: History, Politics, and Salvation*[1] helped popularize the movement in the English-speaking world, set forth its major themes. Christian faith, to Gutiérrez, is prior to theological reflection. Even in the first edition of his celebrated work, written during the heady revolutionary era of the 1960s and 1970s, he affirmed the centrality of God's gifts of creation and grace and the reality of personal as well as social sin. But, as seen by Gutiérrez and others, salvation is not to be understood transhistorically. The world is not just a proving ground for the afterlife. It is the present sphere of God's interaction with humanity. Thus, Gutiérrez insists upon "the radical incompatibility of evangelical demands with an unjust and alienating society."[2] All that enslaves and oppresses humanity stands as an obstruction to God's kingdom of love and justice.

In this context, therefore, Gutiérrez understands theology as critical reflection upon the historical forces and structures that oppress. In part, critical theological reflection has the negative task of exposing all Christian thought that provides an aura of sanctity or legitimacy to these oppressive forces and structures. There cannot be a disjuncture between Christian thought and Christian practice. "Orthopraxy" must accompany "orthodoxy." Any disjuncture between the two is the primary subject for Christian inquiry. Echoing an earlier Marxian theme, Gutiérrez and other liberation theologians call for a theology of praxis. Praxis is action to shape history in accordance with human solidarity and justice. Reflection on praxis entails analysis of what has "worked" and what has not, and why or why not. A theology of praxis does not abandon God for the sake of social goals because the transcendent God is the source of those goals.

Theology can properly take "liberation" as its object since its principal concern is the human realities that oppress and enslave, thereby obstructing God's work of salvation. Gutiérrez and other liberation theologians have made much of biblical symbolism referring to liberation, particularly the Exodus account of the liberation of the Israelites from Egypt. Liberation is not exclusively from social oppression; theologically considered, it is also from personal sin. But to be exclusively preoccupied with personal sin is to overlook the structural embodiments of sin that are at work, objectively, in human history. The liberation theologians would concur, wholeheartedly, in Rauschenbusch's criticism of wicked social orders that make good people do bad things.

The focus upon liberation means special focus upon those who are most oppressed. Therefore, liberation theology has given special importance to what the liberation theologians refer to as the "preferential option for the poor." In part, this can be taken to mean special consideration for the historical plight of the oppressed—for that is the point at which God's kingdom is most under threat. Criticism of the predicament of the poor is the best avenue into overall criticism of the problems of Christian practice. But the "preferential option for the poor" also means giving special attention to the *viewpoint* of the poor. It is to accord a kind of epistemological privilege to the oppressed—giving greater weight to their own experience as a source of knowledge about human society and human history. Among the liberation theologians, Paulo Freire has given greatest attention to the process whereby the oppressed are enabled to think critically about the sources of their oppression.[3] In this process, the oppressed receive "conscientization" or "consciousness-raising." That is, they become aware of the fact and causes of their victimization. Such education is not hierarchal. It respects the role of the community as source of essential knowledge, not just as the receiver of truth handed down by teachers who occupy superior intellectual ground. On the basis of this insight into pedagogy, Latin American liberation theology encouraged the development of "comunidades de base." These base communities are small groups, sometimes directly incorporated in the institutional life of the church and sometimes more informally constituted—with or without the understanding and support of clergy. Their reflection together is grounded in scripture, but it is scripture interpreted in the light of experience and historical circumstances. Through the base communities, Christians think biblically and theologically about their social situation and its causes—and this, in turn, contributes to greater understanding of Bible and theology.

But Christians also think analytically about the sources of oppression. Earlier forms of liberation theology, including Gutiérrez's *Theology of Liberation*, made substantial use of Marxist forms of analysis. Thus, Gutiérrez can write that "only a class analysis will enable us to see what is really involved in the opposition between oppressed countries and dominant peoples."[4] Believing that the economic distress of Latin American countries is a direct result of the economic wealth of North America and Europe, Gutiérrez saw this dependency "within the framework of the worldwide class struggle."[5] Latin American poverty is not caused by the inadequacies or laziness of poor people. It is caused by the alliances between sources of capital in the richer countries and the wealthy elites of Latin America. No amount of "development," understood in conventional terms, can overcome poverty. He concludes that "autonomous Latin American development is not viable within the framework of the international capitalist system."[6] The situation must be understood in frankly conflictual terms. What is required is a revolution through which the poor can become empowered. This does not necessarily mean violent revolution, though Gutiérrez and other Latin American liberation theologians have not generally been pacifists. In respect to violence, they have reminded the church that an unjust order—against which the struggle must be directed—is itself violent. Entrenched power must be expected to respond violently to threats to its continued existence.

Much of this analysis reflects the influence of Marxism, with its themes of exploitation and alienation, class struggle, revolution, and (in the Leninist form) imperialism. José Miguez Bonino, writing in the 1970s, was even clearer in his appropriation of Marxist analysis. Christians, he writes, "confronted by the inhuman conditions of existence prevailing in the continent . . . have been increasingly compelled to seek an analysis and historical programme for their Christian obedience." When they have done so, "the dynamics of the historical process, both in its objective conditions and its theoretical development, have led them, through the failure of several remedial and reformist alternatives, to discover the unsubstitutable relevance of Marxism."[7] But Miguez Bonino, in common with many Latin American liberation theologians, sought to distinguish between Marxism as a method of analysis and program for change and Marxism as a total philosophy. There could be no Christian capitulation to Marxist atheism. And even in its understanding of human nature, Miguez Bonino held, Marxism needs a Christian reminder of the humanity of the enemy and of the temptations of power.[8]

Black Theology of Liberation

While the term "liberation theology" was drawn out of the Latin American context, with its greatest emphasis upon liberation from economic exploitation, the term came to encompass the work of North American theologians responding particularly to racial oppression. Of these, Martin Luther King, Jr., and James Cone were particularly influential.

Martin Luther King, Jr. (1929–1968) is not usually classified among the liberation theologians, but the contributions of the great civil rights leader to Christian ethics anticipate most of the later developments of the liberationists. King, like the others, related Christian theology directly to Christian practice. Indeed, more than any other important liberation theologian, King was directly *involved* in practice. Christian thought, divorced from action, is inauthentic. And King, like other liberationists, was scornful of pious attempts to justify the oppressive status quo. In his classic "Letter from Birmingham City Jail," King responded to white religious leaders who had criticized his movement for evoking violence and for breaking civil laws. In response to the first criticism, he observed that the whole structure of racial segregation, against which his movement struggled nonviolently, was itself violent. "Actually," he wrote, "we who engage in nonviolent direct action are not the creators of tension. We merely bring to the surface the hidden tension that is already alive."[9] Similarly, to criticize the movement for breaking the law—as it sometimes did with acts of civil disobedience—was to forget the important distinction between just and unjust laws. Agreeing with Augustine, King asserts that "an unjust law is no law at all."[10]

Now what is the difference between the two? How does one determine when a law is just or unjust? A just law is a man-made code that squares with the moral law or the law of God. An unjust law is a code that is out of harmony with the moral law. To put it in the terms of Saint Thomas Aquinas, an unjust law is a human law that is not rooted in eternal and natural law. Any law that uplifts human personality is just. Any law that degrades human personality is unjust. All [racial] segregation statutes are unjust because segregation distorts the soul and damages the personality. It gives the segregator a false sense of superiority, and the segregated a false sense of inferiority.[11]

To criticize the civil rights movement, then, on *Christian* grounds for violating the law or for occasioning violent outbursts against peaceful demonstrators is to use Christianity as a support for the unjust order.

King did not specifically invoke a "preferential option" for the poor and oppressed, in the manner of the Latin American liberation theologians. Nevertheless, that was clearly what his theological ethics was all about. Christian ethics is always to be focused first on the victims of injustice. In King's various writings the healing of injustice is understood to be the restoring of the whole "beloved community." The method of nonviolent resistance, largely borrowed from Gandhi, was chosen precisely because it dealt with injustice in such a way as to reconcile the victim with the perpetrator, not to sow new seeds of bitterness.

In one of his last writings, his *Where Do We Go from Here: Chaos or Community?*[12] King defended his dream of a racially inclusive community against militants in the civil rights movement who wished rather to emphasize ethnic identity. The struggle centered on the slogan "black power," which some younger leaders wished to substitute for racial integration as the movement's objective. King himself clearly sought black empowerment—that is what the voting rights campaign was all about. But, he argued, "behind Black Power's legitimate and necessary concern for group unity and black identity lies the belief that there can be a separate black road to power and fulfillment." Such ideas are totally unrealistic. "There is no salvation for the Negro through isolation."[13]

King's nonviolence, though apparently at odds with the revolutionary agenda of many liberation theologians, is similar at least in the sense that it seeks utterly realistic methods for achieving radical social change. King believed the methods of nonviolent resistance to be more effective in gaining the communitarian objective of a society of love and justice than methods heightening hostility and resistance. "The problem with hatred and violence," he writes, is that they intensify the fears of the white majority, and leave them less ashamed of their prejudices toward Negroes. In the guilt and confusion confronting our society, violence only adds to the chaos. It deepens the brutality of the oppressor and increases the bitterness of the oppressed. Violence is the antithesis of creativity and wholeness. It destroys community and makes brotherhood impossible.[14]

King, it should be added, did not disapprove of the use of physical coercion by the state in the preservation of justice through the protection of human rights. His movement sought the replacement of laws upholding racial segregation with laws enforcing civil rights. During the crucial Selma, Alabama, campaign for voting rights, the movement successfully sought a U.S. federal court injunction commanding the government to protect a peaceful march from Selma to Montgomery, Alabama. The state, as such, is not illegitimate to King. It becomes illegitimate only through exercising its powers in unjust ways. King's "pacifism," thus, is qualified by acceptance of the use of force by the state when the latter is on the side of justice.

James Cone's "black theology" is intentionally liberation theology. "Theology," he writes, "is always a word about the liberation of the oppressed and the humiliated. It is a word of judgment for the oppressors and the rulers. Whenever theologians fail to make this point unmistakably clear, they are not doing Christian theology but the theology of the Antichrist."[15] "Truth," he observes, "is that transcendent reality, disclosed in the people's historical struggle for liberation, which enables them to know that their fight for freedom is not futile."[16] Theological truth must therefore be grounded in the concrete experience of a particular people, especially an oppressed people for whom liberation can be the deep word about God. Cone, like the Latin Americans, is dissatisfied with theology presented as universal truth for all times. Invariably such "truth" is really the expression of the interest of a privileged people. Theologians of the Enlightenment, for instance, mask the truth about slavery and the privileges of white people, including white theologians, who ultimately benefit from such oppression. Cone quite unapologetically finds the starting point for his own theological reflection in his personal life experience in the black community. His books convey a sense of the immediacy of black preaching, black prayer, black poetry and hymnody as primary materials for theological reflection.

Cone's black theology is not a simple cultural relativism. His theological conclusions are framed by serious analysis of sociology of knowledge, with its emphasis on the importance of social location in all truth claims. But this very recognition of the relativity of knowledge conveys, ultimately, a respect for the transcendent God. Cone also insists upon the importance of the historical Jesus, without whom, he believes, all christological discussion is meaningless. This historical Jesus is theologically relevant, however, precisely because he also was of an oppressed people. The resurrection was of *this kind of person*, not of an abstract deity come briefly to earth to make a theological point. So Cone can speak of the "black Christ," not to make a racial claim but to characterize the relevance of Christ's own historical existence to black experience.

Cone, more like the Latin Americans than like King, does not shy away from the possible need for use of violence in the struggles of liberation. He points out that "no one can be nonviolent in an unjust society." So "ours is a situation in which the only option we have is that of deciding whose violence we will support—that of the oppressors or the oppressed."[17] He distances himself from King by warning that "we must make clear to them [white oppressors] that we will not be distracted from our liberation with their obscene talk about 'love' and 'forgiveness.' "[18] Black people should concentrate on reconciliation among themselves rather than with the white oppressors. "Reconciliation, like love, must begin at home before it can spread abroad."[19] Still, Cone clearly anticipates a reconciled community in the wake of genuine liberation.

Feminist Theology of Liberation

The feminist movement likewise found expression in the 1970s and 1980s as a theology of liberation. Inheriting much of the enduring agenda of the nineteenth-century feminist movement, theologians like Rosemary Radford Ruether, Dorothee Soelle, and Mary Daly sought to understand Christian theology as expressing and requiring the liberation of women. Some of the feminist theologians—one thinks especially of Ruether and Soelle—give considerable emphasis to economic oppression. Ruether, for example, is a prominent democratic socialist who (like the Latin Americans) is not reluctant to draw upon Marx for specific forms of analysis. Nevertheless, the feminists also emphasize the distinctiveness of oppression in gender relationships. One of the points of distinctiveness is the degree to which the oppression of women enters into everyday speech. Language conveying male dominance is deeply embedded in every culture, blatantly so in most. This is especially obvious in the use of masculine pronouns to include both men and women.

Such linguistic male dominance is especially interesting to feminist theologians because so much of the symbolism of the divine in Christianity is male. Challenging this, a Mary Daly will entitle a book *Beyond God the Father*,[20] and a Rosemary Ruether can seek a new term, "God/ess," to convey equally male and female attributes to the deity.[21] Mary Daly ultimately concluded that Christianity is irretrievably committed to male dominance through its theological language and church structures and, hence, that that religion is not consistent with feminist liberation. Ruether is also critical of the enormous weight of male dominance in the history of Christian thought. Nevertheless, she regards this as an expression of idolatry, not as the essential witness of the church: "If all language for God/ess is analogy, if taking a particular human image literally is idolatry, then male language for the divine must lose its privileged place."[22] Images of God, understood as analogies and not as literal description, help open up "a new community of equals."

> Then language about God/ess drawn from kingship and hierarchical power must lose its privileged place. Images of God/ess must include female roles and experience. Images of God/ess must be drawn from the activities of peasants and working people, people at the bottom of society. Most of all, images of God/ess must be transformative, pointing us back to our authentic potential and forward to new redeemed possibilities.[23]

Ruether, unlike Daly, will not concede patriarchy and privilege as the definitive meaning of the Christian gospel. Rather, these are distortions of which the Christian message must be purified.

Most of the feminist theologians have sought new models of social governance, both within and beyond the church, in which equality and participation replace hierarchy. In this, they have sought to make common cause with the victims of all forms of human oppression. The point has been underscored in special ways by "womanist" theology and ethics, contributed by black women theologians and ethicists who are able to write out of the experience of the double oppression of being black and being women. They, along with most of the other feminist theologians, also emphasize the importance of economic oppression. But feminist theology, in common with black theology, has rarely given this the singular focus common among the Latin Americans.

The Enduring Contributions of Liberation Theology

Toward century's end, it is difficult to assess the long-run significance of the various forms of liberation theology. A number of the principal figures found it necessary to moderate their views in response to criticism, and there was a temptation to write the movement off as another passing fad.

But, as we have seen in the long course of Christian moral teaching, movements can come and go without being inconsequential. Whether or not liberation theology occupies the center of the stage as the second millennium of Christianity gives way to the third, that movement has already made four contributions that are likely to endure:

First, it has underscored (along with the earlier social gospel movement) the importance of structural, institutional moral issues. It will never again be as easy to reduce Christian moral life to personal character alone, important as personal character doubtless is. Christian ethics must henceforth give greater emphasis to the criticism of social power and its consequences.

Second, it has brought into the mainstream of Christian thought the contributions of nineteenth-century Marxism and twentieth-century social science in exposing the links between "social location"—the specific social roles, interests, and privileges or disprivileges—and perceptions of moral truth. It will never again be as easy for Christian ethics to ignore the extent to which theological views serve selfish personal and group interests. Ironically, that also entails searching criticism of the extent to which a social justice cause can itself confer special privilege upon its leaders and the frequency with which revolutionary movements, having gained power, turn to new forms of oppression. That irony has not been lost upon the most penetrating minds in the liberation theology movement, though that by no means vitiates the importance of moral critique of social location.

Third, it has underscored—one may hope, permanently—the full humanity of oppressed people. Since oppression generally deprives people of educational opportunity and physical health, the *appearance* of people in disprivileged groups often supplies superficial evidence of their alleged inferiority. Who could take seriously the views, or the humanity, of unlettered, poorly attired, and physically unattractive people—as defined by the dominant culture? But liberation theology has come also as a movement of empowerment, liberating the oppressed to communicate intelligently and clearly the full extent of their own humanity and their own contributions to the broader society.

Fourth, it has reminded the church that the moral health of the whole community, including that of the worst oppressors, is tied up in the liberation of all of its members. Some of the most astute liberation theologians have recognized that the oppressor is, him- or herself, the first and primary victim of oppression. Even were that not so, it is an enduring insight that any fracturing of the life of the community diminishes that life for all of its members, not just those who are most visibly oppressed. Thus, the "preferential option for the poor," taken in its most general sense, is a constant reminder that the highest priority of any Christian teaching about community must be the plight of those whose condition of oppression or deprivation constitutes its point of greatest vulnerability.

21

ECUMENICAL SOCIAL ETHICS

After centuries of institutional division and theological conflict, the twentieth century marked an extraordinary movement toward unity among the world's Christian bodies. The term "ecumenical," by which this movement is generally known, refers to the church as the "household" of God. The movement considered the disunity of the church as scandal among those who acknowledge themselves to be a part of this "household." The ecumenical movement began among Protestants who had confronted this scandal in the competing mission ventures of the nineteenth century and who had to respond to the bemused non-Christians of Asia and Africa who wondered why so many versions of the truth. The nineteenth century had also witnessed a flowering of unofficial voluntary associations of Christians, like the international YMCA, the temperance movement, and the Student Volunteer Movement, with memberships cutting across denominational lines. But among the greatest impetuses for ecumenical cooperation was the desire of social gospel leaders to address issues of social justice together. Until the middle of the twentieth century, efforts to involve Roman Catholicism were generally frustrated, but Eastern Orthodoxy participated actively from early in the century. The twentieth-century ecumenical movement can generally be taken, thus, to be a movement of many of the branches of Protestantism and Eastern Orthodoxy—and, following the Second Vatican Council, Roman Catholicism increasingly related to it in various ways.

If twentieth-century Roman Catholic social thought is principally registered in the papal encyclicals (and in the documents of Vatican II), ecumenical moral thought is most evident in the preparation for and reports of great conferences.

The first of these, which can be considered the real beginning of the twentieth-century ecumenical movement, was the Edinburgh Conference of 1910. This was an entirely unofficial gathering of prominent mission and social gospel leaders who were determined to work for greater Christian unity.

The Life and Work Movement

Two related movements developed out of Edinburgh: The "Faith and Order" movement, which sought greater unity in church doctrine and polity, and the "Life and Work" movement, which sought greater unity in Christian social witness and action. The Life and Work movement's conferences at Stockholm (1925) and Oxford (1937) were especially important in defining ecumenical social teaching.

The Stockholm Conference reflected both the activism of North American and European social Christianity and frustration over the tragedy of World War I, in which Christian fought against Christian in the greatest military carnage the world had ever seen. In respect to the latter, Stockholm established a very important precedent for all twentieth-century ecumenism: the willingness by the church to repent. The Conference Report stated that "the sins and sorrows, the struggles and losses of the Great War and since, have compelled the Christian Churches to recognize, humbly and with shame, that 'the world is too strong for a divided church.' "[1] And, "we confess before God and the world the sins and failures of which the Churches have been guilty, through lack of love and sympathetic understanding. . . . The call of the present hour to the Church should be repentance, and with repentance a new courage springing from the inexhaustible resources which are in Christ."[2]

The Stockholm Conference was generally eclectic in its conclusions, both as to substantive theological ethics and concrete applications. In the main it reflected the conventional wisdom of the social gospel movement. It announced "that the soul is the supreme value, that it must not be subordinated to the rights of property or to the mechanism of industry, and that it may claim as its first right the right of salvation."[3] The "rights of the moral personality" should stand before blatant individualism. Both the root of evil and the possibilities of redemptive good are located in the human will. The church should state principles and assert the ideal, "while leaving to individual consciences, and to communities the duty of applying them with charity, wisdom and courage."[4]

Perhaps the greatest achievement of the Stockholm Conference was in giving institutional form to the Life and Work movement, preparing the way for the remarkable Oxford Conference of 1937.

The Oxford Conference occurred in the midst of worldwide economic depression and in an international political milieu troubled by the rise of totalitarianism in its German, Italian, and Russian forms. The depth of world economic, political, and ideological struggles in the 1930s challenged Oxford to reach new levels of Christian social thought. The conference's eight preparatory volumes and final report were not disappointing. Reflecting the high-quality contributions of theologians like Karl Barth, Reinhold Niebuhr, John C. Bennett, J. H. Oldham, and William Temple, the Conference's work commanded intellectual respect even among those who disagreed with its conclusions.

Framing its social teaching around the gospel proclamation of the king-dom of God, Oxford understood this to mean "the reign of God which both has come and is coming." The kingdom was established with the coming of Christ and "in the presence of His Spirit in the world." Nevertheless, "it is . . . still in conflict with a sinful world."[5] Christians may not, therefore, identify any human system or institution directly with the kingdom. The Christian ideal of justice as the "harmonious relation of life to life" contains both a negative and a positive aspect. Negatively, it involves restraint of the evildoer. While such use of force is not intrinsically desirable, "it cannot be assumed that the practice of Christian love will ever obviate the necessity for coercive political and economic arrangements."[6] But justice also entails the positive creation of "forms of production and methods of co-operation" that advance "the cause of human brotherhood by serving and extending the principle of love beyond the sphere of purely personal relations."[7] The requirements of Christian love exceed the minimal conditions of justice, but Christians must not allow "individual acts of charity to become a screen for injustice and a substitute for justice."[8]

Such nuanced distinctions are carried into warnings against identifying the kingdom of God directly with human institutions. The language of one passage on this remains worthy of more extensive quotation:

> Every tendency to identify the Kingdom of God with a particular structure of society or economic mechanism must result in moral confusion for those who maintain the system and in disillusionment for those who suffer from its limitations. The former will regard conformity with its standards as iden-tical with the fulfillment of the Law, thus falling into the sin of pharisaism. The latter will be tempted to a cynical disavowal of the religion, because it falsely gives absolute worth to partial values and achievements. Both errors are essentially heretical from the point of view of Christian faith.[9]

The Oxford Conference's analysis of the conflict between communism and capitalism found serious flaws in both. In respect to communism,

Oxford acknowledged that the existence of this movement constitutes a judgment upon the failures of the church to which the church must attend—and that "the Churches must not regard an attack directed against themselves [by movements like communism] as an attack directed against God."[10] Nevertheless, the report continues,

> the Churches must continue resolutely to reject those elements in the actual development of communism which conflict with the Christian truth: the *utopianism* which looks for the fulfillment of human existence through the natural process of history, and which presupposes that the improvement of social institutions will automatically produce an improvement in human personalities; the *materialism* which derives all moral and spiritual values from economic needs and economic conditions, and deprives the personal and cultural life of its creative freedom; and, finally, that *disregard* for the *dignity* of the *individual* in which communism may differ theoretically, but in which it does not differ practically, from other contemporary totalitarian movements.[11]

Oxford's critique of capitalism is no less searching. It is to be judged for its "enhancement of acquisitiveness," its tendency to exacerbate inequalities, its leading to concentrations of economic power "wielded by a few individuals or groups who are not responsible to any organ of society," and the tension it produces between work that is responsive to the will of God (vocation) and work that is required by the economic order. In addition, the report scored the tendency of capitalism to create a "constant threat of unemployment."[12] The report grounded its own commitment to equality theologically, asserting "that all men are children of one Father, and that, compared with that primary and overwhelming fact, the differences between the races, nationalities, and classes of men, though important on their own plane, are external and trivial."[13] Therefore, the report concludes that "any social arrangement which outrages the dignity of man, by treating some men as ends and others as means, any institution which obscures the common humanity of men by emphasizing the external accidents of birth, or wealth, or social position, is *ipso facto* anti-Christian."[14]

Oxford did affirm the right of private property. Nevertheless, it emphasized that all property rights are "relative," that they must be criticized from the standpoint of their origins, that they must be affirmed or judged in light of their social consequences, and that distinctions should be made about forms of property. In respect to the latter, the report notes that when property becomes a form of social power it needs special scrutiny. In a special appeal to affluent Christians, the report emphasizes that they should "put a strong burden of proof on themselves when their decisions coincide with their own economic advantage."[15]

Given the fact that racism was so pervasive in many parts of the world in 1937—even among some otherwise sophisticated Christian thinkers—the message of Oxford on this point has a prophetic ring: "Against racial pride or race-antagonism the Church must set its face implacably as rebellion against God. Especially in its own life and worship there can be no place for barriers because of race or colour."[16]

Aside from the intrinsic merits of its own analyses and conclusions, which were considerable, the Oxford Conference is noteworthy as one of the events leading directly to the formation of the World Council of Churches. At Oxford, and at the Edinburgh Conference of the Faith and Order movement held the same summer of 1937, the decision was reached to join these two movements in such a council. World War II required postponement of the convening of the World Council until 1948, when it was held in Amsterdam. The ideological debates of Oxford remained important, but at Amsterdam the mood was also shaped by new possibilities for the creation of a new world order.

Amsterdam and Evanston

The "Message" of the Amsterdam Assembly addressed the church with soaring rhetoric about its responsibility in a broken world:

> We have to learn afresh together to speak boldly in Christ's name both to those in power and to the people, to oppose terror, cruelty and race discrimination, to stand by the outcast, the prisoner and the refugee. We have to make of the Church in every place a voice for those who have no voice, and a home where every man will be at home.... We have to ask God to teach us together to say No and to say Yes in truth. No to all that flouts the love of Christ, to every system, every programme and every person that treats any man as though he were an irresponsible thing or a means of profit, to the defenders of injustice in the name of order, to those who sow the seeds of war or urge war as inevitable; Yes, to all that conforms to the love of Christ, to all who seek for justice, to the peacemakers, to all who hope, fight and suffer for the cause of man, to all who—even without knowing it—look for new heavens and a new earth wherein dwelleth righteousness.[17]

In its ethical substance, the Amsterdam Assembly clearly reflected Oxford. For example, it repeated and elaborated the even-handed critiques of capitalism and Marxian communism. "The Christian churches," it concluded, "should reject the ideologies of both communism and laissez-faire capitalism, and should seek to draw men away from the false assumption that these extremes are the only alternatives."[18] Noting that communist ideology places major emphasis on justice, assuming that freedom will come as a by-product, and that capitalism does the reverse, the report stated that Christians should "seek new, creative solutions which never allow either justice or freedom to destroy the other."[19] Amsterdam also reflected Oxford's emphasis upon peace and its judgment upon racial discrimination.

The Amsterdam Assembly is, however, best known for its call for a "responsible society." In a brief formulation of this norm, an effort was made to include the ideals of freedom and justice and to emphasize the accountability of both political and economic forms of power—setting all such values in their ultimate theological context. Following is the key passage:

> Man is created and called to be a free being, responsible to God and his neighbour. Any tendencies in State and society depriving man of the possibility of acting responsibly are a denial of God's intention for man and His work of salvation. A responsible society is one where freedom is the freedom of men who acknowledge responsibility to justice and public order, and where those who hold political authority or economic power are responsible for its exercise to God and the people whose welfare is affected by it.[20]

In elaborating the concept, the report registers the now-familiar theme of the Faith and Order movement: "Man is not made for the State but the State for man. Man is not made for production, but production for man."[21] To give substance to its call for a responsible society, the report insists "that the people have freedom to control, to criticise and to change their governments, that power be made responsible by law and tradition, and be distributed as widely as possible through the whole community."[22]

The Second Assembly, convened at Evanston, Illinois, in 1954, continued to elaborate the "responsible society" theme, while seeking to clarify that " 'responsible society' is not an alternative social or political system, but a criterion by which we judge all existing social orders and at the same time a standard to guide us in the specific choices we have to make."[23] As applied to economic questions, Evanston found greater compatibility between "relative freedom in enterprise" than had either Oxford or Amsterdam.[24] Evanston affirmed the importance of the state as a major force in economic life: "When necessary in the public interest, the state must intervene to prevent any centre of economic or social power which represents partial interest from becoming stronger than itself, for the state alone has the power and the authority under God to act as trustee for society as a whole."[25] Still, the document found it necessary to "warn against the danger that the union of political and economic power may result in an all-controlling state," which could be taken to be a caution about socialism.

In general, the tone of Evanston's handling of economic questions is more pragmatic, noting as it does that the ideological debates about capitalism and socialism "disguise the more important issues in the field of economic and social policy."[26]

Evanston's discussion of communism refers to Amsterdam's critique, but by 1954 the Cold War was at its height and, in the United States, popular fear of Communist influence had led to McCarthyism. So the Conference issued the judgment that "preoccupation with the real dangers of subversion in many situations has led to a less widely recognized and more subtle danger to society from those who identify as subversive any unpopular opinions or associations," adding that "enemies of essential human freedom appear on both the political right and the political left."[27] In a broader discussion that produced the report "Communist–Non-Communist Tension," Evanston elaborated the different kinds of questions that persons in communist and noncommunist countries ask.

Evanston laid the groundwork for decades of increasing ecumenical concern for the development of "underdeveloped" regions of the world. The agenda for further study and action included political development, land reform, industrial development, attention to population questions, and the movement toward independence among colonial territories.

Both Oxford and Amsterdam had addressed racism in prophetic terms, but it remained for Evanston to elaborate a definitive Christian response. Section five, on "intergroup relations," especially influenced by the African-American educator Benjamin Mays and the South African novelist Alan Paton, took on a wide front of issues, ranging from legal segregation, or apartheid, to the scandal of separation in the life of the church, to the especially sensitive issue of racial intermarriage. The categorical response of the Assembly, stated in resolution form, was that "any form of segregation based on race, colour or ethnic origin is contrary to the gospel, and is incompatible with the Christian doctrine of man and with the nature of the Church of Christ."[28] The Assembly therefore urged "the churches within its membership to renounce all forms of segregation or discrimination and to work for their abolition within their own life and within society."[29] The section report gave this even greater rhetorical emphasis, asserting that "when we are given Christian insight the whole pattern of racial discrimination is seen as an unutterable offence against God, to be endured no longer, so that the very stones cry out."[30] And, noting the rationalizations often used to justify segregation within the churches themselves, the section report dryly comments that "we often make use of the unregenerateness of the world to excuse our own."[31]

The Evanston Assembly broke ecumenical ground at two other points. The first of these was in its emphasis upon the ministry of the laity, to which a whole section report (six) was devoted. The laity are not "mere fragments of the Church," that report asserts. "They are the Church's representatives, no matter where they are." It is the laity "who manifest in word and action the Lordship of Christ over that world which claims so much of their time and energy and labour."[32] So the report goes on to affirm that "all work honestly done . . . has genuine value and meaning in the purpose of God."[33]

The second point was in the vigorous response to the emerging dangers of thermonuclear war. Warning that "all-out nuclear warfare . . . introduces a new moral challenge," Evanston called for "the elimination and prohibition of atomic, hydrogen and all other weapons of mass destruction" and called upon the nations "to pledge that they will refrain from the threat or use" of such weapons.[34]

The World Council and Revolutionary Social Change

During the 1950s the World Council of Churches embarked on intensive study of the "common Christian responsibility toward areas of rapid social change," with emphasis on the sweeping disintegration of the great colonial empires, the emerging of many new nations in Africa and Asia and important economic and social development in those regions, and rapid technological change worldwide. These points of emphasis had great impact on the Third Assembly of the WCC at New Delhi, India, in 1961. That assembly outlined five ways people react to the bewildering changes of a revolutionary age:

(a) *fear*, because so much that is treasured seems to be in danger of destruction;
(b) *conservatism* that seeks to preserve and defend as much as possible of the old and familiar structures of society;
(c) *passive acceptance* that deplores change, but accepts it as something inevitable that must be endured;
(d) *positive acceptance* that welcomes change as an opportunity to promote self-interest;
(e) *positive acceptance* that welcomes change as an opportunity to provide a fuller and more satisfying life for mankind.[35]

The Assembly commended the fifth of these to Christians, for they know "how heavy are the burdens of poverty and privation carried today by the majority of mankind." Christians must be prepared "to initiate changes and forward reforms that serve the ends of justice and freedom, that break the chains of poverty."[36] And Christians must be willing to cooperate with non-Christians for such ends.

In dealing more specifically with change, New Delhi cautioned that people must not be treated as mere tools for development. In a message implicitly directed alike toward both capitalist and Communist models of development, the Assembly commented that "it is true that part of our duty is to strive to provide the opportunity of a fuller life for the generations that will succeed us, but we must not be tempted to justify present suffering by the hope of benefits entirely in the future."[37] So development must be concerned about the present generation as well as those to follow.

In a message to the peoples of the new nations, New Delhi noted the paradox of nationalism. On the one hand, it was to be seen as a resource in overcoming older cultural and tribal animosities in "constructive nation-building." But the weakness of nationalism was seen "in its possible perversion into policies of antagonism and exclusiveness against other nations."[38]

New Delhi renewed the call of earlier conferences for the development of a more responsible world order, with the admonition that "the evolution of an international order will require of all a measure of surrender of autonomy and sovereignty for the sake of the world community. . . . The aim must be to establish a just system of world order, which provides security through the means to enforce its decisions." At the same time, the Assembly acknowledged that "the absence of a commonly agreed interpretation of law and justice, especially among the great powers, challenges the churches to explore such common ground as exists with a view to bringing them together under effective international control."[39]

New Delhi addressed an appeal to the governments of the world—with a special eye toward the great powers—to work harder at disarmament and peacemaking. "Let there be restraint and self-denial in the things which make for war, patience and persistence in seeking to resolve the things which divide, and boldness and courage in grasping the things which make for peace."[40] At stake in peacemaking in a nuclear age is nothing less than "the future of many generations and the heritage of ages." Both of these "are now easy to destroy, since the actions or miscalculations of a few can bring about a holocaust." The appeal to the great powers had a special poignancy at New Delhi since the Russian Orthodox Church joined the WCC at this Assembly.

The 1966 WCC Study Conference on Church and Society at Geneva, Switzerland, and the Fourth Assembly at Uppsala, Sweden, in 1968 were set in an even more revolutionary milieu. Most of Africa and Asia had become independent, the Second Vatican Council had revolutionized Protestant/ Orthodox/Roman Catholic relationships, the civil rights movement had revolutionized North American race relations, the Vietnam War had put the United States on the defensive internationally while also radicalizing a generation of students, and consciousness of the population explosion and environmental problems was increasing. Primary concern over racism had shifted to southern Africa, where revolutionary movements in Rhodesia (soon to become Zimbabwe) and South Africa attracted world attention.

In this milieu, it is noteworthy that most ecumenical rhetoric abandoned what appeared to be the more static formulations of "responsible society" in order to respond more directly to the demand for revolutionary change. Ecumenical conferences, previously dominated by European and North American church leaders and theologians, were increasingly an arena of confrontation between angry representatives of third-world churches and previously underrepresented women and ethnic minority groups.

The appeal of these conferences was more for action than theological/ ethical formulation. One of the major accomplishments of Uppsala, for instance, was in the adoption of the Special Programme to Combat Racism. That program was destined to place the World Council of Churches in the midst of the racial and political struggles in southern Africa, giving some support to revolutionary movements there.

The deep identification of the WCC with marginalized peoples continued through the 1970s and 1980s. While the "responsible society" theme seldom reappeared as such, it is interesting that the basic concept— expanded now to include environmental concerns—emerged at the Fifth and Sixth assemblies (Nairobi, 1975, and Vancouver, 1983). The new formula was the "Just, Participatory, and Sustainable Society." While not conceptually developed by the assemblies, JPSS represented—in common with the earlier responsible-society theme—a commitment to justice and openness in the power structures of economics and politics. JPSS represented less commitment to the responsible-society themes of order, freedom, and authority, though, unlike responsible society, it now included recognition of the environment. The latter, represented by "sustainable," emphasized the possibility that environmental destructiveness represents a long-run threat to the sustainability of the world—in the loss of which all other values associated with human history would also be ended.

The Vancouver Assembly followed, by four years, the World Council's Conference on Faith, Science and the Future, held in Cambridge, Massachusetts, in 1979. That significant study conference had given high visibility to moral issues arising out of new technologies, such as those associated with genetic engineering.[41] The report of the Cambridge conference expressed considerable appreciation for the "immense fruitfulness of modern science."[42] At the same time, it explored the perils of too much technology in a fragile world and the ways in which science and technology can become instruments of human oppression. The Cambridge Conference and subsequent WCC assemblies have raised important questions in this area without attempting definitive solutions.

New Occasions, New Duties

The JPSS formulation gave way, in the later 1980s, to JPIC: for Justice, Peace, and Integrity of Creation. The difference was not merely semantic. A "sustainable society" can be understood as a human society in a sustainable natural environment that exists for the sake of the human. "Integrity of creation," on the other hand, suggests that the whole of creation—not just the human—has intrinsic value and unity derived from its creator. This JPIC theme was important at the WCC's Seventh Assembly at Canberra, Australia, in 1991. The Assembly's official report made clear that JPIC is not to be understood as a new form of nature worship or pantheism. Nevertheless, it claimed a biblical and trinitarian grounding for appreciation of the intrinsic, not merely instrumental value of creation. "The universe in all its beauty and grandeur manifests the glory of the Triune God who is the source of all life. ... We are accountable before God in and to the community of life, so that we understand ourselves as servants, stewards and trustees of the creation."[43] The Canberra report also records appreciation for the insights gained from science into the immensity and wonder of creation: "our sense of the mystery of life and our awe and wonder at the Creator's handiwork is deepened by what we learn from science. We thank God for all these sources of insight, wisdom and understanding."[44]

In one sense, statements of this kind are so general as to offer very little direct moral guidance. Yet they offer an important corrective to the exploitative attitudes toward nature typical in the era of the Industrial Revolution.

Viewing the Canberra Assembly from the perspective of the decades of development beginning with the Life and Work movement at Stockholm, one can notice substantial continuity as well as change. Commitments to social and economic justice are present from the beginning, and almost from the beginning the importance of political democracy and human rights was being stressed. Toward the century's end the WCC had become much more sensitive to the neglected peoples of the world, both in its teaching and in the inclusiveness with which it ordered its own institutional life. But the impulse toward the marginalized was a consistent theme.

It would be more difficult to locate any one ethical method. Indeed, the whole point of ecumenical theology and ethics is to draw all of the important strains of method into conversation. Most of the assemblies and study conferences reflect, to a substantial degree, the dominant methods and styles of theological and ethical discourse among the churches at the time. Thus, Stockholm was under the influence of the social gospel movement, Oxford and Amsterdam were heavily impacted by what was loosely termed neo-orthodoxy as well as the earlier liberalism, Geneva and Uppsala were influenced to some extent by the secular theology currents of the

1960s, Nairobi and Vancouver by liberation theology, Canberra by a broader eclecticism. If, as John Courtney Murray said, civilization is people "locked together in argument," the ecumenical movement has always been quite civilized! That may be its strength, so long as the member churches and Christian thinkers are challenged to bring to it their very best thinking.

PART VII

Christian Ethics Toward the Third Millennium

Christian ethics is a living tradition. Long as the history is, it always points beyond itself to the present and the anticipated future. Faithful Christians of every generation inherit that history, learning both from its insights and from its failures. But Christians do more than live in the past. They also respond to new problems, new opportunities, new insights. As we have seen, there has never been a time when Christians did not have to address moral problems. We have also seen that almost every generation has added something to the ongoing tradition through its own fresh encounter with reality. Time does not make every ancient good uncouth, but new occasions do teach us new duties.

It belongs to the present generation to round out two thousand years of Christian experience and to embark upon the third millennium of what some have been pleased to call the Christian era. The deepest Christian insight into the meaning of that era will protect the church from too much triumphalism—for there is cause for repentance as well as celebration in that history. Still, the conclusion of two millennia and the beginning of the third is an excellent time for reassessment. Our concluding chapters attempt to stand back from the history we have been outlining, noting some of its enduring tendencies and asking what Christian ethics may be able to contribute in the years to come.

22

CONFLICTING TENDENCIES

What are we to make of the long history of Christian ethics? One should avoid easy generalizations in summarizing the record, for Christian moral tradition is rich and diverse—and sometimes contradictory! Christians have arrived at opposite conclusions about many things, such as war, slavery, the role of women, wealth, sexual relationships, politics, and even the more commonplace virtues. That fact alone would be scandalous if one thought of the tradition as a deposit of truth "once for all delivered to the saints." But if one thinks rather of the tradition as a witness to the transcendent reality of the living God, then is there not room for growth and new insight? Just as in human friendship there is maturing, deepening perception of the reality of the other, so and even more so in the divine-human relationship there is the possibility of development. And our judgments about what is central to the tradition can change.

Nevertheless, the tradition itself has always affirmed the centrality of love in the nature of God and in the character of human life. Christian understanding of the meaning of that love has varied, but the importance of love has almost always been affirmed by Christian ethics. Christians have not always been loving in their actions and decisions, but usually they have known that that is what, as Christians, they are called to be.

In the first chapter of this book we took note of six points of tension in the biblical legacy of Christian ethics. We are prepared, now, to see that those same points of tension have persisted through the two millennia of the history. At certain times one or another of the tensions has been especially important. None of them, however, has finally been resolved. That is so, we must suppose, because each of the truths or values held in tension represents a part of Christian ethics that cannot be dismissed. That can be illustrated by a few comments on each of those tensions:

Tension One: Revelation Versus Reason

How do we *know* what is true or good? In the perennial conflict between revelation and reason it should now be apparent that no final choice between the two could possibly be made, although our understanding of each may vary. One could not choose reason over revelation without reducing Christian faith, and Christian ethics with it, to abstraction. One could not choose revelation over reason without being arbitrary. There is indeed a "givenness" about the Christian story that supplies the basis of Christian ethics. From the beginning, Christian faith centered on the person of Jesus Christ. Christ was understood, one way or another, as the supreme revelation of the nature and purposes of God. In the earliest Christian moral writings, the content of the revelation included the remembered deposit of Jesus' teachings. Most of the early writing was fairly unsophisticated, but even in the earliest times reasoning about the faith is evident. Even the straightforward *Didache*, in calling upon Christians to share, puts this demand in reasonable form: "If you have what is eternal in common, how much more should you have what is transient."[1] Still, as we have seen, it was not enough for Christian ethics to be presented with internal consistency. In the long run, for it to have a formative impact upon the wider world, the moral implications of the faith had to be thought through in relation to other aspects of human culture. This did not mean that Christians had simply to accommodate their faith to external, non-Christian cultural patterns. It did mean that the implications, negative as well as positive, had to be thought out and presented reasonably. So the Alexandrians, Augustine, Thomas Aquinas, Calvin, Erasmus, Jonathan Edwards, Friedrich Schleiermacher, the Niebuhrs, Paul Tillich—to name but a few—sought to make the case for this ethic in reasoned form, utilizing the great philosophical traditions in the process. Occasionally (one thinks of Clement of Alexandria and Joseph Butler), the effort to be reasonable vitiated the deeper implications of the Christian ethic, and the result was to a certain extent a well-reasoned triviality. Occasionally, on the other hand, the content of the Christian ethic was so dependent upon a literal reading of revealed scripture that the result was arbitrary and, ironically, also captive to certain periods of cultural history.

The history should instruct us that the dialectic between revelation and reason will continue as a perennial task of Christian ethics.

Tension Two: Materialism Versus the Life of the Spirit

The struggle against an exclusively "spiritual" interpretation of Christian ethics began in the first century. In one form or another, this, too, has been a perennial conflict. One-sided spiritualism initially appeared as Gnosticism and Marcionism, later as ascetic monasticism and some forms of mysticism. It is a tendency whenever Christianity has been presented as a conflict of spirit against the world.

Had extreme spiritualism prevailed as the interpretation of Christian faith, the consequences for Christian ethics would have been unimaginably great. Whether Christianity itself could have survived is doubtful. For such an interpretation means, in effect, that Christians can have nothing positive to say about the ordering and arranging of life in this world. What could be said about economics, human sexuality, environmental questions, or even politics? What would the implications be for our understanding of God and the doctrine of creation? How would we deal with the Hebrew scriptures, with their strong emphasis on God's creation of the world? It is not surprising that whenever the issue has been drawn clearly, Christian thinkers have generally affirmed that the world is a part of God's creation and that the organization of life in that world is of the essence of Christian ethics.

At the same time, an excessively materialistic interpretation of Christian ethics also poses important problems. If Christian ethics is portrayed exclusively in this-worldly terms, why does it matter? In the end we all perish; the molecules from which we and our environment are formed are dispersed, to be rearranged in new forms. Crude materialism is inconsistent with belief in any enduring values, much less faith in a transcending God. Only rarely have Christian thinkers opted for one-sided materialism. Some versions of the social gospel or liberation theology movements may suggest this, with their very strong emphasis upon social structures as defining the moral life. But most of the social gospel and liberationist thinkers have been careful to combine their concern for the material world with an understanding that human life is not only that. So we have a Rauschenbusch, whose *Prayers of the Social Awakening* combine a sensitivity to suffering in the material realm with profound spirituality. Efforts like Barth's doctrine of creation to formulate the relationship between the material and the spiritual without reducing Christianity to one or the other or to dualism will continue to be important, for this tension is also a perennial one in Christian ethics.

Tension Three: Universalism Versus Group Identity

How are Christians to understand the meaning of their lives? Is it derived from the particular groups to which they belong, or is it given through their relationship with God? The formal answer is clearly the second, in most Christian ethics. God is the ultimate source of meaning of human existence, not some lesser affiliation. Even non-Christians have generally been interpreted by Christians in this way, for non-Christians as well as Christians belong to God, whether they know it or like it or not. That formal understanding of identity is almost inescapable in all Christian ethics—or in the ethic of any other universal world religion.

Nevertheless, there is room for recurrent conflict at two points. First, are we to understand the community of faith, the church, to be the exclusive social sphere for the realization of human identity as seen by Christians? Is the society that exists beyond the church radically fallen, or is there some sense in which that wider society also has positive moral meaning? The question is implicit wherever the monastic impulse is strongest, particularly when one's salvation is considered to be at stake in the monastic vocation. Usually, as we have seen, the church was able to combine the monastic vocation with a positive conception of those not having that vocation. The Anabaptists and later Christian sectarians treat the contrast between the church, as the "company of the committed," and the wider society more radically. As we have noted, that question has resurfaced in the twentieth century for Christian ethics through the work of ethicists who challenge the notion that there can even be a universal community of reference. It has also surfaced in the rigidities of a new fundamentalism that defines Christian identity in accordance with acceptance of specified propositions about the faith.

The other point at which this conflict presents itself is in our understanding of the moral status of lesser, more particular forms of group loyalty. What is or should be the family to us? The ethnic group? The nation? However subordinated to the universal claim of our identity in God, what is the meaning of the other identities comprising the fabric of our lives? Nineteenth- and twentieth-century struggles over racism and sexism have placed this question in bold relief, both in its negative and positive forms. Negatively, Christian ethics has challenged the pretensions and idolatries of particular human groups when these are recognized as exclusive and oppressive of others. To find one's identity as a white person in a society that oppresses persons of color is to invite suspicion. So also is finding one's identity as a man in a world where women are oppressed. But, largely in response to such oppressions, those who have been marginalized have claimed a positive identity and self-worth over against the sources of oppression. In the late twentieth century, Christian ethics had still not fully digested the implications of this form of identity. Was it to be understood as "reverse racism or sexism," or was it to be seen as a corrective for the sake of the more universal identity we all have from God? In any case, even in a world where social oppression has disappeared, there will be a continuing task of relating the more immediate loyalties and communities to the universal community.

Tension Four: Grace Versus Law

It is interesting to note the frequency with which the classic Pauline distinction between grace and works of the law resurfaces in Christian history, with Augustine, Luther, and Barth being among those giving new emphasis to the centrality of grace. It is also interesting that the reliance upon "works of the law" for salvation has continued to appear so often that grace has had to be rediscovered! This tension seems to be built into the very logic of Christian ethics. If this is an ethic grounded in love—God's love for us and our loving response to God—then a purely legal ethic will always be questionable. Obedience to law is conformity to a minimum standard; love is without limit. Reliance upon one's own efforts for one's moral self-esteem does not appear, on the face of it, to be an ethic grounded in love. It is self-centered, not centered in God and others.

Still, the periods of recovery of grace have often given rise to excessive libertarianism. The logic of this, on one level, seems clear: If I can count on God's love, then why should I exert myself morally? And if love is everything, then what is the place of the definition of rules and virtues to guide the moral life? Once made aware of God's saving grace, through justification, what room is there for further moral growth?

Different ways of dealing with this tension have surfaced. Some, like Augustine and Calvin, have treated the moral life as a whole as the gift of God's election. Some people, according to this, are elected to receive and respond to grace; others are not. Some, like Thomas Aquinas, have treated grace as enabling Christians to obey God's universal moral law. Some, like John Wesley, have understood justification as the entry point in a life that will continue to grow in grace through the process of sanctification. Some, like many Lutherans and the twentieth-century situationalists, have treated moral rules as guidelines helping us to live the life of grace. The recurring dilemma is that moral rules and even moral activism, apart from grace, derive from self-centeredness, but grace, apart from moral action, is empty —indeed, it is not even grace. Somehow Christian ethics must link grace and moral action, even while it affirms the priority of grace.

Tension Five: Love Versus Force

We have noted the recurrence throughout Christian history of a debate between Christian pacifism and Christians espousing some form of the just war theory. The conventional picture of this, which depicts the early centuries as mostly pacifist and the centuries following Constantine as corrupted by power, has had to be qualified. In the first place, we have noted that even Christian writers in the first two centuries generally accepted the moral legitimacy of the state, sword and all. And we have noted that

Christian writers subsequent to Constantine do not generally regard war as morally routine or neutral. Still, the tension has persisted. Coercion, not to mention killing, is bound to be problematic for an ethic grounded in God's love for all. At the same time, a disavowal of all forms of coercion appears to leave the most vulnerable members of society hostage to the inclinations of the most unjust. That is so whether the question is raised within the immediate community or nation or at the level of international politics.

Can this tension be resolved? Perhaps not. Love is, and must remain, the foundation of Christian ethics. But justice, as the institutional structure of love, inevitably is dependent upon other incentives including, ultimately, the use of force. The creative resolution of this tension, in Christian history, has generally been represented in institutions where force is seldom necessary.

Tension Six: Status Versus Equality

Here, too, Christian history presents us with such a mixed picture. There has never been a time when *some* commitment to equality was not present, at least within the community of faith. Within that community it was generally understood that even those of highest status might be judged and found wanting by God, while even the lowest are precious to God. That is true of slaves who, from the beginning, were understood to have a moral equality before God even though their social status was very low (and even when Christian ethics taught that their social status *should* be very low). We have given attention in several chapters to the story of women in the history of the church. Very few voices, prior to the nineteenth century, have been raised in support of the social equality of women. But it is interesting that even in the primitive church and in the Middle Ages, when women were always marginalized in church and society, it was still well understood that women could be the bearers of unique messages from God. So a Catherine of Siena could be respected by monarchs and popes alike as one whom God had chosen as a spokesperson. And it is interesting that as the full implications of Christian faith in this regard were registered with the church of the nineteenth and twentieth centuries, even the purely social inequality of slaves and women had to be challenged as inconsistent with the deeper equality before God. In those centuries more penetrating tools of social analysis became available to Christian ethics on the basis of which previous rationalizations of inequality could be criticized.

The tension between status systems and equality remains, in part because every known society (even the church) has had to have leadership and other kinds of divisions of labor. The recurring challenge is to find ways to accommodate the needs of community to the implication of equality at the root of Christian ethics.

To these recurring tensions in the history of Christian ethics we may add another, subtler one. That is the tension between Christian ethics as a discipline in which sure knowledge may be found and as a discipline in which knowledge is partial and tentative. Most writers we have examined are not all that humble about the truth as they have seen it! Often, ethics is forged out of disagreement, in reaction to practices or viewpoints a thinker is eager to correct. Rarely have conclusions been presented in a tentative spirit.

Before judging this aspect of Christian ethics too harshly, we must understand that radical moral relativism would destroy this or any other form of ethics. If all moral viewpoints are equally true and good, then none is really true or good. If we cannot affirm that a moral conclusion is true, then the whole point of Christian ethics—and most of the meaning of human life along with it—is lost.

But having acknowledged this point, too much certainty about God's ways with humanity may not leave enough space for God to be God. Surely the long history of Christian ethics at least shows *us* that many of its leading figures have often been wrong! Are we to conclude that we, at last, occupy privileged ground where greater certainty is to be had? Our enduring problem is to find ways of expressing moral commitment and partial truth while remaining open to correction.

But the last word in summarizing this history surely must be that Christian ethics was so often right, so often a force for good. Most of the tension points referred to in this chapter have been creative ones. In addressing them, Christian thinkers have had to struggle. But the results of the struggle can in so many cases be affirmed: The affirmation of the material world as God's creation, the stress on personal integrity in a life disciplined by love, the judgment against the abandonment of unwanted children, the recognition of the equality of all persons before God, the condemnation of slavery, the recognition of the equality of women, the concept of monogamous marital relationships in a covenant of equals, the negative judgment upon war as a way of resolving human disputes even by those Christians who consider it a sometime lesser evil, the refusal to accept the unregulated market as a sufficient agency for the just distribution of the world's material goods. The list could go on and does go on. But we must turn now to the question of the future of Christian ethics.

23

CAN CHRISTIAN ETHICS
FIND A CREATIVE CENTER?

We have noted, now, some of the recurring points of tension in the history of Christian ethics. Often, something is to be said in support of both "sides" in these perennial conflicts. But this does not mean that a simple compromise is always possible. Sometimes one "side" is more "right" than the other; sometimes both "sides" need to be transcended, in Hegelian fashion, in a higher synthesis. Christian ethics, in any event, cannot be passive; it must struggle, in every age, to understand and teach a faithful Christian moral perspective.

I wish to venture a few thoughts, in this concluding chapter, on the most fundamental challenges facing Christian moral thought as we move into the third millennium of Christian history.

Sources of Christian Ethics

Toward the end of the twentieth century the question of the place of the Bible has reemerged in Christian ethics. Is Christian ethics exclusively biblical? To what extent should biblical insight be supplemented by non-biblical sources, including reasoned reflection on general human experience and the history of Christian tradition? How, indeed, should the Bible's insights be appropriated?

This last question may not be as easy as some suppose. There has been a worldwide resurgence of fundamentalism in all religions, including Christianity, reflecting the yearning of many people for clear sources of moral authority. Faced with an increasingly complex world, many seek definite, unambiguous answers. Often these answers are found in a literal reading of religious scriptures. One effect of such literalism is a studied intolerance of all who disagree. Another is a certain superficiality of approach to the scriptures themselves, for cited "proof-texts" leave no room for interpretation of moral issues in depth. Yet another effect is a fragmentation of the intellectual life, for such literalism cannot honestly address internal inconsistencies within a scriptural canon nor the inconsistencies between ancient scriptures and factual truths now beyond dispute.

In face of this, Christian ethics certainly may not abandon the Bible, for the Bible remains the foundation sine qua non of basic theological insight. But Christian ethics will have no creative center if it cannot utilize the Bible critically, carefully distinguishing between profound insight, on the one hand, and dated cultural perspectives, on the other hand. It is no disservice to the biblical witness to acknowledge that scripture contains error as well as truth. What kind of future could Christian theology, including Christian ethics, have in the world of the third millennium if it insisted upon what thoughtful people know to be false or crude? That was the kind of question the Christian thinkers of the second to fourth centuries had to face. And, with all their foibles, they faced it very well indeed—for their time.

A more open, and deeper, use of scripture commits Christian ethics to responsible exegesis but also to theological reflection that is more than exegetical. Among the mainline Protestant churches there is increasing recognition that the theological task must employ scripture, tradition, experience, and reason. In one sense, scripture is primary, as the basic source. Yet, in the spheres of insight they bring to bear, tradition, experience, and reason can each also be seen as primary. On the basis of creative thought employing each of these four sources, Christian ethics will not hesitate to reinterpret the faith. But those sources themselves provide powerful hedges against subjective relativism. Seen in this way, Christian ethics is very far from being obsolete. It will make very important contributions to the emerging—and inevitable—dialogue of the great world religions. And it promises to be a wonderfully integrative moral influence in the years—and centuries—to come.

Christian Character and Moral Judgment

Toward century's end a debate had begun over whether the proper object of Christian ethics is the moral character of Christians or the ethical analysis of the decisions Christians are called upon to make. Seen in the light of the long history of Christian ethics, such a debate seems quite misplaced: Clearly, Christian ethics must be concerned about both. On one hand, the problem with exclusive preoccupation with judgments and decisions is that we may lose track of the *being* of the Christian, and it is this *being* that is presupposed whenever we ask what kinds of judgments and decisions Christians should make. It is the good will that is assumed whenever we ask what is the good that we ought to will. On the other hand, sole preoccupation with Christian character assumes that such good persons will always know intuitively what they ought to do. To neglect *either* moral character or moral judgment is to collapse the mind and the will in artificial ways. The problem is that we do not always do the good that we know to be good and we do not always know the good that we would do if we could. Christian ethics must continue to struggle with both.

In dealing with moral judgment, the problem is one of translating faith commitments into intelligent decisions. As I have suggested elsewhere,[1] that can often best be done by clarifying moral presumptions. If we understand what are the normal implications of Christian faith, then we know to place the burden of proof against deviations from those norms. Thus, our presumption is for peace, so we place the burden of proof against war. Our presumption is for equality, so we place the burden of proof against inequalities. That is better than the simpler intuitions of situation ethics or an ethic of character because it provides us with intellectual tools for ethical analysis. On the other hand, it is also better than modes of moral reasoning that aim at an elusive certainty. Such "principled flexibility," if one may call it that, will be increasingly important in the decades ahead as Christians confront ever more complex issues in a world with many contending ethical perspectives.

Christian Ethics and the Community of Faith

An equally misplaced debate has centered on whether Christian ethics should pertain to life within the church or to Christian participation in the wider society. Actually, no serious Christian ethicist is willing to limit the sphere of moral witness and action to the church alone. But some do tend toward the rather sectarian position that the church is the only sphere in which one may expect to dialogue seriously about Christian ethics. The church, to this way of thinking, is primarily called to be a demonstration to the world of what it means to be Christian. That is, of course, unarguably a necessary part of the church's vocation as church. The broader conclusion, that the wider society is not a moral dialogue in which we should expect to learn anything, is however questionable. Is not God also at work in that world? And does not the world sometimes, even, improve upon the behavior of the church?

At the same time, tendencies to discount the church as central to Christian ethics should also be resisted. If the church really is the community of moral being, in which Christians share their deepest values with one another and engage in mutual dialogue and hold one another accountable, then the church will continue to be very important.

Christian ethics should therefore, it seems to me, resist both the temptations toward sectarianism and toward accommodating to a society that is never wholly Christian. In the decades ahead, the church will surely continue to be at the center of Christian ethics—but God's intended realm of love and justice is not limited to the church. The church exists both as anticipation and as instrument of that realm. Concretely, this at least means that Christians must be very receptive to dialogue with non-Christians. And the church must not be unwilling to make common cause with those outside the church on issues of mutual concern.

Christian Ethics and Power Politics

This inevitably raises the question of the extent to which Christians can endorse the exercise of state power. That has always been a troubling problem, from the very beginning of the history we have surveyed in this volume. A massive dilemma is built into the problem: On the one hand, is Christian faith not offended, on the face of it, by the violence, the suffering, the destruction, and the arrogance, hatreds, and fears engendered by war? The pacifist case has obvious merit. On the other hand, would it not be equally offensive to Christian faith to allow massive injustices to occur without physical challenge, in a world where the strong are permitted to oppress the weak? Does not the case for some version of just war doctrine also have obvious merit?

We have seen that even advocates of pacifism have often accepted the moral legitimacy of the state, with its ultimate sanctions of coercion. In one sense, this may be equivocation. For, if violence is what pacifists find objectionable about war, violence is also present in police actions required to maintain the state. But lurking behind the equivocation there may be an honest effort to resolve the dilemma.

I do not think Christian ethics would have been very relevant, in the long run, if it had been unwilling to accept the legitimacy of the state. And I do not think Christian ethics will have much of a future moving into the third millennium if it withdraws principled support for the state. The state represents the wider society, acting as a whole. Christians are a part of that society. They of all people must be concerned that society not disintegrate into warring self-interested groups.

But much depends upon what kind of state and how coercion and violence are to be contained. In the post-Enlightenment world Christian ethics has discovered representative democracy with its corollary civil rights and civil liberties. Christian interpretation has added greater depth both to democratic ideology and to Christian ethics itself. Democratic ideology is deepened by Christian insight into the reality of human sin, the need to assure all people of some share in social power, and the possibilities of people—made, as they are in the image of God—to work together toward common creative ends. Christian ethics is deepened by perceiving new possibilities of rising above the sterile alternatives of sectarian rejection of the state and uncritical support for authoritarian, hierarchical forms of government.

This book has been written in the immediate aftermath of one of those sweeping historical changes that always seem to pose new possibilities and new dangers. The collapse, first of the Soviet Empire and then of the Soviet Union itself, brought an apparent end to the Cold War, which has defined so much of the world's thinking about politics for nearly half a century. It suddenly seemed possible to think about constructive politics on the grand scale again. The perennial task of politics is the building of a civil society in which people can dwell together without fear and work together for good ends disclosed in public dialogue. The specific task and opportunity at the beginning of the third millennium is to do that on a world scale.

The Christian church is not dependent upon any particular political order. It has coexisted, in turn, with the Roman Empire, the disintegrated territorial states, the feudal baronies and kingdoms, modern nations and empires, and even totalitarian regimes. But it has been freest to be itself in a democratic environment. Can it help think through the kinds of institutions that may be needed to forge a genuinely *civil* world order? How much local autonomy should be combined with how much central authority? How can democratic participation be maximized in a world with such diverse cultures, religions, and economic interests? Can institutions be crafted—or evolved—that will effectively make war obsolete, at long last? Can ways be found to exercise responsible power at the world level without that power disintegrating into some awful new form of universal tyranny? How can an informed Christian dialogue with the various self-assured religious fundamentalisms help engender the levels of tolerance needed to make democratic politics work at the world level?

These serious questions point to exciting new possibilities for Christian political ethics.

Confronting New Moral Issues

There are not many new issues in Christian ethics, though old issues can be recycled in new forms.

281

But in the latter decades of the twentieth century, some authentically new questions have had to be addressed. Some of these relate to new discoveries and technologies in human biology. Some have to do with the unprecedented rate of growth of world population. Some have to do with threats to the global environment. Sometimes it is possible to address such issues by analogy with older issues that have already been thought through; usually that is not so easy.

We have noted the attention given to some of the new issues in ecumenical literature. Often, in that literature and in the writings of bioethicists or environmental ethicists, problems and dilemmas have been elaborated without conclusion. In effect, an agenda has been marked off for future struggle.

Some of the dilemmas are very real. For instance, how should Christians deal with environmental risks that must apparently be run in poor countries to generate sufficient economic development to raise a whole people out of wretchedness? Is the ecology movement a luxury of rich countries that poor countries cannot afford? In the long run, polluting industries may be very dangerous to the health of third-world people; in the short run even such dangers may be preferable to unemployment and malnutrition. The particular dilemmas suggested here may point to the need for global, not merely national, strategies. But in the absence of international will to address them, how are the people most immediately affected to respond? A related dilemma is posed by the need of all societies for cheaper, less polluting sources of energy. The burning of fossil fuels, which has advanced so rapidly over the past century, threatens the atmosphere in a variety of ways. In any case, such fuels will, over the long run, be exhausted. In light of this, should nuclear energy sources, with all their dangers, be developed more rapidly? How much risk, here, is acceptable?

Or, what are we to make of the new possibilities in genetic engineering? Animal breeding, with an eye toward improving certain desired qualities in cows or sheep or horses, has long been known to animal husbandry. But genetic interventions to achieve specified results in the human species has become much more feasible technically. What kinds of interventions are desirable? What kinds risky? What kinds doubtful? What kinds demonic? Should we de-link procreation from human sexual intercourse, a possibility that already exists? Should we try to remove genetic predispositions to certain congenital defects, such as deafness or blindness or the absence of limbs? Should we deal in this way with Down's syndrome or other genetic patterns that might cause subnormal intelligence? But then, should we manipulate genetic factors to increase intelligence generally? Or athletic ability? Or any other specified quality? If homosexual orientation turns out to be genetically inherited, as some investigators suspect, should genetic interventions be employed to change this to heterosexual orientation?

Two approaches by Christian ethics will not finally do, in my opinion. One of these is to treat all such interventions as contrary to nature and therefore also contrary to Christian understanding of God's purposes. A narrower Thomism may be comfortable with such a natural-law grounding. But that version of Christian ethics has fallen increasingly in disfavor among Christian ethicists, and for good reason. Christian ethics needs deeper theological roots; nature, by itself, is too ambiguous to serve as an ultimate moral norm.

The other unacceptable approach is to forbid any new thing that could be subject to abuse. It could be argued that an acceptable genetic intervention, such as preventing a grotesque fetal malformation, should be rejected because it would place us on the slippery slope leading to unacceptable interventions, such as programming prenatal life for specific kinds of athletic superiority. That approach is questionable because almost *any* moral principle is subject to abuse. The possibility of abuse is not a sufficient reason to reject a morally legitimate practice. An important part of the work of Christian ethics is to make distinctions concerning practices at different points on the "slope."

The larger task, scarcely yet begun, is to sort through the possibilities in new genetic technologies and relate them, positively or negatively, to deeper theological values. We may find ourselves supporting new possibilities for enhancing health, alleviating suffering, making it easier for people to hear and to see and to speak. We may find ourselves rejecting possibilities that diminish the healthy diversities within the human gene pool, that exploit human organisms for subhuman ends, that impose cosmetic features upon the newborn reflecting values specific to a given culture.

There are large moral questions related to the rapid rate of population growth in the twentieth century. Familiar projections demonstrate that that rate of increase cannot be continued for many more decades—not to say centuries—without disastrous effects. But what kinds of interventions can be advocated by Christian ethics, and with what governing criteria? Is procreation to be protected as an absolute right for individual couples? Should entire societies set goals based on agreed optima of population size? If so, what theological norms can contribute to our understanding of optimum population? And then, what means are appropriate and inappropriate to achieving the goals?

A host of economic issues will continue to vex Christian ethics in the future. At century's end, the momentum of the long debate between capitalism and socialism seems to have been gained by capitalism. The collapse of the Soviet system, after seventy years of power, has carried with it a severe discrediting of its socialist economic component. In the years ahead Christian ethics may have to struggle some more with the issues the ecumenical movement has raised: Are there peculiar moral dangers in linking economic and political power, as most socialist models tend to do? On the other hand, are there also peculiar moral dangers in a market economic system that encourages competition and tends to enhance greed? In the long run, I suspect that the momentum will shift again toward more communal ways of organizing many economic problems. If so, what contributions might Christian ethics make to finding the best combination between private ownership and freedom of enterprise and collective power sharing and decision making?

A New Eschatological Perspective

In face of these, and other emerging issues, Christians may well look to the future fearfully, preoccupied more with dangers than with hopeful possibilities. Such an attitude is compounded by new scientific perspectives on the sheer immensities of time and space in which our existence is contained. In a universe of one hundred billion galaxies, each on average with a hundred billion stars and innumerable planets, what is this little indistinguished earth of ours? Even on this earth, now something over five billion years in age, what significance attaches to the mere thousands of years of recorded human history? What difference does our ethics make in a world we know will perish one day, either through loss of energy and atmosphere or through catastrophe?

The Christian perspective can, I suppose, add little to our understanding of the material details of this earth's destiny. For that, we humbly attend to the work of science, confident that scientific insight will increase dramatically through the third millennium. But Christian perspective on the *meaning* of this space and this history already possesses its reference point: In the beginning was God; in the end or eschaton there is God. To proclaim Jesus Christ as Lord of history is to say something about the character of the one who is source of all being; it is to say that the character of God is love. Faithful Christian ethics must do its work in the future, murky though that future may be, confident that it is responding to one whose love is boundless.

NOTES

Chapter 2

1. While the immensity of Socrates's influence is beyond dispute, we cannot be sure which of the thoughts attributed to him by his students are precisely his. The great dialogues of Plato typically use Socrates as the chief protagonist, but the later, more systematically refined writings more likely represent the mature thought of Plato himself.

2. Plato's "Apology," in *Five Great Dialogues*, trans. Benjamin Jowett (Roslyn, N.Y.: Classics Club, Walter J. Black, 1942), p. 56.

3. The "Crito," in *Five Great Dialogues*, p. 73.

4. Ibid., p. 75.

5. The "Republic," esp. Book I, in *Five Great Dialogues*, pp. 221–53.

6. Ibid., p. 236.

7. See esp. Book II, in *Five Great Dialogues*, chs. 1–5.

8. See esp. Aristotle's *Politics*, Book I, ch. 2.

9. Aristotle, *Nichomachean Ethics*, Book II, chs. 5–9.

Chapter 3

1. Ignatius, Bishop of Antioch (b. A.D. 30), wrote seven letters while traveling as a condemned prisoner. While these surviving letters are informal in tone, they deal with a number of important ethical issues.

2. Ignatius, *Letter to the Trallians*, in *Early Christian Fathers*, ed. Cyril C. Richardson (New York: Macmillan, 1970), p. 100.

3. Ignatius, *Letter to the Smyrnaeans*, in ibid., p. 113.

4. Richardson, *Early Christian Fathers*, pp. 53–54.

5. *First Apology of Justin*, in ibid., para. 58, p. 280.

6. Irenaeus, *Against Heresies*, in *Early Christian Fathers*, I.27, p. 367.

7. Ibid., I.27, p. 367.

8. Ibid., I.10, p. 360.

9. *Letter of Polycarp*, in *Early Christian Fathers*, 11.2, p. 153.

10. A product of the second century, the *Didache* has important parallels in other surviving writings and may represent traditions of teaching somewhat older than the document as we know it.

11. *Didache*, 2.8.

12. *I Clement*, in *Early Christian Fathers*, 38.2.

13. *Letter to the Smyrnaeans*, in *Early Christian Fathers*, 6.2.

14. *Letter of Polycarp*, in *Early Christian Fathers*, 4.1.

15. *Shepherd of Hermas*, in *The Ante-Nicene Fathers*, Vol. II, ed. Alexander Roberts and James Donaldson (Grand Rapids: Wm. B. Eerdmans Publishing Co., 1977), p. 20.

16. Justo L. Gonzalez, *Faith and Wealth: A History of Early Christian Ideas on the Origin, Significance, and Use of Money* (San Francisco: Harper & Row, 1990), p. 97.

17. *First Apology of Justin*, in *Early Christian Fathers*, 14, pp. 249–50.

18. *First Apology of Justin*, 66. In a comment on this, Cyril Richardson suggests that Justin's depiction of the contributions as voluntary may have a legal basis. Richardson, *Early Christian Fathers*, p. 287.

19. *Letter of Polycarp*, 4.2.

20. *Didache*, 4.10–11.

21. *Didache*, 3.3.

22. *Letter to the Ephesians,* in *Early Christian Fathers,* 16.1.

23. *I Clement,* 30.1.

24. *First Apology of Justin,* 15.

25. *Letter of Polycarp,* 5.3. The term "homosexual," invented in the nineteenth century, has no exact parallel in the somewhat ambiguous Greek text of 1 Corinthians. It seems clear, nonetheless, that this referred to same-sex relations of males.

26. *Didache,* 2.2.

27. *First Apology of Justin,* 27.

28. *First Apology of Justin,* 29.

29. *First Apology of Justin,* 15.

30. *Letter of Polycarp,* 5.1–2.

31. *Letter to Diognetus* in *Early Christian Fathers,* 5.6.

32. *I Clement,* 1.3.

33. *II Clement,* in *Early Christian Fathers,* 12.2, 5–6; pp. 193–98.

34. *II Clement,* 14.2–3.

35. *I Clement,* 55.3.

36. See esp. Roland H. Bainton's *Christian Attitudes Toward War and Peace* (Nashville: Abingdon Press, 1960), and C. J. Cadoux's *The Early Church and the World* (Edinburgh: T. & T. Clark, 1925).

37. Bainton, *Christian Attitudes,* p. 66.

38. Origen, *Against Celsus* VIII.68 in *The Ante-Nicene Fathers,* Vol. IV, p. 665. Cf. Bainton, *Christian Attitudes,* pp. 68–69.

39. *Didache,* 1.3–5.

40. *II Clement,* 13.4.

41. *First Apology of Justin,* 39.

42. Justin, *Dialogue with Trypho,* CX, in *The Ante-Nicene Fathers,* Vol. I, p. 254.

43. Athenagoras, *A Plea Regarding Christians,* in *Early Christian Fathers,* p. 301.

44. *Letter to Diognetus,* 5.10.

45. *I Clement,* 61.1–2.

46. *First Apology of Justin,* 17.

47. *I Clement*, 49.

48. *Letter to Diognetus*, 5.2–4.

49. *Diognetus*, 5.

Chapter 4

1. Ignatius, *Letter to the Romans*, 3.3, in *Early Christian Fathers*, p. 104.

2. Clement, *The Stromata*, I.5, in *The Ante-Nicene Fathers*, p. 305.

3. Ibid., I.6.

4. Ibid.

5. Ibid., I.29.

6. Ibid., V.11.

7. Ibid., V.12.

8. Ibid., V.11.

9. Clement, *Who Is the Rich Man That Shall Be Saved?* XXXVII.

10. Clement, *Rich Man*, XI.

11. Clement, *Rich Man*, XII.

12. Clement, *The Instructor*, II.1.

13. *Instructor*, II.1.

14. Origen, *De Principiis*, I.3.7, in *The Ante-Nicene Fathers*, Vol. IV, p. 254.

15. Ibid., I.3.8.

16. Ibid., I.3.6.

17. Origen, *Against Celsus*, V.37, in *The Ante-Nicene Fathers*, Vol. IV, pp. 559–60.

18. Ibid., VIII.68.

19. Ibid.

20. Ibid., 73.

21. Ibid.

22. Ibid., 70.

23. Ibid., 72.

24. Ibid., 73.

25. Ibid., VIII.75.

26. Tertullian, *Apology*, 9, 38, in *The Ante-Nicene Fathers*; pp. 25–26, 45–46.

27. Ibid., 39.

28. Ibid.

29. Ibid., 33.

30. Ibid., 30.

31. Ibid.

32. Ibid., 5.

33. Tertullian, *On Idolatry*, 19, in *The Ante-Nicene Fathers*, p. 73.

34. A. Cleveland Coxe, "Elucidations," in *The Ante-Nicene Fathers*, Vol. III (Grand Rapids: Wm. B. Eerdmans Publishing Co., 1976 [1885]), p. 58.

35. The most penetrating analysts of the history of Christian ethics have struggled with this. Cf. esp. Ernst Troeltsch, *The Social Teaching of the Christian Churches*, trans. Olive Wyon (New York: Macmillan, 1931 [1911]), and H. Richard Niebuhr, *Christ and Culture* (New York: Harper & Row, 1951).

36. Lactantius, *Divine Institutes*, I.1.

37. Ibid., III.11.

38. Ibid., III.9.

39. Ibid., V.7.

40. The impressive list of reforms included mitigation of the institution of slavery, an end to use of criminals in gladiatorial shows, declaration of Sunday as a holy day, an end to crucifixions, designation of adultery as a capital crime, severe penalties for consigning one's daughters or female slaves to prostitution, prohibition of exposure or sale of children (with corresponding provisions made for public assistance for those unable to support their children). See George Wolfgang Forell, *History of Christian Ethics: From the New Testament to Augustine* (Minneapolis: Augsburg Press, 1979), pp. 112–13.

41. Basil, *Homily on Psalm XV*, I, in *Message of the Fathers of the Church: Social Thought*, ed. Peter C. Phan (Wilmington, Del.: Michael Glazier, 1984), p. 111.

42. Basil, *Homily on Psalm XIV*, I, in *Message of the Fathers*, ed. Phan, p. 110.

43. Justo L. Gonzalez, *Faith and Wealth: A History of Early Christian Ideas on the Origin, Significance, and Use of Money* (San Francisco: Harper & Row, 1990), pp. 182–83.

44. Gregory of Nyssa, *Homily on Ecclesiastes*, in *Message of the Fathers*, ed. Phan, p. 128.

45. *Fifth Homily on the Beatitudes*, in *Message of the Fathers*, ed. Phan, pp. 129–30.

46. Chrysostom, *Homily XXIII on the Letter to the Romans*, in *Message of the Fathers*, ed. Phan, p. 151.

47. Ibid.

48. Ambrose, *Duties of the Clergy*, I.18, in *Nicene and Post-Nicene Fathers*, Vol. X, ed. Philip Schaff and Henry Wace (New York: Christian Literature Co., 1896), pp. 13–14.

49. Ibid, I.28, p. 23.

50. Ibid.

51. Ibid.

52. Louis J. Swift, *The Early Fathers on War and Military Service* (Wilmington, Del.: Michael Glazier, 1983), pp. 100–102.

Chapter 5

1. John Mahoney, *The Making of Moral Theology: A Study of the Roman Catholic Tradition* (Oxford: Clarendon Press, 1987), p. 68.

2. Peter C. Phan, ed., *Message of the Fathers of the Church: Social Thought* (Wilmington, Del.: Michael Glazier, 1984), p. 194.

3. *The Confessions of St. Augustine*, trans. Edward B. Pusey (New York: Harvard Classics, 1909), Book 3, p. 37.

4. Augustine, *City of God*, XIV.4, trans. Gerald G. Walsh, et al. (Garden City, N.Y.: Doubleday, Image Books, 1958), pp. 300–1.

5. Ibid., XIV.13.

6. Ibid.

7. Ibid.

8. "God's mind," Augustine writes, "does not pass from one thought to another. His vision is utterly unchangeable. Thus, He comprehends all that takes place in time—the not-yet-existing future, the existing present, and the no-longer-existing past—in an immutable and eternal present." Ibid., XI.21, p. 227.

9. Ibid., V.9, pp. 104–5.

10. Ibid.

11. Ibid., XIV.28, Marcus Dods, trans.

12. Ibid., II.21, Walsh, et al., trans.

13. Ibid., V.15, Walsh, et al., trans.

14. Ibid., XV.4, p. 327.

15. At one point Augustine speaks of "the City of God, that is to say, God's Church." *City of God*, XIII.16, Walsh, et al., trans.

16. Ibid., I.35, Walsh, et al., trans.

17. Ibid., XIX.17, Dods, trans.

18. Ibid., XIX.12, Walsh, et al., trans.

19. Ibid., IV.4, Dods, trans.

20. Ibid., XIX.4, Walsh, et al., trans.

21. Ibid., V.21, Walsh, et al., trans.

22. Ibid.

23. Ibid., XIX.7, Walsh, et al., trans.

24. Ibid.

25. *Against Faustus*, 22.75. Quoted in Louis J. Swift's *The Early Fathers on War and Military Service* (Wilmington, Del.: Michael Glazier, 1983), p. 129.

26. *Commentary on the First Letter of John*, 10:7, quoted by Swift in *Early Fathers*, p. 148.

27. Letters quoted in ibid., pp. 143–44.

28. *First Letter of John*, 47.5, quoted in ibid., p. 130.

29. *First Letter of John*, 189.6, quoted in ibid., p. 139.

30. This appears in his writing against the Manichees, quoted by Mahoney in *Making of Moral Theology*, p. 61.

31. Ibid., p. 66.

32. *On Christian Doctrine*, I. Quoted in *Message of the Fathers*, ed. Phan, p. 196.

33. *City of God*, XI.25, Walsh, et al., trans.

34. Ibid., IV.3, Walsh, et al., trans.

35. *Ser.* 39.6. Quoted in *Faith and Wealth*, Justo L. Gonzalez (San Francisco: Harper & Row, 1990), p. 218. In an illuminating discussion of Augustine's treatment of economic issues, Gonzalez notes that in the final analysis "all things belong to those to whom the existing order confers them. If the result is that some are poor and some are rich, that is God's doing and not for us to question" (p. 221).

Part III

1. Christopher Dawson, *The Historical Reality of Christian Culture* (New York: Harper & Brothers, 1960).

Chapter 6

1. The word is derived from the Greek *anachoresis*, for withdrawal.

2. The term is an English corruption of the Greek *koinos bios*, or "common life."

3. The Rule of Benedict was not simply Benedict's own invention. In compiling it, Benedict was heavily dependent upon the Rule of the Master, written by an unknown author around A.D. 500, and upon monastic rules developed by Caesarius of Arles. Benedict's Rule was destined to exert a dominating influence on Western monasticism for many centuries. For an illuminating discussion of Benedict's Rule and its sources, see C. H. Lawrence's *Medieval Monasticism*, 2nd ed. (London and New York: Longman, 1989), pp. 19–40.

4. *The Rule of St. Benedict*, trans. W. K. Lowther Clarke. Quoted in *Christian Ethics: Sources of the Living Tradition*, ed. Waldo Beach and H. Richard Niebuhr (New York: Ronald Press, 1955), p. 157.

5. Ibid., pp. 157–58.

6. *Medieval Monasticism*, ed. Lawrence, p. 7.

7. Ernst Troeltsch, *The Social Teaching of the Christian Churches*, trans. Olive Wyon, vol. 1 (New York: Macmillan, 1931 [1911]), p. 242.

8. Quoted in *Medieval Monasticism*, ed. Lawrence, p. 71.

9. Ibid., p. 247.

10. See Sabina Flanagan, *Hildegard of Bingen: A Visionary Life* (London and New York: Routledge & Kegan Paul, 1989), for a discerning study of the life of this influential figure.

11. Flanagan, *Hildegard of Bingen*, p. 15.

12. Ibid., p. 149. The quotation is from Hildegard's *Book of the Divine Works*, ch. 100.

13. Ernst Troeltsch, for instance, treats mysticism as a separate religious "type," alongside the church-type and the sect-type, with the sect-type encompassing most fully the ethics of monasticism.

14. This work is available in many editions and translations; I shall cite here *On the Love of God* (London: A. R. Mowbray & Co., 1950), which lists the translator—in proper monastic fashion—simply as "A Religious of C.S.M.V."

15. Ibid., pp. 61–62.

16. Ibid., p. 63.

17. Ibid., pp. 64–65.

18. Ibid., p. 65.

19. Ibid., p. 67.

20. Ibid., pp. 68–69.

21. See *Catherine of Siena: The Dialogue*, trans. Suzanne Noffke, O.P. (New York: Paulist Press, 1980); *The Letters of St. Catherine of Siena*, trans. Suzanne Noffke, O.P. (Binghamton, N.Y.: Medieval and Renaissance Texts and Studies, 1988); *The Prayers of Catherine of Siena*, ed. and trans. Suzanne Noffke, O.P. (New York: Paulist Press, 1983).

22. *Dialogue*, 6, p. 37.

23. *Prayers*, Prayer 11, p. 90.

24. *Prayers*, Prayer 22, p. 198.

25. *Dialogue*, 50, p. 103.

26. Catherine continues: "The soul cannot live without love. She always wants to love something because love is the stuff she is made of, and through love I (God) created her. . . . [I]f sensual affection wants to love sensual things, the eye of understanding is moved in that direction. It takes for its object only passing things with selfish love, contempt for virtue, and love of vice, drawing from these pride and impatience. . . . This love so dazzles the eye that it neither discerns nor sees anything but the glitter of these things." Ibid., pp. 103–4.

27. Ibid., 33, p. 74.

28. Ibid., p. 75.

29. Ibid., 47, p. 96.

30. Ibid., 34, p. 75.

31. *Letters*, Letter 78, p. 238.

32. Ibid., p. 239.

33. Ibid., Letter 77, p. 236.

Chapter 7

1. John Mahoney's *The Making of Moral Theology: A Study of the Roman Catholic Tradition* (Oxford: Clarendon Press, 1987) is a particularly clear introduction to the history of confession and its influence in the development of moral theology.

2. *Catherine of Siena: The Dialogue*, 43, trans. Suzanne Noffke, O.P. (New York: Paulist Press, 1980), p. 89.

3. Jan L. Womer, ed. and trans., *Morality and Ethics in Early Christianity* (Philadelphia: Fortress Press, 1987), pp. 24–25, 75–82.

4. Ibid., p. 75.

5. Mahoney, *Making of Moral Theology*, p. 4.

6. Ibid., p. 5.

7. See ibid., p. 5; John T. McNeill and Helena M. Gamer, ed. and trans., *Medieval Handbooks of Penance* (New York: Octagon Books, 1965 [1938]); Henry Charles Lea, *A History of Auricular Confession and Indulgences in the Latin Church*, Vol. II (New York: Greenwood Press, 1968 [1896]).

8. Mahoney, *Making of Moral Theology*, p. 6.

9. C. Plummer, quoted by McNeill and Gamer in *Medieval Handbooks of Penance*, p. 47.

10. McNeill and Gamer, pp. 89–90.

11. Ibid., pp. 101–2.

12. Ibid., p. 103.

13. Ibid., pp. 182–215.

14. Lea, *Auricular Confession and Indulgences*, p. 106.

15. McNeill and Gamer, *Medieval Handbooks of Penance*, p. 157.

16. Ibid., p. 274.

17. Ibid., p. 362. In that same manual a "falsifier of money" is required to observe a bread-and-water penance as long as he lives.

18. An eighth- or ninth-century Irish penitential illustrates the anomalies that could occur in relating objective requirements to spiritual ends: "If he should be in grief and sadness so that he cannot be roused, the monk does penance in another place on bread and water, and returns no more into the community of the brethren, until he be joyful in body and soul." McNeill and Gamer, *Medieval Handbooks of Penance*, p. 168. Of course, even that apparent absurdity may represent psychological insight!

19. The phrase is John Mahoney's. See *Making of Moral Theology*, p. 13.

20. McNeill and Gamer, *Medieval Handbooks of Penance*, p. 48.

Chapter 8

1. Obviously, Thomas Aquinas does not think of "end" or *telos* as the termination of a thing. Rather, it is the "end" as goal or destination. Even that may not wholly encompass his meaning, for he also refers to the "perfection" of a thing—that which marks it as being fully and completely what it is created to be.

2. *Summa Theologica* (hereafter *ST*), I.I, Q. 5, Art. 1. in *Basic Writings of Saint Thomas Aquinas*, ed. Anton C. Pegis, vol. 1 (New York: Random House, 1945), p. 42. Unless otherwise noted, all quotations from the *Summa Theologica* and the *Summa Contra Gentiles* are from the two-volume Pegis edition.

3. *ST* I.I. Q. 48. Art. 2.

4. *Summa Contra Gentiles*, Book III, 37.

5. The allusion here is to Aristotle's classic conception of the "golden mean," virtuous actions avoiding either excess or deficiency.

6. *Summa Contra Gentiles*, Book III, 48.

7. See esp. *ST*, II/I. Qs. 46–55.

8. *ST* II/I. Q. 13. Art. 1.

9. Ibid. Q. 55. Art. 4.

10. Ibid. Q. 13. Art. 3.

11. Ibid. Q. 61. Art. 2.

12. Ibid. Q. 61. Art. 3.

13. Ibid. Q. 62. Art. 1.

14. Ibid.

15. Ibid. Q. 62. Art. 4.

16. Ibid. Q. 63. Art. 4.

17. Ibid. Q. 93. Art. 1.

18. Ibid. Q. 96. Art. 4.

19. Ibid. Q. 95. Art. 4.

20. Ibid. Q. 95. Art. 1.

21. Ibid. Q. 96. Art. 2.

22. *ST* II/II. Q. 40. Art. 1. In *The "Summa Theologica" of St. Thomas Aquinas*, English Dominican Province ed. (London: Burns, Oates, and Washbourne, 1915), hereafter cited as EDP.

23. See Roland H. Bainton's *Christian Attitudes Toward War and Peace* (Nashville: Abingdon Press, 1960), p. 106. Bainton's citation is from Thomas's *De Regno*.

24. *ST* II/II. Q. 64. Art. 7. In EDP.

25. Ibid. Q. 66. Art. 1. In EDP.

26. Ibid. Art. 2. In EDP. Thomas does not quote Aristotle's critique of Plato's *Republic* in this section, but his arguments against common ownership are quite similar.

27. Ibid.

28. "It is not theft, properly speaking, to take secretly and use another's property in a case of extreme need: because that which he takes for the support of his life becomes his own property by reason of that need." *ST* II/II. Q. 66. Art. 7. In EDP.

29. Ibid. Q. 77. In EDP.

30. Ibid. Q. 78. Art. 1. In EDP.

31. Ibid. Q. 152. Art. 4. In EDP.

32. *ST* I. Q. 93. Art. 4.

33. Ibid. Q. 92. Art 1.

34. Ibid. Art. 1.

35. Ibid.

36. Ernst Troeltsch, *The Social Teaching of the Christian Churches*, 2 vols., trans. Olive Wyon (New York: Macmillan, 1931 [1911]), see esp. pp. 257–328.

37. We may note, parenthetically, that Troeltsch's studies set the agenda for much of subsequent twentieth-century sociology of religion as well as social ethics, with endless refinements of his typology.

Chapter 9

1. Certainly the "reward" of goodness portrayed by Thomas Aquinas was itself to be able to contemplate God forever, a vision intrinsically related to a life of loving self-discipline on this earth. Even mortal sin, as the denial of that vision, could be said to have its greatest punishment in one's being cut off from God forever. Nevertheless, even Thomas pictured further physical and spiritual torments. I wish to note that the great Renaissance artist Michelangelo (1475–1564) captured something of Dante's understanding that eternal punishment is intrinsic to sin itself. In his portrayal of the Last Judgment in the Sistine Chapel, Michelangelo depicts a stern Christ standing in judgment over the faithful who are ascending toward Christ on his right hand and the damned who are tumbling down toward hell on his left. The faithful are shown helping each other up toward Christ; the damned are pushing each other further down toward the pit of hell in their selfish struggle to get to the top.

2. Dante, *Monarchy and Three Political Letters*, trans. Donald Nicholl (New York: Noonday Press, 1954). All quotations from *De monarchia* are from this English-language edition.

3. Ibid., Book I, 5.

4. Ibid., 13.

5. Ibid., 14.

6. Ibid.

7. Ibid., Book II, 6.

8. Ibid., 3.

9. Ibid., 4.

10. Ibid., 8.

11. Ibid., 8.

12. Ibid., Book III, 13.

13. Ibid., 14.

14. Ibid., 16.

15. In *Documents of the Christian Church*, ed. Henry Bettenson (New York: Oxford University Press, 1947), pp. 162–63.

16. Dante, *Monarchy*, Book III, 8.

17. Alan Gewirth, ed. and trans., *Marsilius of Padua: The Defender of Peace*, vol. I (New York: Columbia University Press, 1951), p. ix.

18. Marsilius of Padua, *The Defender of Peace* [1324], ed. and trans. Alan Gewirth, vol. II (New York: Columbia University Press, 1956), Discourse I, ch. 4. 3. Quotations from the *Defensor pacis* will be from this edition.

19. Marsilius, *Defender of Peace*, Dis. I, ch. 4, part 4.

20. Ibid., ch. 12, part 3. By "weightier part" he does not appear to mean a simple numerical majority. There is also a kind of qualitative principle that gives weight to citizens of more substantial opinion. Still, he obviously wishes to give weight to all citizens, and numbers matter.

21. R. W. Carlyle and A. J. Carlyle, *A History of Mediaeval Political Theory in the West*, Vol. VI (Edinburgh and London: Blackwood, 1962), pp. 11–12.

22. Marsilius, *Defender of Peace*, Dis. I, ch. 15, part 4.

23. Ibid., Dis. II, ch. 2, part 3.

24. Ibid., part 5.

25. Ibid., ch. 18, part 8.

26. Ibid., ch. 20, part 2.

27. Ibid., ch. 18, part 8.

28. Ibid., ch. 21, parts 3–4.

29. Marsilius appears to have been Ludwig's main source of intellectual inspiration and to have accompanied him when he marched on Rome in 1328. For a brief period Ludwig was able to fulfill a number of Marsilius's ideas, certainly including the antipapalist ones—for one of Ludwig's acts as Holy Roman Emperor was to depose Pope John XXII and to designate a successor. Ultimately, Ludwig was forced to leave Rome, accompanied by Marsilius. See Gewirth, *Marsilius of Padua*, Vol. I, pp. 21–22.

30. From David S. Schaff's introduction to *The Church*, by John Hus (Westport, Conn.: Greenwood Press, 1974 [1915]), p. xxx.

31. Hus, *The Church*, p. 71.

32. Ibid., p. 156.

33. Ibid., p. 160.

34. Ibid., pp. 226–27.

35. The intricate moves and counter moves in this drama are well summarized in *A History of the Christian Church*, 4th ed., Williston Walker et al. (New York: Charles Scribner's Sons, 1985), pp. 371–76.

36. See the particularly insightful discussion of the Conciliar Movement in George H. Sabine's *A History of Political Theory* (3rd ed., New York: Holt, Rinehart and Winston, 1961), pp. 313–28.

37. Bettenson, *Documents of the Christian Church*, p. 192.

38. Ernst Troeltsch, *The Social Teaching of the Christian Churches*, 2 vols., trans. Olive Wyon (New York: Macmillan, 1931 [1911]), p. 376.

39. Niccolò Machiavelli, *The Prince*, Harvard Classics, vol. 36 (New York: P. F. Collier & Son, 1910, 1938), ch. 17. Subsequent quotations from *The Prince* are taken from this English-language edition.

40. Ibid.

41. Ibid., ch. 18.

42. Ibid., my emphasis.

43. Ibid.

Chapter 10

1. Benjamin B. Warfield, "Augustine," in *Dictionary of Religion and Ethics*, II, ed. James Hastings, p. 224.

2. Martin Luther, *Concerning Christian Liberty* [1520], trans. R. S. Grignon, in Harvard Classics, vol. 36 (New York: P. F. Collier & Son, 1938), p. 357.

3. Ibid., p. 347.

4. Ibid., p. 362.

5. Ibid., p. 368.

6. Ibid., p. 372.

7. Ibid.

8. Ibid., pp. 349–50.

9. Such a move, in itself, represented a form of social mobility, although it is also true that one's *status* in the new institutional world of order or cloister usually reflected one's previous status in the secular world. Few peasant boys became popes, and few peasant girls became superiors in their orders!

10. *Secular Authority: To What Extent It Should Be Obeyed*, in *Works of Martin Luther*, Vol. III (Philadelphia: A. J. Holman Co. and The Castle Press, 1930), p. 236.

11. Ibid.

12. Ibid., pp. 236–37.

13. Ibid., p. 237.

14. Ibid., p. 247.

15. Ibid., p. 242.

16. Ibid., p. 269.

17. "Against the Robbing and Murdering Hordes of Peasants" [1525], in *Works of Martin Luther*, Vol. IV (Philadelphia: A. J. Holman, 1931), pp. 248ff.

18. *Secular Authority*, in *Works of Martin Luther*, Vol. III, p. 237.

19. Ibid., p. 251.

20. Ibid., p. 259.

21. It might also overstate the originality of Luther's, for Luther, as well as Calvin, owes much to Augustine. Originality in ethics is less the invention of new ideas than it is the refinement and creative application of enduring ideas to new situations. From that perspective, both Luther and Calvin are highly original thinkers.

22. Ernst Troeltsch, *The Social Teaching of the Christian Churches*, vol. 2, trans. Olive Wyon (New York: Macmillan, 1931 [1911]), p. 586.

23. See esp. *Institutes*, Book II, Chs. II–V.

24. Ibid., Ch. II, p. 8.

25. Ibid., Ch. III, p. 5.

26. Ibid., Ch. II, p. 23.

27. Ibid., p. 24.

28. Ibid., p. 26.

29. Ibid., Ch. III, p. 6.

30. Ibid., Ch. V, p. 3.

31. Ibid., p. 1.

32. Ibid., p. 2.

33. Ibid., Ch. VII, p. 12.

34. Ibid., Ch. VIII, p. 58.

35. Ibid., Book III, Ch. X, p. 6.

36. Ibid.

37. Ibid., p. 2.

38. Ibid., p. 3.

39. Ibid.

40. Ibid., p. 4.

41. Ibid., p. 5.

42. Ibid.

43. Ibid., Book IV, Ch. XX, p. 1.

44. Ibid., p. 2.

45. Ibid.

46. Ibid.

47. Ibid., p. 4.

48. Ibid., p. 6.

49. Ibid., p. 8.

50. Ibid., pp. 25–26.

51. Ibid., p. 10.

52. Ibid., p. 11.

53. Ibid., p. 12.

54. In an illuminating, though complex, discussion of the relationships between Calvinist religious conceptions and their political and economic effects, Troeltsch carefully reminds us that Calvinism was not so much democratic as theocratic. The covenant is between God and the nation. It is not a covenant among citizens to form the state, as the later contract theorists and earlier Stoic theorists maintained. See Troeltsch, *Social Teaching*, vol. 2, pp. 617–34. Nevertheless, the absoluteness of God has the effect of leveling humanity, despite the elitism of Calvinism's doctrine of election. If God is king, then no human being is king. The covenant binding humanity together in civil society is through God, but it is no less real. We should not be surprised that those nations most heavily influenced by Calvinism also tended toward democratic theory and practice. See also James Hastings Nichols's *Democracy and the Churches* (Philadelphia: Westminster Press, 1951).

Chapter 11

1. Erasmus, *The Praise of Folly*, in *The Essential Erasmus*, ed. John P. Dolan (New York: New American Library, 1964), pp. 148–49.

2. Erasmus, "Letter to Paul Volz," in *Christian Humanism and the Reformation: Selected Writings of Erasmus*, ed. John O. Olir, revised ed. (New York: Fordham University Press, 1975), p. 111.

3. Ibid., p. 112.

4. Erasmus, *The Complaint of Peace* (La Salle, Ill.: Open Court, 1974), pp. 2–3.

5. Ibid., p. 54.

6. Erasmus, "Letter to Paul Volz," in *Christian Humanism*, p. 115.

7. Erasmus, *On the Freedom of the Will*, in *Luther and Erasmus: Free Will and Salvation*, ed. E. Gordon Rupp and Philip S. Watson (Philadelphia: Westminster Press, 1969), p. 41.

8. Thomas More, *Utopia*, Harvard Classics, vol. 36 (New York: P. F. Collier & Son, 1938 [1910]), p. 240. Quotations from *Utopia* are from this edition.

9. Ibid., p. 167.

10. Ibid., p. 236.

11. Ibid.

12. Ibid., p. 231.

13. Ibid., p. 143.

14. Ibid.

15. Ibid., p. 197.

16. Ibid.

17. Henry Bettenson, ed., *Documents of the Christian Church* (New York: Oxford University Press, 1947), p. 368.

18. Bettenson, ed., *Documents of the Christian Church*, pp. 369–71.

19. Bettenson, ed., *Documents of the Christian Church*, p. 373.

20. Quoted in John Mahoney, *The Making of Moral Theology: A Study of the Roman Catholic Tradition* (Oxford: Clarendon Press, 1987), p. 136.

21. Loyola, *Institutum Societatis Jesu*, I, in *Christian Social Teachings*, ed. George W. Forell (Garden City, N.Y.: Doubleday & Co., 1966), pp. 204–5.

22. Ibid., p. 205.

23. Francisco de Suarez, *A Treatise on Laws and God the Lawgiver*, Book III, Ch. II, in *Christian Social Teachings*, ed. Forell, p. 207.

24. Ibid., p. 208.

25. Ibid., p. 212.

26. Ibid., p. 211.

27. Ibid.

28. Ibid., p. 213.

29. Ibid.

Chapter 12

1. Quoted by Eric W. Gritsch in *Thomas Müntzer: A Tragedy of Errors* (Minneapolis: Fortress Press, 1989), p. 99.

2. Ibid.

3. John Denck, "Whether God Is the Cause of Evil" [1526], in *Spiritual and Anabaptist Writers*, ed. George H. Williams (Philadelphia: Westminster Press, 1957), p. 106.

4. Melchior Hofmann, "The Ordinance of God," in *Spiritual and Anabaptist Writers*, ed. Williams, p. 198.

5. Menno Simons, "On the Ban: Questions and Answers" [1550], in *Spiritual and Anabaptist Writers*, ed. Williams (Philadelphia: Westminster Press, 1957), p. 264.

6. Ibid., p. 267.

7. "The Trial and Martyrdom of Michael Sattler," in *Spiritual and Anabaptist Writers*, ed. Williams, p. 143.

8. *Rules of Discipline*, in *Christian Social Teachings*, ed. George W. Forell (Garden City, N.Y.: Doubleday & Co., 1966), p. 239.

9. Ibid., p. 241.

10. See William Penn, *Some Fruits of Solitude*, in Harvard Classics, vol. 1, ed. Charles W. Eliot (New York: P. F. Collier & Son, 1937, 1909).

11. "The Putney Debates," in *The Levellers in the English Revolution*, ed. G. E. Aylmer (Ithaca, N.Y.: Cornell University Press, 1975), p. 100.

12. Ibid., p. 102.

13. Hobbes's *Leviathan*, a more pessimistic version of contract theory, was published only four years later. The second of Locke's *Two Treatises on Government*, which better reflects Leveller political sentiments, was published in 1690.

14. Ibid., p. 109.

15. "The True Levellers Standard Advanced," in Lewis H. Berens's *The Digger Movement in the Days of the Commonwealth* (London: Holland Press and Merlin Press, 1961 [1906]), p. 96.

16. "The Law of Freedom," in *Digger Movement*, Berens, p. 216.

17. Ibid., p. 217.

Chapter 13

1. Joseph Butler, *The Analogy of Religion,* in *The Works of Joseph Butler,* Vol. I, ed. W. E. Gladstone (Oxford: Clarendon Press, 1896), p. 188.

2. Gladstone, W. E., *Works of Joseph Butler,* I, p. 197.

3. Ibid., p. 195.

4. Butler, "Sermon I: Upon the Social Nature of Man," from *Fifteen Sermons Upon Human Nature* in *The Classical Moralists,* ed. Benjamin Rand (Boston: Houghton Mifflin Co., 1937), p. 369.

5. Ibid., p. 374.

6. Ibid., p. 375.

7. Ibid., p. 377.

8. Butler, "Sermon II: Upon the Natural Supremacy of Conscience," in *Classical Moralists,* ed. Rand, p. 381.

9. Ibid., p. 388.

10. Ibid., p. 392.

11. Butler, "Of the Nature of Virtue," in Gladstone's *Works of Joseph Butler,* I.

12. Butler, "Upon the Love of Our Neighbour," in *Christian Ethics: Sources of the Living Tradition,* ed. Waldo Beach and H. Richard Niebuhr (New York: Ronald Press, 1955), p. 341.

13. John Wesley, "The Character of a Methodist," in *Christian Perfection as Believed and Taught by John Wesley,* ed. Thomas S. Kepler (Cleveland: World Publishing Co., 1954), pp. 13–14.

14. Wesley, "Further Thoughts on Christian Perfection," in *Christian Perfection,* ed. Kepler, p. 96.

15. Wesley, notes from 1764, in *Christian Perfection,* ed. Kepler, pp. 137–38.

16. Quoted by Max Weber in *The Protestant Ethic and the Spirit of Capitalism* (New York: Charles Scribner's Sons, 1958 [1904–1905]), p. 175. Weber, in citing this passage, treats Wesley as a prime example of the ascetic Protestant spirit which unleashes the pursuit of wealth from earlier ascetic constraints while placing even greater constraints upon consumption. Weber found this combination of a strong vocational drive toward production with an equally serious emphasis upon stewardship to be highly functional in the development of modern capitalism.

17. Wesley, "Thoughts on the Present Scarcity of Provision," in *Christian Social Teachings*, ed. George W. Forell (Garden City, N.Y.: Doubleday & Co., 1966), p. 286.

18. Ibid.

19. *Journal*, Feb. 9–10, 1753. Cited in *Good News to the Poor: John Wesley's Evangelical Economics*, Theodore W. Jennings, Jr. (Nashville: Abingdon Press, 1990), p. 55.

20. Quoted by Jennings in *Good News to the Poor*, p. 85.

21. Wesley, "Thoughts on Slavery," in *Christian Social Teachings*, ed. Forell, p. 284.

22. Ibid.

23. Quoted by Richard M. Cameron in *Methodism and Society in Historical Perspective* (Nashville: Abingdon Press, 1961), p. 53.

24. Wesley, "A Calm Address," cited in Jennings's *Good News to the Poor*, p. 217.

25. Wesley, "Some Observations on Liberty," in Jennings's *Good News to the Poor*, p. 217.

26. Wesley, "The Doctrine of Original Sin," in *The Works of John Wesley*, Vol. IX (Grand Rapids: Zondervan Publishing House, 1958 [1756]), p. 222.

27. Ibid., p. 223.

28. C. T. Winchester, *The Life of John Wesley* (New York: Macmillan, 1906), p. 80.

29. Jonathan Edwards, *The Nature of True Virtue*, in *Christian Ethics: Sources of the Living Tradition*, ed. Waldo Beach and H. Richard Niebuhr (New York: Ronald Press, 1955), p. 390.

30. Ibid., pp. 391–92.

31. Ibid., p. 399.

32. Ibid., pp. 399–400.

33. Ibid., p. 396.

34. Ibid., p. 398.

35. Ibid., p. 402.

36. Ibid., pp. 402–3.

37. Ibid., p. 412.

38. Edwards, "Obligations to Charity," in *Christian Social Teachings*, ed. Forell, p. 304.

Chapter 14

1. Immanuel Kant, *Critique of Practical Reason*, trans. Lewis White Beck (Chicago: Univ. of Chicago Press, 1949 [1788]), p. 146.

2. Schopenhauer, *The World as Will and Idea*, trans. R. B. Haldane and J. Kemp (London: Routledge & Kegan Paul, 1883). Quoted from *Approaches to Ethics: Representative Selections from Classical Times to the Present*, 3rd ed., W. T. Jones et al. (New York: McGraw-Hill Book Co., 1977), p. 270.

3. Ibid., p. 274.

4. Ibid.

5. See esp. Marx's *Economic and Philosophical Manuscripts of 1844*.

6. Marx, "Contribution to the Critique of Hegel's *Philosophy of Right*," in *The Marx-Engels Reader*, ed. Robert C. Tucker, 2nd ed. (New York: W. W. Norton & Co., 1978 [1844]), p. 54.

7. John Stuart Mill, *Utilitarianism*, in *The English Philosophers from Bacon to Mill* , ed. Edwin A. Burtt (New York: Modern Library, 1939 [1863]), p. 903.

8. Ibid., p. 902.

9. Friedrich Nietzsche, *Twilight of the Idols*, in *Approaches to Ethics*, ed. Jones et al., p. 326.

10. Ibid., p. 328.

11. Nietzsche, *The Antichrist*, in *Approaches to Ethics*, ed. Jones et al., p. 332.

12. Friedrich Schleiermacher, *Introduction to Christian Ethics*, trans. John C. Shelley (Nashville: Abingdon Press, 1989 [1826–27]), p. 46. This volume is the most complete English translation of Schleiermacher's ethics, but it must be noted that it is derived from notes and transcripts of his academic lectures. Schleiermacher was never able to write his complete systematic ethics as he had hoped to do.

13. Ibid., p. 53.

14. In an illuminating interpretation of Schleiermacher, James M. Gustafson contrasts Schleiermacher's moral self as one whose "action *expresses the personal history that it has accumulated* through its past experiences and associations" with Kant's moral self whose "action is a *free self undetermined by its phenomenal history* . . . acting out of this freedom to determine the future." *Christ and the Moral Life* (New York: Harper & Row, 1968), p. 92.

15. Ibid., p. 42.

16. Ibid., p. 63.

17. Schleiermacher, *Introduction to Christian Ethics*, p. 60.

18. Ibid.

19. Ibid., p. 57.

20. Ibid., p. 58.

21. Ibid., p. 43.

22. Ibid., p. 54.

23. Ibid., p. 88.

24. Ibid., pp. 88–89.

25. Søren Kierkegaard, *Either/Or*, Vol. II, trans. Walter Lowrie (Garden City, N.Y.: Doubleday, 1959 [1843]), p. 167.

26. Ibid., p. 171.

27. Kierkegaard, *Fear and Trembling*, in *A Kierkegaard Anthology*, ed. Robert Bretall (Princeton, N.J.: Princeton University Press, 1946), p. 130. The emphasis is Kierkegaard's.

28. Ibid., p. 134.

29. Kierkegaard, *Attack Upon "Christendom,"* trans. Walter Lowrie (Princeton, N.J.: Princeton University Press, 1944 [1854–55]), p. 21.

30. Ibid., p. 83.

31. Ibid., p. 42.

32. Ibid., p. 95.

33. Ibid., p. 84.

34. F. D. Maurice, *The Kingdom of Christ*, Vol. II (London: SCM Press, 1958 [1842]), p. 335.

35. Ibid., p. 284.

36. Ibid.

37. Ibid., pp. 284–85.

38. Ibid., Vol. I, pp. 197–201.

39. Maurice, *The Conscience: Lectures on Casuistry*, 3rd ed. (London: Macmillan, 1883), pp. 50–56.

40. Maurice, *The Kingdom of Christ*, Vol. II, p. 337.

41. Ibid.

42. Frederick Maurice, ed., *The Life of Frederick Denison Maurice: Chiefly Told in His Own Letters* (New York: Charles Scribner's Sons, 1884), p. 35. In a letter to a friend, Maurice exclaimed, "we must not beat about the bush."

43. Ibid.

44. Albrecht Ritschl, *The Christian Doctrine of Justification and Reconciliation*, trans. H. R. Mackintosh and A. B. Macaulay (Clifton, N.J.: Reference Book Publishers, 1966 [from the 3rd ed., 1888]), p. 15.

45. Ibid., p. 8.

46. Ibid., p. 10.

47. Ibid.

48. Ibid., p. 11.

49. Ibid., p. 107.

50. Ibid., p. 211.

51. In making this point, H. Richard Niebuhr treats Ritschl as a prime example of the "Christ of culture"—the easy identification of Christian faith with the highest moral ideas and values of the dominant culture. See H. Richard Niebuhr, *Christ and Culture* (San Francisco: Harper & Row, 1951), pp. 98–99.

52. Ritschl acknowledges the close association of his views of Christian ethics with those of Kant. But he argues that "these ideas are valid in Christianity also, or rather it was on Christianity that Kant modelled them." Ibid., p. 530.

53. Adolf Harnack, *What Is Christianity?* 2nd ed., rev. (New York: G. P. Putnam's Sons, 1904), p. 55.

54. The publication in 1906 of Albert Schweitzer's *Quest of the Historical Jesus* sharply focused the methods of critical biblical scholarship upon the Gospel portraits of Jesus and raised substantial doubts about the extent to which an uncritical use of Jesus' reported teachings could be the basis for Christian ethics. Used in more sophisticated ways, of course, those teachings were to remain very important in the subsequent development of twentieth-century Christian ethics.

55. Leo Tolstoy, *My Religion* (New York: Crowell & Co., 1885).

56. Tolstoy, *The Kingdom of God Is Within You*, trans. Leo Wiener (New York: Farrar, Straus & Cudahy, 1961 [1905]), p. 72. This book is a collection of Tolstoy's writings evoked by response to *My Religion*.

57. Ibid., pp. 100–101.

58. Ibid., p. 102.

59. Ibid., p. 117.

60. Ibid., p. 171.

61. Ibid., p. 267.

62. Ibid.

63. Ernst Troeltsch, *The Social Teaching of the Christian Churches*, 2 vols., trans. Olive Wyon (Louisville: Westminster/John Knox Press, 1992 [1911]).

64. Ernst Troeltsch, "My Books" (unpublished trans. by Franklin H. Littell, 1960).

Chapter 15

1. John Woolman, *The Journal of John Woolman*, in Harvard Classics, vol. 1 (New York: P. F. Collier & Son, 1937), p. 281.

2. Richard M. Cameron, *Methodism and Society in Historical Perspective* (Nashville: Abingdon Press, 1961), p. 97.

3. Ibid., p. 99.

4. I. L. Brookes, *Defense of the South Against the Reproaches of the North* (1850), quoted in ibid., p. 144.

5. George Fitzhugh, *Sociology for the South* (1855), cited in ibid., p. 145.

6. William A. Booth, M.D., *The Writings of William A. Booth, M.D. During the Controversy Upon Slavery* (Sommerville, Tenn.: Reeves and Yancey, 1845), p. 7. Booth wrote that "we believe the condition of the slaves at the South to be equal to that of the servants at the North, and better than that of the lowest classes of people in any other nation." Acknowledging that ultimately emancipation could be affirmed, this more moderate southern spokesperson nevertheless argued that "ultra-abolition strengthens the fetters of slavery and augments the misery of the slave." Ibid., p. 20.

7. Quoted in John R. McKivigan, *The War Against Proslavery Religion: Abolitionism and the Northern Churches, 1830–1865* (Ithaca, N.Y.: Cornell University Press, 1984), p. 31.

8. Charles G. Finney, *Lectures to Professing Christians* (New York: John S. Taylor, 1837), p. 55. Quoted in Lawrence Thomas Lesick, *The Lane Rebels: Evangelicalism and Antislavery in Antebellum America* (Metuchen, N.J.: Scarecrow Press, 1980), p. 175.

9. Quoted by McKivigan in *War Against Proslavery Religion*, p. 97.

10. Ibid., p. 103.

11. Quoted in ibid., p. 67.

12. Quoted in Lesick's *The Lane Rebels*, p. 176.

13. Ibid., p. 175.

14. Frederick Douglass, "An Appeal to the British People," in *The Life and Writings of Frederick Douglass*, Vol. I, ed. Philip S. Foner (New York: International Publishers, 1950 [1848]), pp. 162–63.

15. Ibid., p. 163.

16. "Captain John Brown Not Insane," from *Douglass' Monthly* (November, 1859), in *Life and Writings of Frederick Douglass*, ed. Foner, p. 460.

17. See Clarence C. Goen, *Broken Churches, Broken Nation: Denominational Schisms and the Coming of the American Civil War* (Macon, Ga.: Mercer University Press, 1985).

18. Miriam Schneir, ed., *Feminism: The Essential Historical Writings* (New York: Random House, 1972), p. 78.

19. Ibid., pp. 78–79.

20. Ibid., p. 77.

21. Lucretia Mott, "Not Christianity, but Priestcraft," in ibid., pp. 100–102. This address was delivered extemporaneously.

22. Donna A. Behnke, *Religious Issues in Nineteenth Century Feminism* (Troy, N.Y.: Whitston Publishing Co., 1982), p. 123.

23. Frances E. Willard, *Woman in the Pulpit* (Boston: D. Lothrop Co., 1888), p. 33. Quoted by Behnke in *Religious Issues*, p. 124.

24. Behnke, *Religious Issues*, pp. 130–31.

25. Ibid., p. 133.

26. Ellen Carol DuBois, ed., *Elizabeth Cady Stanton/Susan B. Anthony Correspondence, Writings, Speeches* (New York: Schocken Books, 1981), p. 233.

27. Ibid.

28. Ibid., p. 245.

29. Sojourner Truth, "Ain't I a Woman?" in *Feminism*, ed. Schneir, pp. 94–95.

Chapter 16

1. Charles Howard Hopkins, *The Rise of the Social Gospel in American Protestantism: 1865–1915* (New Haven, Conn.: Yale University Press, 1940), p. 175.

2. Washington Gladden, *Applied Christianity* (Boston: Houghton, Mifflin, 1886), p. 161.

3. Ibid., p. 87.

4. Ibid., p. 20.

5. Ibid., p. 22.

6. Washington Gladden, *Working People and Their Employers* (New York: 1876), cited in Hopkins's *Rise of the Social Gospel*, p. 30.

7. The most complete biography of Walter Rauschenbusch is Paul Minus's *Walter Rauschenbusch: American Reformer* (New York: Macmillan, 1988).

8. Walter Rauschenbusch, *Christianity and the Social Crisis* (New York: Macmillan, 1907), p. 111.

9. Walter Rauschenbusch, *A Theology for the Social Gospel* (New York: Macmillan, 1917), p. 151.

10. Ibid.

11. Ibid., p. 97.

12. Ibid., pp. 97–98.

13. Ibid., p. 77.

14. Ibid., p. 78.

15. Ibid., p. 267.

16. Ibid., pp. 267–73.

17. Ibid., p. 273.

18. Ibid., pp. 273–74.

19. Walter Rauschenbusch, *Christianizing the Social Order* (New York: Macmillan, 1912).

20. Ibid., p. 125.

21. Ibid., p. 131.

22. Ibid., p. 136.

23. Ibid., p. 156.

24. Rauschenbusch, *Christianity and the Social Crisis*, p. 195.

25. Ibid., p. 407.

26. Rauschenbusch, *Christianizing the Social Order*, pp. 402–3.

27. Ibid., p. 63.

28. Ibid., pp. 63–64.

29. Ibid., p. 403.

30. Walter Rauschenbusch, *For God and the People: Prayers of the Social Awakening* (Boston: Pilgrim Press, 1910), p. 97.

31. Richard M. Cameron, *Methodism and Society in Historical Perspective* (Nashville: Abingdon Press, 1961), pp. 323–24.

32. Ibid.

33. The English translation of the Blumhardts' work is *Thy Kingdom Come: A Blumhardt Reader*, ed. Vernard Eller (Grand Rapids: Wm. B. Eerdmans Publishing Co., 1980). This material is taken from a collection of the Blumhardts' writings, *Der Kampf um das Reich Gottes in Blumhardt, Vater und Sohn—und weiter!* edited by Leonhard Ragaz. It is not always possible to identify which Blumhardt was responsible for particular passages, and for our more general purposes it is not necessary. In the quotations that follow, I assume authorship by the son, Christoph Friedrich Blumhardt.

34. *Thy Kingdom Come*, ed. Eller, p. 3.

35. Ibid., p. 4.

36. Ibid.

37. Ibid., p. 173.

38. Ibid., p. 20.

39. Ibid., pp. 20–21.

40. Ibid., p. 21.

41. Ibid., p. 22.

42. Ibid., p. 23.

43. Ibid., p. 25.

44. Ibid.

45. Ibid., p. 26.

46. Ibid., p. 158.

47. Ibid., p. 70.

48. Leonhard Ragaz, *Signs of the Kingdom: A Ragaz Reader*, ed. and trans. Paul Bock (Grand Rapids: Wm. B. Eerdmans Publishing Co., 1984), p. 22.

49. Ibid., p. 15.

50. Ibid., pp. 10–11.

51. Ibid., p. 6.

52. Ibid.

53. Ibid., p. 54.

54. Ibid., p. 55.

55. Ibid.

56. Ibid., p. 63.

Chapter 17

1. Pope Leo XIII, *Rerum novarum*, 35. In citations from papal encyclicals, numbers refer to sections. Quotations from papal encyclicals referred to in this chapter are taken from *Seven Great Encyclicals* (Glen Rock, N.J.: Paulist Press, 1963).

2. Ibid., 34.

3. Ibid., 40.

4. Ibid., 42.

5. Ibid., 27.

6. Ibid., 38.

7. Ibid., 26.

8. Ibid., 28.

9. Ibid., 41.

10. Ibid., 28.

11. Ibid., 29.

12. Ibid.

13. Ibid., 12.

14. Ibid., 7.

15. Ibid., 5.

16. Ibid.

17. Charles E. Curran, "The Common Good and Official Catholic Social Teaching," in *The Common Good and U. S. Capitalism*, ed. Oliver E. Williams and John W. Houck (Lanham, Md.: University Press of America, 1987), p. 112.

18. Pope Pius XI, *Quadragesimo anno*, 79.

19. Ibid., 94.

20. Ibid., 88.

21. Ibid., 105.

22. Ibid., 74.

23. Ibid., 112.

24. Ibid., 113.

25. *Divini redemptoris*, 58.

26. Ibid., 19.

27. Ibid., 22.

28. Ibid., 23.

29. Ibid., 49.

30. Ibid., 44.

31. Ibid., 54.

32. Ibid., 59.

33. Ibid., 64.

34. Ibid., 75.

Chapter 18

1. Reinhold Niebuhr, *Moral Man and Immoral Society* (New York: Scribner's, 1932).

2. Ibid., p. xi.

3. Reinhold Niebuhr, *The Nature and Destiny of Man*, vol. I (New York: Scribner's, 1941), p. 251.

4. Ibid.

5. Ibid., p. 252.

6. Reinhold Niebuhr, *The Children of Light and the Children of Darkness* (New York: Scribner's, 1944), p. xiii.

7. Reinhold Niebuhr, "Why the Christian Church Is Not Pacifist," in his *Christianity and Power Politics* (New York: Scribner's, 1940), pp. 1–32.

8. Ibid., p. 31.

9. Ibid., p. 18.

10. See esp. Karl Barth's *Church Dogmatics* II/2 (Edinburgh: T. & T. Clark, 1957), Section 36, "Ethics as a Task of the Doctrine of God."

11. Ibid., p. 509.

12. Karl Barth, *Church Dogmatics*, III/I (Edinburgh: T. & T. Clark, 1958).

13. Ibid., p. 97.

14. Ibid.

15. Barth, *Church Dogmatics*, III/4, pp. 116–240.

16. Ibid., p. 166.

17. See *Karl Barth and Radical Politics*, ed. George Hunsinger (Philadelphia: Westminster Press, 1976).

18. Barth, *Church Dogmatics*, III/4, p. 460.

19. Ibid., p. 455.

20. Ibid., p. 460.

21. Ibid., p. 462.

22. Ibid., p. 463.

23. Ibid., p. 458.

24. One of the best brief summaries of Barth's complex views of the relationships of church and state is his 1946 essay "The Christian Community and the Civil Community," published in English in his *Community, State, and Church* (Garden City, N.Y.: Doubleday, Anchor Books, 1960), pp. 149–89.

25. Ibid., p. 154.

26. Ibid., p. 156.

27. Ibid., p. 158.

28. Dietrich Bonhoeffer, *The Cost of Discipleship* (New York: Macmillan, 1963 [1937]), p. 59.

29. Ibid., p. 69.

30. Ibid., pp. 133–34.

31. Ibid., p. 137.

32. Ibid.

33. Paul Tillich, *The Protestant Era*, trans. James Luther Adams (Chicago: University of Chicago Press, 1948), p. xii.

34. Ibid., p. xiv.

35. Ibid.

36. Paul Tillich, *Systematic Theology*, Vol. I (Chicago: University of Chicago Press, 1951), p. 151.

37. Paul Tillich, *Love, Power, and Justice* (New York: Oxford University Press, 1954).

38. Ibid., p. 71.

39. See esp. Tillich's *Systematic Theology*, Vol. I, pp. 164–65, 174–86.

40. H. Richard Niebuhr, *Christ and Culture* (New York: Harper & Row, 1951).

41. H. Richard Niebuhr, *Radical Monotheism and Western Culture* (Louisville: Westminster/John Knox Press, 1993 [1960]).

42. H. Richard Niebuhr, *The Responsible Self* (New York: Harper & Row, 1963).

43. Joseph Fletcher, *Situation Ethics: The New Morality* (Philadelphia: Westminster Press, 1966).

44. Paul Lehmann, *Ethics in a Christian Context* (New York: Harper & Row, 1963).

45. Ibid., p. 159.

46. Paul Ramsey, *Basic Christian Ethics* (Louisville: Westminster/John Knox Press, 1993 [1953]), p. 340.

47. Paul Ramsey, *Deeds and Rules in Christian Ethics* (New York: Charles Scribner's Sons, 1967).

48. See esp. Paul Ramsey's *War and the Christian Conscience: How Shall Modern War Be Conducted Justly?* (Durham, N.C.: Duke University Press, 1961).

49. See Edgar S. Brightman's *Moral Laws* (Nashville: Abingdon Press, 1933); L. Harold DeWolf, *Responsible Freedom: Guidelines to Christian Action* (New York: Harper & Row, 1971); and Walter G. Muelder, *Moral Law in Christian Social Ethics* (Richmond: John Knox Press, 1966).

50. Walter G. Muelder, *Foundations of the Responsible Society* (Nashville: Abingdon Press, 1959).

51. Ibid., p. 9.

52. Anders Nygren, *Agape and Eros: A Study of the Christian Idea of Love* (New York: Macmillan, 1932–1938).

53. DeWolf, *Responsible Freedom*, p. 108.

54. John C. Bennett, *Christian Ethics and Social Policy* (New York: Scribner's, 1946), p. 120.

55. See esp. W. A. Visser 't Hooft and J. H. Oldham's *The Church and Its Function in Society* (Chicago: Willett-Clark, 1937), p. 210.

56. Ibid.

57. See esp. J. Philip Wogaman, *A Christian Method of Moral Judgment* (Philadelphia: Westminster Press, and London: SCM Press, 1976) and *Christian Moral Judgment* (Louisville: Westminster/John Knox Press, 1989).

58. See esp. John Howard Yoder's *The Politics of Jesus* (Grand Rapids: Wm. B. Eerdmans Publishing Co., 1972).

59. See, e.g., Stanley Hauerwas's *A Community of Character: Toward a Constructive Christian Social Ethic* (Notre Dame, Ind.: Univ. of Notre Dame Press, 1981), and James Wm. McClendon, Jr.'s *Ethics: Systematic Theology* (Nashville: Abingdon Press, 1986).

60. Bernard Haring, *Free and Faithful in Christ*, Vol. I of *General Moral Theology* (New York: Seabury Press, 1978), p. 6.

61. Ibid., p. 323.

62. Ibid., p. 324.

63. Ibid., p. 312.

64. Ibid., p. 74.

65. Ibid., pp. 75–76.

66. Bernard Haring, *The Law of Christ*, Vol. II of *Special Moral Theology* (Westminster, Md.: Newman Press, 1963), p. 94.

67. Ibid., p. 94.

68. Ibid.

69. Ibid., p. 399.

70. Haring, *Free and Faithful in Christ*, p. 2.

71. Ibid.

Chapter 19

1. Pope John XXIII, *Mater et Magistra*, 113. Quotations of the encyclicals of John XXIII are from *Proclaiming Justice and Peace: Documents from John XXIII to John Paul II*, ed. Michael Walsh and Brian Davies (Mystic, Conn.: Twenty-third Publications, 1984). Numbers in the citations from papal encyclicals refer to numbered paragraphs in authorized editions.

2. Ibid., 115.

3. Ibid., 116.

4. Ibid., 117.

5. Ibid., 189.

6. Ibid., 152.

7. *Pacem in terris*, 137.

8. Ibid., 135.

9. Ibid., 145.

10. Ibid., 112.

11. Ibid., 51.

12. Ibid., 73.

13. Ibid., 56.

14. *Gaudium et spes*, 4.3.

15. Ibid., 21.2.

16. Ibid., 17.

17. Ibid., 31.1.

18. Ibid., 29.

19. Ibid., 66.

20. Ibid., 71.

21. Ibid., 71.5.

22. Ibid., 82.

23. *Declaration on Religious Freedom*, 2. In *The Documents of Vatican II*, ed. Walter M. Abbott (New York: America Press et al., 1966).

24. Ibid.

25. Ibid., 3.

26. Ibid., 1.

27. *Declaration on the Relationship of the Church to Non-Christian Religions*, 2, in *Documents of Vatican II*, ed. Abbott.

28. *Populorum progressio*, 31, in *Documents of Vatican II*, ed. Abbott.

29. Ibid., 37.

30. Ibid., 78.

31. Ibid., 79.

32. *Octagesimo adveniens*, 23, in *Documents of Vatican II*, ed. Abbott.

33. Ibid., 13.2.

34. *Humanae vitae*, 7–10, in *Documents of Vatican II*, ed. Abbott.

35. Ibid., 11.

36. Ibid.

37. Ibid., 17.

38. Ibid., 23.

39. Ibid., 15.

40. John Paul II, *On Human Work: Encyclical Laborem Exercens* (Washington, D.C.: U.S. Catholic Conference, 1981), 6.

41. Ibid., 12.

42. Ibid.

43. Ibid., 14.

44. Ibid.

45. Ibid., 41.

46. Ibid., 46.

47. John Paul II, *On the Hundredth Anniversary of Rerum Novarum (Centesimus Annus)* (Washington, D.C.: U.S. Catholic Conference, 1991), 19.

48. Ibid., 24.

49. Ibid., 19.

50. Ibid., 35.

51. Ibid., 40.

Chapter 20

1. Trans. Caridad Inda and John Eagleson (Maryknoll, N.Y.: Orbis Books, 1973). The Gutiérrez lecture "A Theology of Liberation" in Chimbote, Peru, in July, 1968, appears to be the origin of the name of the movement.

2. Ibid., p. 145.

3. Paulo Freire, *The Pedagogy of the Oppressed*, trans. Myra Bergman Ramos (New York: Seabury Press, 1970).

4. Gutierrez, *A Theology of Liberation*, p. 87.

5. Ibid.

6. Ibid., p. 88.

7. José Miguez Bonino, *Christians and Marxists: The Mutual Challenge to Revolution* (Grand Rapids: Wm. B. Eerdmans Publishing Co., 1976), p. 19.

8. Like most of the Latin American liberation theologians who continued to write after the 1970s, Miguez Bonino's use of Marxist tools of analysis became much more circumspect. See esp. his *Toward a Christian Political Ethics* (Philadelphia: Fortress Press, 1983).

9. Martin Luther King, Jr., "Letter from Birmingham City Jail," in *A Testament of Hope: The Essential Writings of Martin Luther King, Jr.*, ed. James M. Washington (San Francisco: Harper & Row, 1986 [1963]), p. 295.

10. Ibid., p. 293.

11. Ibid., p. 293. King here illustrates the enduring influence on Christian ethics of ancient Stoic distinctions between natural law and civil law.

12. Martin Luther King, Jr., *Where Do We Go from Here: Chaos or Community* (New York: Harper & Row, 1967).

13. Ibid., p. 48.

14. Ibid., p. 61.

15. James H. Cone, *God of the Oppressed* (New York: Seabury Press, 1975), p. 83.

16. Ibid., p. 17.

17. Ibid., p. 219.

18. Ibid., p. 246.

19. Ibid., p. 245.

20. Mary Daly, *Beyond God the Father* (Boston: Beacon Press, 1973).

21. Rosemary Radford Ruether, *Sexism and God-Talk: Toward a Feminist Theology* (Boston: Beacon Press, 1983), pp. 46, 68–71.

22. Ibid., pp. 68–69.

23. Ibid., p. 69.

Chapter 21

1. "The Message of the Universal Christian Conference on Life and Work, Stockholm, 19–30 August, 1925" in *Ecumenical Documents on Church and Society (1925–1953)*, ed. John W. Turnbull (Geneva: World Council of Churches, 1954), p. 2.

2. Ibid.

3. Ibid., p. 3.

4. Ibid., p. 4.

5. *The Churches Survey Their Task: The Report of the Conference at Oxford, July 1937, on Church, Community, and State* (London: George Allen & Unwin, 1937), p. 92.

6. Ibid., pp. 93–94.

7. Ibid., p. 94.

8. Ibid., p. 58.

9. Ibid., p. 96.

10. Ibid., p. 102.

11. Ibid., pp. 102–3.

12. Ibid., pp. 104–9.

13. Ibid., p. 106.

14. Ibid.

15. Ibid., p. 124.

16. Ibid., p. 58.

17. *Man's Disorder and God's Design: The Amsterdam Assembly Series* (New York: Harper & Brothers, 1948), n.p.

18. Ibid., "Report of Section III," p. 195.

19. Ibid.

20. Ibid., p. 192.

21. Ibid.

22. Ibid.

23. *The Evanston Report: The Second Assembly of the World Council of Churches 1954* (New York: Harper & Brothers, 1955), p. 113.

24. Ibid., p. 117.

25. Ibid., p. 116.

26. Ibid., p. 117.

27. Ibid., p. 121.

28. Ibid., p. 158.

29. Ibid. Such declarations came in advance of the U.S. civil rights movement, but it is noteworthy that they were adopted in the very same year (1954) as the landmark *Brown vs. Board of Education* decision by the U.S. Supreme Court, which declared racial segregation in public schools to be unconstitutional.

30. Ibid., p. 155.

31. Ibid., p. 154.

32. Ibid., p. 161.

33. Ibid., p. 167.

34. Ibid., pp. 132–33.

35. *The New Delhi Report: The Third Assembly of the World Council of Churches 1961* (New York: Association Press, 1962), p. 94.

36. Ibid.

37. Ibid., p. 95.

38. Ibid., p. 106.

39. Ibid., p. 107.

40. Ibid., p. 280.

41. See *Faith and Science in an Unjust World: Report of the World Council of Churches' Conference on Faith, Science and the Future*, 2 vols. (Philadelphia: Fortress Press, 1980).

42. Ibid., vol. 2, p. 17.

43. World Council of Churches, *Signs of the Spirit: Official Report, Seventh Assembly . . . 1991* (Grand Rapids: Wm. B. Eerdmans Publishing Co., 1991), pp. 238–39.

44. Ibid., pp. 240–41.

Chapter 22

1. *Didache*, 2.8 in Richardson's *Early Christian Fathers*, p. 173.

Chapter 23

1. J. Philip Wogaman, *Christian Moral Judgment* (Louisville: Westminster/John Knox Press, 1989).

FOR FURTHER READING

The old saying that "history is long and life is short" takes on new meaning when one writes a general history of Christian ethics. One must be highly selective in the choice of subject matter and sources. In respect to sources, I have relied upon the actual writings of major figures and movements in this history. Citations from these works are generally taken from standard and accessible English-language translations. Interested students are invited to read more deeply in the primary sources cited in footnotes.

In addition to these, I wish to note some of the secondary sources that have been especially useful to me for reference purposes.

Ernst Troeltsch, *The Social Teaching of the Christian Churches*, 2 vols., tr. Olive Wyon (Louisville: Westminster/John Knox Press, 1992 [1911, 1931]) remains the great classic in the field eighty years after its initial German publication. Generations of scholars in Christian ethics and sociology of religion were tutored on this work. It remains important despite the many corrections made necessary by twentieth-century historical scholarship. Its pages obviously do not encompass the actual developments in Christian ethics during this century.

H. Richard Niebuhr, *Christ and Culture* (New York: Harper & Row, 1951), significantly influenced by Troeltsch, is a typological study of the history of Christian ethics. While scholars have quibbled over its classifications of various thinkers, the volume is helpful in delineating some of the perennial contrasting tendencies in the history of Christian ethics.

Waldo Beach and H. Richard Niebuhr, *Christian Ethics: Sources of the Living Tradition* (New York: Ronald Press Co., 1955), presents a variety of selected readings from the history of Christian ethics with Beach and Niebuhr's thoughtful introductions and commentaries.

George W. Forell, *History of Christian Ethics*, vol. I, *From the New Testament to Augustine* (Minneapolis: Augsburg Press, 1979), is the first in a projected three-volume history to be completed by Forell and others. John Mahoney, *The Making of Moral Theology: A Study of the Roman Catholic Tradition* (Oxford: Clarendon Press, 1987), is the best general introduction to Roman Catholic moral theology. Michael Keeling, *The Foundations of Christian Ethics* (Edinburgh: T. & T. Clark, 1990), is an insightful recent introductory text in Christian ethics containing useful commentary on a number of important figures in the history.

James F. Childress and John Macquarrie, *The Westminster Dictionary of Christian Ethics* (Philadelphia: Westminster Press, 1986), contains many articles on significant figures and movements in the history of Christian ethics and presents the work of a rich cross-section of contemporary contributors from North America and the United Kingdom.

General histories of the Christian church and of Christian thought are indispensable accompaniments to the history of Christian ethics. Especially valuable is Williston Walker's classic work, now available in updated form as Williston Walker, Richard A. Norris, David W. Lotz, and Robert T. Handy, *A History of the Christian Church*, 4th ed. (New York: Charles Scribner's Sons, 1985). Kenneth Scott Latourette, *A History of Christianity* (New York: Harper & Brothers, 1953), with its extensive historical interpretations, remains useful forty years after its publication. Justo Gonzalez, *A History of Christian Thought*, 3 vols. (Nashville: Abingdon Press, 1970; rev. ed. 1987), is an excellent reference work on the development of Christian theology and doctrine.

General or "secular" histories of ethics and political thought are often useful as reference works. R. W. and A. J. Carlyle, *A History of Mediaeval Political Theory in the West*, 6 vols. (Edinburgh and London: W. Blackwood & Sons, 1903–36), is a rich source on the early development of Christian political thought and its relationship to ancient philosophical movements such as Stoicism. George H. Sabine, *A History of Political Theory*, 3rd. ed. (New York: Holt, Rinehart & Winston, 1961), also contains a wealth of commentary on Christian political thought. Radoslav A. Tsanoff, *The Moral Ideals of Our Civilization* (New York: E. P. Dutton, 1942), is encyclopedic in its coverage of minor as well as major figures in the history of Western ethics (including Christian ethics) to the date of its publication. Francis William Coker, *Readings in Political Philosophy* (New York: Macmillan, 1929), is another useful source of selections and commentaries drawn from Western political history.

The number of studies of particular periods of history or of particular themes and issues is too extensive for full listing here. But I wish to acknowledge the particular helpfulness of several titles. C. J. Cadoux, *The Early Church and the World* (Edinburgh: T. & T. Clark, 1925), provides a comprehensive summary of early Christian thought on social issues, exhaustively organized by topic and period. Justo Gonzalez, *Faith and Wealth: A History of Early Christian Ideas on the Origin, Significance, and Use of Money* (San Francisco: Harper & Row, 1990) is an excellent introduction to Christian economic thought in the early centuries. Roland H. Bainton, *Christian Attitudes Toward War and Peace* (Nashville: Abingdon Press, 1960), continues to be acknowledged as the premier history of Christian thought on war. Bainton classifies most of the contributions to that history in three general types: pacifism, the just war, and the crusade. Charles Howard Hopkins, *The Rise of the Social Gospel in American Protestantism* (New Haven: Yale University Press, 1940), is a detailed history of the social gospel movement. Paul Bock, *In Search of a Responsible World Society: The Social Teachings of the World Council of Churches* (Philadelphia: Westminster Press, 1974), is the most complete history of the World Council's social thought, although it does not encompass the important developments of the past twenty years. Two volumes by Edward LeRoy Long, Jr., *A Survey of Christian Ethics* (New York: Oxford University Press, 1967), and *A Survey of Recent Christian Ethics* (New York: Oxford University Press, 1982), analyze the work of major Christian ethicists of the twentieth century typologically. Most of the authors dealt with in these volumes are North American.

The twentieth century has been an unusually productive period for work in Christian ethics. The many volumes dealing with particular issues and problems often include a substantial number of historical references of various kinds. That fact is a reminder that all work in Christian ethics is dependent upon centuries of previous thought.

Secondary sources such as these are useful, but we must be reminded once again that serious study in the history of Christian ethics drives us back to the primary writings of its principal thinkers and movements.

INDEX